Until the World Shatters

Until the World Shatters

Truth, Lies, and the Looting of Myanmar

DANIEL COMBS

MELVILLE HOUSE
BROOKLYN
LONDON

Until the World Shatters
First published in 2021 by Melville House
Copyright © Daniel Combs, 2020
All rights reserved
First Melville House Printing: March 2021

Lyrics to Side Effect songs "Meikhtila" and "The Change" reprinted with
permission of Darko C

Disclosure: The views expressed in this work are are the author's own and do not
necessarily represent the views of the Department of State or the United States.

Melville House Publishing
46 John Street
Brooklyn, NY 11201
and
Melville House UK
Suite 2000
16/18 Woodford Road
London E7 0HA

mhpbooks.com
@melvillehouse

ISBN: 978-1-61219-887-3
ISBN: 978-1-61219-888-0 (eBook)

Library of Congress Control Number: 2020950398

Designed by Richard Oriolo

Printed in the United States of America

10 9 8 7 6 5 4 3 2 1

A catalog record for this book is available from the Library of Congress

That which is real they know as real,
that unreal, to be unreal;
roaming fields of thought well-formed
they at the real arrive.
—THE DHAMMAPADA

I know what I have to do. For every one step that they
walk, I have to walk five.
—PHOE WA, PHOTOGRAPHER

The truth is simple: To make a bullet, you need money.
Without any money, you won't have any bullets.
—BUM TSIT, KACHIN HUMANITARIAN

Contents

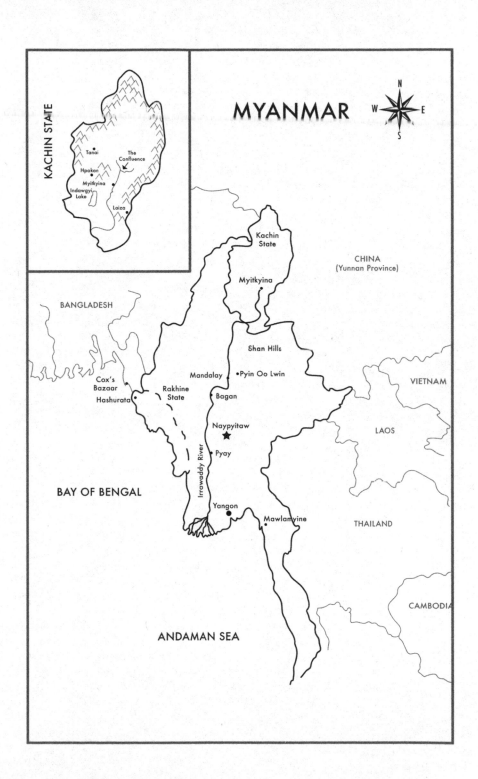

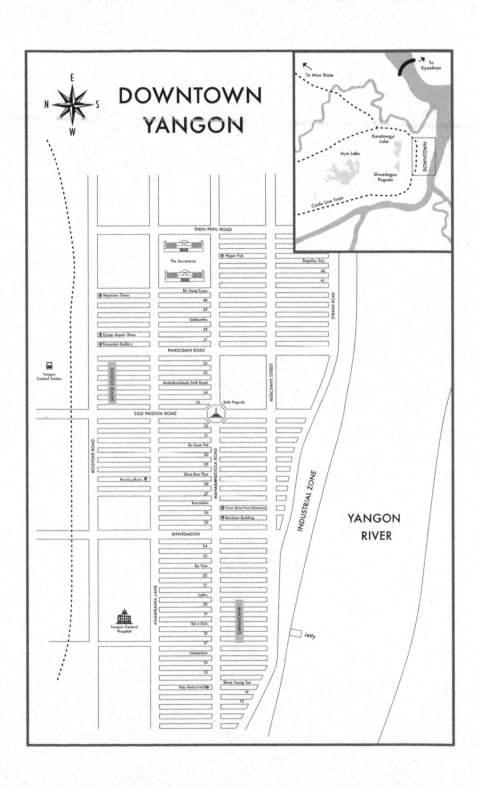

A Note on Names and Pronunciations

L ike so much else in Myanmar, the very name you use for something can have political connotations. Burma vs. Myanmar. Rangoon vs. Yangon. Old vs. New. Often, these arguments are more emotional than practical. Burma and Myanmar mean roughly the same thing in Burmese. And Rangoon is simply the anglicized version of Yangon.

In this work, I have tried to stay consistent to what I heard while I was in the country. I use the name "Myanmar" to describe country, and "Bamar" to describe its dominant ethnic group. Those are the words most people used while I was in the country, and that is the name officially recognized at the United Nations. However, in conversation some people still use the word

"Burma" to describe the country and "Burmese" to describe its majority population, and I have not altered any of these direct quotations. Likewise, I have chosen not to alter the many direct English citations from Myanmar-based writers that are in this text, despite occasional misspellings and grammatical errors.

This is a work of nonfiction, and I've used real names wherever possible. However, as many in Myanmar still do not trust the state system to have their best interests at heart, I have changed names where requested. Bum Tsit, the Kachin businessman at the heart of this story, asked me not to use his real name. Bum Tsit means "Green Mountain" in the Kachin language.

Burmese is a complicated and beautiful language that doesn't always translate well into the Roman alphabet. The below pronunciation guide may be helpful for some readers:

Aung San Suu Kyi . . . *kyi* is pronounced like *ch* in "cheese"

Myitkyina . . . *kyi* is pronounced like *ch* in "cheese"

Bo Aung Kyaw . . . *kya* is pronounced like *j* in "jaw"

Rohingya . . . *gy* is pronounced like the soft *g* in "engine"

Pyay . . . *yay* is pronounced like *ee* in "see"

Hpakan . . . *hp* is pronounced like the breathy *p* in "power"

Phoe Wa . . . *ph* is pronounced like the breathy *p* in "power"

Until the World Shatters

Introduction

The train to Kachinland clacks thirty hours north from Mandalay on old colonial tracks. The heavy rhythm of the metal wheels beats a mantra for change as the train passes from one world to another: from the river valley to the mountains; from the center to the periphery; from the heart of state control to an invisible border world.

Along the way, the train stops in Shwebo, Hopin, Mogaung. Places with old names that hold memories and forgotten truths. When a column of British colonial soldiers passed this way in 1888 on a mission to subjugate the warrior hill tribes and secure the famed Kachin jade mines, Major Charles Adamson lamented the fact that locals kept so many secrets from the foreign military men. "Of the road from Mogoung to the Jade mines little could be learnt," he reported. "As those people who knew the road were almost invariably interested in keeping the knowledge from us."

Secrets have always held power in a place like Kachin, where the interests of governments, businessmen, and local militias have been colliding for over a century. The treacherous mountain geography and dangerous malarial jungles impede both invading armies and the flow of information. The land is secretive for a reason. Kachin State, in Myanmar's far north, is home to unimaginable wealth. Every year, billions of dollars worth of jade spill down from the mountains that Adamson's men labored to find, driven by a ravenous, mystically attuned demand from China.

In the Kachin hills, locals and outsiders still battle for control over those resources, and for much more. In many ways, it is a fight for Myanmar's soul.

∎

I arrived in Myanmar in the beginning of September 2017, on a one-year fellowship to study Burmese and do research on the country's civil war. The fellowship and the research were tied to the master's degree I was working toward at Columbia University—where I was studying international security policy—but the decision to come back to Myanmar was just as much personal as it was professional.

I first visited the country in 2012. It was easily the most complicated, interesting, and difficult place I had ever been, and I wanted to learn more. That first time, as a twenty-three-year-old traveler living out of a backpack, I had been fascinated by a country that seemed to have stepped sideways in time. After five decades spent isolated from the rest of the world under a series of authoritarian rulers, everything about Myanmar felt unique—the people and their politics far more preoccupied with their own convoluted history than with what was happening outside their borders. There were no Western brands in Myanmar, no cell phones, no ATMs in the entire country. It felt like a story that hadn't finished telling itself—even names weren't settled. Was it Rangoon or Yangon, Burma or Myanmar? That sense of mystery and unsettled history was compelling.

I remember coming from Thailand with two thousand dollars hidden between the pages of different novels in my backpack, waiting to be changed into local currency at the black market money changers my friends had told me could be found around a pagoda in downtown Yangon. I remember walking through a Shan marketplace and encountering a psychedelic rainbow of fruit I had never seen or smelled or tasted. I remember making a phone call to a friend back home. Shut off from the global telecommunications boom, there were no SIM cards in Myanmar. So to dial out I had to stand on a street corner at a table run by an old lady, where twelve old rotary phones snaked together in a tangle of wires to plug into the telephone pole leaning out over the busy road. When I was done, a man passing by with a towering plate of desserts on his head handed me an orange cake and thanked me for visiting his country. I was hooked.

Myanmar in 2012 was in the throes of a renaissance. My arrival in March of that year, when the country held its first relatively free elections in fifty years, was possibly the most optimistic period in Myanmar's postcolonial history. The pro-democracy icon Aung San Suu Kyi, who had been censored and held under house arrest by the country's military dictatorship for most of the last two decades, was elected to parliament, and the feeling was that nothing could stop the forward march of progress. In all the major cities I visited, people were upbeat and eager to share their story with someone from outside. After spending half a century living in fear and forced to hide their activities and opinions from shadowy intelligence services, Myanmar's citizens were finally celebrating the ability to speak their minds. Truth was the currency of the day, and people shared it freely. They told me that a history of secrecy and violence was finally being sloughed off, that it would be replaced by a new world where people had the freedom to speak truth to power.

But it soon became clear that for some, life in Myanmar was still defined by violence and economic exploitation.

During that same trip, I took the train north to Kachin State, where I went to report on the ongoing civil war that had displaced 100,000 people in the previous year. Young men belonging to the Kachin Independence Army explained that the rebel group was fighting to uphold the Kachin people's rights for equal representation, and that the Myanmar military was bent on destroying not only their traditional systems of governance but their very ethnic identity. That ethnic hatred had fueled decades of violence in Myanmar's borderlands. But the Kachin war, they told me, was also about natural resources. The northern region was replete with hydroelectric power, valuable teak forests, and billions of dollars of untapped mineral wealth.

By drinking with the soldiers in Kachin State, and by reading the history books I was able to find in dusty old shops when I returned to Yangon a week later, I learned that the northern civil war was not a new phenomenon. Since Myanmar won its independence from Britain in 1948, the country has been torn apart by a single question: Who has the right to rule?

Minority ethnic groups living in the country's borderlands, averse to being ruled by the majority Bamar population, have waged sporadic insurgencies since 1948. Myanmar is one of the most diverse places on the planet, and seemingly every distinct group has had its own armed faction fighting against the central government at some point in its modern history, whether it be over ideology, religion, or resources. After seventy years of civil war, Myanmar's ongoing struggle between the central government and its fringes is the longest lasting armed conflict in the world today. The war's character and temperature have evolved throughout that time. During some years, the fighting is isolated to the resource-rich northern mountains. Other times, the entire borderlands can be under siege. The conflict's changing landscape builds its own narratives about rights and representation, forcing people to make impossible choices that shape their identities for life.

I left in 2012 having only glimpsed the country, and for five years I searched for a way to come back and continue learning about the Kachin war, Myanmar's intricate history, and its peoples' longing for their own truth.

•

When I returned to Myanmar in 2017, the unresolved issues of ethnic conflict and governance in the borderlands were threatening to undo all the progress and hope of 2012. The country had begun opening to the world and was flirting with democracy, but was still reckoning with deep-seated racial hatreds and a military juggernaut that was allergic to truth telling and afraid of losing power.

I found a guide, and a friend, in a young man named Bum Tsit. In Kachin State, where the thirty-year-old jade businessman lives, the armies fight for political power, for territory, and for their version of the truth. But most of all they fight for the land and what is buried underneath.

Jade is Myanmar's most valuable resource and its biggest secret. Over the past two decades, hundreds of billions of dollars of the green stone have come down from its northern mountains. For the armies battling in the jungle, jade is the perfect commodity through which to launder secrets. It is untraceable. Its value is fungible. A handful can be worth millions of dollars. And when it flows through the ungovernable reaches of Myanmar's borderlands, that money moves the needle toward war.

As an extractive industry, it can sometimes feel like jade is taking something from everyone it touches. For the ethnic Kachin people living in the area, the loss of local ownership has become linked to their very identity. For miners, the chase for jade can lead to death. And for businessmen like Bum Tsit, following the green vein can cost everything.

In the Kachin mountains, governance has all but collapsed under the relentless trauma of war between ethnic militias and the national army. In the vacuum, powerful military groups are perpetrating one of the largest natural resource heists in the history of the world. Kachin State is home to some of the country's most bountiful natural wealth. The hills are awash in gold, teak, amber, and jade, worth many billions of dollars. Yet the majority of that wealth is systematically siphoned away from both local communities and government tax collectors into the hands of shadowy business groups.

At the same time, armies use their access to the region's natural resources to fund their military operations and enrich themselves. Local grievances about these abuses of power fuel a conflict without end. Like many issues in Myanmar, the war in the north feels like a deadly cycle of blame, greed, and violence. One that is largely ignored by the outside world.

Only those on this northbound train seem to be paying attention.

∎

Toward the end of the train ride, passengers disembark in Mogaung, the starting point for the trip to the jade mountains. Kyin Aye, a twenty-five-year-old Buddhist from Rakhine State, in the country's southwest, remarks that this is the farthest north he's ever been. "I don't know anything about this place, about Kachin," he says. "I only come for one thing, to make money in the jade mines."

He is one of hundreds of thousands of migrant workers that come to Kachin State every year toward the end of the summer rains, when the water levels go down and the roads open up. In these northern mountains, they can live off the leftover jade scraps from the large mining companies and still earn three to four times more money for their manual labor than anywhere else in the country. But what really goes on in the mines is unknown to most of the young men heading that way. The promise of wealth is a gemstone hidden in the rough. Many go into the mountains but never return.

In Mogaung, the would-be miners are held up. The road to the mines is closed. This happens periodically, as tension between the national army and the local Kachin insurgents heats up or cools down. A battalion moves across the road, an artillery piece drags along. Traffic slows. People wait. "You don't realize until you get to Kachin, because no outsiders can really tell you about this life, but you have to be very patient to work here," says Aung Min, another miner who is coming to Kachin to work for the third straight year. "But you also have to be ready to act fast. Stop, start. Stop, start. That is life in the mines."

Myanmar's secrets might decide the country's future. But another group of citizens hopes otherwise.

Perhaps no group celebrated the country's would-be reforms more than its journalists and artists. Beginning in 2010, when the government began loosening its censorship rules, photographers and writers began chronicling the evolution of a country waking up from a long, self-imposed nightmare. These stories were as much for a domestic audience as an international one, as Myanmar's truth tellers tried to help their compatriots grapple with new social upheavals against a backdrop of five decades of propaganda and fear-mongering.

Phoe Wa, a young photojournalist from southeastern Myanmar, benefited greatly from those reforms. As a high school student, he enrolled in a journalism workshop, and eventually found a job in a local newspaper. After another round of elections in 2016, when Aung San Suu Kyi's reformist National League for Democracy, known everywhere in Myanmar as the NLD, took power, he naturally thought that these freedoms would keep increasing. But within the first year of the NLD takeover, those expectations started to founder. Journalists, student groups—anyone who was overtly critical of the government or military—were forced back into silence. As the army embarked on ever-more aggressive campaigns against the country's minority groups, the promise of democracy was turning into despair.

My return to Myanmar coincided with the most divisive moment for Myanmar's truth tellers since the country gained independence. No issue was more polarizing than the fate of the Rohingya Muslims, a minority group living in Myanmar's far west. Long persecuted by their Buddhist neighbors, the Rohingya's voices were nearly silenced in September 2017, when the national military began a coordinated campaign of rape, murder, and arson that drove over 700,000 people from the country in the world's largest refugee exodus since World War II. The United Nations called the campaign "a textbook example of ethnic cleansing," but the Myanmar government has successfully hidden that truth from its own people. The country's leaders deny that the Rohingya are citizens of Myanmar. Military officers claim that Muslim villagers torched their own homes to dupe the international community into supporting them. Politicians enlist hordes of anonymous online commenters to praise them as the defenders of Myanmar's traditional culture in the face of "Islamic terrorists" that want to destroy Buddhism.

In Myanmar, the truth is malleable.

Over the course of a year, I watched Phoe Wa's journey to report the truth despite the forces working against him: government propaganda, religious nationalist fanatics, and his own spiritual doubt. As his journalistic responsibility grew, he was forced to ask himself what he was willing to sacrifice to tell the truth.

•

This book tells the story of how people like Bum Tsit and Phoe Wa traffic in truth and secrets. In a fractured society like Myanmar, where civil war, repressive government, and dark money have shaped life for decades, it can sometimes feel like everyone is fighting for their own version of the truth. Information means power in Myanmar, and whether you keep secrets or campaign for the truth, the stakes are high.

The story alternates between two parallel narrative threads.

Bum Tsit's journey into the hidden world of jade—with its soldiers and spies—exemplifies the connection between Myanmar's civil war and its natural resource trade. Through historical records, oral testimonies, and my own reporting, I have tried to show how Myanmar's government and armed opposition groups in the far north are colluding to siphon billions of dollars away from state coffers, leaving a swath of devastation and suffering in their wake. Bum Tsit's story illustrates the human cost of this organized theft and shows how everyday people are forced to make extraordinary choices when traditional social structures have been eroded through decades of ethnic and economic oppression.

Phoe Wa's narrative gives context to the crisis in northern Myanmar by exploring how the country as a whole is battling over the issue of the truth. As Myanmar transitions from an authoritarian state to a semi-democratic one, free speech, and the responsibility that comes with it, has become the country's defining issue. Myanmar is one of the fastest changing places in the world, and its journalists, artists, and religious leaders all hope to shape its future by expounding their version of the Truth. That debate is taking place in an environment where public trust has been eroded through decades of censorship and propaganda, a situation that is both exacerbated and exploited by a government that has wholeheartedly embraced the twin strategies of discrediting local media and sounding the dog whistle of ethnic nationalism.

I spent a year chronicling the lives of Bum Tsit and Phoe Wa, and I've remained in regular contact with them as I wrote this book. This narrative follows each of them through Myanmar's three seasons—Cold, Hot, and Rain—as the two young men grapple with the country's most deep-seated problems, find new ways to contend with them, and ultimately face the consequences of their actions. During that year, their lives changed in extraordinary and strangely parallel ways, and the seasonal shifts often coincided with major life events for each of them.

In Myanmar, life follows the seasons. The winds shift; the air gets cool. Things move slower when it's wet. The seasons mark the passage of time in a country where most people's lives are still tied directly to the land and its bounty. Myanmar is shaped like a kite, with its head in the snowy peaks of the Himalayas and its tail sweeping south across the Andaman Sea. Mountains and jungles and dessicated plains furrow the landscape and help create a nation that is nearly unrivaled in its biological, ethnic, and political diversity. Yet the rhythm of the seasons—Cold, Hot, Rain—Cold, Hot, Rain—builds a cycle of change that connects all who live in Myanmar, no matter their differences. Life drives endlessly forward. Across it all, the massive Irrawaddy River carves a long north–south backbone across the country, giving nourishment and energy and economic power to those who can lay claim to its mighty twists and turns.

Some strains of Buddhist philosophy in Myanmar consider time to be a wheel, with human beings rolling forward through a cyclical existence of hunger, thirst, separation, desire, and eventual death. But humans are also uniquely positioned to elevate themselves above this relentless pursuit of survival and achieve something greater—something closer to thriving. The crushing cycle of the wheel of time is both suffering and flourishing. Each revolution of the seasons is another chance to connect with the Truth of the world and its movement through time.

In my reporting in Myanmar I also met many other secret keepers and truth tellers who followed this cycle—priests and monks and punks and drunks—whose lives and philosophies further illustrate the struggles faced by both Phoe Wa and Bum Tsit. These stories of sacrifice and struggle in modern Myanmar are intertwined with the journeys of the book's two main characters to show what it means to live in a country that prizes, above all else, survival.

In Myanmar, life follows the seasons. The winds shift; the air gets warm. Things move quicker when it's dry.

•

The Kachinland train's rails are old—they were laid down at the end of the nineteenth century. They are twisted and warped with age, and have seen few repairs. The train bounces up and down as it chugs forward along the tracks. Every so often, a train car will bounce too high and derail.

This is known as "jumping the rail."

When a car jumps the rail, it marks a sudden and violent deviation from the set path. Everything crunches to a halt. Some things have to move in reverse to fix the problem. Power systems fail. Everyone waits and watches while the conductors try to avoid blame and figure out how to put the train back where it's supposed to be. But the scenery is beautiful. Yellow fields of sunflower, and distant mountains on the blue horizon.

PART 1—COLD

August 2017–December 2017

BO AUNG KYAW STREET

Bo Aung Kyaw Street is busy in the mornings, and it smells like smoke. It starts outside the mosque, where the imam gets on the loudspeaker every morning at 5:30 to begin his call to prayer. The tea shop ladies that work outside start their charcoal brazier, and the scent wafts up into the apartment buildings above. Soon, the imam's chants are mingled with the droning fog horns of the container ships moving down the Yangon River—the never-ending flow of commerce and the endless cry of faith weaving together in a droning echo that reverberates through the block.

From my third-floor balcony, the next sound is always the Buddhist nuns carrying their megaphones. Robed in pink and ochre, they parade barefoot down the sidewalk in groups of twenty or more, bestowing luck and long life through the amplified speaker, each nun carrying a small bowl to collect donations of food and small monies.

Soon, the mobile vendors show up. By 9:00, the corn lady usually appears, balancing a basket of steaming yellow ears. "Corn! Corn!" she shouts into the still morning air. "Hot corn with salt!" Anyone wanting a morning snack can call down from their balcony. Most apartments in Yangon are connected to the street with a long string. At the end hangs a small bag or a strong metal clasp. Passing vendors can load up their wares, wait as the bag is hauled upward, filled with the appropriate small bills, and lowered again. Religiously minded residents can send down donations to the passing nuns every morning. The simple innovation saves everyone from climbing up the steep staircases in Yangon's oppressive, wet heat.

Newspaper boys use the ropes to make their deliveries, clipping black and white newsprint to the appropriately labeled string, and giving it a yank to ring the bell attached inside. If you walk down the sidewalk early enough, you can learn a lot about who lives where. The second-floor apartment, above the hardware store at number 197, likes to read *Daily Eleven*, a paper known for its good business coverage. My neighbor in building 167 subscribes to *The Voice*, which is notable for its extensive translations of regional and international news. My other neighbor only ever seems to read *Kicker*, a local soccer magazine. Strolling up and down the sidewalk, headlines flash out. A pedestrian can get his fill of the day's news long before arriving at the newsstand.

•

Downtown Yangon has a deliberate geography. The long east–west grid marches along the riverfront in a kind of steady, crowded cadence. From First Street in the west to Sixty-Fifth in the far east, there is a calming regularity to the long, narrow blocks. Every third street has a name, while the rest are numbered. Two numbers and a name, and you can describe any downtown neighborhood:

Ninth Street—Tenth Street—Hledan Street

Eleventh Street—Twelfth Street—Monk Street

Thirty-Seventh Street—Thirty-Eighth Street—Pleasant Port Street

If you want paint or fishing nets, you go to Twenty-Sixth Street.

Plumbing supplies are found at the top of Fortieth. All of the eyeglass stores line Shwe Bon Thar Street. The upper block of Thirty-Sixth Street houses movie production studios.

It feels both ordered and ramshackle. Unplanned and perfectly deliberate. Newcomers to the city have to ask to find anything, but then will never forget where to go the second time. It can make shopping both inconvenient and strangely straightforward. You might have to cross town to find your glasses. But then if the first store doesn't have what you need, you know there are at least ten others on the same block that you can check.

Commerce all takes place in public. Shopfronts spill out onto the sidewalk displaying their wares. On the lower block of Twenty-Seventh Street almost every store sells wire mesh. Thick wire, plastic wire, bendy wire—chicken wire, green wire, blue wire. Three-foot rolls, four-foot rolls, six-foot rolls. When someone picks a product, a small crowd gathers as the overweight owner brings the wire out into the sunny sidewalk and uses a pair of ancient shears to cut through the metal. His daughter gives a business card to the customer while the workers from the nearby shops look on. "Please remember to come here for all your metallic wire needs," she says with a smile.

■

The city's methodical downtown planning belies a hot, tropical mess. Growth is defiant in Yangon. Trees burst out of the sidewalk and crawl over the sewer. Everywhere you look, new green leaves push through the gray soot that covers the old city. In every spare, scratched-out pocket of dirt, a palm tree or flower bush or vine manages to take root and flourish in the wet heat. Buildings themselves become nourishment for plants. The mold and dirt caked onto the facades of Yangon's old apartments host bright green patches of viney growth. Small trees launch themselves out from windowsills, while old ladies tend to the orchids hanging on their balconies. The air is heavy with the breath of living things.

Downtown Yangon is busy. And it is loud. Taxis honk constantly as they push through the traffic. Trishaw drivers ring their little bells while making deliveries of people, construction materials, and food in the baking midday sun. Buddhist devotees drive through the streets with amps and loudspeakers attached to their trucks, blasting out prayers to anyone living nearby. Street vendors hawk their products as they prowl down the narrow blocks. Generators hum all through the day, coughing diesel fumes into the crowded pedestrian alleyways. It is cramped and colorful and defiantly alive. Rats scamper around the gutters, and packs of crows flit between buildings, screaming at each other. The city is bursting with dirty, sweating, thriving life.

But it is also a place of quiet corners and contemplation. A sunset seen from the jetty. The smell of grass after a summer downpour. The aura of a gilded pagoda shining through the black night. Yangon is a nerve center, a giant artery, a place where people come to feel something.

The city has always been a place of change. People have been living along the water here for nearly fifteen hundred years. Yangon is at the confluence of five different small rivers, which flow together into the rich waters of the Andaman Sea. In the middle of town is the only hill for miles in any direction, a crucial vantage point in a region historically beset by military conquests.

As the area has transformed, its name has changed with it. For most of its history, it was known as Dagon, nothing but a small fishing village founded in the sixth century by the Mon people, who ruled much of what is today southern Myanmar. When the Bamar king Alaungpaya came south and smashed the Mon in 1755, he optimistically renamed the town Yangon, meaning "End of Strife." A century later, after the British routed the Bamar in the Second Anglo-Burmese War, the city transformed again. The new rulers, unable to consistently pronounce the local name, changed it to Rangoon. In 1989, after the military took control of the government, they changed practically all of the anglicized names in the country, and the city reverted back to Yangon.

■

As the sun dips below the roofs on Bo Aung Kyaw Street, it casts long shadows across the colonial-era facades. U Myo Tun, the doorman to my building, is smoking a cigarette with a newspaper spread out across his lap. U Myo Tun gets paid 130,000 kyats a month—around one hundred dollars—to sit on a stool in the sidewalk and unlock the gate for the building's six residents. He makes a few extra bucks each week selling cigarettes and sodas and betel nut to day laborers who work nearby. Seeing me, he coughs, readjusts his longyi—a long tube of fabric tied around the waist, without any pockets—and stands up to unlock the gate with the tiny key he keeps hidden in an electrical conduit.

He points to the paper he's reading. An article about new construction projects covers the front page.

"They talk about this city like it's turning into some paradise." U Myo Tun laughs and pulls on the cigarette. "But you just need to open your eyes to see how hard it is in Yangon."

1.

HEARTBEAT OF THE NATION

Downtown Yangon

E ach morning, I pulled up the string to my apartment on Bo Aung Kyaw Street and opened up two newspapers. The first was the *Myanmar Times*, a privately owned, English language daily with offices just up the street from my house. The second was the state mouthpiece—*The Global New Light of Myanmar*. Together, the two papers gave a refractory view into the day's events: a little bit of truth, and something else kind of like it. Sometimes, I would read a news story in one paper, only to read in the other that everything I had just been told was wrong. One morning, the *Myanmar Times*'s big story came on page three: "ASEAN seeks long-lasting solution to Rakhine crisis." It read, in part:

Foreign Ministers of the 10-country Association of South-East
Asian Nations (ASEAN) repeated its calls for a durable solution to
the northern Rakhine crisis in Myanmar, one of its member states.

The ASEAN foreign ministers also want a speedy and safe
return of the over 650,000 Muslim residents who fled northern
Rakhine to neighbouring Bangladesh to escape violence.

Renewed violence in northern Rakhine erupted on August
25 . . . when Arakan Rohingya Salvation Army (ARSA) fighters,
which the government labels a terrorist organization, attacked
government outposts that killed several security forces.

The Myanmar armed forces, locally known as Tatmadaw,
retaliated with ferocity, launching "clearing operations" that killed
hundreds of people.

The international community, including the United Nations,
accused the Tatmadaw of excesses and human rights abuses, while
human rights organisations accused government security forces of
systematic "cleansing" of Muslims.

Most Myanmar people do not consider the Rohingya to be one
of the country's ethnic groups, but consider them illegal immigrants
from neighbouring Bangladesh even though they have lived in
Rakhine for generations.

In *The Global New Light of Myanmar*, the same meeting was reported
on the front page under the headline "ASEAN expresses support for
Myanmar":

ASEAN foreign ministers pledged their support for Myanmar's
humanitarian relief effort in Rakhine State, according to the Union
Minister for International Cooperation of the Republic of the
Union of Myanmar U Kyaw Tin, who returned to Nay Pyi Taw
yesterday after attending the ASEAN Foreign Ministers' Retreat
held in Singapore on Tuesday.

In a statement issued by the ASEAN Chair, the ASEAN

Ministers expressed their continued support for Myanmar's humanitarian relief programme in Rakhine State and welcomed the ASEAN Coordinating Centre for Humanitarian Assistance on disaster management (AHA Centre)'s ongoing work with the Myanmar Government–led mechanism to deliver humanitarian assistance to all displaced inhabitants without discrimination . . . The ASEAN Foreign Ministers, among others, expressed their support to the Myanmar Government in its efforts to bring peace, stability, rule of law and to promote harmony and reconciliation among the various communities, as well as sustainable and equitable development in Rakhine State.

Taken together, the papers told two important versions of the truth: what happened, and what the government thought about it. While *The Global New Light of Myanmar* focused on government ministers, their official statements, and the proceedings of the legislature, the *Times* helped put some of those events into context.

Context is everything in Myanmar. News never happens in a vacuum, but Myanmar's peculiar, isolated history and complicated politics made learning about ongoing issues particularly intimidating. The headlines carried months of political baggage—the result of a convulsive national crisis centered around the military operations in Rakhine State.

The inner pages of the morning news contained other important truths. In the *New Light*, you could read full transcripts of government speeches and official statements made by state ministers or agency directors. The paper also covered the quotidian bureaucratic proceedings that affected everyday life in Yangon, like the fact that the Ministry of Education had suddenly mandated new identity cards for students taking their matriculation exams. The newspaper made it very clear to the reader what mattered: the government; its narrative; its rules. Background, opinion, and analysis had no place in its pages. The most exciting thing in the paper was usually the sports section on the back page, with color photos of international soccer and tennis stars.

The *Myanmar Times* called itself the "heartbeat of the nation." It cost thirty-seven cents for the daily edition, five times more than *The Global New Light of Myanmar*. It had robust business, photo, and lifestyle sections; occasionally it published a juicy crime report for Yangon. It also listed the domestic flight schedule every week. For someone who wanted a reliable snapshot of the things that most people really cared about in Myanmar, the paper was a good source. Although it had courted significant controversy over its coverage of the Rakhine crisis, it was still one of the only newspapers that printed the word "Rohingya," albeit only in reference to the fact that most locals considered it a fabricated identity.

Seven hundred thousand people in Rakhine State had been driven from their homes in the past few months, but living in Yangon it was sometimes easy to feel completely detached from the violence. According to the *Times*'s travel section, if you wanted to see ancient Buddhist ruins in Rakhine, you could still fly direct to the state capital three times a day.

·

Every weekend, the *Times* also published a photo essay. One week, it was a dozen eye-catching photos detailing the practice routine of a local dance troupe, the Sky Dragon Lion Club.

The photographer, Phoe Wa, was only twenty-two years old. As the *Myanmar Times*'s photo intern, landing the weekend photo essay was a big deal. In the seven months he had been working at the paper, he had only published four major stories. Phoe Wa's pictures were easy to spot in print, and I always looked for them in the newspaper. The young photographer captured a Yangon in motion. He had a way of documenting human movement that felt very immediate and voyeuristic. In his pictures the viewer always seemed to be looking at someone during a critical instant. Even generic photos meant to fill up page space—like a shot of a man talking on a mobile phone for a story about a new telecom company—felt somehow urgent and made an impression.

To shoot the Sky Dragon Lion Club, Phoe Wa had spent a week following the dancers around while they practiced, taking over a thousand photos.

During their training, he watched as three of the dancers injured themselves. In his images, both the elegance and the violence of the dance became clear: a concussion; a broken tooth; teammates huddled together to help a friend stretch out a pulled hamstring.

Phoe Wa was perfect for shooting the dancers, and it was clear why his editor had chosen him for the assignment. The head of the paper's photo section, Kaung Htet, was one of the country's most well-known and respected photojournalists. He was part of a group of six or seven photographers who had spent the last decade documenting the country's breakneck pace of change. Kaung Htet specialized in conflict reporting. He had spent years covering the internal conflicts in Myanmar's borderlands, embedding with both rebel militias and Myanmar government troops to bring some of the realities of constant war home to the country's safe spaces. His work had inspired Phoe Wa to quit his job and move to Yangon to become a photojournalist.

Phoe Wa was new to the art form. He had only been taking pictures for a year. Before that, as a reporter for a small distribution paper in Mon State, in the country's southeast, he had written articles in Burmese about local politics. But the first time he saw a photo essay, when Kaung Htet came to his city to give a photography workshop, the young journalist decided to switch career paths. I could understand why. Phoe Wa and I attended one of Kaung Htet's presentations together. The subject was conflict reporting, and the images that garnered the most attention from the young audience were the photos of the Kachin Independence Army soldiers in the far north, and of the famously dangerous jade mining area in Hpakan. Most people in Myanmar heard of these distant, difficult regions through newsprint, radio, and word of mouth. But a photo taken behind rebel lines could show the reality of the civil war far better than any seven-hundred-word story.

Later, I talked to Phoe Wa about why he thought photojournalism was so powerful. "When you see a photo story, with fifteen or twenty photos, you can really get to know inside the story," Phoe Wa told me. "Photojournalists can see the invisible things. These issues would disappear, but a good photojournalist can bring them out for people to learn."

■

Phoe Wa and I lived only a few cramped blocks from each other in downtown Yangon. We often met for drinks at Hyper Pub, where the *Myanmar Times* photographers liked to grab beers after work. I liked hanging out with Phoe Wa because he was just as interested in exploring his new city as I was. He sometimes asked me what subjects foreigners found interesting in Myanmar so that he could pitch them as photo story ideas.

Phoe Wa told me that he usually slept with his camera under his covers. It was his most prized possession. The small media company he had worked for in his hometown in Mon State had leased him the camera, which he paid off in installments over several months. Phoe Wa slept in a one-room hostel with thirteen other young men, all migrants to Yangon who came to the city for work. The hostel was on the seventh floor, in a building with no elevator. The room had no mattresses or pillows, just mats laid out on the floor, with power strips stretching in all directions. The longest-term resident earned the right to sleep against the far wall. Phoe Wa slept next to him, with the camera against his body.

Every morning, Phoe Wa woke up at 7:30 to shower and eat breakfast. He missed cooking his own food at home and didn't like the taste of most meals in Yangon. "They can't make mohinga right here," he told me, referring to the fish noodle soup that is a breakfast staple across the country. "It's not as good as in Mon State."

By 8:30, Phoe Wa usually arrived at the *Myanmar Times* office, an hour and a half before any of his colleagues in the Photography section. He used the time to practice his English online, using one of the office computers while they were available. Phoe Wa also stayed an hour and a half later than anyone else, because that was his best chance of scoring an assignment. The news jobs tended to go to photographers in descending order of seniority. Phoe Wa received assignments when there was no one else to do them, or if he successfully pitched an idea to Kaung Htet.

Phoe Wa relished the opportunity to work the long hours. Any time spent working as a journalist was training, and validation of his choice to move to Yangon. He went in to work on Saturdays, Sundays, and every holiday. "There are no days off," he said. "No free time."

Part of the photojournalist's job was to provide captions for photos, so Phoe Wa knew that he needed to improve his English if he wanted to land a full-time gig at the *Times*, or *Frontier Myanmar*, or one of the other few reputable news outlets in the country. In the evenings, before going to bed, he spent another three hours lying awake between the other hostel residents, listening to downloaded English lessons on his headphones. He fell asleep at 11:00 most nights, to the snores of the migrant workers sleeping a few inches from him. "Everyone just stays quiet, in their spot," Phoe Wa told me when I visited the hostel one night. "Everyone is very tired from work. No one really talks so much."

His one solace was the balcony, where residents hung their clothes and bedsheets to dry. Standing between the billowing white shirts, Phoe Wa liked to look out into the Yangon evening. "This is my favorite spot," he said to me one night while we both squeezed onto the small space. "The air is nice out here, and it is quiet." He paused and stared at the night sky. "It's like freedom."

However brutal Phoe Wa's self-imposed regimen was, it was a major improvement from his first few months in Yangon. When he first arrived by train from Mawlamyine with only $150 in his pocket, he slept for free on the floor of a monastery. A monk from Phoe Wa's hometown, whom he knew through a friend, ran the monastery. The room and board didn't cost anything, but he had to chip in and work according to the monks' rigorous schedules. That meant waking up at 3:30 every morning to prepare breakfast so that the abbot and his followers could eat after their early morning meditation. Up so early, Phoe Wa would then go and explore the city while everyone else still slept.

Phoe Wa was a devout Buddhist, and he spent his first weeks in Yangon praying at the city's famous pagodas every morning in his free time. But money soon started wearing thin. Even though the monastery was free to stay in, he still needed to pay for transportation around the city and had to feed himself when he wasn't with the monks. He had limited himself to only

1,000 kyats per day—about seventy-five cents—and his health had suffered as a result.

"My nutrition was very bad," he remembered. "When I ran, I felt light-headed. And if I was sitting and stood up quickly, I would get so dizzy." But spending more money was out of the question. After only a few months in the city, he was down to only 50,000 kyats—less than forty dollars—and knew that he didn't have many more chances before he'd have to go home with nothing to show for his time in Yangon.

Phoe Wa didn't have a strategy for finding a job when he arrived in Yangon. He hadn't made any real friends in the city. He was still living in the monastery, cleaning and cooking for the monks every morning. He still had not reached out to Kaung Htet, the man who had inspired him to quit his job and pursue a career in photojournalism. But now, after months living in the monastery, pacing the streets alone, his money dwindling every day, Phoe Wa showed up at the *Myanmar Times* office one morning and waited for the older photographer to show up for work.

"I was really afraid to reach out to U Kaung Htet," Phoe Wa remembered, using the honorific title "U." "He and I are too far apart. He is a big person in Yangon. I was afraid to talk to him."

"He just kept coming back every day," Kaung Htet told me, when I asked about the meeting. "Every morning he was there waiting for me. We already had two photography interns, but he ended up working kind of like an unofficial intern."

"He was just so nice to me," Phoe Wa recalled while we sat together at Hyper Pub one day after work. "There was no position for me at the *Myanmar Times*, but he told me to just go take pictures and that I should come show them to him. So during the day I'd go take pictures, and then in the afternoon U Kaung Htet would teach me."

For a month, Phoe Wa kept showing up in the Kaung Htet's office in the afternoon, until finally he got a lucky break. One of the *Myanmar Times* photo interns landed a job offer from *Frontier* magazine, a prestigious English-language weekly in which big glossy pictures accompanied most stories. Phoe Wa became the *Times*'s official photo department intern, moved out of the monastery, and started sleeping with his camera next to his body to protect it from thieves.

·

While Phoe Wa's decision to take an unpaid internship was unusual in a place like Myanmar, where personal ambitions are often cast aside for the sake of finding food to eat, he was far from alone in migrating in search of better work. Few economic opportunities exist in the countryside besides farming and body-bruising labor in extractive industries like logging, mining, and oil work. For women, there are even fewer work options, and often an expectation to stay at home and maintain the household. Migration for work has a long tradition in Myanmar. Throughout the country's decades of self-imposed isolation, the only option for many families was to seek work abroad. In 2017, one out of every twenty-five men from Myanmar worked in Thailand. Phoe Wa's father was one of them. In the ten years he had lived in Bangkok, he had only been home to see his son twice. He had spent several years working on a construction crew before landing a more comfortable job in an ice factory. Phoe Wa talked to him on the phone occasionally, but for the most part, his father's only presence in his life had been the money he sent to the family.

For all the men and women that went abroad for better paying work, just as many turned up in Yangon. The city is Myanmar's largest by far, and the country's only real metropolis. For the hundreds of thousands of young migrant workers that made the move each year from the rural countryside, the city could be overwhelming. Yangon had a man-made tumult that didn't exist elsewhere in the country. The volume of daily life was orders of magnitude higher than in other cities in Myanmar. Living in the city was also expensive, and there were more opportunities to spend money than at home. Sports bars, movie theaters, and fancy new stores all threatened to siphon away a migrant's hard-earned cash.

But for all its distractions, Yangon could still be a lonely place for newcomers like Phoe Wa. The city's cosmopolitanism also held an anonymity that was impossible to find in the small villages and towns that most migrants came from. Even Phoe Wa, who had grown up on the outskirts of a large town, felt disoriented by Yangon's impersonal attitude.

He saw it as a problem with the people themselves: "Yangon people are just rude," he told me one day. "There are so many alcoholics here. You never know who you can trust. That makes it lonely."

When we met in the evenings for drinks, Phoe Wa would sometimes treat it like a confessional. He said that I was the first person he had told about his controlled starvation during his first months in the city, and about how grueling his daily schedule was.

"Many of the things I'm telling you, I haven't told my colleagues," he said to me one night. "It's difficult to talk about my life here. But I know what I have to do. For every one step they walk, I have to walk five."

■

Phoe Wa had chosen a difficult time to become a journalist in Myanmar. During the past year, the military had charged and imprisoned at least twelve journalists and media personnel on arbitrary, sometimes obscure, legal grounds. The move was a significant backtrack for freedom of information in a country undergoing a difficult transition from military to civilian rule.

For most of its history after achieving independence from the British in 1948, Myanmar was ruled by police states and military juntas that had made free information the enemy of the regime. The Press Scrutiny and Registration Division, part of the Ministry of Information, strictly controlled all news. Prior to publication, every newspaper and magazine had to be vetted by the censors, who would remove or redact entire articles, leaving only a whitewashed set of stories that the government approved. Hundreds of journalists and independent dissidents were arrested over the decades. They faced years of torture and the special hell of Insein Prison, where they were pressured to divulge information about their sources. Myanmar was a black hole of secrecy. Little information got in, and even less came out. Journalists that focused on the country often reported from abroad. Some of the most knowledgeable foreign writers were blacklisted from ever receiving entry visas. Dissidents that fled the regime's terrors founded news outlets and advocacy groups outside the country. Other writers published under pseud-onyms. Those that did manage to get into the country legally were heavily restricted in their movements, followed by shadowy military intelligence officers, and monitored by an enormous network of anonymous informants. Speaking to the press could mean a lifelong prison sentence for you or your family, and all reporters had to go through strenuous steps to protect sources.

But after 2010, when the military junta began the slow process of tran-sitioning Myanmar toward civilian-run democracy, press freedoms began to blossom. Between 2010 and 2017 Myanmar climbed up the World Press Freedom Index from 174th in the world to 131st. It was a far cry from the free flow of information found in Norway or the Netherlands, but a remark-able change in a country where people were once afraid of greeting the wrong person in public for fear of being overheard by secret informants.

Phoe Wa remembered the changes of 2010. "We had very few journal-ists before then. Almost no one wrote the truth about the government. Most people just wrote what the government told them, just saying that the gov-ernment was very good."

But with the reforms, new stories about Myanmar started flooding the country, and Phoe Wa's generation had a window to the world that his par-ents' generation had forever been denied.

"We can learn about our country in school, but some lessons you cannot learn in a classroom," he said. "We need journalists to teach us."

The second big change came in August of 2012, when the Ministry of Information dropped its requirement for newspapers to go through a censor-ship process prior to publication. Now, theoretically, what a paper printed was up to its own editorial discretion. But according to more senior journal-ists like Kaung Htet, this change came with its own difficulties. "Now there's no censorship board approval, but self-censorship is part to the job," he said. "So all journalists have to toe a careful line. Photojournalists can do more stuff now. We can cover things like sectarian violence, but we have to be re-ally, really careful. Photojournalists, me included, have been threatened."

Despite the occasional threats, information seemed to be getting slowly freer. Photographers like Kaung Htet were able to openly report about the county's civil wars without fear of being killed by their own government. He had made eight trips to Kachin State to document the prolonged conflict between the Kachin Independence Army and the national military, known in Myanmar as the Tatmadaw. In the past, these borderland wars, which were struggles for the very definition of the country, would only be reported on from dissident journalists abroad, or else made it to Yangon only as whispers and hearsay. Now the photos of the guerrilla soldiers in Kachin State could grace the front page of the *Myanmar Times*.

In 2016, Aung San Suu Kyi's National League for Democracy, or NLD, took power, becoming the first democratically elected civilian government since 1962. At the time, most people thought that these freedoms would only increase. But within the first year and a half of the NLD takeover, those expectations started to founder.

In January of 2017, a group of high school students were charged under a vaguely defined law known as 66(d), the anti-defamation clause of the Telecommunications Act. During a local peace dialogue in the Ayeyarwady Division in southern Myanmar, the students had put on a satirical play about the country's civil wars, with one group portraying military officers, and another playing the ethnic opposition groups. The humorous depiction of the Tatmadaw, was too much for an army officer somewhere, and the students were charged with "damaging the reputation of the army." While it was the Tatmadaw itself, and not the civilian government, that brought the defamation charges against the students, the NLD did nothing to publicly oppose the move.

As the year progressed, however, it became obvious that the NLD had an even less favorable outlook toward truth tellers than the previous quasi-military government. In June, the state arrested three journalists from *The Irrawaddy* magazine and the *Democratic Voice of Burma* and charged them under the colonial-era Unlawful Associations Act. The law, written in 1908 to help the colonial government combat nationalist opposition in the borderlands, states that "Whoever is a member of an unlawful association, or takes part in meetings of any such association . . . or in any way assists the operations of any such association . . . shall be punished with imprisonment."

The three reporters had gone to the borderlands of Shan State, in Myanmar's mountainous northeast, to cover a drug eradication program put on by a local insurgent group. In doing so, the government claimed, they had taken part in a meeting of an unlawful association. Reporting on the borderland wars had suddenly gone from a civic service to a national security threat.

The most high-profile arrests took place toward the end of 2017. Since late August, when the Tatmadaw began its large-scale military operations in Rakhine State, the government had forbidden all journalists from entering the area. During that time, hundreds of thousands of Rohingya Muslims had fled across the border to Bangladesh, where aid groups and reporters interviewed them. They told of horror stories: indiscriminate executions, torched villages, rapes, and mass graves. In December 2017, two local reporters from Reuters, Wa Lone and Kyaw Soe Oo, were invited to dinner with two police officers in Yangon to follow up on a lead about a massacre of ten Rohingya villagers, in which security forces and a local Buddhist militia allegedly worked together to murder the Muslims and bury them in a mass grave. At the restaurant, they were approached by two policemen whom they had never met before and handed a pile of documents. Almost immediately afterward, the two reporters were arrested. The next day, they were charged under the Official Secrets Act, another colonial-era law that makes illegal any action in which someone "obtains . . . or communicates to any other person any . . . note or other document or information which is calculated to be . . . directly or indirectly, useful to an enemy." In this case, the enemy was the Rohingya militant group the government was fighting. By attempting to publish information about the Tatmadaw's classified operations, the reporters were aiding the so-called "terrorists."

This arrest attracted widespread media attention of its own. The US State Department issued a statement saying that, "the media freedom that is so critical to rule of law and a strong democracy requires that journalists be able to do their jobs," and called for Wa Lone and Kyaw Soe Oo's immediate and unconditional release. Every news outlet in the country followed the case of the detained reporters, with the exception of *The Global New Light of*

Myanmar and *Kicker*. The arrest raised fears of entrapment and arbitrary crackdowns among local journalists. A third local Reuters reporter that worked on the story—a photographer—fled to Thailand when he heard the police were looking for him. He wasn't even supposed to be indicted on the same charge as his colleagues. His official crime: importing drones without a license.

In Myanmar, the rule of law was often used as a tool of political convenience. Even the most innocuous activities could be marked on your permanent record and brought back out when it was time for the state to make an example of you. People broke the law every day without even thinking about it, but that was because there were laws against everything. Every samosa sold on the side of the road was a violation for vending without proper permits. Every journalist that went to report on what the opposition groups were doing was risking jail. And in that way, very little had changed from the darkest days of the military junta.

When I asked Phoe Wa if this climate of restricted press freedoms caused him to second guess his career path, he was stalwart. "We have to be careful, of course. But we learn from what they did, how they worked, why they were arrested. But journalism is too important. We need to tell the truth. We need to open people's eyes and ears."

.

One Saturday, Phoe Wa and I went to visit the small town of Kyauktan, on the outskirts of Yangon. Our taxi driver told us that he was nervous—he had only been driving for two weeks and had never been that far outside of the city. Our destination was only twenty miles from the seven-million-person metropolis, but the hour-long drive felt like a time warp stretching back into the days before Myanmar ever opened up to the wider world. Advertisements for mobile phones with high definition selfie cameras quickly disappeared, replaced by signs for local fertilizer products. Ubiquitous billboards displayed Myanmar Beer's slogan: *Brimming with optimism*. Almost as soon as we crossed the river that marks Yangon's boundary, the gray cityscape morphed into electric green rice fields and thatched-roof shacks. Instead of trishaws gathered on the sidewalk, water buffalo plowed through the fields just off the edge of the highway. It was a sharp reminder that most of the country still lived in rural, desperately poor conditions.

Phoe Wa loved getting out of the city. "It's like we could be anywhere else in the country," he said when we passed through a little farming village. "It makes me wish I could go home to my village."

The roads grew congested as we got closer to our destination, and our driver's inexperience started to show. Drivers in Myanmar have an impressive disregard for safety, part of which is structural: steering wheels are on the right side of cars, but people drive on the right side of the road. So when taxi drivers want to pass, which is often, they have to veer all the way out into oncoming traffic to see if it's safe. This presents a dangerous gamble for passengers: sit in the passenger seat, which is generally the only one with a seatbelt, but which practically guarantees death if the taxi driver doesn't time his maneuver right; or take a seat in the back, behind the driver, where you can bounce around the inside of the car like a ping-pong ball when it swerves away from headlong collisions.

On this day, I sat seatbeltless in the back with Phoe Wa, who was going on about our destination. Kyauktan was famous for having a pagoda in the middle of a river. Almost every small town in Myanmar has a famous pagoda. This one was accurately named "Midstream Kyauktan Pagoda."

When we got to the jetty, small wooden boats plied back and forth, ferrying passengers between the island and the busy shore. The pagoda was a popular place for weekend picnicking. On the water, the wind brought the steamy temperatures down by fifteen degrees, and it was packed with hundreds of families who brought pots of rice and curry to eat on the temple's cool marble floors. Other visitors supplicated themselves in front of various shrines, working their way in an auspicious clockwise circle around the center of the pagoda. Some groups of people just seemed to enjoy being out on the river, and never set foot inside the pagoda, but instead just lounged on the island's banks.

One of the most well-known features of the river temple was the downstream bank, where visitors could throw balls of puffed-up rice husks into the muddy chocolate water. Enormous leathery catfish patrolled the eddies, waiting for the visitors. Young women in colorful formal dresses posed for selfies in front of the trash-filled river, with the leaping catfish in the background fighting for the rice balls.

"Everyone in Myanmar knows about this pagoda," Phoe Wa told me. "Not because of the stuff inside, but because you can feed the catfish here." He walked down to the water's edge to photograph a young woman throwing rice balls.

Like many other holy places in Myanmar, the hallways of Midstream Kyauktan Pagoda were decorated with a series of painted panels, which told stories associated with the temple's origins. For a non-Buddhist, these murals could often be the most fascinating part of visiting a religious space. They usually recalled local histories and colorful legends from Buddhist scripture, and often explained the town's relationship to the site.

In one panel series, the king had a dream where everything was backward: frogs were eating snakes; bulls refused to fight; cows drank milk from their calves; and women could criticize men. Distraught, the king went to the Buddha for help interpreting the dream and was told that his vision prophesied great change in the world. Reading the script underneath the panels, Phoe Wa summarized the story's simple lesson: "In the future, everything will be different."

We continued our clockwise tour of the Midstream Pagoda. In the last hallway hung a group of paintings depicting the various stages of Buddhist hell. Colorful cartoon demons performed imaginative tortures on those who had committed grave sins in their life. A mother paused with her daughter in front of the mural that Phoe Wa said commemorated "*Raurava*," the fourth hell, which was reserved for those who disrespected their parents and teachers. The name *Raurava* is supposed to sound like the shrieks made by those being tortured. In the painting, a horned demon was gleefully stabbing a sinner's body while another demon held his head underwater in a boiling cauldron.

The most extreme tortures were reserved for the mural of the eighth hell, which Phoe Wa called "*Avici*," where you go if you commit crimes against the Buddha. The eighth hell was the largest and most colorful paint-ing in the temple and was the last picture we saw before circling back to the boat launch. Those cursed to the eighth hell were depicted drowning in a sea of fire, while green- and blue-skinned demons impaled screaming humans on spears and roasted them over the flames. It was as though the pagoda was explicitly reminding visitors to remain pious after they left the site, lest they end up in one of the murals one day.

Several years previously, the small village of Sinmakaw, on the outskirts of Kyauktan, had declared itself free of all Muslims and Christians. Outside the small enclave, there was a big green sign with Buddhist flags in the cor-ners. It read:

> THIS IS A BUDDHIST VILLAGE
> Other religions are not allowed
> We are honest
> Racially Superior
> Sinmakaw Village
> Must be a purely Buddhist Village.

Sinmakaw was one of about two dozen spots around the country where residents had declared Muslim-Free Zones. In other such villages through-out Myanmar, Muslims were prohibited from owning property or selling goods within the village boundaries. Even though Muslims and Christians make up only a small minority of the country's population, these villages forbid them from staying overnight. Towns posted large signs on their out-skirts, warning visitors. Many of the signs referred to unwanted outsiders as "*kalar*," a racial epithet that originally referred to dark-skinned people of South Asian descent, but which in Myanmar sometimes applied to any Muslim person.

I asked Phoe Wa if he wanted to visit the village, but he put a finger to his lips and pointed to the back of our taxi driver's neck, where the number "969" was prominently tattooed. The numbers referred to an anti-Islamic movement that advocated for the boycotting of Muslim-owned businesses and spread incendiary rumors about jihadist plots to replace the country's Buddhist majority through higher birth rates and polygamy. The movement had been accused of inciting extremism and violence. The 969 group was led by a radical monk named Ashin Wirathu, who had been jailed for his extremist teachings during the military regime, but was freed in 2012 along with hundreds of other political prisoners. The movement represented the most virulent forms of Buddhist hate, and Wirathu's infamous sermons railing against the spread of Islam had landed him on the cover of *Time* magazine in 2013. In the interview, he described himself as "the Burmese bin Laden," and said that "You can be full of kindness and love, but you cannot sleep next to a mad dog." Failure to stand up to Muslims, he said, would lead to a jihad in Myanmar, and a destruction of the country's Buddhist heritage. 969 had significant support in the country, and the government banned the *Time* edition that showed Wirathu in a negative light.

Yangon could often feel like a cosmopolitan bubble, where the ethnic and religious tensions in the rest of the country disappeared. Stories filtered in about violence and killings in Myanmar's periphery, and there were occasional rallies in support of Wirathu, Aung San Suu Kyi, or the Tatmadaw, but no one really spoke openly about the conflicts in the borderlands or the sectarian violence in Rakhine State. A strange cloud of silence had descended on the city, muffling most attempts to address the defining issues of the day. The long shadow of secrecy that had defined life in the country for so many decades still obscured public discourse and hid certain truths.

A quick trip outside the city could change that. But the most surreal part of the trip was the fact that our racist taxi driver wasn't from Kyauktan, but from downtown Yangon. We had hailed the cab right in front of my apartment, next to one of the oldest mosques in the city.

■

No issue was more divisive in Myanmar than the violence against Rohingya Muslims in the far west. Like many other newsrooms, the *Myanmar Times* had to figure out how to properly cover an unprecedented national crisis while appealing to both local and international readers. Since the paper's birth in 2000, it had generated controversy and attention, with connections to military intelligence officials and a mix of foreign and local owners who could tally a handful of arrests between them for ruffling the wrong feathers in Myanmar's military extablishment.

Despite its sometimes-convulsive changes in management, the *Times* nevertheless thrived during periods of national drama. In March 2015, the paper moved from a weekly to daily circulation, and became the paper of record for many people in Myanmar for that year's election cycle. During the country's first free national election in over fifty years, the *Times* was the definitive source for information in the run-up to the vote and provided a live-updated feed for over a week as final voting results were tallied. Freed in 2012 from the shackles of prepublication censorship, it flourished during the most important and scrutinized transition period in the country's modern history.

But self-censorship came with its own issues. There was no longer a black pen redacting whole articles, but the barrier of what was acceptable to print was now invisible. How do you know whether you've crossed it or not? How much truth is too much for the faceless government authorities? In late 2016, the *Times* found out. That October, a militant group known as *Harakah al-Yaqin* (known in English as the Arakan Rohingya Salvation Army, or ARSA, but translated directly as "The Faith Movement"), which claimed to represent the fight for Rohingya salvation, launched a coordinated attack on three military outposts on the Bangladesh border, killing nine security personnel. In response, the Tatmadaw began what they called "clearance operations" against the militants. These back-and-forth clashes with armed ethnic opposition groups have a long history in Myanmar's borderlands. The Tatmadaw had been fighting ethnic militias on fronts throughout the country's periphery for the past seventy years. In other parts of Rakhine State, the Tatmadaw had spent the last seven years skirmishing with the Arakan Army, an armed group fighting for the autonomy of the local Buddhist population.

But something about the October 2016 response was different. The government blocked UN food aid meant for eighty thousand internally displaced people from reaching northern Rakhine State. Journalists were prevented from entering the area. Within weeks, tens of thousands of Rohingya Muslims had fled to Bangladesh, where they reported extrajudicial killings and torture by the military, a chilling forecast of what would take place again ten months later. Amid the upheaval, the *Myanmar Times*'s editor for special investigations, Fiona MacGregor, filed a report in which she relayed claims that members of the Myanmar security forces had raped women during their operations in Rakhine. Several days later, after a phone call to the paper by the Ministry of Information, she was fired. According to an exposé published by *Frontier* after the fact, the *Times*'s management claimed that MacGregor had "breached company policy by damaging national reconciliation and the paper's reputation."

With a new civilian government finally in place, journalists across the country had expected a continuation of the past six years' reforms. The hope had been that new press freedoms might usher in a younger generation of reporters that could tackle the country's increasingly complex issues. But the government's strong-arming of the paper to fire MacGregor had demonstrated how wrong those expectations had been. The *Times* was now facing pressure from the government not to publish anything that would harm the national interest. New editorial guidelines were put in place: any article that mentioned Rakhine State had to be vetted by the editor-in-chief before publication. Editors were expected to choose stories bearing in mind that one of the paper's responsibilities was to "promote national reconciliation."

Throughout late 2016 and early 2017, many foreign reporters and editors resigned from the paper over its handling of the worsening Rakhine crisis. By this point, international outlets were doing almost all the substantial reporting on Rakhine State. The paper that called itself the "heartbeat of the nation" was no longer reporting on the country's most important issue. When I talked with people in Yangon about the *Myanmar Times*, the most common response from both foreigners and locals was something along the lines of: "What happened to that paper? It used to be good."

For the *Times*'s senior local staff, like Kaung Htet, the changes in the paper's editorial process had become suffocating. Previously, the photo editor had been able to go on reporting trips to the borderlands without asking permission. He would pay for the trips himself, and then get reimbursed when he returned to the office. But under the new ownership, all of his reporting had to be approved beforehand. "They don't understand what it's like to do journalism," he complained to me one day. "They are just businesspeople."

The paper had instituted a policy whereby employees had to scan their fingerprint when they entered and exited the building as a way to clock in and out. If the reporters didn't work their allotted hours, they wouldn't get their full pay, regardless of how thoroughly they did their jobs as journalists.

▪

Whenever Phoe Wa and I met in the evenings, he would talk about his obligations, goals, and hopes for the future. "If I just keep trying, I know that I will succeed," he told me once. But for the moment, trying hard meant working without pay in an expensive and alien city. For Phoe Wa, the decision to take an unpaid internship was an especially fraught one. "I am the oldest, I should be supporting my parents now. But I cannot," he said. "I feel very *A Na*." He grimaced as though he was revealing something unpleasant.

A Na is a universal human feeling for which the Burmese language has found a name. My Burmese–English dictionary defines the term as "being embarrassed by feelings of respect." That description only led to more questions. What kind of respect? What sort of embarrassment? It didn't seem to fit with Phoe Wa's use of the term.

But *A Na* is a vague and very personal feeling, and English words have a hard time pinning down the exact meaning. In Phoe Wa's case it might be better described as a feeling of humility or modesty stemming from strong social obligations. *A Na* is the feeling you get when you show up to a party and don't want to be the first one to eat from the buffet, or when you realize that you haven't called to check in with your parents in three weeks.

Phoe Wa felt *A Na* because he wasn't able to send money back home to his mother and sister. He felt *A Na* about asking for help or receiving anything that seemed like a handout. When I paid for the drinks the first time we met, he told me, "Daniel, you make me feel very *A Na*, because you are a guest here and I should pay." Suddenly, his slow, measured sips of beer made more sense: I had finished two glasses over the course of an hour and a half, while he had only sipped from the top of his while it got warm. *A Na* was part of living a Buddhist life, Phoe Wa told me once. It was an integral part of his identity.

But *A Na* worked both ways. I had a fellowship with a monthly stipend fifteen times greater than Phoe Wa's life savings. I had my own feelings about letting him buy me drinks. Occasionally, I would relent and let him pay. But I felt *A Na* in my own way around Phoe Wa.

Social pressures regarding family obligations are especially strong in Myanmar, where Buddhist traditions dictate much of one's personal responsibilities regarding family. Every day that Phoe Wa spent in Yangon, working without pay, a heavy sense of humility and accountability hung over him, while his small bankroll shrank day by day.

Phoe Wa was thrifty by necessity. He didn't yet have the network he needed to do freelance work in the city, so he hustled for extra cash and benefited from occasional charity from Kaung Htet. When he had an assignment from the *Times,* the paper would give him a stipend to pay for the taxi. When the assignment was not urgent, he would take the bus instead, and pocket the remainder of the cash. "But of course, when it is an important story and I need to get there fast, I will just take the taxi," he assured me.

It was clear to me that Kaung Htet really believed in Phoe Wa and was going out of his way to help the young photographer succeed. "I think of him like a little brother," Kaung Htet told me once. He would occasionally bring Phoe Wa small presents from his trips, but the young photographer always refused to accept them.

Other photographers had occasionally borrowed cash from Kaung Htet, but Phoe Wa, the one unpaid staff member, had never asked for anything. When colleagues offered to buy him lunch or drinks when out on assignment, Phoe Wa would always say that he'd already eaten. Phoe Wa had a profound sense of shame and embarrassment about asking for help, and Kaung Htet was worried that it would end up harming him. "I don't really understand it," said Kaung Htet. "Why he doesn't just accept some help. We just want to help him."

Even successful photographers like Kaung Htet had to hustle on the side to make ends meet. "The salary at the newspaper is so low," he said to me one day. "Bro, you wouldn't believe it. I also do freelance work for the *Wall Street Journal*. If I work for them for two days, it covers my entire month salary at the paper."

Freelance work had dried up in the past few years. "From 2010 to 2014, everyone was paying attention to the country," Kaung Htet said. "But now no one cares anymore. There just aren't many opportunities to do freelancing." While the international media's attention on the Rohingya crisis had brought the country back into the spotlight, for local journalists like Kaung Htet the inability to visit the affected area meant missing out on lots of paid opportunities.

Kaung Htet's own transition to photography had been unorthodox. His business cards said Dr. Kaung Htet, because he had trained in internal medicine for several years. In 2007, during the last year of his residency, he was working in a government hospital when the Saffron Revolution took place. In that year, the country's Buddhist clergy protested en masse against the military government. The military sent out the soldiers to turn back the monks, and the streets ran red. "At that point, they just didn't care," Kaung Htet said. "If you said the wrong thing, they would just shoot you like it was nothing."

Kaung Htet rushed down and saw monks being beaten to death by military and police officers. He tried to save two of them, but both died there on the street.

"As a doctor, we take the Hippocratic oath. You treat everyone. It is just a patient. Religion, politics, nothing else matters. But that is not how it was on the ground at that time."

Also on the street, Kaung Htet saw other concerned citizens—people secretly taking photos, recording the events to smuggle the truth out of the country and tell the world what was happening in Myanmar. He decided at that moment that he could no longer work as a government employee. He saved his money for a year, bought a camera, and taught himself how to take pictures. He landed an internship at the *Myanmar Times* in 2009 and had been with the newspaper ever since.

Today, as the paper's photo editor, Kaung Htet mostly worked to train the younger generation of photographers. He told me that he had considered quitting many times. He called the *Myanmar Times* a sinking ship, but one that he had a real emotional connection to, having spent his entire career there. The *Times*'s photo department was the largest of any in the country, with nine full-time staff, and arguably the most well-respected part of the newspaper. Kaung Htet had a lot of latitude to run the department as he saw fit, and it gave him an important creative outlet. "I want to run the most stable aspect of a failing newspaper," he told me, laughing.

He also knew that it was one of the best ways he could help train the next generation of photographers. Many of the young journalists, like Phoe Wa, were drawn to Kaung Htet's war photography. He gave workshops throughout the year on conflict photojournalism, talking about what he learned, strategies for staying safe, and the way to take pictures when bullets start flying.

Phoe Wa told me that his big dream as a photojournalist would be to emulate Kaung Htet. But the older photographer thought that if Phoe Wa wanted to succeed in Myanmar's journalism world, he would have to break out of his shell. Phoe Wa had ambition and concrete goals—he had given up his job as a reporter because it wasn't close enough to his dream of being a photojournalist—but his shyness and modesty stood in direct contrast to that drive.

It made sense that Phoe Wa's favorite movie was *Forrest Gump*. He had watched it over and over since moving to Yangon. He liked the fact that the main character was modest and hard working, but still managed to be on the frontlines of history.

∎

I kept my eyes peeled for Phoe Wa's photography in the *Myanmar Times*. Every morning, the corn lady passed by the apartment on Bo Aung Kyaw, the nuns chanted their prayers, and I pulled the newspaper three floors up on a string. The next photo series of his I saw was from late October. Phoe

Wa had visited an orphanage in northeastern Yangon and published a photo essay called "Longing to be Reunited." The photos were rough and gloomy. Phoe Wa had photographed swaddled infants lying in neat little rows in their stainless-steel cribs, and a group of motherless toddlers crawling around together in a large empty room.

Phoe Wa told me that he wanted to focus less on the day-to-day news items and more on the neglected aspects of life in Yangon. He said photographing the orphans was about giving a voice to people who couldn't speak up for themselves. That attitude set him apart from his peers, so many of whom were set on capturing the positive, sparkling changes that came along with Myanmar's economic development. "Kaung Htet tells me to photograph what I'm interested in," Phoe Wa said. "These forgotten stories are more interesting to me."

Just as he had intended, Phoe Wa's pictures were a respite from the day's other news, which was still breathlessly following the Rohingya crisis. That morning, one of the *Myanmar Times*'s headlines was "Peace, stability restored in northern Rakhine, some troops withdrawn." Under the headline, a photo showed a burning house in the forest—a common tactic of the Tatmadaw's clearance operations.

The article started with excerpts from the Tatmadaw's official statement describing the end of its operation against "terrorist groups." As hundreds of thousands of Rohingya Muslims continued to flee, creating the world's largest refugee camp across the border in Bangladesh, the army was reporting that "since the areas in northern Rakhine State are quite stable in terms of rule of law, some of Tatmadaw columns have been withdrawn from the two townships."

The *Times* article also described the international community's ongoing response to the Tatmadaw's actions in Rakhine State, including decisions by the United States to suspend military assistance and by the European Union to cancel meetings with Myanmar's leaders. The newspaper highlighted that Myanmar's campaign against the Rohingya was costing it support, and that the country was becoming more and more isolated over this issue.

After Tatmadaw carried out military operations in retaliation against the ARSA attacks, the government received fierce criticisms from the international community over alleged widespread human rights [abuses]. Both the government and Tatmadaw denied the accusations.

That same day, *The Global New Light of Myanmar* ran articles about government activity in the same region:

Villages destroyed in terrorist attacks by the Arakan Rohingya Salvation Army (ARSA) are being rebuilt. A stake-driving ceremony was held yesterday to officially start construction of 86 houses in Thittonenargwa village tract.

With the Rohingya gone from the area, government officials had begun rebuilding some of the torched villages and issuing new national ID cards to residents. The very reason the Rohingya had been the target of such fierce animosity and attacks was because they weren't considered citizens of Myanmar, and to some, the new ID cards felt like a way to further solidify the Rohingya's otherness. The *Global New Light* article explained that the IDs would be important for the verification of any refugees returning from Bangladesh.

In the same edition, there was an article detailing a recent loss for the Myanmar national soccer team, followed by the team's slogan, which felt conspicuously inaccurate: *We are one. We are Myanmar.*

Taken together, the two papers gave a refractory view into life in Myanmar: a little bit of truth, and something else kind of like it.

2.

KINGDOM ON THE COAST

The Beach, Rakhine State

August 30, 2017, started out like any other morning in the village of Hashurata. Zahura Bekam woke up to the rooster's third cry and washed her face. She went about cooking a simple meal of rice with dried fish for her husband, Mohammed, and her two small children. After breakfast, Zahura put on her headscarf and went outside to spend a few hours repairing Mohammed's fishing nets in the morning sun. The languid coastal winds shifted the palm trees back and forth while she worked the nets. It was a tedious but important chore for any family in the fishing village. Mohammed normally went out on the water every two or three days; his catch was the family's only real source of income.

Hashurata is a small village on Myanmar's southwest coast, home to only three hundred Rohingya families. (Hashurata is the Rohingya name for the village. On most maps, it is labeled with the Burmese name of the larger township area—Ah Lel Than Kyaw.) The village is situated on one of the most idyllic stretches of beach in the world. Azure waters from the Bay of Bengal lap the sand, and coconut trees line the narrow dirt roads. Just inland, a lush belt of rainforest glows an electric shade of green.

Zahura was twenty-two years old, and had only left Hashurata a few times in her life. She had grown up in the village and knew practically everyone there by name. Zahura and Mohammed had married when she was thirteen, a normal age for girls in the Rohingya community, which tends toward the more conservative strains of Islam. Mohammed had been twenty-five at the time, and at first the age gap was scary for Zahura. "It was difficult," she remembered. "Our two families decided on our marriage. But I came to love him very much."

Zahura adjusted to her new role, and once she gave birth to their daughter, she came to enjoy the daily routine of motherhood. Zahura usually spent the mornings doing housework, and then often lounged with her neighbors during the afternoon. Like many other Rohingya women, Zahura's husband forbade her from leaving Hashurata by herself. She also wasn't allowed to work outside the home, so after she tended to the fish pond, where the family kept Mohammed's catch, she would visit with the other village wives and watch the children together.

On Wednesday the thirtieth, Mohammed stayed home. There was a sense of fear in the air. Everyone in Hashurata knew about the violence that was sweeping across Rakhine State. Five days earlier, a group of ARSA militants had attacked thirty border posts controlled by the Myanmar police and military, killing fourteen men. According to statistics released by the government, three hundred and seventy-one of the attackers died. The act was done in the name of the Rohingya people. But according to Zahura, none of the Hashurata villagers had any affiliation with the attackers.

"No one in Hashurata was ARSA," she said. "We are just a fishing village."

The Tatmadaw's response to the attacks was a vicious crackdown against the Rohingya in general. They called these "clearance operations," which were supposedly to apprehend "terrorists" planning more attacks. The villagers in Hashurata had heard stories of what these clearance operations entailed, and knew that some Rohingya were fleeing to Bangladesh. They hoped that, as a small, out-of-the-way fishing village on a neglected strip of coast, they might be spared.

But if recent months were an indicator, the Tatmadaw had a more aggressive form of retribution in its sights. The quality of life in the village had steadily deteriorated as the military had moved more and more soldiers into the region. No one in Hashurata knew what prompted the sudden troop buildup, but rumors had spread through the community of a campaign to push the Rohingya out of their homes. The day-to-day oppression from the government in the form of curfews, beatings, and killings had grown significantly worse.

"We were bothered by the Tatmadaw and police for a long time before they came to kill us," Zahura remembered. "They started putting more pressure on us six months before they came, because of events in other places."

That summer, as the pressure intensified, Zahura sat down with Mohammed one night when the kids were asleep and they talked about their situation. "How will we survive," she asked him. "If I cannot go outside for rice or if you cannot go catch fish, how will we eat?"

The fear started in earnest then. It was a feeling that would never leave.

On the evening of the thirtieth, soldiers wearing the dark green battle dress of the Tatmadaw entered Hashurata. Zahura estimated that there were close to one hundred soldiers. One group came to Zahura's house. "They entered our home and told us not to move. We didn't understand why. I took my two children and we huddled together. Then they bound our hands together."

Zahura and Mohammed could hear what was happening outside. In nearby houses, women were being raped in front of their families. Children were screaming. Gunshots echoed in the still night air.

The family huddled together in the middle of the room while the soldiers ransacked their belongings.

"They took all of our fishing nets and dragged them outside," Zahura remembered. "Then they locked the doors."

The family thought that they may have gotten off unscathed, but the nightmare was only beginning. Zahura heard the soldiers conspiring outside, then the unmistakable whoosh of dry fibers going up in flame. The family's bamboo-constructed house was on fire, and they were locked inside. As the blaze climbed the walls of the house, the roof, made of thatch and palm, lit like a torch. The children started screaming.

"We ran to the kitchen," Zahura recalled. "Then we cut a hole in the wall by breaking down the bamboo. Then we just ran into the jungle. All four of us escaped together. We stayed in the forest and watched."

They hid with other families from the village that had fled into the jungle and watched as their house burned to the ground. The men, women, and children gathered there stayed hidden until 3:00 a.m., watching the soldiers sift through their belongings, hoping that they would leave.

"They took all of our boats," Zahura remembered.

But then, once the looting was over, the soldiers formed into a line, walked toward the jungle, and opened fire with their assault rifles. "The army just started spraying bullets—rat tat tat tat tat," Zahura said. Her husband Mohammed was near the front of the group, watching with their one-year-old son, Mohammed Sulim.

"First my baby was shot in the head," Zahura said. "Then I lost my husband. I was further into the forest with my daughter. I saw them fall. I thought—What will I do? I could not go to him because there were so many army men. So I just fled for my life with my daughter and did not look back."

Zahura ran through the jungle with six-year-old Shrau Bibi and a group of neighbors. She would never see her village again. "Everyone was leaving. Lots of people from Hashurata were with me. None of us tried to go back to our houses because we knew we would die. We just started moving towards Bangladesh."

Zahura had also been hit with a bullet—a graze above her left eye—but she could not stop and clean the wound. During that night and into the next day she slowly trekked through the jungle, sometimes carrying her daughter, who had gone still and mute from the shock. Finally, they arrived at the Naf River, about five miles to the west, which marked the border with Bangladesh. There, they joined a group of forty other Rohingya who together paid a man with a boat $250—a month's worth of savings for most people in Myanmar—to take them across the river. Despite living on the beach, many of the Hashurata villagers did not know how to swim. Other boats were capsizing in the current. People were flailing as they waded through the water. But Zahura's boat made it safely to Shapuree Island, at the mouth of the river.

"We stayed on that island for eight days," she remembered. "We had no food and no water." The villagers lay there on the naked spit of land, exposed to the elements at the height of the rainy season. "I just remember thinking that we would never make it." Zahura said.

Finally, on September 8, Zahura and Shrau Bibi crossed the border. "When I arrived in Bangladesh I felt good, because it is a Muslim country. I thought: We can survive here."

•

Zahura's story is emblematic of the horrors that practically every Rohingya man, woman, and child living in Myanmar in the autumn of 2017 went through. From August to January, more than 700,000 Rohingya Muslims were forced to flee their homes in Rakhine State following a coordinated campaign of killing, rape, and arson by Myanmar's security forces. Thousands of Rohingya men, women, and children were killed in these "clearance operations." Satellite imagery of western Rakhine State showed that hundreds of Rohingya villages had been burned to the ground. Once in Bangladesh, refugees told remarkably similar and consistent stories about the atrocities they had experienced. To most of the world, this exodus bore all the hallmarks of a state-sanctioned genocide. The American secretary of state and the UN high commissioner for human rights both described the Myanmar military's campaign as an act of "ethnic cleansing." But beyond funding humanitarian response operations, there was little that the international community could do to curb the violence. China and Russia had long supported Myanmar's government in multilateral venues (in part because they have long-established policies opposing any international "interference" in domestic affairs—including alleged abuses within their own countries) and continued to use their veto powers on the UN Security Council to prevent any sort of muscular international response.

Myanmar felt like a place cut off from the rest of the world—a place with its own history, its own dialogue, and its own version of the truth. The national narrative was all about heroism: elite troopers fighting off terrorists who sought to destabilize the country. The Tatmadaw's operations had been nominally sparked by the ARSA attacks on August 25. The attacks were seen as part of a jihadist uprising, but were mostly carried out by angry, desperately poor farmers wielding machetes and homemade weapons led by a group of militants from abroad and a few radical locals. The leader of ARSA, a man named Ata Ullah, was a Rohingya born in Pakistan who spent most of his life in Saudi Arabia. Security analysts believed that ARSA's operations were partly funded through Saudi-linked groups, and that Ata Ullah received guerilla training from jihadist groups in Pakistan and perhaps Libya. Once back in Rakhine State, Ata Ullah recruited angry young men to fight the well-equipped Tatmadaw with nothing but makeshift weapons and a healthy dash of faith. The Islamist links gave ARSA an infamous reputation in Myanmar, but they were far less organized and less well-funded than the country's other insurgent groups.

As Zahura remembered, and as all of the Rohingya refugees I spoke with attested to, the Myanmar military had begun a troop buildup in the area months prior to the ARSA attacks. The United Nations, Reuters, and Amnesty International later confirmed the slow and deliberate nature of this military buildup. One UN official I spoke with in New York said that local UN officers had been issuing reports of troop buildup in Rakhine state for six months prior to the August 25 ARSA attacks, but that the warnings went unheeded. "We told people that this would be a slaughter," the UN official said. "But no one did anything."

To the world, this looked like a preplanned massacre of the poorest, most desperate, most maligned ethnic group in Myanmar. A stateless people without hope cut down by an army without mercy. But to most people in Myanmar, the truth was a different story—one that morphed constantly, that lived on social media and in politicians' speeches, and which wouldn't be changed from the outside.

■

Like most writers covering Myanmar, when I first started reporting on the Rohingya, in outlets like *Asia Times* and *The Diplomat*, I quickly became the target of repeated, anonymous online harassment. The most common post was just two words: "Fake News."

Other responses were more elaborate. On a story about Rohingya protests in Bangladesh, one commenter wrote, "This is a distraction made by USA and it's media to fend off bombing of Yemen bus full of school children which they and Saudi Arabia are in toghedar."

Some responses singled me out for fabricating stories. A poster with the name "Truth and Justice Myanmar" sent me a message with the subject "You Are Wrong."

> The testimonies you publish are fake.
> You faked them or those dirty Bengali lied to you.
> Tatmadaw did not burn any Bengali villages. The ARSA terrorist
> burne their own houses in order for world support of their hidden
> jihadist agenda.
> Do not suport the liars

That same accusation permeated all levels of public discourse. In newspapers and on radio and on television the message was the same: The "Bengalis," as the Rohingya are often called in Myanmar, were duping the rest of the world into supporting a terrorist uprising. The Tatmadaw was protecting Myanmar from these jihadists.

When a group at the United Nations General Assembly jointly accused Myanmar of ethnic cleansing and attempted genocide, the country's ambassador to the UN responded that the military was fighting an arm of the global Islamic terrorist menace, and that the rest of the world was being hypocritical.

"Terms such as atrocities, ethnic cleansing, and genocide must not be used lightly," he said. "When it comes to terrorism, there can be no choices. The world cannot condone terrorism in any form or manifestation for whatever reason. We must stand together to remove the scourge of terrorism."

As more Rohingya escaped Myanmar, newspapers, TV stations, and radio across the world ran stories about the atrocities committed against the Rohingya. Outlets seemed to compete to see who could publish the most shocking anecdotes. One headline that ran on the front page of *The New York Times* read: "Rohingya Account Atrocities: 'They Threw My Baby Into a Fire.'"

But for every story that described Myanmar's security forces destroying Rohingya lives, there was a separate domestic narrative to counter it.

Throughout the month of September, the state mouthpiece, *The Global New Light of Myanmar*, ran a series of editorials castigating negative media coverage as "fake news." In one essay from September 19, columnist Khin Maung Myint wrote that only naïve readers would believe the stories coming out of the refugee camps, and that this coverage was part of an effort to aid the ARSA militants:

> All along, I have thought that journalists are well educated,
> intelligent and well informed, know their jobs thoroughly, and
> credible people, until lately. I couldn't understand why, not
> everyone, but some international media persons want to deceive
> the readers with fake stories that only gullible and naive persons
> would believe, but not me . . . [M]any of the well known TV
> channels in the world including those in the West, are frequently
> airing fabricated fake news about the plights of minority people in
> Rakhine. They had been persistently advocating for the cause of
> the Arakan Rohingya Salvation Army (ARSA), using false and
> fabricated news and depicting irrelevant photos, which I presumed
> were fed to them by the international lobbyist groups.

Sometimes, it could feel like the government assertions were meant to counter specific allegations from the foreign press and human rights groups, as though they were sparring in a public debate. When Human Rights Watch published an account on September 9 showing before and after satellite imagery of burned Rohingya villages, the government responded quickly. On September 11, the Ministry of Information published an interview with Police Brigadier General Thura San Lwin, commander of the Border Guard Force in the affected area. A large portion of the interview was devoted to the case of arson:

Q: Is there still any arson cases up to now since the terrorist activities on 25th August?

A: We find the fire outbreaks everyday while area clearing operation is being carried out. It is found the fire outbreaks become less after the Bengalis have deserted their villages.

Q: Could you please make it clear whether the terrorists burnt the villages or the Bengali villagers burnt their house by themselves and fled?

A: We found in every instances that the terrorists and Bengalis were burning their houses by themselves and fled. According to security forces, when they went on clearing operation to villages the improvised bombs were set to explode and gunfire were heard. Then the houses were seen burning. Then, they fled. The sequence of the incidents indicate clearly that the terrorists and the collaborators set the fires so as to give the false impression that the security forces were burning the Bengali villages.

The complete and utter refutation of every story that painted the military in a negative light resulted in these kinds of increasingly bizarre assertions. When police and military gave the first group of international journalists a tightly controlled tour of some of the conflict areas on September 7, they took them to Zahura's village. When asked about the still-smoldering wreckage of the village, Aung Kyaw Moe, a local police officer, said that, "They burned their own houses and ran away . . . We didn't see who actually burned them because we had to take care of the security for our outpost . . . But when the houses were burned, Bengalis were the only ones in the village."

When I wanted to gauge how regular people reacted to the national media, I would talk to U Myo Tun, who owned a street stall outside my apartment in Yangon. U Myo Tun made a living selling betel nut, cigarettes, and soda to the day laborers and porters who worked on the crowded streets in downtown Yangon. He was an excellent person to talk to about the media, because he spent all day reading newspapers. He kept a stack of the day's news on a little stool and would slowly work his way through the stories as the shadows slid across the buildings. U Myo Tun was a Bamar Muslim who shared a religion and little else with the Rohingya, but he had lived in Rakhine State for a year when he was young.

During the height of the crisis, when thousands of refugees were pouring over the border to Bangladesh every day, I visited U Myo Tun and asked him about the Rohingya. He held up a finger. "There are no Rohingya people in Myanmar," he told me. "Only illegal immigrants from Bangladesh who call themselves that name." We were standing on a busy part of the sidewalk, and people walking by turned their head and scowled when they heard a foreigner using the word "Rohingya."

But then U Myo Tun went on to describe the childhood relationships he had with Rohingya kids.

"I remember when my family lived there. Relationships were good then. The Bengali and Rakhine students went to school together. Back then we did call them Rohinyga, but now the government has shown that there are no Rohingya. They are all Bengali. The situation in Rakhine is so difficult. It's sometimes hard for outsiders to understand."

When I asked him if he believed everything he read in the newspapers, U Myo Tun said, "We know that they lie about a lot. All the media has an agenda. The Tatmadaw has an agenda. For decades, all they did was lie to us. But we have to choose what to believe. I read all the newspapers in order to develop my own viewpoint. What choice do I have? There's no other news for me to turn to."

∎

The government could easily deny the accuracy of international coverage, because with the exception of very rare and heavily monitored trips to specific villages, foreign reporters were not allowed into northern Rakhine State to report on the violence. Occasionally, the military would invite a few local journalists deeper into Rakhine State to report, and even brought in several Chinese reporters. The coverage from these visits uniformly praised the Myanmar security forces for their professionalism and restraint. Most concluded that Islamic jihadists perpetrated the violence, that they had destroyed their own homes in order to dupe the rest of the world, and that the military had uncovered a dangerous plot to destabilize the country.

When I asked Aung Hla Tun, the deputy minister for information, why journalists weren't allowed into the area, he said that, "we have to restrict the number because of the limited resources, logistic problems, and security concerns."

Denied access to the site of the violence, foreign journalists could only observe from afar and were forced to rely on the oral accounts told by refugees like Zahura. As the detail and consistency of these accounts grew, media outlets and human rights groups began publishing detailed stories of Tatmadaw assaults on individual villages.

To combat this "fake news" coming in from abroad, the Tatmadaw dispatched an agency called the True News Information Team, which promulgated its own facts: "There was no death of innocent people." When "women and children were fleeing their homes, not a single shot was fired on them."

On September 30, a headline in *The Global New Light of Myanmar* ran: "More Muslim Villagers Emigrate to Bangladesh of Their Own Accord."

The article stated calmly that, "Starting on Tuesday, they left their region, claiming that they felt insecure to remain because they were now living in a sparsely populated area, as most of their relatives had left for Bangladesh."

This narrative found a ready readership among most people in Myanmar for several reasons. For one, the crisis in Rakhine had a complicated history, which was difficult to distill into a seven-hundred-word article. If a reporter made a small mistake, the government would highlight it as evidence that the journalist was uninformed and unprofessional and was simply reciting the Rohingya's side of the story. Secondly, because these international reports were rarely syndicated in any local media, people didn't have the luxury of deciding for themselves which stories were real or fake. Like U Myo Tun said, "What choice do I have? There's no other news for me to turn to."

The eighteen million people in Myanmar with regular access to social media had more information to digest, but they also had to wade through the bewildering flood of allegations and stories being shared on Facebook, many of which were fabricated or greatly exaggerated. Online troll teams would overwhelm news stories, commenting and posting on anything related to Rakhine State. Mostly their profiles were newly created, lacked any identifying information, and bore most of the hallmarks of coordinated information warfare campaigns seen in places like the United States and Germany. But enough regular people shared these semi-anonymous posts and comments, however, that links to things like "terrorist lists," which included names of Rohingya children, quickly spread across Myanmar's online population.

In November, *The Global New Light of Myanmar* published official findings from the Tatmadaw True News Information Team, which had conducted its own investigation into the behavior of its security forces. The report concluded that soldiers and police had acted according to legal rules of engagement and did not commit any war crimes. It then detailed specific actions that the Tatmadaw *did not* do:

According to the answers of 2,817 villagers from 54 Bengali villages in interviews and confessions of 362 villagers from 105 Muslim villages, security forces did not commit shooting at innocent villagers and sexual violence and rape cases against women. They did not arrest, beat and kill the villagers. They did not totally destroy, rob and take property, gold and silver wares, vehicles and animals of villagers from the villages and displaced villages. They did not set fire to the mosques in Bengali villages. They allow the Bengali villagers to perform their faiths in freedom without banning them to attend the mosques and join prayers. They did not threaten, bully and drive out the villagers not to be able to live in the villages and they did not set fire to the houses. They are joining hands with relevant administrative bodies in systematically supervising the tasks to protect the remaining houses in villages against destruction and stealing of unscrupulous persons. It is found that mobile medical teams gave health care services to the locals in villages for 291 times, and rice, edible oil, salt and foodstuffs weighing 234 tons were provided to the locals for 273 times.

The vast majority of people in Myanmar, who get their news from TV, radio, and newspapers, received this one consistent narrative, the one that was being strictly controlled by the very same people who were responsible for the violence.

■

As September wore on, and the stream of refugees kept pouring into Bangladesh, the international outcry grew. There were repeated calls for Aung San Suu Kyi, the head of the civilian government, to speak out against the military's campaign. Under Myanmar's constitution, which was written by the Tatmadaw in 2008, the civilian head of government has no direct control over the armed forces. However, Aung San Suu Kyi occupies a moral high ground in Myanmar that is perhaps unique among heads of state. She is both the daughter of the country's founding father and an international human rights icon in her own right. She endured fifteen years of house arrest and emotional toil in her nonviolent struggle for democracy in Myanmar, for which she was awarded the Nobel Peace Prize in 1991. During her imprisonment, she was forbidden from participating in national politics, unable to visit her dying husband, and absent from her children's lives. Parts of the constitution were expressly written to bar her from power, but her personal sacrifices for the people of Myanmar, and the deep support she enjoys across the country, allowed her party to sweep national elections in 2015. After her ascendance to power, many observers hoped that she would use her moral authority to try to curb the already well-documented persecution of the Rohingya. After the 2017 "clearance operations" began, the cries came for her to do something, anything, to try to stop the violence.

But instead, the human rights icon sided with the military and with the overwhelmingly popular opinion in Myanmar—that the campaign in Rakhine State was a necessary part of protecting the nation. She joined the chorus blaming "fake news" and "an iceberg of misinformation" for exacerbating the crisis.

Then, in late September, she gave a speech to assembled diplomats in the capital city of Naypyidaw. International observers hoped that she would reassert herself as the champion of the downtrodden. This was a politician, after all, who had written, "The struggle for democracy and human rights in Burma is a struggle for life and dignity."

In the nation's former capital, Yangon, thousands turned out to show their support of The Lady. I joined a crowd of young rally-goers in Mahabandoola Park. The atmosphere was charged. People were angry that the world was slandering their icon, and they wanted to share their displeasure. A group of men and women stood in the middle of the crowd, holding up signs that said "We Stand with Aung San Suu Kyi." Organizers gave speeches that blasted out of enormous speaker walls. A few police stood on the outskirts of the crowd. They didn't seem to care if the rally got out of hand. That seemed to be the point of the whole event.

As a man on the platform shouted to the crowd, I spoke with a young woman who was wearing a T-shirt with The Lady's picture on it. Aye Aye was twenty-eight and worked as a bank teller in downtown Yangon. She had never been to Rakhine State, but had strong opinions about its Muslim inhabitants.

"These people do not belong here. They are illegal immigrants," she told me. "Aung San Suu Kyi and the Tatmadaw are protecting us from the terrorists. We will support them no matter what."

I asked Aye Aye how she knew that and she looked shocked. "Everyone knows it. You just have to read a newspaper."

"I've never seen anything like that in the newspaper," I said to her.

She took her phone and showed me a post on Facebook. It was an image that had been widely shared during the past several weeks. It showed a group of South Asian–looking men armed with rifles, encamped in a lush green field. "These are the illegal Bengalis," Aye Aye said, using the common term for the Rohingya. "They are preparing to invade. This is their jihad against the Buddhists."

The BBC had researched the photo and identified that it was indeed a picture of armed Bengalis. But the picture was from Bangladesh's 1971 war for independence. The fact that the clothing, equipment, and landscape around the photo's subjects was indistinguishable from that of northern Rakhine in 2017 showed just how limited development had been in the neglected Rohingya communities. When I told Aye Aye about the real provenance of the photo, she turned to me: "How can you be sure that is not fake news?"

Aung San Suu Kyi's statement about "an iceberg of misinformation" was largely directed toward Western governments who rushed to highlight the persecution of the Rohingya without conducting the proper due diligence. On August 29, the Turkish vice prime minister, Mehmet Simsek, posted photos on Twitter that he claimed documented massacres of Rohingya. But none of the photos had actually come from Rakhine State. One was a picture of people from Myanmar who had drowned in a river boating accident in 2016. Another was a group of Thai Muslims taken in 2004. One showed a river in Pakistan. The photos were accompanied by a caption that said, "Stop turning a blind eye to ethnic cleansing." The vice prime minister urged that the "Int'l community must act now."

Aye Aye had a point. Fake news *was* exacerbating the crisis. For the people of Myanmar, there was no way to discern who was telling the truth and who was lying, or who were themselves being deceived by fake news.

In her speech, Aung San Suu Kyi stood by the military. She refused to use the word "Rohingya." She assured the world that "The security forces have been instructed to adhere strictly to the code of conduct in carrying out security operations, to exercise all due restraint, and to take full measures to avoid collateral damage and the harming of innocent civilians."

This was a woman, after all, who had also written, "It is not power that corrupts but fear. Fear of losing power corrupts those who wield it and fear of the scourge of power corrupts those who are subject to it."

■

The account of 2017's sectarian violence was not the only thing in dispute. Practically everything about the Rohingya—their history, their name, their very identity—was contested by others in Myanmar. The truth about an entire people seemed to be in flux.

Despite ample evidence that most of the Rohingya had lived in the country's far west for generations, the majority of people in Myanmar consider them to be illegal immigrants from Bangladesh. The fact that most people in Myanmar even had an opinion on the Rohingya was itself noteworthy. Other ethnic groups of comparable size, like the Lisu in the far north or the Pa'O from the Shan hills, some of whom maintained standing armies and had waged civil wars against the central government for decades, garnered little public attention. None of them were considered "terrorists," and for the most part, people in Myanmar didn't think they should leave the country or even disband their militias. But the national discourse around the Rohingya had been so manipulated over the decades that the poorest and most powerless group in the country had fueled a national hysteria over security.

In most official government and military statements, the Rohingya were referred to as Bengalis. People who wanted to appear more accommodating would call them "Muslims in Rakhine." The government campaign against them had a singular goal: to convince the people of Myanmar that the Rohingya do not actually exist.

But historical records paint a different picture. Most historians believe that Muslims have lived in what is now Rakhine State since the arrival of Arab traders in the ninth century. The Arakan Kingdom, as it was then called, was a Buddhist theocracy, but relationships with the Muslim community were warm. Some Arakan kings even took honorific Muslim titles to maintain the communal relationship. There is also evidence that at least some of the Muslims living in the region have referred to themselves as "Rohingya" since the eighteenth century. The first written appearance of the word comes from an East India Company document dated to 1799. Dr. Francis Buchanan was a surgeon who attempted to compile one of the first categorized lists of all of Myanmar's ethnic groups. He distinguished several groups in Arakan, including a group of Muslims "who have been long settled in *Arakan*, and who call themselves *Rooinga*, or natives of *Arakan*." Buchanan noted that these Muslims "call the country *Rovingaw*."

Not long after Buchanan's report, the Myanmar kingdom (which had absorbed Arakan in the 1780s) launched an ill-advised war against the British. By 1826, Arakan was part of the growing British Empire. The new rulers encouraged immigration flows that would characterize the next century of colonial rule in Myanmar—each year bringing millions of people from other parts of the empire to work and settle in what was until that point a small, isolated country. On top of that, as historian Thant Myint-U points out, the British also instituted a racial hierarchy, differentiating "native races" from "non-native" ones, and apportioning benefits accordingly. Together, these practices would have profound effects on the attitude of the native population toward outsiders.

Throughout colonial rule, the British maintained fastidious records of the people living across their territories. In 1917, the *Akyab District Gazetteer* was published. It covered the area around Zahura's village and contained a section about the provenance of the Muslims (whom the British called "Mohamedans") living in the northern part of the district. The authors were cheerfully condescending about the Muslim community and the ease with which they intermingled with the local Buddhist population. The report made it clear that by 1879 the population included both permanent residents and migrant workers. Many were descendants of Muslim slaves captured by the former Arakan kings, whose empire had stretched well into modern-day Bangladesh. But the *Gazetteer* made clear that the Muslims had integrated well into the local society and "differ but little from the Arakanese except in their religion and in the social customs which their religion directs."

Today, critics of the Rohingya in Myanmar often point to the fact that the word "Rohingya" never appears in the official British colonial records. There are only references to "Muslims in Rakhine," or "Mohamedans." There is nothing to distinguish these people, the argument goes, from the thousands of Bengali Muslims who came across the border at that time. And even though records clearly describe "bona fide" Muslim residents, the more attention-grabbing detail for most people in Myanmar was the description of the Muslims as the "men who come down for the working season."

It is true that after Buchanan's 1799 report, the word "Rohingya" doesn't appear in published documents until the second half of the twentieth century. But by that point, in the early years of independence, it had become an accepted term in Myanmar. The central government came to recognize the Rohingya identity, and even employed Rohingya men as civil servants. Burmese government documents from the 1950s use the term "Rohingya," and radio programs from the era broadcast in the Rohingya language.

But by the 1980s, the socialist regime, which ruled from 1962 to 1988, had begun denying that the Rohingya existed at all. This effort was part of a broader campaign of xenophobia that sought to cast the majority Bamar population as above Myanmar's many minorities, and to categorize all ethnic groups in the country according to government-mandated criteria.

In 1982, the socialist regime passed a new citizenship law, which defined full citizens as members of those ethnic groups that had settled in Myanmar prior to 1823, the year before the first war with the British Empire. The government deemed eight ethnic groups—the Bamar, Shan, Kachin, Chin, Rakhine, Karen, Mon, and Kayah—"National Races," and granted them full citizenship. Groups like Chinese, Nepalese, and mixed-race people who were not part of the National Races, but who could demonstrate "conclusive evidence" of ancestry dating back to 1823, fell into a second tier of citizenship. Other requirements for citizenship were deliberately vague. People applying for citizenship had to be able to "speak well one of the national languages," be "of good character," and be "of sound mind."

Ethnicity as a defining characteristic of citizenship was further cemented into the national discourse the following year. During Myanmar's census, the government divided the eight National Races into 135 different subgroupings. Census takers asked respondents to categorize themselves according to these criteria. The number 135 has since come to be seen as the defining characteristic of Myanmar's ethnic makeup. Everything from policy documents to tourist brochures describes Myanmar's diversity with reference to its 135 different ethnic groups.

But the provenance of the number 135 is disputed, and many people consider it to be completely arbitrary. Some analysts point to a 1931 British colonial census that listed 135 different languages in Myanmar. Another explanation is that the number comes from a senior Tatmadaw general who, when asked why the military was having so much trouble combatting ethnic insurgencies in the country's periphery, noted that it was because there were so many ethnic groups: 135. Some people believe that the number 135 arose from the former dictator Ne Win's well-known obsession with numerology and the number nine, reportedly due to an astrologer's recommendation to the leader. Several policy decisions around this time were based around the number nine. (At one point, much of the national currency was devalued and replaced with bills that were multiples of nine, to devastating effect.) Supposedly the number of ethnic groups satisfied the same numerological criteria because 1 plus 3 plus 5 equals 9.

Most experts say that the list of 135 ethnic groups is both inaccurate and inconsistent. A 2012 analysis of Myanmar's ethnic makeup found only fifty-nine distinct ethnic subgroups. Representatives from the Chin ethnic minority, which on the official list supposedly contains fifty-three different subgroups, have said that there should only be eight. In some instances, the official list highlights small clan or dialect differences, taking them as representative of entirely different ethnic subgroups. Some groups appear multiple times under different names.

The list conspicuously ignores the Rohingya. Other Muslim minorities from Rakhine State, like the Kamein, are included. But the Rohingya, who make up the largest Muslim population in the country, are missing. When census takers came door-to-door and asked people to pick an identity, the Rohingya had to fill in the blank.

However the government determined this list, the legalized categorization of ethnicity successfully suppressed the political power of minority groups by highlighting their fractures while maintaining the illusion of a more uniform Bamar population making up the majority of the country.

For the Rohingya, the passage of the 1982 citizenship law and the reification of Myanmar's "135 ethnic groups" accelerated their disenfranchisement. Many Rohingya families had emigrated into Myanmar during the colonial period, which automatically excluded them from full citizenship under the new laws. But even for those who could trace their lineage in Myanmar back to before 1823, the burden of proof was so difficult and vague—"conclusive evidence"—that all but the most well-documented Rohingya families were ineligible for any form of citizenship under the new rules. Instead, for all intents and purposes, they were treated like foreigners.

In 1991, the government began a new policy of mandating annual photos of every Rohingya family. In these pictures, every member of the family had to be present, and the picture was used to verify each individual's legal status. If the family failed to comply, the consequences could be severe. Noor Mohammed, a grocer from Maungdaw city, in Rakhine State, described the dangerous situation this created for his family: "Every year we had to supply a family photo. One year we would have eight people in the picture. But the next year, one person could not make it. He had to work in the farm. So that year we only had seven people in the photo. The government worker I gave the picture to told me, 'That guy who is not here, now he is no longer a resident of this country. We will arrest him if we find him, because he is here illegally.'"

Noor Mohammed had a handful of the old photos in his breast pocket, creased and worn. In each, his family stood arrayed against a plain wooden backdrop. No one smiled. The stiff formality of the pose made it feel nothing like a family photo. He showed me a pair of pictures, one in which a young boy was present and another where he was missing. That year he had been sick and missed the photo. He was stricken from the government rolls.

Likewise, identification documents became tools of oppression. Local administrators would call in Noor Mohammed's family to update their National Identity Cards, which listed things like citizenship status, ethnicity, and "identifying marks." But when they turned in their cards, which had said "Rohingya," they were confiscated and replaced with cards that said "Bengali/Muslim." Later, those cards were replaced with a third identity document, which didn't say anything about ethnicity, effectively removing any legal status.

Throughout this time, the Rohingya also contended with regular military incursions into their villages. Rakhine State has always been a restive place. Since the late 1960s, both Rohingya Muslims and Rakhine Buddhists have maintained sporadic insurgencies against the central government. But in Rakhine State, the Rohingya have borne a disproportionate level of retribution from the Tatmadaw.

By the early 2000s, Rohingyas in Myanmar were systematically excluded from all the basic elements of citizenry. Being Rohingya meant being unable to travel freely, apply for certain business licenses, or register the birth of your child. A Rohingya student accepted to a university in Yangon would never be able to relocate in order to enroll. Rohingya men and women that needed to be hospitalized were kept separated from other patients.

Once ARSA began attacking the Tatmadaw in the name of liberating their people from an apartheid regime, the government's coordinated campaign of disenfranchisement had taken its toll. The government had effectively changed the reality of Myanmar, and had written Rohingya out of history. By 2017, the word "Rohingya" had become taboo. During the height of the refugee crisis, even newspapers like *The Irrawaddy,* which once proudly thumbed their nose at the government by printing "Rohingya," succumbed to pressure and began to write "Muslims in Rakhine State" instead.

■

Many Rohingya went out of their way to prove their historical claims to the land they called home. Shan Shau Din, a Rohingya photographer whose photos have appeared widely in Myanmar media since the 1980s, documented more than a century of his family's ownership claims in their village of Boli Bazar. (The Burmese name for the village is Kyein Chaung.)

Each year, when the government demanded photographs of Rohingya families to prove their residency, Shan Shau Din opened his photography studio. Speaking from the floor of a UN shelter in a refugee camp in Bangladesh, he estimated that he photographed fifteen hundred families annually across eight villages for more than twenty years. "Because of this, I was able to feed my family," he said.

Despite his personal quest to prove the legitimacy of his own well-documented life in Myanmar, Shan Shau Din had long prepared for disaster. In June of 2012, when riots between Rakhine Buddhists and Rohingya Muslims in Maungdaw city left more than eighty dead, he remembered thinking, "That was the beginning of the hate. Day after day, I thought: This disease can come into my area as well."

Not long after, Shan Shau Din received warning that the police were looking for his son. They had word that Zayed was affiliated with a new group of militant Rohingya calling themselves "The Faith Movement." Zayed swore to his father that it was not true, but Shan Shau Din knew better than to leave justice up to the Myanmar police. He sent Zayed to Bangladesh, one of nearly 100,000 Rohinyga who fled that year.

For the next five years, Shan Shau Din continued trying to make a legal case for his identity. Every year, he brought his binder full of papers to the local magistrate and pleaded his case for citizenship. Other photojournalists he knew through his membership in the national photographic society tried to help.

But none of his connections or family history mattered when the violence started in August of 2017. "It was like lighting fuel in a bottle," Shan Shau Din said. "It just exploded." When he heard of the Tatmadaw attacks spreading across Rakhine State, he sent the rest of his family across the river to Bangladesh, but stayed himself in order to document the destruction that he knew was coming.

"If everyone leaves, no one will see what happens. So I needed to stay and witness. I will have to die at some time. Today, tomorrow, whenever. So as a result, I decided to take the risk."

By early September, Boli Bazaar village had been completely emptied. One morning, Shan Shau Din walked down the road to pray at a mosque in a nearby town. His neighbors had all fled to Bangladesh, and Shan Shau Din remembered the eerie silence of the building. His prayer echoed in a chamber that had once resonated with the chants of hundreds of men. He had never prayed in a mosque alone before.

His reverie was short-lived. "As I finished my prayer, I heard the bullets—rat tat tat tat."

Shan Shau Din went outside and started taking pictures with the little handheld Canon camera that he carried everywhere. Across a paddy field, a line of Rohingya men, women, and children were carrying their belongings on their backs as they headed west to the Bangladesh border. Behind them, flames consumed the village. He moved to get closer, and took photos of a thatch roof on fire, with thick smoke etched in black against the flat blue sky.

"Then after a few minutes of taking pictures, my body collapsed on the inside. Something was wrong. I knew that there was going to be a real problem."

He took the memory card with all of the photos out of his camera. "I held it in my fingers like this," he demonstrated, placing the card between his second and third fingers. "And I put in a spare memory card with nothing stored on it into the camera. Then, next thing I knew, I felt it." The barrel of a soldier's assault rifle was pressed in his back.

"They demanded to know who I was and where I was from. I didn't say anything, I just showed them my card from the Myanmar Photographic Society, and they said OK, no problem."

Once the soldiers left, Shan Shau Din took the memory card containing the photos and buried it under the mud on the side of the road. He marked the spot with a rock and then ran home to collect the pieces of his life he couldn't leave behind: a small bag of clothes and the historical documents about his family that he had painstakingly organized. Then, under the cover of darkness, he returned to collect the memory card and took a boat across the Naf River to safety in Bangladesh.

A year later, the old photographer still clung to the idea that he might be able to return to the home he had spent years documenting. In his house in the Balukhali refugee camp, he kept the papers in a blue plastic bucket donated by the World Food Program. The documents were faded and halfway illegible. They had been folded and unfolded so many times that the four-way creases were beginning to tear.

At first, as Shan Shau Din was showing me his documents and recounting the story of his escape, he asked that I not use his name, because it might cause him trouble when he eventually returned home. Then he thought for a moment. "If we return, they will kill us. I don't know how it's possible, but please help us. It is important that the world hears the story." Then he gave me copies of the photos he had taken before fleeing Myanmar.

In the refugee camp, Shan Shau Din busied himself documenting his new life. "I used to have thirteen cameras, but now only this," he said, holding up the little Canon that had captured the destruction of the Rohingya village. "It helps," he said. "I spend all my time with the camera, photographing. I do not want to hang out with anyone."

He kept saying to me, "I want to go home. I want to go home. But I cannot see any hope."

As far as most people in Myanmar were concerned, Shan Shau Din was home. He had been an illegal refugee from Bangladesh and now he had gone back to his homeland. Plus, the house he and his family had left behind in Myanmar, like most Rohingya homes, was likely burnt to the ground.

·

Seeing the camps firsthand was humbling. From a tall hill in the center of Kutupalong refugee camp, the sight of a million lives stretched out in an endless wave of sandbags and misery. Tens of thousands of white tarps fashioned into temporary roofs glinted in the tropical sun, and five times a day, the call to prayer rang out from the loudspeakers of hundreds of mosques—a pulsing roar of faith carried on the wind.

A massive humanitarian response accompanied the refugee crisis, and the camps were well run and relatively clean. Wells and latrines were easy to find, and charity-run clinics and schools advertised their services on the main roads. But certain problems are inescapable when one million people huddle month after month in temporary shelters. Rivers of mud and sewage flowed through the steep canyons that twisted through the camps. Old men made their way over rickety bridges made from bamboo and twine. The steep hills of ochre mud that gave the camp its geography seemed held together with a mixture of sandbags and hope. The refugees had chopped down all the trees that once stood there, so the rains threatened to wash everything away toward the sea. Plastic detritus poked out of the mud everywhere, pounded into the earth by the thunder of two million flip-flops. Endlessly recycled canvas tarps stamped with the emblems of UN organizations were used for everything from roofing to staircases to garbage bags and playthings. My first morning in the camps, I saw a naked boy using an empty sack stamped *International Organization for Migration* as a makeshift sleeping bag on the floor of a little cigarette shop.

I interviewed Zahura in her new home: Kutupalong Camp 5—Block C1. She lived on one of the camp's nicer blocks, made up of newly constructed houses built with Turkish aid money. Every building came with a flashlight, a solar powered phone charger, and a radio. The block was situated near the top of a hill, and the fresh sea breeze kept the noxious fumes from the lower parts of the camp at bay. The house itself was a simple two-room construction of bamboo, with a UN sheet covering the roof and blue tarpaulin lining the walls. Very little light entered the house and without any windows, the air in the dark room was stifling. As we spoke, dust from the sandbags holding down her roof sprinkled through the ceiling, staining the pages of my notebook.

Zahura still looked very young. She was wearing a purple hijab that framed a long, oval face and sharp nose. A diagonal scar ran through her left eyebrow, a daily reminder of where the Myanmar soldier's bullet grazed her face the night she lost her husband and baby boy. While we talked, she played with the fringe on her brightly colored floral dress.

Like many Rohingya women, she kept most of her personal wealth on her body: she had four gold bracelets on her right wrist, and another two on her left, along with a pair of gold earrings and three rings. She used to have more jewelry, she said, but would periodically sell a piece to the Bangladeshi pawnshops in the camps. These stores were everywhere, and were one of the only sources of cash in the refugee camps. The other way to get money was through the informal system of Muslim moneylenders scattered across Southeast Asia called Hundis. This unregulated system connected the refugees to the Rohingya diaspora across Malaysia, Indonesia, and the Gulf states, where they often worked as cheap laborers and repatriated money to family stuck in the camps. A lot of money also came from Rohingya jade traders who lived along the Chinese–Myanmar border. But these networks depended on family connections, and for a small fishing family like Zahura's they were as elusive as everything else in the camps. Cash was a precious commodity for everyone, so she sold her jewelry and slowly watched her personal wealth diminish.

Zahura sat in the far corner while we talked. Two men from nearby houses sat with her. My translator told me that their presence would make her more open to talking with a foreign man. Otherwise, my questioning might be inappropriate.

Her daughter, seven-year-old Shrau Bibi, was at one of the religious madrassas, where she spent a few hours every afternoon. Twice a week the young girl also attended a two-hour class at one of the learning centers sponsored by foreign aid groups, where teachers gave instruction in both Burmese and Bengali languages.

The family lived off donations. Every month, Zahura and her daughter received a shipment from the World Food Program: Thirty kilogram of rice, four kilograms of lentils, and two liters of cooking oil. The food was more than enough to survive, but was hardly a well-balanced diet for a seven-year-old girl. With the help of a local community leader, Zahura sold the surplus to Bangladeshi buyers, who resold the donated food on the local black market. The extra cash went toward things like phone credit and fresh food. "Sometimes I want to eat chicken or fish or vegetables. I cannot raise my daughter on just rice and lentils."

Her life had changed dramatically. The slow-moving paradise of the fishing village and its coconut trees was gone. The restrictions and fear that accompanied her life as a Rohingya woman in Myanmar were gone too. "I know I can survive here," she told me more than once.

But her new life was depressing and diminished. She hadn't left the Kutupalong camp since her arrival, as the Bangladesh government tried to prevent Rohingya from traveling to other parts of the country. Some young Rohingya men could make it to Cox's Bazar or Dhaka, where they worked as informal laborers. But for Rohingya women, travel was doubly difficult. Zahura rarely left her home. Instead, she sat in her donated shack and flipped through the pictures on her phone—the only mementos of a life gone forever. "Whenever I think of my husband and child, I feel so bad," she said.

And even though the Tatmadaw was no longer an existential threat, Zahura was nervous about other dangerous forces. During the day, the UN and aid groups ran the camps, but after they left at 4:00 p.m., criminal gangs reigned. There were fifty Bangladesh police officers for every 100,000 refugees, and the camp's residents often took the law into their own hands. While I was there, there was a string of murders in the camps as gangs battled for territory, and a makeshift gun factory had been discovered not far from where Zahura lived. Residents said that young men affiliated with ARSA would run drills and practice combat at night. There were rumors that the militants were planning another attack on Myanmar.

One of the most noticeable aspects of visiting the camps was the degree to which misinformation and conspiracy theories had also permeated the Rohingya community. During my time there, a rumor was filtering through the refugee population, spread by group messaging apps like WhatsApp and Viber. The Myanmar government had recently completed a series of "Transition Camps" in which up to 30,000 Rohingya were supposed to be housed once they had been returned to Rakhine State as part of an official repatriation program between the Myanmar and Bangladesh governments. None of the Rohingya I spoke to wanted to live in these new buildings. Initially I thought that this reluctance was due to the fact that the camps weren't connected to their ancestral land or houses. But I learned that there was another reason: The Myanmar government had paid construction companies to plant explosives under the buildings. It was an absurd allegation, but one I heard dozens of times during my interviews in Bangladesh. "Once we return to these concentration camps, they will detonate the bombs, and we will all die," one young man said. "It is their plan to kill us all." When I asked him how he knew this, he said, "All the Rohingya groups share news with each other. It is the only news we can trust."

Zahura's small family was learning to live a new life as refugees, but she feared that unless they left the camps soon her daughter might forget her home on the beach and come to see life here as normal.

As we talked, other men from Block C1 would poke their head in, see a foreigner, and walk into the house, uninvited. By the end of the interview, seven men were surrounding Zahura, and they were eager to tell their stories as well. When I asked a question about why she sold the donated food, it was a man with a long, henna-stained beard who spoke up.

"She wants chicken or fish. But she has no husband. She probably has some plans to make money though, but without a husband she cannot. So she just wants to say thank you to the Bangladesh government for giving her this home."

Each time she was interrupted, Zahura would stop talking, wait patiently, then continue her story. Her voice never wavered, but recounting her exodus was clearly a painful experience.

Reliving the night of the attack, she kept trying to reassure me that she was telling the truth. Like other Rohingya, she knew that most people in Myanmar didn't believe the stories coming out of the refugee camps. The term "fake news" had permeated everything about the Rohingya exodus, including the way the refugees talked about themselves. Zahura responded confidently to my question about the Myanmar government's allegations that her lived experience was false: "This is the truth. What I am saying is one hundred percent honest answers. Nothing that I am saying is fake. I don't understand why they would say that. This is one hundred percent honest. What I say to the Myanmar government is: I am not lying. I am telling you what really happened. They gave this to me," she pointed to the scar above her eye.

Zahura paused for a second, and none of the men tried to talk over her. Her voice shook for the first time. "I didn't even bring anything with me. Nothing but the clothes on my back," she yelled. "They say I burned down my own house! Who would do such a thing?"

3.

THE CONFLUENCE

Myitkyina, Kachin State

The northbound train trundled to a halt in downtown Myitkyina under gray skies. All through the thirty-hour journey, the men and women on the train from Mandalay had tried to protect themselves from the harsh tropical sun streamimg through the dirty windows. But as soon as we entered Kachin State—the northern borderlands of Myanmar, where a civil war had raged for decades—clouds began gathering heavy and low. Normally by mid-October the northern skies have cleared, and Kachin residents can begin to reap the benefits from four months of downpour. The farmers and fishermen were celebrating the continued rain. The fields were green with growth, and the stream banks were high. In Myitkyina, the state capital, city life pressed on beneath overflowing gutters.

I disembarked and hitched a ride across town to a large compound on a leafy boulevard. The well-dressed attendees to the Red Cross promotion ceremony had to carefully navigate a muddy track to reach the banquet hall. Ascending the wooden steps into safety, the uniformed men and women assembled in the dry building. Family and friends were not invited. This promotion ceremony was an internal affair, held only once every few years. A solitary local cameraman was the only one in attendance to document the event.

Inside the hall, brigade members milled about quietly, waiting for the VIPs to arrive. The younger male cadets pressed their dun-colored dress uniforms down flat and carefully adjusted their hat brims in the window reflection, while the few older officers sat in chairs, checking their phones with a kind of studied boredom.

While we stood together, listening to the rain drum on the big metal roof, I spoke with one of the young women up for promotion. Like the other female members of the brigade, her uniform was all white—dress and stockings and shoes—and it made the Red Cross emblem on her chest and shoulders stand out. Compared with the army-inspired livery of her male colleagues, it looked much more compassionate. I remarked that the whole event felt strangely militaristic for the Red Cross, which after all was an independent humanitarian organization.

"Yes, we are organized like a small army," she acknowledged. "But it helps. We are four thousand volunteers, and the Red Cross has a difficult mission in Kachin. And we do work in the war zone."

Hsu Myat Thandar had lived in Myitkyina since age two. Her family had been in Myanmar for three generations, after her great-grandfather had migrated from Nepal during the colonial era—part of the small army of civil servants, military police, and merchants that moved from the subcontinent when Myanmar became a British colony and a province of India. Hsu Myat Thandar had studied medicine at university. "But here your studies and occupation may not match," she said. After graduation, she wasn't able to gain entry into the small residency class required to continue medical training, and she had to give up her dreams of being a doctor. But other opportunities presented themselves. Myanmar was opening to the world, and enterprising young people were creating new professions in the changing economy. She found a job as a teacher, training adults to use computers, mobile phones, and other technologies that were novel to most people in the country. But she didn't find the job fulfilling and wanted to do something to help people.

She changed paths, taking a job as a local program officer for the Danish Red Cross, and she now worked in camps for internally displaced people scattered across the state, where Kachin people whose villages had been destroyed in the northern civil war lived in primitive conditions and received only the most minimal services. There, Hsu Myat Thandar ran workshops educating the men, women, and children on the risk of land mines.

"I like the job," she said, "but it can be quite sad sometimes. We don't know exactly where all the land mines are. I'm always worried when people go back to their villages. They want to cultivate their land again after being away, but with all the fighting, some parts of their land could be mined."

Hsu Myat Thandar turned and looked at a map hanging on the wall showing the townships of Kachin State. Nearly half the townships were colored green, indicating that the Red Cross had done mine risk education there during the first half of the year. "We tell them to be careful," she said softly, "but you never know what will happen."

The chief of police finally arrived, and the ceremony began. One by one, the men and women were called up to receive their promotion. Each time a name crackled over the worn-out loudspeakers, the officer would leap to attention at his or her seat, and shout "Here!" Then the emcee would call them to the stage, and they would march solemnly to the front of the hall. The whole event had a forced, put-on quality. Whenever someone walked from their seat to the stage they swung their arms and legs stiffly, as though they were goose-stepping in a military parade. It was clear that no one had rehearsed the formal walk before coming to the event, and the well-intentioned marchers made frequent missteps.

Later, the commander offered words of wisdom and encouragement to the officers and new recruits assembled in the room: Protect the weak. Be prepared to sacrifice. Work together. We have much to accomplish. He looked tired and spoke softly into the microphone. Sitting in the front row, the police chief took pictures on his tablet.

▪

By October 2017, there were an estimated 120,000 internally displaced people, or IDPs, in and around Kachin State. Since 2011, irregular but intense fighting between the Tatmadaw and the Kachin Independence Army, or KIA, had crippled life across the northern hills, forcing entire villages to flee into the jungle. The majority of these migrants lived in squalid camps on the far edge of civilization, in the high mountains where the Myanmar government's authority effectively ends and the Kachin self-administered territory begins. Most of Kachin State was off limits to foreign workers and humanitarian groups. Special permits and travel authorizations were required to visit, which could only be approved by military-controlled government offices. The International Committee of the Red Cross had been prevented from visiting the camps.

Instead, it was the Kachin State branch of the Myanmar Red Cross that worked with the IDPs. As a local organization, they could access areas that outside groups were banned from. A corps of volunteers ran the entire organization. They rode vans and ambulances into the mountains to attend to the sick and those injured from the war. The volunteers were organized into brigade-style detachments, complete with field and dress uniforms. Bum Tsit, a twenty-nine-year-old ethnic Kachin from Myitkyina, headed the youth volunteer brigade. He had joined the Red Cross movement as a university student in 2008, when his professors selected him to attend a national convention for the Myanmar Red Cross Society. The purpose of the event was to promote youth chapters in universities across the country. At the university, students were under particular scrutiny by the military's secret intelligence services, as most previous protest movements had started on school campuses. Even book clubs and study groups were banned. For Bum

Tsit, the Red Cross provided an outlet for participating freely in a large youth group for the first time. Later, when the war started, it became a way for him to help other ethnic Kachins affected by the fighting.

With the Red Cross, Bum Tsit made regular trips to the IDP camps in the border regions. His youth volunteer teams provided humanitarian services that international NGOs could not deliver, like first aid training and HIV awareness education. Without a robust public health infrastructure, virulent strains of malaria had been coursing through the jungle camps, and the Red Cross presence was crucial to combating its spread. The volunteers also provided livelihood and psychosocial training for the displaced, some of whom had been stuck in the remote IDP camps for six years, unable to work, and had lost most of their self-sufficiency. The volunteers sometimes traveled to jade or amber mining regions, where the fighting could be particularly fierce as the KIA and the Tatmadaw battled for control of Kachin State's valuable resources. Locals in these areas were often trapped in camps, prevented from returning home because their villages had become grounds for sporadic back-and-forth assaults between the two militaries.

I asked Bum Tsit about the Red Cross's military style and he laughed. "Yes, it is a little weird," he said. "But many things in this country are run like the military, especially the old organizations."

Allegiances to various armed groups were worn with pride in the borderlands, and in Kachin, most people backed the KIA over the Myanmar military. It was common to see shirts with the KIA flag, or bumper stickers showing loyalty to the rebel army. Civilian life meant living among military structures, and that culture had permeated into many organizations, even humanitarian missions like the Red Cross.

After the ceremony, Bum Tsit invited me for a drink at his family's restaurant. We drove to a shady corner of the city, where the restaurant's garden sprawled across a walled compound. It had a big sign in English that said *Red House*, and I asked Bum Tsit what the significance was. "It's because the building is red," he said.

Inside the restaurant, the walls were covered with large oil paintings. One showed the Confluence—the meeting of the two rivers that formed the

Irrawaddy. The land between was known as the Triangle and was considered the homeland of the Kachin people. It had long been a major KIA stronghold. Another oil panting showed a naked Western woman poised next to an enormous glass of beer. "That's the place most men want to sit," Bum Tsit said, laughing.

A few young girls were running around the restaurant, playing and shouting. Bum Tsit told me that most of the clients were part of his big, extended family. "We all come here every evening to eat." Two girls, playing tag, wore red-and-green-striped shirts with the crossed-sword emblem of the KIA.

At the restaurant, away from the brigade, Bum Tsit was candid about the difficulties of working within such a military culture:

"There are not many Kachin youth volunteers in the Red Cross. It's mostly Burmese, Indian, Nepalis. And it is because of the uniforms and the military style. The Kachin see the uniforms and think we are like the Tatmadaw. You know, Kachin people hate the Burmese—well, not the Burmese, but the military. But it's kind of the same thing to most people. So when they see us in the uniform they think we are part of the government or the military and they would not want to join."

He paused to think.

"We really need to change the uniforms and culture," Bum Tsit said. "I always tell this to the brigade, but the old members are resistant to change."

Occasionally, Bum Tsit and the other volunteers would make trips to what they officially called "armed group controlled areas"—jungle camps defended by the KIA, beyond the control of the Tatmadaw. To gain access to these regions, the Red Cross had to negotiate with both the Myanmar government and the rebel army's political arm. For several years, the volunteers were unable to negotiate access. The Myanmar government didn't have a problem with their making the trips, but the KIA was suspicious of the Red Cross. The volunteers wore army uniforms, and the organization was loaded with representatives and close contacts of the central government; the executive committee's president was the military-appointed state minster of health, and the vice president was the state police chief. The

Kachin rebels were afraid that the trips would be used to gather intelligence for the Tatmadaw. "It was impossible for the KIO to trust us," Bum Tsit admitted, referring to the Kachin Independence Organization, the KIA's political wing.

The Red Cross's board was reorganized. The minister and police chief were given advisory roles, and new blood came into the top ranks of the organization. Bum Tsit, as head of the Youth Brigade, was given a place on the executive committee, along with heads of public health agencies, powerful police sheriffs, and wealthy, philanthropic businessmen. "To help others is very noble," Bum Tsit told me. "To have humanitarian virtues is part of our ethnic heritage. More Kachin need to volunteer, to help their own people. I try to tell my people."

At one point, Bum Tsit's brother-in-law, who managed the restaurant, came and sat down with us, and asked me how the food was. Red House served Kachin-style food. A lot of it was very spicy, and Bum Tsit kept ordering rounds of beer to the table. Only two types of beer were available: Myanmar Beer and Tuborg, and the Kachin men never drank Myanmar Beer. A military-run conglomerate owned the brewery, so it was an act of resistance to order a Tuborg instead.

Bum Tsit said that most evenings he sat at Red House and had five or six drinks, but assured me that this was normal for someone from Kachin. "Most Kachin men, and the women too, once work is over, we just drink and enjoy ourselves." He had recently read an article online that discussed the correlation between heavy drinking and famously intelligent people, and he gave frequent toasts by saying "For the intelligence!"

Over the Tuborg, Bum Tsit talked to me about the difficulty of life in Kachin:

"It used to be that one person could provide for his entire family through his work. Kachin people are blessed with abundant natural resources—gold, amber, wood, jade—and these provided people living in the rural area with good work. But now, resources are gone, or they have been mismanaged, or bigger outside companies have taken control, and now it is much more difficult for people to provide for their families. The entire family has to work sometimes. So one person will come to Myitkyina and look for work. It is difficult and they are alone, and now there is much more crime in the city."

Other stories revealed the simple day-to-day corruption of life in Myanmar. Myitkyina was in a difficult economic situation: young people were having a hard time finding jobs, and drug abuse was rampant in the city. Many young Kachins believed that the central government was deliberately encouraging the drug use to weaken the next generation of Kachins and hamper the armed resistance. Bum Tsit, who had worked with the state police, waved away this conspiracy theory. The truth was simple, he said. Policemen weren't paid enough by the government, so they accepted bribes to look the other way from the drug trade.

Later, other members of Bum Tsit's extended family came and sat with us, munching roasted peanuts and drinking beer. Everyone wanted to know if I golfed, and if so, what my handicap was. Not really knowing, I made up a number that sounded respectable if believable—twenty—and we set plans for a golf outing later in the week. "For the intelligence!" Bum Tsit called, and we all clinked glasses.

•

Like many people that lived in the borderlands, Bum Tsit was a natural with languages. He was fluent in Jinghpaw, the lingua franca of the diverse Kachin tribes, as well as Burmese and English. He also spoke a little bit of Chinese, and despite living far from Thailand, had learned some phrases in Thai. In addition to the restaurant, Bum Tsit owned a jewelry store in town with his brother-in-law, and they hired a goldsmith from Thailand to spend several months at a time working at the shop. They communicated in a pidgin mix of Burmese and Thai and seemed very happy with the arrangement.

Bum Tsit described himself as "self-employed," and had fingers in a lot of different projects, including the shadowy jade industry that was central to the region's civil war. For a long time, Bum Tsit wouldn't tell me much about his jade business or how involved he might be in the underground economy. The industry was notoriously secretive and corrupt, and he was wary about sharing details. I learned quickly that Bum Tsit could be quite guarded about some aspects of his life—an important quality in a society fractured by civil war.

Bum Tsit knew how to move effortlessly between different groups, and I always marveled at his ability to put people at ease. He was a natural politician, and it seemed clear to me that he was bound for something larger than just local Myitkyina affairs. He had been to France, Switzerland, and Germany for Red Cross conferences, and had visited countries across Asia both for work and for pleasure. He was preparing to fly to Turkey for another Red Cross convention. On his phone, he showed me pictures of a recent trip he took to Yunnan province, in southern China, to meet some of the Red Cross brigades working on the other side of the border. Many ethnic Kachins live in China, where they are called Jingpho. Some of them were displaced by the war in Myanmar, and Bum Tsit was able to communicate with them in Jingphaw. In the pictures, he was posed in a hotel lobby with the brigade commander next to an enormous boulder of bright green jade.

My first trip to Myitkyina, Bum Tsit brought me with him to meet a wealthy Chinese jade merchant named U Maung Chin, who was an advisor for the Kachin State Red Cross. Both of us had an interest in the stone—mine was academic, Bum Tsit's was mostly commercial—and he told me that it was impossible to learn about the jade business if you didn't know the right people.

"The black market is much bigger than the legal one," was the first thing U Maung Chin said. "There's a Myitkyina black market, a Myanmar black market, a worldwide black market. Everywhere, every business has its own black market. Here in the local level of Kachin, the government doesn't have so much control. Rules and laws are not so strong."

Jade is not a commodity, like copper or gold. It isn't used for anything but art and jewelry. Its value is purely aesthetic, based entirely on a perception of beauty. But unlike other precious stones, like rubies or diamonds or emeralds, there is no way to estimate a jade stone's value. With a diamond, you can evaluate clarity and carat weight to estimate a price. But not with jade. Its value lies entirely in the eye of the beholder, and it is impossible to assign a market-standard value to a single rock. That makes it a perfect vehicle for laundering money and evading taxes. U Maung Chin told me that he would often sell a jade ornament for two thousand dollars but write a receipt for twenty dollars, because there was no way for regulators to check.

The walls of U Maung Chin's house were lined with glass cabinets filled with ivory tusks and heavy old iron Chinese swords. One glass case was just filled with elephant molars—giant rock-like things that seemed to serve no purpose other than to look enormous and powerful. U Maung Chin was part of Myitkyina's Chinese community, and unlike his Kachin and Bamar compatriots, he actually saw an intrinsic value in jade. In addition to carving it, he had filled his living room with the stone. As we spoke, intricately wrought jade dragons and Buddhas stared down at us from their display cases.

When I asked U Maung Chin more about how a jewelry maker could skirt the taxes, he grew evasive. "The taxes are very complicated," he said. "We would be here all night if I tried to explain it to you."

The enormous profit margins around jade and low governance in the border region make it a tempting vehicle for illicit deals and smuggling. For the Kachin rebels, jade has been a major source of wealth since the mid 1960s. As China's rocketing economic reforms propelled hundreds of millions of people into the middle class starting in the late 1980s, jade has become a luxury item for the largest market in the world and demand has skyrocketed. And for China's new über-rich, the stone has become an investment akin to fine art. In 2012, a record was set in a Hong Kong jewelry auction, when a necklace of green jadeite from Myanmar was sold for $27 million.

In modern China, jade has also become a tool of bribery. Instead of an envelope of cash, someone wishing to bribe a general or high official can offer a valuable piece of jade jewelry or a jade sculpture as a gift. In 2012, as Chinese president Xi Jinping embarked on a sweeping crackdown of graft in the Communist Party, the jade trade slumped. But such disturbances are relative to the size of the market. By 2014, the jade trade between the two countries was valued between $15 and $40 billion, a sum that would represent somewhere between 23 and 62 percent of Myanmar's GDP.

Yet somehow jade means little to people in Myanmar. The aesthetic value and desire for the green stone lies entirely outside the country's borders. For Myanmar, the stone is nothing but a tool for the rich and powerful, and a vehicle for the dreams of the poor.

•

Bum Tsit referred to his childhood as "a bitter history." He was born in 1988—Myitkyina Township, Dugahtawn ward. Bum Tsit's father was a manual laborer and gold miner, but he died suddenly when his son was only four months old, leaving the family without an income. To survive, Bum Tsit's mother left shortly thereafter, to work as a cook in the jade mines, where money flowed more freely. Bum Tsit didn't see her again until he was sixteen years old. Instead, he lived with his father's parents in their small compound on the outskirts of the city. Aside from his grandfather's negligible government pension and a trickle of money that his mother sent, the small plot of land was their only source of income. Bum Tsit helped his grandmother plant vegetables and care for the pigs and chickens. "She worked hard, digging holes every day until she was seventy-four," he recalled. "But when my grandfather died, she slowed down, and I had to do most of the work myself."

Bum Tsit had siblings, but hardly ever saw them. His grandparents couldn't care for all of them, so his brother and sister lived with an aunt. "It was very difficult for us," he said, "I had to take care of myself."

Despite the bitter history, some parts of Bum Tsit's life were normal for a Kachin boy growing up in Myitkyina. He went to church on Sundays, spent time helping his grandmother, and tried to stay safe. His family, like most in Kachin, had deep ties to the KIA. Many of the men in his family had fought for the rebel force during the long war that had turned parts of Kachin into a semiautonomous enclave. In the past, the army would draft young men and women into its ranks, but by the time Bum Tsit was fighting age, a ceasefire had reigned between the KIA and the Tatmadaw for over ten years. Instead of picking up a gun and heading to the mountains, Bum

Tsit went to Myitkyina University and studied English literature. He could speak and write the language well and liked Shakespeare. "As soon as I was accepted to university, I started tutoring to earn money," Bum Tsit remembered, "so I never had to ask for anything from anybody."

He got his first exposure to something larger in 2006, when his professors nominated him to attend a youth conference for the Association of Southeast Asian Nations. He traveled to six different Southeast Asian countries as a representative for Myanmar. The experience left him with mixed feelings. Traveling abroad and meeting other young people was enjoyable, but he also felt left out. At a time when youth in other parts of the region were flourishing under prosperous economies, the eighteen-year-old English student was representing one of the poorest countries in the world. He was there at the behest of a military junta with decades of documented human rights abuses and social repression. Standing for such a backward regime was difficult, and after the trip Bum Tsit came back to Myitkyina unsure if he would do it again. "Sometimes when I'm abroad, and don't want to say that I'm from Myanmar, I tell people that I come from Kachinland," Bum Tsit said, using the local name for the Kachin nation. The next opportunity to attend a youth group was with the Red Cross, a much less morally troublesome experience, and for the rest of his time at school, he concentrated on building the humanitarian organization's local youth chapter.

Bum Tsit graduated in 2010, during one of the most profound social transformations in Myanmar's history. After forty-eight years of authoritarian rule, a civilian party took power from the military government. While the military still controlled powerful levers of the state, and the new Union Solidarity and Development Party, or USDP, was mostly made up of ex-commanders, the loosening of social controls transformed everyday life in Myanmar. In a country with a young population, many people were now able to speak freely for the first time in their lives. The face of government changed everywhere in the country. For twenty years, successive leaders of the Tatmadaw's Northern Command, who were generally despised by the local population and accused of widespread corruption, had run Kachin

State. Now, a new post of "Chief Minister" was created. The central government appointed Lajon Ngan Hsai, a smiling Kachin businessman with an
engineering background, to the post.

During military rule, a talented young person's only guaranteed means
to success had been to join the Tatmadaw—and benefit from its far-reaching
corruption. The military had stakes in all the country's industrial areas, and
an officer was assured a wealthy life. High-ranking generals were all extremely rich, with holdings in everything from beer production to jade mining. But for a smart young Kachin, the military was rarely a viable option.
Not only did the Tatmadaw have a long history of war crimes committed
against the Kachin, but it was also a jingoistic organization, conditioned by
decades of civil war against ethnic militias to see minority groups as outsiders and enemies. The enmity went both ways. When talking about the war,
Kachin people normally described their antagonists as "the Burmese army,"
rather than "the government."

As the military's grip lessened, new opportunities for public service became available, and with them, new avenues to turn a family's "bitter history" into a new life. When the new chief minister took office, he overhauled
the state government's administration, and began a hiring push. His staff
sent word to Myitkyina University that promising students should apply to
work with the new government. "Everyone knew that USDP was just the
army in different clothes," Bum Tsit told me, but he still applied to work on
the minister's staff. He was up against stiff competition; a few high-ranking
military officers were also interviewing for the position. But the chief minister wanted someone on his staff that could represent the younger generation of Kachin State, and at age twenty-three Bum Tsit became his personal
assistant.

"Getting the government job was a life-changing experience," Bum Tsit
told me. As right-hand man to the highest government official in northern
Myanmar, he was suddenly thrust into a position of power. He sat in on
conversations with some of the country's richest businessmen, worked on
the periphery of the national peace process, and liaised with politicians from
across Myanmar and southern China. He accompanied his boss on trips

throughout Kachin State and built his own relationships with township leaders, local business communities, and, importantly, the police force. The job gave him a feeling of agency, that he was doing something good for the people of Kachin. The USDP, being as it was the "army in different clothes," had deep connections throughout the state, built on decades of patronage relationships. Constructed on the back of the military, government was effective and fast, and Bum Tsit had a seat at the table. The experience was exhilarating, and showed the man who had struggled through poverty for all his young life the economic and political influence available to those who held positions of power and knew the secrets of governance in Kachin. But the job got much more difficult when civil war reignited a year later.

∎

Modern history had been dramatic for the Kachins. For most of the eighteenth and nineteenth centuries, independent, distinct tribes in the Kachin hills had maintained regular, if sometimes violent, relationships with their valley-dwelling neighbors. They were small, mobile populations that rubbed up against the much larger Bamar kingdom to the south, and the massive Indian and Chinese empires to the west and east. The mountains—steep peaks wreathed in malarial jungle—were too hostile for outside armies to occupy or control. When they did fight, the Kachin were excellent warriors with a long martial history, and they largely succeeded in keeping other civilizations at bay. Interdependent economies provided linkages to the outside world. Kachin chiefs traded amber, jade, and gold to Chinese merchants and Bamar court officials. They raided into the lowlands and forced weaker chiefs to pay protection money. Without the agricultural base needed to support a large population, Kachin tribes would occasionally boost their numbers by kidnapping Shan women and girls to carry back up into the mountains as slaves.

After the British annexed Upper Myanmar in 1886, subsuming it into the Indian Empire, resistance to the colonial government was fiercest in the hills, and some Kachin chiefs held out longer than anywhere else in the territory. The mountains were perfect ground for guerrilla warfare, and insurgent chiefs hid in the jungle, terrorizing British patrols and persuading other clans to oppose the occupation. The British had identified the Kachin hills as strategically vital territory; the rugged terrain held some of the most valuable resources in the country. Colonial administrators also hoped that by subjugating the Kachin and bringing Victorian order to the region, they would be able to open a backdoor trading route into China's interior market.

But the mountains east of the Irrawaddy River are so remote, with so few people living there, that parts of the frontier remained contested well into the twentieth century. The region was simultaneously remote, hostile, and strategically valuable, and outside designs continued to turn life upside down for the hill tribes. During World War II, American generals were fixated on the idea of building a road across northern Myanmar in order to keep resupplying the Chinese troops. Both the British and American militaries armed the Kachin warriors and trained them to spy on the Japanese. The same prowess in guerrilla warfare that had stymied the British occupation now bled the Japanese, building time for the allied campaign to retake Myanmar.

After Myanmar gained independence in 1948, many of the minority ethnic groups, already heavily armed from fighting the Japanese and their Bamar sympathizers, turned their guns on the new government. Insurgencies of every stripe cropped up along the periphery of Myanmar. There were armies for devout Communists, Baptist separatists, and Buddhist nationalists. Remnants of the old Chinese Nationalist Army still encamped in Myanmar, in the hope that they would eventually retake China from the Communists. Narco gangs set up private mercenary forces in the jungle and constructed opium empires. The Kachin people didn't take up arms en masse until 1962, when the central government attempted to make Buddhism the state religion. The Kachin, by then largely devout Baptists, launched the Kachin Independence Army, and spent the next thirty-two years battling the Tatmadaw.

Although it was a religious spark that started the rebellion, the root political cause of the Kachin's grievances was the central government's failure to concede autonomy to the region. After centuries of relative independence, the Kachin were now under the control of a government dominated by the ethnic majority, and decided to fight rather than acquiesce. Throughout the last decades of the twentieth century, the Kachin undertook one of the most successful insurgent campaigns in Southeast Asia. They built a self-sustaining mini-state in the remote northern hills, with functioning health, education, and road-building departments. The Kachin were able to fund and feed a ten-thousand-strong army, largely by trading the area's mineral and forest wealth. KIA leaders built networks with like-minded partners against the Myanmar government. They were able to work with both the Chinese Nationalists and the Communists; they looked for support in Europe. Together with other ethnic militias, they were part of a front that united insurgencies all across Myanmar's periphery into an alliance of convenience against a moribund government in the faraway capital.

By the early 1990s, the Myanmar government had signed a ceasefire with the Kachin rebels. Chinese money and Bamar migrant workers started flowing into Kachin State, as the region's timber, mineral, and agricultural resources were finally open for business. But despite the accord, the KIA refused to disarm and continued to maintain a parallel government apparatus in its stronghold areas throughout Kachin hills. The balance produced some strange arrangements. The KIA had secured hydropower access by damming mountain rivers, and in 2007 Myanmar's military government signed a contract with a KIA-owned power company to be the sole electricity supplier in parts of Kachin state. Elite members of both the Myanmar army and the KIA profited immensely from the ceasefire, but everyday Kachin saw few benefits. Grassroots protest movements started cropping up. Throughout the 2000s, tensions came to a head over several high-profile development projects, including a plan for a Chinese company to dam the Irrawaddy River and create a reservoir that would flood several villages in the heart of Kachin State. While that project had been put on hold, others were in full swing, including another dam project in the mountains east of the Irrawaddy. In the face of mounting local opposition to the dam, the KIA announced that as the sole legitimate representative holding the Kachin nation's interests at heart, it would fight for the right of the Kachin people to determine the use of their own natural resources. In June 2011 the Kachin Independence Army went back to war against the central government.

∎

The war complicated Bum Tsit's life. "In Kachin, every family has some ties to the KIA," he told me. "When you hear someone's last name, you automatically know how his family is related to the KIA. Anyone that hears my name knows that we have a long history with KIA."

Soon after the fighting broke out in 2011, when Bum Tsit was a year into his government job, his brother quit his job as an engineer and joined the rebel army. As a new recruit, he had to list a next-of-kin that would take his place on the battlefield in the event that he was killed. He listed Bum Tsit. "I said to him, 'Are you insane? I work for the government you are fighting against.' But that's how it went."

Bum Tsit made the trip to the KIA headquarters in Laiza, in the mountains near the Chinese border, to attend his brother's graduation ceremony at the end of basic training. The strangest part of the journey was the transition from the government-controlled part of the road into the rebel-held territory. "You just drive to the checkpoint and there is a bar in the road with some soldiers. You stop and get out of the car, walk to the other side, and get in the car that's waiting for you on the other side." The whole thing was seamless. The soldiers on either side were not firing at each other. Beside the change in uniform, there was nothing to indicate that the two groups were enemies, much less that there was a war going on. It spoke to how Myanmar's civil wars had so warped life in the borderlands, and how success depended on the ability to navigate colliding and divergent issues.

Bum Tsit's complicated life highlighted how nuanced the country's ethnic divisions could be. Myanmar's never-ending civil war tended to grind away at any narrative that didn't highlight ethnic fault lines, and people rarely acknowledged similarities between different groups. It was easy to spot the differences: The Kachins were mostly Christians and lived in the mountains; the Bamar were primarily Buddhists that lived in the valleys and lowlands. But as an outsider, it was sometimes harder to see the overlaps between groups that were supposedly antagonistic toward one another.

Territory was a muddled issue. There were definite KIA strongholds, which mostly corresponded to historical bastions of Kachin power. The rule of thumb was that the central government controlled the major towns and the roads between them, while the rebels held the mountains and jungles in the empty parts of the map. But in Myitkyina, overlapping power centers frequently mingled. KIA intelligence officers moved openly about the city, while the Tatmadaw's Northern Command generals perused military plans in the sprawling army base west of the airport. Across Kachin State, companies had to pay taxes to both the KIO and the central government.

When I asked a KIO official about the organization's tax policy, he described the matter as one part of a broad issue. "The KIO collects taxes from everyone, but it is negotiable," he said with a wry smile. "Sometimes we call it a donation, sometimes tax. You know, on the other side, the central government doesn't call it a tax. They say it is war funding. . . . Sometimes businesses don't like to pay, especially in downtown Myitkyina, because this is considered to be a central government–administered zone. But we insist."

The central government had even contracted a KIO-owned and operated business to supply power to large portions of Kachin State. The company, called Buga, had signed an agreement with the then-military government in 2007, during the ceasefire years. The contract was set to last until 2027 and supplied the KIO with a steady stream of revenue. I had seen the large Buga office in downtown Myitkyina, as well as Buga technicians in uniforms driving around the city. It seemed strange that all these men sauntering around the state capital were employees of one of the most heavily armed and best-organized rebel groups in Asia. If the state parliament had electricity problems, they had to call a Buga repairman. The company also supplied power to the Northern Command military base. As part of the Myanmar government's attempt to forge peace deals with dozens of armed opposition groups across the country, they had declared the KIA and all other organizations who refused to sign the ceasefire to be "illegal" groups.

Foreign NGO workers caught associating with any of these militias could be thrown out of the country. But in Kachin State, the government had hired them to keep the lights on.

I told Bum Tsit that to an outsider, it seemed strange that the KIA and the Myanmar government could simultaneously be at war with each other and also work together on something as bureaucratic and paper-heavy as power supply. "We fight, but we also do business together." he shrugged. "That's just the way it works."

We were sitting on the second-floor balcony of Bum Tsit's house, sipping *sapi*, the sweet local rice wine, as we chatted. In his government job, he had witnessed firsthand the complicated web of personal contacts and shared secrets between state officials, private businessmen, and military and police leaders that made things tick. In the business of politics, he explained to me, there were few absolutes. Despite an initial guardedness about his personal business, Bum Tsit was open about the corruption and insider dealing he'd seen in government, and I got comfortable asking him questions that I might not ask others.

When I asked him to describe how politicians and businesspeople worked together, he was frank about the governance problems in Kachin. "Low salaries are part of the reason we have so much corruption. A state minister does not make real money, so when the businessman comes to him and asks for approval for a project, the ministers will say 'give me shares of your company—for free,' then he will give approval very quickly."

The highest-level civil servants for Kachin State wielded significant administrative power, but only made about $450 a month. Lower-level employees earned about $120. "It's not enough to support a family, or even rent a decent apartment," Bum Tsit shrugged. During his time working for the chief minister, the state government had built several high-rise condo blocks near the parliament building to house employees for free, a move that was especially useful for representatives and their staffs that came to Myitkyina from far away. "How else could they afford to come and work in the parliament?" Bum Tsit pointed out. "They can't afford to rent an apartment or stay in a hotel. They would have to resort to other means."

But a minister or director of a state agency has the power to approve business licenses and grant permits, processes that mostly happen behind closed doors. Some agencies, like the ministries of forestry, agriculture, and planning, made decisions worth hundreds of millions of dollars. The temptation to skim off the top was enormous. "So if the minister or director has shares in several companies he has a lot of interest in making them more profitable, so then paperwork moves much quicker all of a sudden."

Bum Tsit's house was palatial. The ceilings were fourteen feet high and the floor was made from teak stained in warm shades of honey and copper. His grandparents had lived on the property in a small wooden house for several decades, but at the age of twenty-six, after five years of professional work experience, Bum Tsit started building a new home for his family. "I had a house design catalogue from Thailand," he explained as we nibbled at a large spread of salads brought over from Red House. "I sat with an architect and just picked pieces out and he designed all this." He paused. "When we were building the house, we didn't have room for the pigs anymore, so now we pay a neighbor to take care of them."

I wondered what Bum Tsit's other cash flows might have been besides his paltry government salary. Ten other people were living in the compound he built. One of them was the goldsmith from Thailand he employed in the jewelry store. His brother-in-law, who slept downstairs, ran Red House. Neither business seemed busy enough to pay for everything. Bum Tsit's ninety-three-year-old grandmother, who had spent most of her life digging holes, now slept in a king-size bed with lots of throw pillows, and spent most of the day reading the bible or watching TV shows on an iPad. She seemed to approach the indulgences of modernity with the muted enthusiasm of someone who had never been comfortable before.

After a few glasses of *sapi*, Bum Tsit began to loosen up and hint at some of the outlandish corruption stories centered around Kachin State's valuable jade mines—and the underground power structures that operated in parallel to the official government ones. The Kachin hills are the only significant source in the world of top-quality green jadeite, and in China's luxury markets the stone can outprice diamonds. A single boulder of top-quality jade smuggled across the border could fetch hundreds of millions of dollars. It has been a major revenue stream for generations of Kachin elites that could navigate the difficult political waters and establish connections with Chinese trading partners.

Prior to the 1994 ceasefire between the KIA and the Tatmadaw, the jade mining town of Hpakan, in the middle of the Kachin mountains, had been one of the KIA's most important strongholds. But with peace came new opportunities for well-connected investors from outside Kachin: military leaders and Chinese businessmen with significant access to capital soon arrived in the mines. Mining contracts also became much larger. Solitary local miners and family-owned tracts were swallowed up by large industrial companies that could rip apart entire mountain ranges. The rules around jade changed as well. In mining centers, companies now had to pay taxes to both the central government and the KIA. While the government's taxes were based on official accounting of the firm's records, Bum Tsit said, the KIA made an estimate based on a company's ability to pay. "They see you are a big business, so they ask for a big fee. Sometimes as much as one billion kyats." (About $750,000.) "The business people just want to make money. They don't want to be in the middle between the two sides and be responsible for starting a fight. They just pay quietly and go back to work."

Even large jade mining companies, owned by "cronies" who were close to the former military government, paid taxes to the KIA. The payments were an open secret. Paying a "tax" to what was officially an unlawful group would leave the companies open to state prosecution. So they described it as a "donation" for the KIO's charitable work, such as relief for the IDP camps. It put the "legitimate" businessmen and the "illegitmate" rebels in the same network, and made the distinction between political, economic, and ethnic concerns feel murky.

Bum Tsit knew a state police officer working in Myitkyina who sometimes brought Chinese businessmen to Hpakan. All foreigners need special travel permits to visit the jade mining site, but when they didn't want to go through the official process, which involved heavy scrutiny and required connections with the military, they could just pay a policeman. "For him it was very easy to bring them through all the checkpoints. As a high-ranking policeman, he could just go right through the roadblocks without them asking any questions. And the Chinese can very easily blend in. They don't even have to pretend to be Burmese or Kachin. There are so many Chinese-Burmese people who look very Chinese."

Chinese-owned companies reap a large share of money from Kachin State's jade deposits. Some jade businessmen that I interviewed reported that Chinese owners, through local partners, control around 80 percent of mines around Hpakan. A small cohort of Bamar businessmen, generally with connections to the military government, owned most of the rest. All companies, regardless of size or owner, are adept at skirting government taxes. As U Maung Chin had explained to Bum Tsit and me, jade's value is set by the buyer, not by a market, and he could easily sell a piece of jade for two thousand dollars but write a receipt for twenty dollars, or not write a receipt at all. As a result, the government has a difficult time collecting meaningful revenue from the jade trade, despite its value. While no one knows exactly how much the jade industry is worth, it is clear that the stone is one of—if not the—single largest chunks of the country's gross domestic product. The KIA was able to skim hundreds of millions off the illegal jade trade by taxing the smuggling routes and shaking down mine operators. The KIA made more money from the jade trade than the central government, which meant even less filtered down to the citizens of Kachin State through official channels. What the KIA did with this revenue wasn't shared publicly. *They say it's war funding.*

"That's why there is fighting," Bum Tsit said, sipping his *sapi*. "No resource sharing. Jade is supposed to go from Hpakan straight to Naypyidaw. It's technically illegal to bring it to Myitkyina, but you see all this jade here. One hundred percent of revenue is supposed to go to the central government. Of course that doesn't happen, but the point is that none of it is supposed to come to Kachin State, and that's not fair."

I wanted to make sure I understood what he was saying. "So even though the central government doesn't really have the capacity to collect the revenue, the fact that it's not supposed to go to Kachin is enough to justify the fighting?"

"Now you understand Myanmar," Bum Tsit said. "For the intelligence!"

.

There are two golf courses in Myitkyina. One is close to the town center, owned by and open to the public. The second, Northern Star Golf Course, is out by the airport and is owned by the Tatmadaw's Northern Command.

We teed off under a heavy rain at Northern Star. Myitkyina is still far from the global supply chain of name brand sports equipment, and Bum Tsit and his in-laws Min Tun and Zawng Ting only had used, refurbished golf balls to play with. The course had been hacked out of the jungle, and the rough was impenetrable. If your ball rolled even a couple yards off the fairway, it was basically impossible to find. I lost five of Bum Tsit's precious golf balls by the third hole. But on the side of the fourth hole, there was a half naked, barefoot child sitting in the weeds, ready to sell me some scavenged balls for 1,000 kyats.

The three of them had just started playing a year ago, but they were good, consistent golfers. I admitted with no small level of embarrassment that I had been playing since I was a child, but still couldn't really hit the ball straight. We made for a mismatched foursome. Not only was I by far the worst golfer, but I was also the only one without any connection to a rebel army. Bum Tsit's brother was a cadet. Min Tun and Zawng Ting's father was a high-ranking KIA general. Min Tun worked for the KIO's Technical Advisory Team. On paper it was a nonprofit group that advocated for the Kachin within the architecture of the national peace process. In reality, it was an arm of KIA military intelligence, run by an active duty colonel. Min Tun smoked a lot and was quick to laugh.

We played with caddies: young women paid to carry the golf bags, clean the clubs, and cheer us on. My caddy was named Su Su, and she caddied barefoot. I looked down at my sneakers, already completely soaked with water, and thought that she had the right idea.

After nine holes, we stopped for beer and peanuts and waited for a fifth player to join. When a gold-colored Toyota sedan rolled quickly into the parking lot, Bum Tsit shot out of his seat. "He's here; let's go." I had noticed that when around his friends and family, Bum Tsit was relaxed, smiley, and quick to crack jokes. But as soon as someone in a position of power showed up, he snapped to attention and became very formal and respectful. Before the driver's-side door of the car had opened, Bum Tsit was standing next to it, with his hand outstretched.

The man that stepped out of the car was tall and fat for someone in Myanmar. His big belly was almost perfectly round, and the belt of his tan slacks went right around the middle. He wore white New Balance sneakers and a pale yellow polo shirt that clung to his arm when he reached out to shake our hands. His grip was soft and warm.

Bum Tsit introduced him as the Kachin State Director of City Development, and he came with his own caddie. The Director was friendly. He had a big, tenor belly laugh, which he let out whenever anyone made the simplest joke. He was also a very good golfer, and clearly came to Northern Star often. All the staff recognized him and jumped to greet him when he walked by. His caddie was also barefoot.

Halfway through our second nine, Min Tun came up to walk next to me. We were about twenty paces in front of the Director, and he said under his breath, "Don't mention that I work for the opposition groups. It is a sensitive subject, with the Director here."

"Does he know and not care, or just doesn't know?" I asked.

"I think he knows," he said, and chuckled through his cigarette smoke. "He was high in the army, in the Northern Command. But now he was put as a civilian into this position."

.

The Tatmadaw's Northern Command and the KIA had been fighting each other in the jungles of Kachin State since the Kachin insurgency began in 1962. Decades of war between the two armies had not only killed thousands of young soldiers on both sides, it had paralyzed civilian life and contributed to the poverty and lack of development throughout Kachin territory.

In 2015, the quasi-military government announced a ceasefire agreement with eight of the country's ethnic militias. Most of the signatories were small, relatively insignificant forces or armies that had not been fighting for some time. (The one notable exception was the Karen National Union, a five-thousand-man force that had controlled the mountains near the Thai border since 1949.) Following the initial success of the ceasefire, the government pushed other groups to join. While most of the country's opposition militias had been in de facto ceasefires for years, or sometimes decades, the government's push for them to sign onto a single nationwide agreement, with little room for bilateral negotiation of terms or recognition of local conditions, soured relations.

Once Aung San Suu Kyi and the NLD took power in 2016, many of the polices of the military-aligned USDP were pushed aside as a new civilian government, detached from the military, took power. The Lady made ending the country's civil wars the top priority of her administration and began overhauling the peace process. Her administration fired many of the technocrat civil servants that had been working on the previous government's peace process and replaced them with NLD members, who were perceived to be more loyal.

The KIA refused to sign the ceasefire, in part because it did not address local grievances about sharing the region's natural resources, and instead shored up their bargaining position by allying with other active combatant groups in the north. In 2016, the KIA joined with three other militias to form the Northern Alliance–Burma. Together, the group had been able to successfully fight the Tatmadaw to a draw, and by 2017, some analysts claimed that the Myanmar army was losing the fight in the north.

Later, when I talked with a KIO spokesman away from the golf course, he told me that the KIA and other ethnic groups had tried to approach the NLD leadership about negotiating directly. "We wanted straight talk, outside the regular process," the spokesman, named Dau Hka, told me. "We expected [Aung San Suu Kyi] to use her credit and people power to make change, but there have been no changes to the country's rule of law, to law enforcement." When The Lady's government refused to negotiate outside the set dialogue process, the KIA moved closer to the Chinese-led coalition. "The Kachin public is pushing us to negotiate without signing a ceasefire,"

Dau Hka said. "The northern groups still have a very strong power to threaten the Burmese government . . . we can keep this fight going for years."

On Northern Star, the two sides of Myanmar's civil war were playing for 5,000 kyats a hole and seemed to be splitting it pretty evenly. The Director cheered when the enemy intelligence officer holed a birdie putt and ribbed me good-naturedly when my shots careened off into the bush.

The more I hung around Bum Tsit, the harder it became to really understand why the two sides were fighting in Kachin. It seemed more and more like they weren't two sides at all, but merely participants in a game with very high stakes.

Far from the Northern Star course, Min Tun told me more about this incongruity over a Tuborg.

"Some people think that the KIA and the Burmese army are keeping the war going on purpose, that it's more profitable for them if the war continues. Because with the fighting maybe they can do certain business without people looking over their shoulders. But I don't really believe this."

He paused and lit a cigarette.

"The real cash cow for the KIA is the electricity. Jade, timber, gold, agriculture—all those can be impacted by politics and fighting. But people always need to light their homes. Businesses and government offices and hospitals need to keep running. And they charge exponentially more for power used. You know our office, they call it the Technical Advisory office, but still effectively it is the KIO. And Buga still charges us for power. They make us pay, but they give it to Northern Command for free. Go figure."

Later, I asked Bum Tsit about the connection between the KIA and the military, wondering if he felt a contradiction in the fact that he worked for the USDP chief minister, and his brother was fighting on the other side.

Bum Tsit shrugged. "I just do not care; it is that simple. And he doesn't care either. I am good at my job. Of course the chief minister knew. He just didn't care. It's important to understand that. It's not one side or the other. There are middle grounds."

■

On a cool, misty morning in October, I accompanied Bum Tsit on a trip to Myitsone—the Confluence—where the Mali and N'Mai Rivers come rushing together to birth the Irrawaddy. The place had special significance to the Kachin people, and to Bum Tsit.

The area above the Confluence, between the Mali and N'mai, is called "the Triangle" and is widely recognized as the territorial heartland of the Kachin people. There are no written records that provide a reliable account of the Kachin people's ancestral migrations. Instead, clues come from the oral tradition. During important religious ceremonies, professional story-tellers recite the Kachin creation myth. These stories recall a place called *Major Shingra Bum*, which can mean "Naturally Flat Mountain," or "Central Plain." Most scholars now believe that the Kachin originated in Mongolia, before migrating to the high plateau of Tibet, and then continuing south to settle in the Triangle around the fifteenth or sixteenth century.

Until very recently, the area was largely isolated from outside forces. Ever since the Kachin pushed down from the Tibetan highlands to occupy the Triangle, forcing the Shans and other ethnic groups further south, this inhospitable jungle has been a place where old traditions still flourished and strangers had a difficult time surviving. The high mountain passes, steep valleys, and vast wilderness contributed to the tough, independent mindset of the local people, and to their martial prowess. During the KIA's long fight against the Tatmadaw, the Triangle had been one of the few areas that the rebels were able to keep consistently secure. The protection provided by the Triangle allowed the KIA to exercise the political and social programs that made Kachinland viable as an autonomous region.

Bum Tsit liked the area because of its poor mobile phone reception. From 2011 to 2016, when he worked for the chief minister, he was expected to work six days a week: Monday through Friday in the office, then all day Saturday at his boss's house. Days started at 7:30 and lasted until 10 or 11 at night. The work uniform for Myanmar civil servants is a formal Burmese cotton jacket and a longyi. The jacket has four to six pockets lining the front and interior, and when Bum Tsit went to work, each pocket was filled with a different phone. He carried his two personal phones, the chief minister's two work phones, and one of his boss's personal phones.

"My whole day was just ringing phones, nonstop," Bum Tsit said as we drove around Myitsone. "I'd have to talk with multiple people at once, while also doing the other parts of my job. It was exhausting."

They would travel throughout Kachin State for work, and in these remote areas, Bum Tsit also had to carry mobile Internet routers and chargers, along with multiple SIM cards from different providers, and a short-wave radio. "Because you can never be sure where you'll have service in the countryside."

On Sundays, Bum Tsit was free to do what he liked. "But I still needed to carry my phones. And if my boss calls and I don't pick up, he'd be angry with me."

At Myitsone though, there was zero reception. "If someone called me, they would just get the message, *This user is unavailable,*' and they'd know that I was out of range. And I would finally be able to relax."

Bum Tsit would come up to the Confluence nearly every Sunday to relax and eat lunch by the river. Sometimes he would pay a few dollars to lounge at a nearby hotel for the day. On the weekends when his girlfriend would come up to visit from Mandalay, the couple could rest quietly on these Sunday outings.

The Triangle is now identified as Injangyang Township. It is a sparsely populated area bordered by the two rivers, defined by sharp mountains and poor infrastructure. Like most of Kachin, it is strictly off limits to foreigners without special travel authorization from the government. In this case, the prohibition on travel was because the KIA occupied large parts of the township, and there had been active fighting throughout the previous spring in the northeastern reaches. But from the banks of the river at Myitsone, it was a thirty second, two-dollar boat ride away, with no one to check any papers.

We motored across and up the current of the Mali Kha, the pounding outboard motor making it impossible to speak. From the spit of sand in between the two rivers, you could land a rock on the Myitkyina Township side with a good throw. The land was heavily forested, right up to the water, but at the top of a small hill, overlooking the Confluence, was a small Christian shrine decorated with multicolored LEDs and a picture of the Virgin Mary. An old man lived behind the shrine with his pigs and chickens and tended the holy place for a small salary. "He is old and still never married," Bum Tsit remarked with a hint of sadness. Bum Tsit took his shoes off, walked up to the shrine, and said a quick prayer with his eyes closed. The shrine could occasionally get busy on Sundays, when Kachin residents around Myitsone came to pray. There was also a full-sized church on the busy right bank of the Irrawaddy, where we had taken coffee. But the government had recently built a large Buddhist stupa, painted gold, right on the bank of the river. It occupied a much nicer piece of land than the church and many Kachins were unhappy with such a visible Buddhist religious structure being built in an area imbued with deep traditional meaning for the local Christians. But in the small forest chapel, where I watched Bum Tsit pray, the rest of the world felt cut off. The lush forest canopy kept the ground cool and soft. The only real sound was the rush of the two rivers coming together.

■

For the 2020 elections, the USDP leadership in Kachin State asked Bum Tsit to run for state parliament as a representative from Injangyang Township. Bum Tsit was well versed in party politics from his time working with the chief minister and knew that he would have to consult with other stakeholders before deciding whether to run. The matter of who wins usually depends more on conversations with community leaders over beer and *sapi* than it does voter turnout. Injangyang Township is dominated by the KIO, and whomever the organization supported had an overwhelming advantage in the vote. Dau Hka, the KIO spokesman, told me that in 2015, "there was a force behind the scenes," in the Kachin electorate. "The KIO showed the green signal to people to vote for the NLD, because we also expected Aung

San Suu Kyi to make change. That's why NLD won so much in Kachin."

Bum Tsit had sat down with the KIO leaders in Injangyang and asked if he could count on their support. "The KIO knows me, and they said that they would support me over the NLD."

Support for the NLD was waning here in the borderlands. "People are upset that they haven't been able to get anything done," said Bum Tsit. "Where is the NLD chief minister? No one ever sees him."

Bum Tsit went on: "One good thing about everyone voting for NLD in 2015 is that people will be able to see the difference between USDP and NLD and then make a more informed decision next time. There's a lot of mismanagement with the NLD. They had to start everything from scratch. Take the peace process for example. The USDP government had been working for five years building a deal for peace, and it was going well. But then the NLD had to start building those relationships from scratch all over again. And many of them have no political experience before. Lots were prisoners for the past twenty years."

The KIO had become disillusioned with the NLD, too. "If Aung San Suu Kyi is out, our position will be stronger," one officer told me. Bum Tsit himself was particularly upset about the lack of momentum in the country's peace process. The Kachin rebels had refused to sign on to the civilian government's ceasefire agreement, and the NLD had made it a policy that they would not hold any level of negotiations with what they were calling "non-signatory" armed groups.

Dissatisfaction with the NLD government was a common complaint among the Kachin people I spoke with. "Neither party cares about the Kachin," one young businessman told me, "so we might as well have the party in power that is more effective."

In Myanmar, institutions matter much less than relationships, and Bum Tsit had seen how government could work when everyone knew each other on a first name basis. He wanted to be back, close to that seat of power, and took seriously the offer to run for parliament in 2020. But if he was elected, he would only be thirty-two years old by the time he took office. That was fine for serving as a legislator, but Bum Tsit couldn't be appointed to a ministership until age thirty-five. "I would only be an MP. It would be kind of boring, and I would have to give up my position in the Red Cross brigade. So I won't run now, but I will later."

Bum Tsit's experience in government had shown him that the key to power in Kachin State lay not in someone's title, but in their portfolio. People in official positions were the public face of authority, but they negotiated and shared their power with military leaders, rebel commanders, and businessmen. What connected each of these players was access to resources and the ability to profit in a system where civil war and what side you were on defined your opportunities. Bum Tsit liked being in the middle of that web—with chips scattered in the various baskets of independence politics, business, and humanitarian aid. He knew that even if he turned down the political offer there were other options available to him, deeper reservoirs of power that ran through the mountains of Kachin.

4.

THE GREEN VEIN

Hpakan, Kachin State

Gold is valuable; but jade is priceless.
—CHINESE PROVERB

Most days, Hkun Myat wakes up at 4:30 to get to the hillside before the sun comes up. On his hands and knees, bundled in a cheap jacket to protect against the cold mountain air, he searches through the slag and rubble left over from the night before. Hkun Myat gets up early because if any of the other miners missed something valuable the previous evening, he might have a chance of snagging it when fewer people are on the slope. He is looking for jade, the precious green stone that can mean the difference between going hungry and feeding his family for the month.

Hpakan, the sprawling, ramshackle mining town where Hkun Myat lives and works, in the sharp mountains in the center of Kachin State, is the heart of Myanmar's jade trade. At twenty-seven years old, he has been pick-ing jade there for nearly ten years. Hkun Myat is at the bottom rung on the jade ladder. He is what is known as a yemase (*"yay-ma-say"*). The word means "not to wash with water," and refers to the customary rule that jade stones should not be tampered with when the miners sell them. But it can also refer to the lifestyle surrounding the lower levels of the jade trade. There are hun-dreds of thousands of young men like Hkun Myat picking through rubble in Hpakan. Many come from other war-torn parts of Myanmar, hoping to strike it rich and start anew in the mines.

Almost all the jade mined in Myanmar ends up in China, where there is a nearly limitless demand for the stone. Jade has long been associated with supernatural powers and luck in China, and as a result, the highest quality pieces can fetch enormous prices in the Chinese luxury markets. Mean-while, the yemase live in squalor, hoping to scavenge a shard of valuable stone from the leftovers of the wealthier jade players. The stone means noth-ing to them except as a way to get paid. When large mining companies dump their waste into the enormous slag piles stretching across the scarred, lunar landscape, the yemase race each other to search through the refuse.

■

Sitting in a small restaurant, Hkun Myat explained the details of his work-ing life. His two main tools are a flashlight and a hammer, he explained. He holds the bright flashlight in his mouth while he works at night. "Then I take a small hammer and hit the stone and listen to the sound. By listening to the sound, you can tell if it is jade or not."

In an average day, he said, he would hit close to a thousand individual stones, looking for the right sound. "It took me a long time to understand what it really sounds like. But once you know, you will never forget. Jade is a sweet sound."

Holding a glass of beer, Hkun Myat's rough fingers recalled the concus-sive, bone-wearing labor of the rocks he works with all day long. It was winter, and Hkun Myat wore a big jacket, but even under the clothes, his broad shoulders were clearly evident—strong but also worn into a semi-permanent slump—the burden of a life spent bent over, searching the ground.

The freelance jade mining that Hkun Myat and other yemase do is extremely dangerous. Lax safety regulations and torrential rainstorms lead to frequent landslides that can bury the young men under tons of rubble. Yemase deaths are not uncommon. Without any kind of insurance, families are rarely compensated for their losses. The work is also illegal. The yemase operate without licenses, and without the official consent of the mining companies from whose cast-offs they make a living. But because most stones the yemase recover eventually end up in the hands of larger trading companies, they are tacitly tolerated as a necessary, if expendable, part of the jade supply chain in Myanmar.

Despite working around the mines for most of his adult life, Hkun Myat still chalked up most of his fortune to chance. "It's always a guess," he said, and admitted readily that he didn't know what determines where the good jade is buried. "The stone is like a stream underground," he said. "The jade stays in the stream, like a vein. So it depends on the place you search. We follow the companies. When they go to a new area and tap into a stream, yemase hear about it and follow. But for us, it is all about luck whether or not we succeed."

Imperial jade, the highest quality stone, makes up only one hundredth of one percent of all the jade mined in Hpakan. For every ten thousand kilograms of jade mined, one kilo will be graded as "imperial," worth tens of millions of dollars per kilogram. These were the "life-changing stones" that Hkun Myat and the other yemase were looking for. Every day on the hillside was a race to find the stone with the slice of bright translucent green that would carry them out of poverty. But most days, all that turned up was low-grade slag.

In a good week, Hkun Myat might find a jade stone every day. But he can also go long periods without unearthing a single piece worth keeping. Income was irregular. When he did find some jade that he thought might be worth selling, he brought it to his older brother or uncle, who helped him polish the stone and determine if it was valuable or not. The true value of a jade stone can only be determined once it has been cut open. The weathered exterior hides the color and clarity of a stone. Yemase like Hkun Myat will shave off a small corner of the rough shell to advertise the contents within. If a buyer—usually a middleman, like the jade merchants Bum Tsit knew, who will resell the stone to a larger trading company—likes what he sees, he will haggle with the yemase about the quality and try to buy the stone for a cut-rate price. When he slices the stone open, and the coloring is revealed, he may have lost everything, or he may have made a fortune.

For Hkun Myat, the only thing that mattered was that initial transaction, which could be hard to arrange alone. Like many parts of the jade industry, it relied on informal connections and access to information. Hkun Myat relied on his uncle's advice to navigate the tricky world of the middlemen traders, who did their best to cheat the yemase out of valuable stones. Whenever he did make a sale, he'd split the profit with his uncle. "I don't know the people that buy the stone," Hkun Myat admitted. "That's why I need my uncle's help. I just know that they are rich men."

Most months, Hkun Myat made three to four hundred dollars, which he shared with his parents and younger siblings. It was two or three times what he could hope to make as a day laborer anywhere else in the country and is the reason hundreds of thousands of migrant workers had poured into Hpakan in the last decade to search for their personal fortunes. But with more money also comes a higher cost of living; Hpakan is one of the most expensive places in Myanmar, and Hkun Myat's monthly take never went far. Habits could often outrun income in the sprawling mining town, where overnight millionaires could purchase imported French champagne and hundred-dollar bottles of whiskey. Hkun Myat admitted to being a frequent drinker, but swore that he had never touched the heroin that destroys the lives of so many freelance miners.

"My life as a yemase is much better than the people from lower Myanmar that come to work in Hpakan," Hkun Myat told me. "My family is there. I have my home, a place to stay. It is no problem for me to live in Hpakan."

Migrant miners are often forced to room in flophouses run by local businessmen. Hkun Myat called these men the "rich owners" of Hpakan. Like most aspects of the jade industry, the arrangements were predatory. House rent is free, but any jade stones that the workers find are then the joint property of the owner and the yemase. Without a strong local network or detailed knowledge of the opaque industry, it is difficult for the yemase to defend themselves, and they are often cheated out of their jade money.

"Some of the lower Myanmar yemase are very good at picking jade stones," Hkun Myat said, referring to the migrant workers from Rakhine State who make up a disproportionate amount of the labor at the mines. "I know one friend who found a stone worth $100,000. But the rich owner he was working for only gave him $1,000. He was betrayed. Some yemase, like my friend, they become very humble and won't fight for themselves. So instead of standing up to the rich owner, they will just go and live in another rich person's house and try to start over. They end up going from one house to another, never having a home."

Many yemase told similar stories. Everyone seemed to have a friend that had struck it lucky and found a life-changing piece of jade, only to have the fortune slip away into the hands of someone much more powerful.

Hkun Myat didn't see himself falling into the same trap. When I asked him about his life plans, he said that he hoped to find a high-quality piece of jade and sell it. If he found the right stone, he could become a millionaire overnight. Then he would leave the mining town and resettle in Myitkyina. With the jade profit, he said, he would open a mobile phone shop that earns money more regularly.

"Then I could get married and start a family, and get away from jade."

•

Some of the earliest Chinese artifacts are circular jade carvings, known as 璧 (*bi*), or annular discs. The Neolithic-era objects are large and crude. Some of them are six to eight inches in diameter: simple, unadorned circles with small holes punched in their centers. They were used in royal ceremonies, in ritual sacrifices, and were buried with the dead. The *bi* were the physical manifestation of heaven itself and were supposed to guide the deceased to the afterlife. Today, *bi* are no longer part of religious ceremonies, but their memory can be seen in the jade pendants given to Chinese children, and in the expensive jade bangles that upper class women wear on their wrists.

There is no object in the West that approaches the same level of cultural significance as jade does in China. "Jade is heaven!" declared the writers of the *I Ching*, a divination manual from the Zhou dynasty. Since the Neolithic cultures around the Hangzhou Bay first started mining jade in 5500 B.C.E., the stone has played a foundational role in Chinese life, retaining both religious and aesthetic significance for nearly seven millennia. Jade embodied the union of man and god, allowing humans to communicate with heaven. In some Chinese myths, it was the benevolent Jade Emperor who fashioned humans out of mud, and who ruled over the realms of Earth, Heaven, and Hell.

Jade has been used in totem worship, religious musical ceremony, and in medicine. Court documents were written on jade tablets, whose supernatural qualities allowed the writing to be "transmitted indefinitely, forever preserved and unalterable." Jade was fashioned into weapons and clothing and currency. A Han dynasty poem illustrated the stone's many values:

> Benevolence lies in its gleaming surface,
> Knowledge in its gleaming quality,
> Uprightness in its unyieldingness,
> Power in its harmlessness,
> Eternity in its durability,
> Moral leading in the fact that it goes from hand to hand without
> being sullied.

Because of jade's supernatural powers, the stone was long associated with immortality and burial rites. Chinese emperors, obsessed with achieving eternal life, would ingest powdered jade mixed into a tonic. When rich people died, they would have jade stones sewn onto their burial robes and put into their mouths. Jade statues were placed in strategic locations throughout the burial chamber. In death, the jade objects were functional deities, guiding the deceased toward eternity. It is no wonder that jade is still called the stone of heaven.

Gemologists differentiate between two types of jade. Nephrite is a softer, gentler stone. It mostly appears in shades of pale gray and ivory, although also presents as bright white or deep green. The Chinese have mined nephrite for millennia, with the most prodigious deposits coming from the Khotan region in the country's far west. Sculptors praise nephrite for its workability and gentle texture. The feeling of high quality "mutton fat" nephrite is often compared to the touch of a woman's skin. Thousands of years of craftsmanship has contributed to a highly advanced skill set among Chinese artisan carvers. They can work nephrite into delicate, almost gossamer three-dimensional shapes. The stone expresses something pure and amorphous.

The second type of jade is called jadeite. It has a vitreous feel and is harder and more brittle than nephrite, and its colors can be much more vibrant. Jadeite can be a brilliant, translucent shade of emerald green. In Chinese, it is known as 翡翠 (*fěi cui*) which is often translated as "emerald." Its finest specimens appear almost like that precious stone, a vivid green that is unforgettable. Jadeite can also appear in shades of pale lavender, jet black, and speckled green and white. It is also much rarer than most varieties of nephrite. Geologists have found jadeite deposits in limited quantity in California, Turkey, and Guatemala. But there is only one place in the world where the high-quality green jadeite known as Imperial Jade is found on a large scale: the Kachin hills of northern Myanmar.

It is difficult to say exactly when the Chinese became aware of the green jade from Myanmar. Figurines of jade excavated from Pyu-era archeological sites indicate that civilizations along the Irrawaddy River valley were mining and using jade as far back as the sixth century. But it is unlikely that the stone moved from Myanmar to China until much later.

A story frequently cited in the history of Myanmar jade is that of a nameless merchant from the mountains of Yunnan, in southern China, who ventured to the southwest sometime during the thirteenth century. On his way home from a trading trip in what was referred to as the barbarian lands of *Mien*, the load on one of the merchant's ponies was unbalanced. The man supposedly picked up a large stone from the side of the road and used it to even out the burden. Later, when the merchant dropped the stone on the ground, it split open to revel a brilliant, translucent green interior. After his discovery, a party of merchants returned to *Mien*, or Myanmar, to search for more of the stone, but was unsuccessful.

While that origin story may or may not be true, what we do know is that officials stationed in Yunnan during the Ming dynasty (1368–1644) purchased jade from the Bamar kingdom. The Ming court had a fabulous infatuation with precious stones, especially rubies and sapphires, and was wealthy enough to buy them in large quantities. Eunuchs, who functioned as magistrates and power brokers in the Chinese court, were dispatched to the borderlands to secure gems and riches for the imperial court in Beijing. Records of court expenditures show that jade was being purchased from Myanmar at least as early as the 1560s. It shows up in the Ming annals as "green jade."

The eunuchs sent merchant caravans into the southern jungles to find and purchase rubies, amber, gold, sapphires, and jade. The merchants had to travel in groups—a minimum of ten people—because the trip was so hostile. The jungles held poisonous snakes, roving highway bandits, and deadly malaria, as well as headhunting mountain tribes. For every ten-man caravan that made the trek to Myanmar, six or seven travelers would die. Fevers and illness claimed the lives of thousands of intrepid adventurers.

Despite difficulties, the jade trade grew quickly and steadily. Throughout the eighteenth and nineteenth centuries, Qing dynasty aristocrats kept up a rabid consumption of the stone. Merchant caravans laden with Chinese goods trekked into the hostile mountains to trade with the Kachin chiefs that owned the mines. Occasionally, as warrior hill tribes waylaid supply trains or held roads hostage, the merchants would have to find new avenues to and from the jade mines. By 1805, the flow of goods had settled into a pattern that would persist until World War II: Chinese merchants carried silver to the Kachin hills, which they used to pay for jade. Porters took the stones by foot or river to the trading center of Mogaung, halfway between the mines and the mighty Irrawaddy River. There, someone representing the Bamar king collected a value-added tax, and recorded the stone's weight. After that, the stone could travel freely anywhere in the country. Small boats loaded with jade moved downriver toward Bhamo, where the stones were carried with the caravans of cotton traders that made the overland trip to Yunnan with mules.

Much of the jade business was subject to customary rules. Each ethnic group involved in the trade operated within a particular niche: Shan middlemen arranged nearly all purchases between the Kachin miners and the Chinese buyers. Prices were negotiated in secret and in silence, with the buyers and middleman using a complex system of finger taps that took place under a cloth or in the sleeves of a merchant's robe. The covert deal-making prevented the Bamar king's taxman from knowing the exact price negotiated, so the government representative instead demanded one tax based on the stone's weight, and another for every stone that entered or exited the trading town of Mogaung.

These rules produced odd relationships. The king's tax collector was normally not Bamar, but rather someone from Yunnan who had well-established connections with the rest of the Chinese merchants. State control of jade revenues was always difficult to secure, so the king would often lease out the position for an annual fee, and then the tax collector could run the operation like a personal business. The Bamar king got a steady, annual source of revenue, and was assured that his power was well represented in the far north: once the tax collector had paid for the position in advance, he was sure to tax the stone as much as possible.

The desparate isolation and harsh geography of the mines also shaped trading practices. While every group involved wanted to control as much exchange as possible, no group was able to contest Kachin ownership of the mines. The Bamar and Chinese power centers were too far away to extend authority into the mountains, and the valley-dwelling Shan could not compete against the Kachin warriors in the hills.

These customary rules ensured that everyone got some slice of the pie, but those who could get their stones into the Chinese markets quickest always reaped the most profit. Often this meant allying with whichever war-lord held sway in that region. In that way, the jade trade brought together business and military interests that might otherwise be at odds with each other. Jade was pure profit, and it made for strange bedfellows.

The enormous profitability of jade meant that only the most cataclysmic events could dry up the green vein. When Mao's Communists took Beijing in 1949, closing off China to outside trade, the jade business faltered. But the magnitude of the Chinese appetite for the stone, as well as the porous state apparatus in Myanmar, meant that smugglers willing to take risks could still follow the green vein to unimaginable wealth. From the 1960s to the mid-1980s, as the government in Yangon embarked on the "Burmese Way to Socialism," black market economies like the jade trade contributed to up to 60 percent of the country's income. But with Communist China no longer importing luxury goods from its neighbors, circuitous alternatives had to be found to get the stone to market. Caravans laden with opium and jade stones made their way from the Kachin hills to the Thai border in the southeast. From there, smugglers bribed Thai border guards and intelligence officers to authenticate customs reports, and the contraband stones became legal goods. Traders then shipped boulders of jade from Bangkok to the auction houses of Hong Kong.

The stone has managed to find a way to market no matter what political or geographic obstacles stand in its way. "Jade is always changing," Richard Hughes, an American gemologist who has been studying the jade trade for decades, told me. "The rules change, and the industry adapts to it. It's a lot like the drug trade in that sense. The police go this way; it changes and goes that way. Jade always finds a way."

.

Hkun Myat and I had mutual friends. We were introduced through Bum Tsit's small Kachin business empire, and first shared drinks at Red House. Whenever I got the chance, I would buy Hkun Myat drinks and talk about jade. At first, he was soft-spoken and reserved. But after a few beers, Hkun Myat would open up and become expressive. Then he would talk about his life and the struggle of being a yemase in lucid, almost poetic language.

"Jade is the stone of luck," he told me once. "When you find the stream, a life of possibility will open for you."

We were sitting outside, not far from the Manau Park in downtown Myitkyina. The sky was cloudless, and seemed to stretch far beyond the Kachin peaks on the horizon, and Hkun Myat looked up frequently, as though he wasn't used to its beauty. We were eating a pack of J Donuts I had brought from Yangon. Like most people who lived far from the metropolis, the sweet snacks were an impossibly rare treat for the yemase. I usually brought several packs whenever I traveled north and gave them to people I interviewed.

The young miner stared back at the package, where the J Donuts logo was printed in English: "Always Fresh. Always Share. Always Health." Hkun Myat sounded the words out under his breath. Unlike many of the yemase in Hpakan, he rarely left the mining town and had few opportunities or reasons to practice his English. But far from being jealous of the other itinerant miners, he was deeply sympathetic to them. The miners that came from outside of Hpakan lacked the family and safety net of the locals.

Some nights, young women from the city would come and sit in the bar and chat with the men. Hkun Myat was modest and shy around the girls from Myitkyina. While they wore fashionable denim and tops with designer labels, the yemase was usually bundled in the same pair of thick red sweatpants and flip-flops. The black and white plaid coat he wore was scraggly and stained from exposure on the mountains. He was a country boy, they were city girls, and it was obvious that he felt like an outsider. He confided in me once that he was jealous of the life of his peers in the city, that he was sacrificing part of his youth chasing after jade stones every day.

Hkun Myat told me he didn't plan on staying a yemase. His life goal was to settle down in Myitkyina—jade could bring wealth, but rich people lived in the city, not in the mines. And Hpakan was no longer the home that his family had hoped for when they moved there.

Every morning, after picking through rubble for three hours, Hkun Myat returned home around 8:00 to eat breakfast with his parents and rest for a few hours. The *yemase* lived with his parents and three siblings. He supported the household with his sporadic jade earnings. Both of Hkun Myat's parents were ethnic Kachin, part of the post-independence generation that had lived their entire lives in a land consumed by civil war.

Hkun Myat's father was originally from the far north of Kachin State, in the mountains of Sumprabum Township, where the fingers of the Himalayas reach down into the Southeast Asian jungle. In the 1960s he moved south to Myitkyina, where he met Hkun Myat's mother, and settled down to start a family and a farm. They grew bamboo, bananas, and pineapple, which they picked in the morning and sold at the afternoon markets in the city.

The family grew quickly. Hkun Myat's mother eventually gave birth to seven children. At the time, the KIA was fighting a multifront war against both the Myanmar central government and the Communist Party of Burma. The KIA controlled large parts of the north and drafted young ethnic Kachin men and women into the insurgent army. Hkun Myat's parents supported the rebels, but they lived in Myitkyina, a stronghold of the central government, and had to live and work among the city's diverse population of Bamar, Shans, Chinese, and Indians. They straddled two worlds: the city, connected to the state and all its diversities and prejudices; and the Kachin land, the peripheral, semi-autonomous hills, and a centuries-long tradition of resistance to outsiders. Life split across such disparate, invisible boundaries was an everyday reality in the borderlands.

In the mid 1970s, as the KIA solidified its gains in the rural areas of the north and began reaping large profits from the jade mines they controlled, Hkun Myat's parents saw a twofold opportunity. They would move out of the city, both to search for the family's new fortune and to begin a life that was more firmly rooted in Kachin tradition and culture. The family pulled up stakes and moved to Hpakan. At the time, the trip from Myitkyina took days, rather than hours. Ensconced in the mountains, they felt insulated from the ethnic divisions that plagued much of the north. They were part of the first group of migrant workers to the mining boomtown, and over the next forty years they watched as Hpakan's physical and social landscape changed dramatically.

Throughout the 1970s and '80s, the jade trade was a primary source of funding for the Kachin war effort. Civilians like Hkun Myat's parents that came to work at KIA-controlled mines did so at the pleasure of the rebels. For the most part, the army only allowed Kachin miners to work in the pits. The KIA made it a policy to deny access to ethnic Bamar, Shans, Chinese, and others. This prohibition was part of the jade mines' strategic importance to the insurgency. KIA battalions that passed back and forth across the Kachin Hills would dispatch runners to Hpakan, where they could procure supplies and contraband unavailable anywhere else in the north.

The KIA cultivated an air of regulation and control over the mines. But at its heart, the jade business is a trade for those comfortable with high levels of risk. Gamblers and middlemen also flocked to the town, along with the drugs and sex workers that tend to crop up in mining centers. Hpakan became a hub for illicit goods in Myanmar, a central node in the flow of black-market capital during the dark days of Myanmar's socialist experiment.

But it was also a place where a Kachin family could make a living. For nearly twenty years, Hkun Myat's family did well living off the KIA-run mines. Several of Hkun Myat's older brothers went into the mining business. They bought small plots of land and searched the dirt for green stones. No one struck it rich, but the family was able to afford a comfortable life, buy a home, and manage to stay away from most of the fighting in northern Myanmar.

Growing up around the jade mines, Hkun Myat and his brothers were cut off from the rest of the world. The politics of Yangon rarely filtered up to Hpakan, where the entire town was consumed by a single-minded pursuit of the green stone.

"I never know what's happening outside Hpakan," Hkun Myat told me. "It's like a bubble. All day I just go and search for stones. I never have news from outside, and it is hard to stay informed. But it is worth it for the money."

Most yemase I spoke with didn't know who the American or Chinese presidents were. When I asked them about the Myanmar government's Nationwide Ceasefire Agreement, they usually shook their heads and said that they didn't know anything about it. But when it came to jade news, yemase could recall events with pinpoint accuracy, even for incidents that happened before they started digging for the stone. Kachin miners that made it rich by finding high-quality stones were treated like local celebrities. Everyone remembered 2011, when Brang Di, a Kachin mine owner from Myitkyina, found his purple jade worth $24 million.

And even though they didn't follow the national peace process, the miners always kept an eye on the local fighting between the government and the KIA. People had to know when the roads would be closed. The jade companies had to pay bribes to both militaries to keep the jade stream flowing.

Certain dates held special significance for all yemase. Starting in 1994, things began to change dramatically in Hpakan. The ceasefire between the KIA and the central government allowed large mining companies to finally move into the area. Jade mining had mostly been the preserve of small time Kachin prospectors, but it quickly transformed into an enormous state-sponsored industry. Chinese investors brought in gargantuan earthmoving equipment, and mine owners adopted new strategies to find the stone. Instead of digging tunnels through the earth and searching for the green streams running underground, mining companies simply started dismantling entire mountains. The exercise was highly destructive to the environment, but also highly profitable. Hills could disappear into a pile of rubble within days or weeks, and mine operators could extract million-dollar boulders every day.

With more money came more fortifications. Mining companies hired private guards or police to protect their investments. The Tatmadaw invested heavily in the jade business. Army-owned conglomerates operated mines scattered across Hpakan and entered into profit-sharing arrangements with private Chinese companies. Jade money started directly funding the Myanmar military, and the mines once again became a strategically vital position for both big business and the military. Only now, for the first time in Myanmar's history, the central government was in control of the jade stream.

For the Kachins who lived in Hpakan, like Hkun Myat's family, the idyll of a life in the mountains away from the heavy hand of the state had disappeared. Now, the family was living in one of the most heavily securitized parts of the country. Military checkpoints dotted the roads in every direction, and Hkun Myat often had to deal with aggressive young Tatmadaw soldiers and policemen on his way from his home to the mines. It was one of the contradictions of life in Hpakan: where the dream of wealth was all around him, but the landscape of denial and despair was all he could see.

Myanmar's transition toward civilian government in 2016 did little to curb the military's influence in the jade business. Army-owned companies still controlled vast swaths of Hpakan, and security was tight. Foreigners were still prohibited from visiting the area. When Aung San Suu Kyi and the NLD took power in 2016, the Ministry of Mines embarked on a policy review process to overhaul the country's gemstone rules. While they debated, the government imposed a moratorium on new mining licenses. The process was laced with bureaucratic delays and moved slowly, and the government stopped renewing concessions for all except the most well-connected companies. Those with expiring licenses saw a limited window to suck as much wealth as possible out of the ground, and the result was a rapid acceleration in mining activity; Hpakan's landscape was changing faster than ever.

·

At 11:00 a.m., Hkun Myat goes back out to the hillside to tap more stones with his hammer. The daylight reveals the mining center's lunar landscape. Where two-thousand-foot mountains once stood, only craters remain, with enormous excavators sifting through the rubble. After detonating explosives to blast the tops of mountains, backhoes comb through the debris, pulling out boulders of jade. Hkun Myat and the other yemase stand aside and try to eke out a living on the leftovers.

Despite the industrial transformation of Hpakan, some customary rules still carried weight in the jade business. Middlemen were still employed to arrange purchases, yemase shared profit with diggers who helped them unearth large stones, and buyers still followed the strict traditional rules about when and where jade stones could be cut open.

Other rules were more modern. Instead of the old hidden-finger method, jade merchants used mobile phones to video chat with prospective buyers in China and show off their stones on camera.

The yemase and the dump truck drivers had also developed their own customary procedures to keep people safe in the mines: Before dump trucks deposited their slag on a hillside, they were supposed to honk their horn several times and flash their lights to warn the yemase on the slopes to watch out. But sometimes the truck drivers were in a hurry, or forgot to honk, or were just plain careless. Falling rocks could easily crush yemase that were in the wrong place at the wrong time.

The yemase could be highly unified in their outrage to such negligence, and directed their frustration at the large mining companies. Civil disobedience was more visible in Hpakan than most other places in Myanmar. Area newspapers often carried stories of locals and migrant workers protesting together against the behavior of the mining companies. In addition to safety concerns like those that Hkun Myat voiced, many locals abhorred the environmental degradation of the area. "There used to be mountains everywhere in Hpakan. It used to be beautiful," said Steven Tsa Ji, the head of a local organization that promoted grassroots development policy. "The Uru River was clean and filled with fish. Now the rivers are poisoned. The mountains are gone. They can take whole mountains down in a matter of weeks."

The industrial mining practices could also destabilize the ground and cause landslides. The yemase worked on hills that could suddenly and violently move, and most of them had stories about narrow misses from falling rocks and debris. One yemase I interviewed, Naw Aung, had worked in Hpakan for four years. In 2016, he was on a steep hill with hundreds of other yemase when an explosion at a nearby mine caused the slippery ground to start sliding under his feet.

"The land was shaking, and there were so many people on the hill that it was too much weight. It happened so fast, and it's so easy for the land to fall. Four of my friends got caught and they were buried by the falling rocks. I tried to dig them out, but almost no one would help me. When the land moves like that, a lot of the jade stones that are buried come up to the surface, so everyone just runs to try and find the jade. They focused on the stones, and no one came to help us."

Fourteen men died during the landslide. Four of them were Naw Aung's friends. He said that he warned younger yemase about the dangers of landslides, but the incident hadn't done much to change his working style. Other friends of his had found valuable jade stones that had allowed them to quit, but Naw Aung was waiting for that one life-changing stone. He still worked the steep slopes every day and had been caught in two more landslides. One had buried him partway and the other had sent a large boulder flying right past his head. "I'm lucky to be alive," he admitted.

For many miners, the only way to stomach the bone-shattering, dangerous work was by staying doped up. Myanmar has long been one of the largest opium producers in the world, and cheap, dangerously pure heroin has been a fixture in the jade mines for decades. So-called "shooting galleries" line the streets of Hpakan, where miners can get hits of heroin for less than five dollars a pop. Heroin dulled the pain and monotony of hammer strikes, broken bones, and angry soldiers that defined the day-in day-out life of the yemase. Hkun Myat described the herion use as a symptom of hoplessness, another side effect of the complete lack of economic opportunity that drove miners to take greater and greater risks in the pursuit of jade. Even when government inspectors closed down mining sites that were deemed unstable, yemase often broke into the areas to pick through the debris on the steep hills.

Hkun Myat had also narrowly avoided being crushed by falling rocks several times. In November of 2016, he was working on a steep hill with about fifty other yemase when a landslide started. "The whole hillside was moving down very fast, crushing people," he recounted. "People ran to get to the side to get out of the way, but my friend got caught and he was buried in the stones up to the top of his head. I had to dig him out with another person. The stones were crushing even his face."

After a visit to the hospital, Hkun Myat's friend survived. But not all yemase were so lucky, and accidents were common. In January of 2018, outrage grew in Hpakan over a mining accident in which fifteen yemase were killed by a landslide. Later that year, dozens were killed after an explosion collapsed a mountainside filled with miners. Often, these deaths were the only part of the jade world that landed on the front pages of the Yangon newspapers.

∎

For the past few years, Hkun Myat had worked in an area of Hpakan called Mo Wan Gyi. The site was well known for its high-quality jade deposits and was popular with yemase. But in 2017, most mining companies suddenly abandoned the area. Like many events in Hpakan, the rationale felt secretive, and no information filtered down to the yemase. But the effects were simple and clear: "They moved away from there very quickly," Hkun Myat recalled. "So we moved with them."

He and four other friends had begun scavenging in a new area, called Gataimaw, where Tatmadaw-affiliated companies were scaling up enormous mining operations. "We don't have any profit yet, but I hope that we will have a better chance in the area," he told me. "Sometimes we search in a group, but mostly I search by myself."

The new worksite produced regular deposits of high-quality jade for the mining companies, and word spread. More yemase flocked to the area to try to siphon off the leftovers. Officers from the KIA also had a knack of appearing in the mines whenever an especially valuable stone was unearthed. Even though mining companies tried to keep these finds secret, the KIA paid spies throughout Hpakan to alert their intelligence officers to these jades. That information could be deadly. When the KIA showed up, the threat of violence was real. Mine owners were ordered to pay the "tax" determined by the KIA official, and in return received a piece of official paper that only held value to the rebels. But the alternatives to paying were far worse.

In 2014, one such mining company found an enormous boulder of extremely high-quality jade. Normally whoever found such a stone would immediately smuggle it to China, but in this case the piece of jade was so large it couldn't fit on a truck. The single rock was worth hundreds of millions of dollars. The company that unearthed the stone refused to inform the KIA, but the rebel tax collectors learned about the stone through their informants and demanded payment. When the company refused, the KIA sent a truck bomb into the mining area, destroying millions of dollars worth of jade and killing more than eighty people.

Even though most jade mining was controlled by the Tatmadaw and businessmen close to the army, the KIA's continual presence in the mines highlighted the other eternal truth about Myanmar's secret world of jade: whoever controlled the land was in control of the jade. The central government may have secured most of the mining areas after the 1994 ceasefire, but the rebel army still controlled some of the mountainous territory around Hpakan, and they had no intention of giving up their share of the jade profit.

.

Hkun Myat was aware of the power politics around jade, but he told me that these things didn't really affect him. Those were questions for "big people," he said. People with connections, influence, and power, who could actually change things in Kachin and maybe bring peace and order to the mining centers.

Instead, the way Hkun Myat saw the jade business, everything was about luck. Jade was supposed to be the stone of luck. His life plan was "to get lucky and find a valuable stone." Whichever army controlled the mines didn't matter so much to him. The best he could hope for was that the underground vein of green stone was prodigious enough that a little bit of jade would trickle downhill to him. That meant following the mining companies around and racing through the rubble to find jade before the other miners.

Occasionally, when yemase heard about a new site and tried to gain access to the leftover slag heaps, the large mining companies would prevent them from entering.

On October 20, 2017, a group of fifty yemase like Hkun Myat tried to gain entry to a mining dumpsite owned by a firm called the 111 Company. Even though yemase picking is technically illegal, mine owners typically let the workers in without issue. In this case however, police officers employed by 111 Company prevented the miners from entering the site. Most mining companies hire private security outfits to protect their concessions, but companies connected with the military sometimes use state police or military to guard the mines.

An hour after being turned away, the yemase returned. But this time, there were six hundred of them. The group destroyed mining equipment, burned dump trucks, and attacked the police with knives and digging tools. Five officers were reportedly injured, and they turned their guns on the miners in response. Five yemase died, and another twenty were sent to the hospital with injuries.

When I asked Hkun Myat about the incident, he said that it was an especially high-profile example of an issue that happens all the time. "If a yemase doesn't find stones, his life collapses," he explained. "We do what we must to find it."

·

When I spoke to a mine owner about security in Hpakan, he was also frustrated by the town's disorder. "There is no rule of law in Hpakan!" yelled Bum Yun, a Kachin businessman who owns the Jinghpaw Academy Company, which operates 115 acres of jade mines in the Hpakan area. "That's why thousands of yemase can just go to the company's mine areas with no permission. The company pays tax to the government, but the government says it's not their problem. They just tell us, 'go to the police or the army with your problems.' So then we have to take the issue into our own hands."

Bum Yun started working in Hpakan in the early 1970s, around the same time Hkun Myat's parents moved to the town. The young man traveled to the mining town from Myitkyina during his school vacations. "Jade was already very famous in Kachin when I started," he remembered. "People were rich because of jade. They could afford an education because of jade."

Bum Yun worked his way up the jade ladder to become one of the most successful mine owners in Kachin. But when he looked at the industry, all he could see were problems. At many of his sites, his company had to work in partnership with the Myanmar Gems Enterprise or Tatmadaw businesses, whose aggressive mining practices he disliked.

When the NLD government began to reform the jade industry, Bum Yun and other ethnic Kachin jade bosses argued that companies with links to the military were able to consolidate ownership claims and continue operating without government oversight. Large Tatmadaw-linked companies would surround groups of smaller, Kachin-held mines. Once the larger companies excavated, it became physically impossible for the small-scale mine owners to gain access to their sites, and they were forced to sell their concessions to the larger companies.

Despite the risks to Kachin mine owners, jade had made Bum Yun a rich man. We were sitting in his house, an enormous three-story building in the middle of Myitkyina. The building was covered in jade. Green mosaics covered the columns that supported the second-floor balconies. Inside, big boulders on pedestals were scattered about the house. Many were veined with bright green, translucent jade, worth tens of thousands of dollars. In the living room, beaded jade seat covers spread across three enormous leather couches. On the wall over one couch, someone had hung up a large framed landscape of the Kachin mountains. The whole picture was green, white, and brown—a meticulous construction of tiny jade rocks. Outside, a high perimeter fence topped with barbed wire surrounded the property, and in the driveway, he had used old car tires to construct an eight-foot-tall yellow "Minion" from the *Despicable Me* movies.

For yemase, jade is a life of gambling and risk. But for mine owners like Bum Yun, the stone was a safe bet, albeit one that needed protection.

The businessman told me he employed private security guards at his mines to stand at every corner of the perimeter fence. Myanmar law prohibits such security personnel from carrying firearms, and when I asked him if they were armed, he refused to answer directly.

"The Tatmadaw owns its own mines, and of course they protect those," he said. "But for us, we are on our own."

A photo album on the table recounted a career of success. In one picture, Bum Yun and a colleague crouched in an underground tunnel. Behind them, a bright green vein of jadeite shined out from a rock wall. "For me, there is no gambling," he said, pointing at the picture. "This is 160 feet underground. I only dig when I am very sure. With jade like this, you can be quite sure of success. It takes work to find, but when I see this in the tunnel, I know that I will make money."

According to Myanmar law, Bum Yun and other jade merchants are supposed to sell all of their jade at the annual emporium in Naypyidaw, the capital. But with stones of such high quality, Bum Yun said, there was very little incentive to follow the rules. Cumbersome tax regulations, which most merchants say do not align with the jade industry's business model, encourage underground trade. And it is easy to skirt the government's tax collectors by smuggling the rocks out of the country. "We send it to China, because Myanmar's policies don't fit in with the business," Bum Yun said matter-of-factly. "Besides, people never send quality stones to the emporium. Everyone sends it illegally to other countries."

But Bum Yun did still spend time in the capital. In the photo album, there was a picture of him standing in Naypyidaw, posing with a forty-ton boulder of jade in front of a government building. "That is my jade," he said. "I didn't sell, just gave it to the government." He shrugged. "That's the price of doing business."

The jade sales in Naypyidaw also served another purpose: they were essential for laundering money from illegal jade shipments to China. A jade mine can pull out tens of thousands of tons of jade per year, but only a tiny portion will be the highly valuable "imperial" quality stone. Industry experts estimate that 95 percent of the value of a jade mine comes from less than 3 percent of stones. And because so much value can be stored in such a small amount of jade, moving enormous amounts of wealth through the mountains into China can sometimes be as easy as driving a motorbike along a jungle path. The problem for mine owners like Bum Yun was repatriating that money. The annual jade emporiums provided a vehicle.

A mine owner could reserve a portion of jade stones each year—usually enormous boulders that would be difficult to smuggle across the border. These huge stones look flashy but tend not to be such high quality. Then at the annual jade emporium they would sell these stones to foreign buyers and put that money on the company books. Some of the largest mining operators, those affiliated with high-ranking generals in the Tatmadaw or with Chinese financing, would even establish dummy companies to buy stones back from themselves as a way to wash their money from black-market jade sales in China.

"The money from the official sales, we call it white money. You just use it for official expenses," Bum Yun said, sitting underneath a framed portrait of himself, another picture of him standing in the capital city with a large piece of jade from his mine. "No one sells jade in Naypyidaw unless they need to clean their money." There were other money laundering options as well, he said. Some jade magnates reinvested into real estate in Naypyidaw or Yangon. Others sent money abroad to Thailand or Singapore.

Sitting at the top of the jade ladder, risk virtually disappears. At Bum Yun's level, the stone represented security, not risk. With its benefit, he could look down at the industry and think about the millions of lives it has affected.

"There is a perspective that jade is the only thing that makes people rich quickly," he said. "So yes, it is important. It is very valuable and can bring Kachin people money. But because of jade, Kachin has suffered a lot. There is so much mismanagement."

•

For policymakers trying to reform the jade industry, one of the most difficult tasks is figuring out who exactly profits from the stone. With so much of the trade operating in the shadows, billions of dollars go untracked. Secret agreements between businessmen and armed groups mean that the stone is never far from the front lines of Myanmar's civil war, and indicate that political considerations are often less important than financial ones in the ungoverned borderlands.

In the past decade, several groups have tried to map the jade trade using available economic data, interviews with industry experts, and trips to the Naypyidaw emporium. The results have been highly variable, but also highly revealing, with estimates of the industry's annual value ranging from $8 billion to $40 billion. Together, these studies paint a picture of Myanmar's most valuable resouces being systematically divided among a shadowy cabal of current and former Tatmadaw generals, KIA leaders, Chinese fianciers, and crony businessmen, with hardly any money making its way into official government coffers.

When the United Nations Fact-Finding Mission on Myanmar investigated the Tatmadaw's economic activities, the team reported that the military was heavily involved in Myanmar's jade trade, an industry they estimated could be worth up to $31 billion, making up nearly half of the country's GDP. The UN report concluded that the military's jade business "directly contributed to international human rights violations in conflict-affected areas of Kachin State." Yemase voices were featured prominently in the report. One jade picker interviewed said that Tatmadaw had tortured him for information about jade mines in KIA-controlled areas. Other yemase testified that soldiers would detain them walking through Hpakan and demand any jade stones they were carrying. When the yemase didn't have stones, the soldiers would beat them unconscious. Because the vast majority of jade commerce was underground, untraceable, and had a global reach, the report cautioned that international companies involved in the industry could be unwittingly implicated in the industry's many abuses.

The most recent analysis on Myanmar jade came from the Natural Resource Governance Institute. In Yangon, I met with Maw Htun Aung, NRGI's Myanmar country director, who told me that any analysis that claims to measure the jade industry with certainty is being dishonest. "It's a gray economy," he said, "which makes it incredibly difficult to estimate." NRGI's own valuation of the industry was around $8 billion per year—still an enormous amount of money in a country with a GDP of less than $70 billion.

NRGI had also worked with the Myanmar Gems Enterprise to build a database of stakeholders in the jade industry with the aim of showing the public where jade revenue comes from and how mining concessions get parceled out. However, the database, called Open Jade Data, only has access to data from legal jade channels, totaling roughly $500 million per year. Maw Htun Aung told me that's how much of the multi-billion-dollar industry the Myanmar government is actually able to get its hands on. The government and the Tatmadaw were often thought of as one and the same, due to the military's continued dominance over most of the economy and security operations. But Maw Htun Aung highlighted that the civilian, NLD-led government was more like an unsophisticated third party in the jade war—locked out of the river of wealth by the military that supposedly answered to it. There is enough money in jade to build hospitals and pave roads and help bring Myanmar out of the economic hole wrought by five decades of mismanagement and isolation. But due to a complete lack of governance in the north, driven by the neverending civil war, so far the stone has only lined the pockets of the country's most powerful families. Regardless of whether jade in Myanmar is worth $8 billion or $40 billion a year, this systematic and secretive siphoning of money away from the state is one of the largest natural resource heists in the history of the world.

Another study, from Harvard University, used Chinese trade data from the UN to estimate underground jade exports from Myanmar. In a policy paper titled *A Grand Bargain*, economist David Dapice values Myanmar jade at $15 billion annually, which he calls "a conservative estimate." The paper argues that two-thirds of this money actually ends up in the hands of outside investors—mostly Chinese—who finance the largest mining companies. Meanwhile, the Tatmadaw and its affiliated cronies pull in more than $2.5 billion of untaxed jade money each year—money that pads the army's unofficial budget and lines the pockets of its top generals. The Harvard analysis also estimates that the KIA earns a little more than 5 percent of all jade revenue—totaling roughly $800 million annually—mostly by shaking down jade producers and charging fees along smuggling routes. It is impossible to trace where that money goes. The Kachin Independence Organization refers to this revenue as a "tax," reflecting their ownership of the local resources, but most people see it as funding for the war effort.

Dapice writes that "The KIA's ten tax agents in [Hpakan] . . . collect more than their thousands of counterparts working for the Ministry of Mines." The story, while anecdotal, is very significant. The Ash Center analysis shows that all told, less than 7 percent of jade sales go through legal channels, and the government only recoups 3 percent of revenue from the jade trade. The lack of governance in the jade industry highlights one of the historic truths about the trade: money is made in the shadows, and both business and armed groups are interested in keeping it that way. The reason the KIA and Tatmadaw have such enormous stakes in the status quo, the paper argues, is that more effective government control of the industry would likely result in a drastic reduction in their profit. For both sides, perpetual civil war is still a better deal than losing out on billions of dollars of jade revenue.

Taken together, the reports show that war means profit in the jade mines, and that elites profit at the expense of the country's poorest. The leaders and friends of the KIA and the Tatmadaw have more in common economically than they have differences politically. And in the complicated calculus of civil war, both sides had decided that billions of dollars worth of jade carried more value than all the lives of the doped-up yemase or the young soldiers with nothing to lose or the civilians caught in between.

•

The night shift is when most of the yemase's business takes place. Like a worker going in to punch the clock, Hkun Myat returns to the hillside every evening around 11:00 p.m.—his third shift of the day—with his hammer and flashlight, alongside thousands of other stone pickers. The large jade companies keep operations going around the clock, and at night, buyers set up a long, ramshackle market on the ridgeline. Flashlights, which the yemase hold in their mouths, are the only sources of light once the sun disappears, and from the stalls, all you can see is a thousand white circles probing through an invisible landscape of rock.

During the day, when Hkun Myat found a good jade stone, he would bring it to his uncle and brother to look at. But often at night he could go directly to a buyer's kiosk, show a stone under the light, and sell it for around 10,000 kyats. Most of the jade he sold this way was probably not worth much—low grade stones that a buyer took a risk on, hoping to be surprised when he cut the stone open. But the cutting never happened in front of Hkun Myat. He never knew whether or not the stone he sold could have been the life changing one. He just knew that it was enough money to help feed his aging parents.

He said that one day he would find the stone that would change his life—a universal conviction among the yemase. Sitting in the bar one evening, we looked at Facebook photos from a mutual friend, a Kachin woman that had married into a Chinese jade trading family. For their engagement photos, the couple had flown to Europe along with a team of photographers and makeup designers. They had photo shoots in Italy, Switzerland, and France. The bride's outfits cost more than $20,000. One photo of the couple in the Swiss Alps had won an award from a prestigious wedding magazine. The ostentatious display of wealth was the dream for most people in the jade business. In comparison, it made Hkun Myat's goal of opening a phone shop in Myitkyina seem quaint.

The yemase scratched at his puffy jacket and shook his head while we looked at the pictures. He asked me how far away Europe was, and I told him that they probably had to travel most of the day on an airplane to get there. Hkun Myat nodded slowly; he had never been on a plane. The young man finished his beer in a single gulp. Before leaving that night, he asked to take a picture with me on his phone, to prove to his parents that he had met someone from the outside.

SAPI

Four men sit in the middle of a field on a raised wooden platform, sipping rice wine. It is late afternoon and the rice wine is pink and cool and faintly sweet. The Kachin call it *sapi*, and it tastes excellent with grilled skewers of pork intestine and chicken legs.

The winter sky is a high, sharp blue, and Yenawsi, the man who owns this field, has just finished his work for the day. He has spent the last few hours staking out different plots of land and marking them with rope and flags. It is simple work, but physically difficult. The land is close to a small stream, and Yenawsi sinks into the muck when he walks back and forth. His feet have the strong, splayed-out toes of someone who has spent most of his life working outside without shoes on. Yenawsi is nearly fifty, but he radiates youth. His shock of thick black hair stands straight up from his forehead. He is less than five feet tall, but his body is rippling with muscles. The only place you can see his age is around his eyes, which are wrinkled from spending so much time in the sun. But it might also be from smiling and laughing, which he does often and loudly, slapping his knees and guffawing. You can see it in his teeth as well, which are stained red from chewing so much betel nut.

The men talk about how difficult it is to sell land these days. A couple of years ago, when prices kept going up and up, there was so much speculation that it was impossible to lose money in real estate. But sometime after the war restarted, the bubble burst, and most people blamed the Tatmadaw for their financial losses.

Yenawsi has strong feelings about the army.

"We lived in the forest for a long time," he says. "Me and my brother. We fight for Lisu people. But then they shot my brother." He raises his hands up, holding an imaginary rifle, and pulls the trigger. "Boom! I hate the army. I will kill the army."

Yenawsi encourages everyone to drink the *sapi*. He keeps using the Chinese toast, "Gambei," which means everyone has to finish their glass. The *sapi* isn't much stronger than beer, but it goes to your head quickly.

Yenawsi is particularly excited because I am the first foreigner he has spoken to. Actually, he corrects himself, "You are the second foreigner I spoke to. The first one was last year in the city, and someone came up to me and asked me something. But I didn't understand. I was afraid and so I ran away." He laughs and refills my *sapi* glass, and invites me to dinner the next evening.

▪

Yenawsi lives out to the east of Myitkyina, at the end of a very long dirt road filled with potholes. Normally it's only a twenty-five-minute drive from the city center in Bum Tsit's luxury sedan, but when the cows refuse to move out of the road, it can take up to an hour. It is a beautiful slice of northern farmland. The rice fields glow under a lilac sky and birds chase each other through the bamboo canopies. Yenawsi lives in the only cement house in the neighborhood, and he is proud of how far he's come. His house is surrounded by magnificent flowering fruit trees that he and his wife have planted, but the first thing he points out to me is the new satellite dish on the roof.

Si Thu Aung, Yenawsi's eight-year-old son, is too shy to talk. "Speak English to him," Yenawsi tells him in Burmese. "Show him how you love to study English." But Si Thu Aung buries his head in his mother's dress and only peeks out when he thinks I'm not looking.

Yenawsi parades me around the neighborhood, shouting at his mother, who is asleep, that there is a foreigner here to visit him. "That's my mother's home," he points across the road. "I built it for her."

Over there is the first car he bought, moldering in the grass. And over here is the new puppy that he just got the family.

Slowly, we walk down the narrow dirt lane, which is pitch black now that the sun has set. Yenawsi has a hand-crank flashlight, which he gives to me. He holds my soft hand in his two rocklike ones, as male friends often do in Myanmar, and says in English, "Thank you. I love you," over and over. Eventually, we reach a clearing, with a small building in the middle. A narrow stream runs nearby, and Yenawsi says that he sometimes stands in the water and catches fish with a net, but the stream is too low now.

Yenawsi's farm is filled with pomelo trees, and he has put together a basket of fruit on a small table. The grass has been freshly cut, and he tells me that he came up here last night to prepare the area. He hadn't hosted any guests for over six months, and the grass was knee high, so he and a friend cut it by hand. They started at 9:00 p.m. and kept going until one in the morning. I tell him that he shouldn't have done so much work for me, but he waves his hand dismissively. Of course he should. He is hosting someone new. It would be disrespectful to do anything less.

Yenawsi is wearing slacks and a starched button-down shirt, his business uniform for when he has to go into the city and meet with prospective land buyers. But when he sees that I am in shorts and a T-shirt, he changes to a longyi and tank top. Then he busies himself setting up the lights. He wires it all by hand, chewing off the end of the rubber insulation and twisting the copper wires together before flipping a switch and bathing the yard in a fluorescent white glow.

We sit outside and eat chicken curry and pomelo. Yenawsi and his wife are both Lisu, one of the subgroups within the Kachin nation. The chicken recipe is a Lisu classic that his wife makes for special occasions. It is earthy and delicious. Yenawsi tells me he ate like this every night when he was a fighter in the jungle—when he and his brother fought for Lisu independence against both the KIA and the Tatmadaw.

But Yenawsi doesn't want to talk about the past. The seven of us sit around the table—Yenawsi and his wife and son and his wife's sister, Bum Tsit, another of Yenawsi's friends, and me—and Yenawsi asks me about life in America and how much land costs there.

Mostly we talk in Burmese, but occasionally he needs to say something in Jinghpaw, which Bum Tsit translates for me. He speaks to his wife entirely in Lisu, which is unintelligible to the rest of us. The only thing I learn is "Akeeshimo." Thank you. The Jinghpaw men laugh when I say it. In their language it sounds like, "Eat a fart."

Someone brings up Ohn Myint, the Tatmadaw general who headed the Kachin State government for many years. Most people in Kachin hate Ohn Myint, who was deeply involved in granting natural resource concessions to the military and crony companies. He was one of the most corrupt players in the jade business and made millions from the region's natural resources. He was the local commander of the military when they shot Yenawsi's brother in the jungle.

But Yenawsi loves Ohn Myint. Under the general, the military seized thousands of acres of land from poor farmers across the state, including Yenawsi's father. But when the land went back on sale later, it was incredibly cheap, and Yenawsi was able to buy back all of his father's land, plus much more. He suddenly went from a poor farmer to a rich one, and that was all that mattered.

The two Jinghpaw men sitting with us shake their heads. They both hate Ohn Myint. But Yenawsi, having finished his glass of *sapi*, switches to English briefly. "Ohn Myint very good. Number one for Yenawsi!"

Later, on the drive back into the city, I ask Bum Tsit why he had asked me to meet Yenawsi. "He is just a nice man who works hard for his family," Bum Tsit says while we drive back to Myitkyina. "I wanted you to meet him to see that. Not everyone in Kachin thinks the same thing. Not everyone cares about the war and jade. There is more than one way to live here."

The moon sets over the rice fields; the sun comes up with the twittering of a thousand birds. The river flows forward and the wheel of time keeps turning. In Myanmar, life follows the seasons. Things move quicker when it's dry.

PART II—HOT

January 2018–April 2018

BANYAN TREE

There are banyan trees everywhere in Myanmar. Small villages in the countryside sometimes use them as meeting places, and plan their streets around trees growing in the center of town. In parts of downtown Yangon, they are the only trees that survive. The spreading roots seem to be able to sustain the tree no matter how hostile the environment. They crunch through paving stones in search of sustenance, and grapple onto nearby buildings to stretch toward the sunlight. Many narrow dead-end alleyways in Yangon terminate with ancient banyans spreading their shade over the nearby houses. These neighborhood guardians are often adorned with offerings and small shrines. Golden Buddha statues placed in the trees decades before peer out through the weathered brown exterior, partially swallowed and crushed by the tree's growth. People treat the banyans like communal points of worship; often dressing them in golden Buddhist sashes.

The banyan is part of the fig family. Biologists classify the tree as an epiphyte. It has difficulty germinating on the ground, so most banyans start life as a parasitic vine that grafts itself onto a host. Normally that host is another tree. But when the banyan seed falls in an area like Yangon, it can graft onto a dirty building covered with nutritious black mold. From there, the small plant can send roots down to the ground in search of nutrients. As they reach down from above, these roots sometimes hang like ropes in the air, swaying in the wind. As the vine grows and multiplies, it can wrap itself over large portions of the host, a behavior that earns it the name "strangler fig."

The banyan is an aggressive tree. As it matures, it takes on the appearance of a bundle of ropes wrapped painfully around an unwilling core. Eventually, the banyan sends its own branches up into the air. They twist and spread, searching for sunlight and a chance to unfurl their heavy leaves, which cast a lovely shade on the ground and therefore crowd out any other potential sunlight competitors. Eventually, the branches become so thick that they are too heavy for the tree to support on its own, and the aerial roots that extend to the ground thicken to become buttressing supports. When they stiffen and solidify over the decades, these vertical roots become indistinguishable from the trunk itself.

The Buddhist scripture known as the Pali Canon makes reference to the banyan. The text highlights both the good and bad qualities of the tree. A hospitable person is described as being like a great banyan tree on the side of the road, one that "welcomes weary travelers with its cool shade and soothes their tiredness."

But the banyan can also represent some of humanity's worst impulses. Its aggressive parasitic structure and unyielding thirst recall the dangerous temptations that appear to those with power. As it grows, it needs more. Like untempered human avarice, the tree is never satisfied. Only the enlightened mind can let go of these worldly attachments and live at peace.

The Buddha was supposed to have seen in the tree an archetype for humanity's suffering. "Just as a tree that has been cut down can grow again if its root is undamaged and complete, in the same way this suffering returns again and again if the tendency to craving is not removed."

In Myanmar, you can see the banyan's roots everywhere. In village centers, alongside jungle roads, on top of Yangon's dirty sidewalks, the trees have grafted themselves into the rich land. They look like a permanent part of the landscape. Immovable. Awe inspiring in their growth and resilience. They only fall during earthquakes and fires. Or if a great group of people come together with a single-minded intention.

Sometimes, the twisting roots of the banyan tree become so strong that they completely corrupt and envelop the host tree, crushing it. Eventually, the host rots away, leaving a hollow column inside an exterior webbed shell. The only thing supporting the giant structure is the roots. The center has completely disappeared.

5.

RICE BOWL

Lower Myanmar

O n a steamy, mosquito-filled evening in February, I accompanied Phoe Wa to the awards ceremony for the tenth annual Yangon Photo Festival, held in the garden of the French Institute. Some of the country's best photographers had submitted work to be judged by an international panel. The first-place winner would receive a new camera, while the second prize was a trip to the World Press Photo awards in Amsterdam. Everyone agreed that second place was more desirable. "You can get a new camera any time," said Phoe Wa, "but going to the awards and meeting those people is a once-in-a-lifetime opportunity."

The competition was the culmination of two weeks of events across the city celebrating photojournalism and studio photography. During the festival, galleries and public spaces across Yangon had displayed local and international photography, and I had gone to see several of the exhibits with Phoe Wa. We had met in the crumbling old Secretariat Building one day to see a collection of photos from Myanmar's colonial period and early independence. Phoe Wa had never used a film camera before and was fascinated by old techniques and the masters who used them. He said that the stories of the photographers inspired him. He was part of a long line of native artists and intellectuals who had documented his country's difficult history. Memory and truth were preserved in the fraying black and white films that decorated the walls of the old building.

At the awards ceremony, Phoe Wa was on assignment, photographing guests during the cocktail hour and taking down their details for a photo spread in the *Myanmar Times*'s events page. Before the ceremony started, he and I walked around the courtyard, looking at some of the photo stories displayed. The panel of competition judges contained three foreign photographers whose recent work was being highlighted that evening prior to the event. One was a seven-year project about refugees migrating to Europe. Phoe Wa and I paused at one picture—the moment of impact when a Muslim refugee was intentionally struck by a furious driver on a Greek island. The young man, airborne alongside the glass from the car's shattered windshield, spun through the air with a grimace of agony on his face.

The dynamism of the photo reminded me of the kinds of pictures Phoe Wa might take one day if he got the chance to photograph real news stories.

The young photographer turned to me. "You know Aung San Suu Kyi used to be the head judge of this competition," he said. "Every year she came here to the ceremony. But this year she said no. This year, the government is not so friendly with the journalists."

First as the country's preeminent opposition figure, and later as head of the civilian government, Aung San Suu Kyi had supported the photo festival not just as a judge, but also by lending her public support to the efforts of photographers and journalists to document Myanmar's changing social landscape.

Before the ceremony started, the big projector screen displayed a slide-show of past years' festivals. The Lady was present in many of the pictures, which made her absence all the more conspicuous. Milling about the French Institute's garden, Phoe Wa and I eavesdropped one some of the attendees gossiping about The Lady's absence.

"The EU delegation asked her to come," one man told his friend. "But she complained that everyone there would be talking about human rights, and it wouldn't look good for her."

During the previous year's festival, The Lady was still a global human rights icon leading one of the world's most promising democratic transitions. This year was different. In the months since the Tatmadaw's operations began in Rakhine State, Aung San Suu Kyi had faced immense international condemnation over her government's handling of the crisis, as well as over the draconian restrictions placed on journalists trying to cover the issue. A month earlier, the Committee to Protect Journalists described her as one of press freedom's biggest backsliders in 2017. It wasn't surprising that she refused the invitation to join the judging panel, which included several journalists well known for their work covering the plight of the Rohingya.

The ceremony started with a small speech from the organizers, high-lighting the effectiveness of the photography workshops they held throughout the country. The amateur artists that were showing their photo essays were all graduates of the program, where they had learned to think like photographers.

"Now photography is easy," the emcee said. "We are all photographers; you just press the button. What is important is the thinking. What do you want to say?"

The competition was a lighthearted affair. Ten amateur photographers presented their work in three-minute photo essays set to ambient electronic music. Most took place in the borderlands, and many were about the hardships of life on the outskirts of Myanmar. None of the stories addressed the Rohingya issue. The one story set in Rakhine State was a profile piece about a horse that couldn't find a job pulling carriages anymore, now that fewer tourists were coming. For a celebration of photojournalism, it felt like some punches were being pulled.

But there were still some excellent photo essays. There was a heart-wrenching story about a leper colony in Karen State. Another was a self-portrait by a nine-year-old girl with partial paralysis living in a camp for internally displaced people. My favorite was a profile of a village in Shan State that still lived entirely off the opium trade. The rugged mountains and bright green-gold poppy field landscapes were some of the most visually stunning pictures of the night.

After the amateurs, six professional journalists shared their photo stories. In all, more than one hundred photographers had submitted entries to the competition.

The judges awarded the first-place prize to a woman named Seng Mai, the editor of a local news journal in Kachin State. Her story about female soldiers in the Kachin Independence Army had all been shot in a single day—the constraints of photographing an illegal army in their mountaintop outpost. Second place went to one of Phoe Wa's colleagues at the *Myanmar Times* for a photo essay about the lives of laborers who dismantle old container ships. When Phoe Wa saw the pictures he gasped. "Their life is too difficult to stand," he told me. Along with the commendation, the *Times's* photographer also won the trip to Amsterdam.

"One day, that will be me," Phoe Wa said. "I will submit my photos next year. Hopefully I will win second place."

•

A few weeks later, two journalists were hunched together over an old computer terminal in the photography office of the *Myanmar Times*. From the second-floor windows of the whitewashed colonial building, the lights on St. Mary's Cathedral lit up like a beacon in the night sky, and the bells from a Hindu temple next door mixed in with the bustle of evening foot traffic on Bo Aung Kyaw Street.

Kaung Htet was helping Phoe Wa edit photos he had taken that afternoon of a protest against the government's war on the KIA in Kachin State.

Student activists in Yangon had marched through the streets with signs that said *Stop Bombing Kachin State* and *I Stand with the Kachin Youth Movement*. The photos would be on the front page of tomorrow's edition, and Phoe Wa was on a deadline to get the pictures to the layout department before they left for the night. Together, the two photographers were trying to find the best caption to run with a photo of a group of students chanting antiwar slogans. I looked at the screen.

Kachin students join in a demonstration against fighting in their home state, in Kamaryut Township of Yangon.

"It is a few characters too long," Phoe Wa told me. "It won't fit as a caption."

Behind us, Kaung Htet was puffing on his vaporizer, letting huge clouds of smoke roll out from behind his twisted-up moustache. "You were there, Phoe Wa," he said. "It's your caption."

"What about this," I asked, and typed in:

Students join in a demonstration against Kachin State fighting, in Kamaryut Township of Yangon.

The new caption fit the character limit, and Phoe Wa rushed a flash drive with the edited picture to the team doing the layout down the hall. I felt an embarrassing amount of pride thinking about how tomorrow some words that I chose would be part of the morning news, and I realized that that was what Phoe Wa and Kaung Htet must feel every day.

While Phoe Wa worked with the layout team, I stood with Kaung Htet on the sidewalk outside. The veteran photographer puffed on his vaporizer and talked about his protégé. "He has come far, Phoe Wa," he said. "But I am worried that he might not have what it takes. Now he has been here one year without a real job. That's a long time for anyone, and he is really still this countryside boy who has come to the big city. Does he have that competitive drive that is necessary?"

∎

Phoe Wa and I went for a drink. It was last call at Hyper Pub, which closed at 11:00 p.m. on weeknights. Then the photographers and other reporters from the *Myanmar Times* would finish their Myanmar Beers and shuffle home through Yangon's semi-deserted streets. Phoe Wa hated going back to the hostel at night. Nothing there felt like home and all he had to look forward to was a cold shower before curling up on the floor between twelve other men. So sometimes we would take slow walks back from the pub to his dorm, enjoying a moment of quiet in the city.

It was also nicer to walk at night. The hot-season sun in Yangon is suffocating. It's the kind of heat that makes you question why you are doing something, rather than nothing. It's a heat that demands exertion, whether you're ready to give it or not. For the millions of farmers across Myanmar tilling the field, like the men and women from Phoe Wa's village, these painful hours of labor under the sun can determine success or failure for the year. The hot season is a time for sacrifice, and a time for suffering.

Despite having lived in Yangon for nearly a year now, Phoe Wa still thought of the city as an alien and aggressive place. He felt like he was losing part of himself. Being in Yangon meant being disconnected from the customary way of life and the daily rituals that had defined his family for generations, especially religious rituals. At home, he was used to spending hours practicing local meditation techniques, often with his grandfather. But in Yangon, it felt like there was no personal space, and in the crowded downtown dormitory, he was limited to just fifteen minutes of meditation. Phoe Wa told me that the morning meditation was critical to his mental health, and he credited many of his personality traits to the practice: "It helps me to not get angry, not get upset when I'm in trouble, avoid rude behavior," he listed. But it was also a way to hold onto a connection with his home

The longer Phoe Wa went in Yangon without finding a paying job, the more of a sacrifice it became for him. He was giving up his spiritual health in order to concentrate on his professional dream. But without having anything concrete to show for it, he was embarrassed.

He told me that he felt grateful that he got to keep learning from his mentor, Kaung Htet. But he still felt extraordinary *A Na* for not being able to send money home to his mother and sister, and the job search hadn't progressed at all in the past few months. He told me about recently applying for a job at *The Irrawaddy* with Kaung Htet's help. For weeks, Phoe Wa had held out hope that the prestigious newsmagazine would hire him as a photographer. But in the end it turned out that someone in *The Irrawaddy* office had made a mistake and left the job advertisement up online even though they had already filled the position. Despondent, Phoe Wa would sometimes text me his thoughts from the dorm room. "Nothing is feel like my home in Yangon," he wrote to me in English one night.

Most evenings, he would lie alone and listen to his headphones, alternating between his English audio courses and soft, classic Burmese rock that reminded him of Mon State. He especially liked the songs of Htoo Eain Thin, one of Myanmar's most famous musicians from the '80s and early '90s. "Ever people who away from home like this song," he wrote to me on Facebook, with a link to the music video for a song called "Mom's Home."

Since coming to Yangon, Phoe Wa had only made the trip home twice. Kaung Htet thought that it was important for Phoe Wa to visit his family and remember how far he had already come. But without any reliable income, Phoe Wa found it hard to justify spending the money for a round-trip ticket. And he didn't feel like he could afford to miss too much time at the newspaper, in case it somehow led to paying work. Part of it was dedication to his career dreams. But another part of it was that he still felt like he hadn't made it in the city. Whenever his girlfriend, who had a good paying job as a nurse, asked to come visit, he made up excuses about why she should wait. "I don't want her to see where I live," he explained. "I want to wait until I have a nice apartment and then she can see the city that way."

But at night, Phoe Wa would hum the chorus to "Mom's Home" and think of his village: "Walking the streets of life / I'm so wasted / My heart is lingering for Mom's home. . ."

■

The 7:15 train to Mawlamyine was crowded. Crows swooped through Yangon's central station, flitting through the shafts of early morning light that spilled through the old building's giant windows. Phoe Wa met me with a large backpack stuffed with gifts for his family and friends, and led me to the train. We boarded just as the long line of rusty beige cars pulled out of the station. The young photographer had reserved us seats at the front of one carriage. "Just wait until you see Mon State," he said, beaming. "My home is so much more beautiful than Yangon."

At Kaung Htet's urging, Phoe Wa had finally decided to take a trip home. During a lull in the middle of hot season, when the only news seemed to be how quickly the flies buzzing around the *Myanmar Times* office were dying from heat exhaustion, Phoe Wa and I went to visit his family.

For the first hour, the train was flanked on both sides by hillocks of trash and poverty as it plodded through Yangon's urban sprawl. Small communities of squatters had pitched tents and makeshift shacks near the refuse. Everywhere was plastic and human filth. The train felt like a long, dirty knife slicing though the waste. Inside the train car, old ladies held rags to their noses as we passed a patch where the city's sewer had clogged and overflowed down toward the tracks. Above us, old cement housing complexes blocked out the sun. But once we passed through the city limits, the horizon expanded into the distance, the train picked up speed, and the fields started rushing by in a hazy, dun-colored stream.

Phoe Wa displayed a nervous energy about going home. He kept talking about how different it would be. And he stood up often to adjust the old sliding window. The metal catch on one side was broken, and the thing lay crooked in its frame. Phoe Wa spent twenty minutes at the beginning of the ride trying to wedge it back up into position. "So you can see the countryside more clearly," he said, giving me the window seat. He seemed determined that I enjoy the ride and experience his hometown the way he saw it. "All you see every day in Yangon is buildings. This is much nicer."

Every train line in Myanmar is an economic artery stretching from an urban center out into the rural countryside where more than 60 percent of the country lives. Populations near the train lines are more likely to have access to electricity and reliable services, and are generally better off than the groups who live farther out in the remote mountains and jungle.

Along these economic highways, every traveler in Myanmar is a potential customer. Throughout the trip, vendors walked up and down the aisles, calling out their wares, selling anything travelers might have forgotten in the city. One skinny young man carried a handful of wire-frame eyeglasses in assorted styles, which he was selling for 1,500 kyats each. Other sellers carried headphones, cold drinks, and small snacks. One woman had a steaming basket filled with whole-roasted quails, still glistening with cooking oil. At one point Phoe Wa grabbed a man walking by, and told him that he wanted chicken and rice for two people. At the next station, a young boy hopped on the train, gave us two styrofoam boxes filled with food, and jumped back off as we were pulling out of his little town.

All this unlicensed commerce was technically illegal, and the vendors had to bribe the conductor to get on the train to sell their wares. Halfway through the journey, a new trainman took charge, and ordered all the vendors to re-up their payment. A young man walking up the train selling corn and hard-boiled eggs told me that everyone was supposed to pay another 1,000 kyats, or they would be thrown off the train. When the new conductor walked through our car, two old women hid in the toilet with their drinks and snacks until he passed, then hurried down into the next car before he saw them.

At least once every hour, Phoe Wa would look up from the novel he was reading and tell me how beautiful it would be when we arrived. "Wait till you see the Thanlwin bridge," he said three or four times. "It is the longest bridge in Myanmar. That is how we will know we are almost there. You will see it. It is so beautiful, going over the river."

∎

Mawlamyine is not so far from Yangon—only one hundred miles in a straight line—but the train journey took a whole day, and described a wide arc around the country's southern coast. Bago, Kyaiktyo, Thaton: towns came and went as a series of hand-painted signs on station platforms. Then, as we entered Mon State, and the train began chugging south, the landscape grew steadily more lush and tropical. Even in the driest weeks of the hot season, the rice fields here were swampy and green, a far cry from the farms around Yangon, which were already dusty and burnt. The air smelled like black mud. Palm trees swayed in the breeze along one side, and the sharp limestone peaks of the Danwa mountains framed the other, marking the border of the Karen hills and the path east toward Thailand.

Mon State forms a narrow strip of land sandwiched along the Andaman coast. The region's fortunes have risen and fallen in cycles over the past twelve hundred years. Blessed by naturally fertile land surrounding the area where the Thanlwin River empties into the Indian Ocean, the Mon kingdoms that cropped up along the coast in the ninth century prospered from their rich agriculture base and easy access to sea trade. But starting in 1057, seven hundred years of successive wars with the Bamar kingdoms to the north left the region at times thriving and independent, and at other times as a crippled vassal state to the warrior kings of the Bamar. By the time the British came to call in the early nineteenth century, the Mon readily allied with the invaders as a way to regain power in lower Myanmar. Afterward, the port city of Mawlamyine became the capital of Britain's colonial outpost for a time. The rubber and timber industries flourished, and the Mon regions prospered once more.

And always there was rice. This part of the country is much more fertile than the dry zone in the center of Myanmar. While most famers along the Irrawaddy River valley have to contend with brutal seasonal changes and only get a single rice harvest per year, in the southern part of the country they harvest the paddy once in December and again in April. The natural productivity of this southern rice belt helped make Myanmar at one point the largest rice producer in the world. From 1950 to 1964, the country shipped an average of 1.52 million tons of milled rice overseas annually—accounting for a quarter of the world's rice exports.

The country's prosperity in the 1950s wasn't limited to agriculture. As most of Asia was still crawling out of the devastation of World War II, Myanmar, from the outside, looked poised to emerge as the continent's next economic powerhouse. Its prodigious stocks of valuable natural resources meant that it could always be a supplier to the rest of the world. Its universities were some of the most competitive in Southeast Asia, and the country boasted more social mobility and higher quality of life than anywhere else in the region. But Myanmar was already grappling with many of the unique internal issues that would define it for the rest of the century. By the early 1950s, armed insurgencies had seized control of much of the frontier lands. The government's sovereign territory was functionally limited to Yangon and the surrounding countryside. Infrastructure arteries like the train lines denoted corridors of government control, but rural areas outside of the Irrawaddy River valley were functionally independent.

Where government was able to rule, it was relatively effective. There was a concerted effort on the part of the post-independence regime to transform the country's economy into one that served its citizens. An enormous agricultural tax base allowed the government to spend on health, education, and infrastructure. Most of the British-built infrastructure had been decimated by World War II, and government investment was essential to restarting the newly independent country's economy.

As the country fell deeper into civil war through the 1950s, the military's response to the insurgents became more and more a part of everyday life in the country. The pressure to defeat the insurgents grew, until in 1958 the democratically elected government voluntarily gave up power to the military for a two-year caretaker arrangement. In 1960, the military returned government to the civilians, but not before General Ne Win, the army chief, had acquired a taste for power.

In 1962, Ne Win's military forcefully deposed Prime Minister U Nu and retook control of the country, marking the end of Myanmar's short experiment with parliamentary democracy. Throughout the next decade, the government embarked on a sweeping collectivization program, wrapping up all of the country's major industries into state-run enterprises. Almost no one was exempt from this economic revolution, which came to be known as the "Burmese Way to Socialism." Families rich and poor were forced to give their land up to the state.

The reforms ushered in a generation of darkness, as the country closed itself off from the world and productivity slaked behind the rest of the region. Myanmar went from a beacon of economic hope to being considered the Sick Man of Asia—a diagnosis that sadly defined life for most people in the country. Whereas twenty years previously, Myanmar had fed the entire world, by 1973 the country couldn't even feed itself.

Forty-five years later, many people in southeastern Myanmar still lived a destitute, agrarian lifestyle more reminiscent of the nineteenth century than the twenty-first. Rice, rivers, and religion defined daily life in the area and molded the region's young men like Phoe Wa.

As we chugged south through the fields, deeper into Mon State, the young photographer got out of the train seat and started bouncing on his toes in anticipation. He stuck his whole head out the window and gazed into the distance. Water buffalo standing knee-deep in the rice paddy stared gloomily at the passing train, and the sun dipped low beyond the western sea.

■

Phoe Wa became a different person once he was home. The shy migrant that was too humble to ask for help was gone, replaced by a bigger fish in a smaller pond—someone who knew every street corner and could name all the important players in town. "I know everything about Mawlamyine," he said with a swagger when he picked me up at my hotel the next day on his Honda Wave motorbike.

As we toured around the city, he talked with a louder voice and looked people in the eye. He made statements instead of asking questions. Whenever we met in Yangon, Phoe Wa would ask what we should do together, but once he was home, he was suddenly comfortable setting the schedule. "We should go see my old office at Hinthar Media," he said on our first day.

I asked Phoe Wa if he ever felt like coming back to Mawlamyine and being a journalist here. He was clearly much more comfortable in his hometown than he was in Yangon. The slower pace of life and more relaxed feel of the seaside town seemed to suit him. "That is what we can talk about with my former colleagues," he said as he revved the Honda.

Hinthar Media's newsroom was run out of the second floor of an old wooden house, a few blocks up from the river. The garage next door functioned as the printing press and makeshift photography studio. The paper was owned by the son of a powerful Mon politician and was dedicated to the regional politics of Mon State. It described itself as a "Mon State based media housing that focuses on regional issues and ethnic perspectives." Phoe Wa had been a reporter with the paper for two years before he saw Kaung Htet's talk on photojournalism and decided to change career paths and move to Yangon. The office was quiet when we entered. Upstairs, the paper's photo editor was busy on a computer, retouching pictures of a political rally. A reporter was on the phone talking with a local politician.

The journalists were excited to see Phoe Wa, and immediately dropped what they were doing to talk with him.

"We all want to go to Yangon," the editor told me. "Of course we do."

"That's why we are so happy for Phoe Wa," said the reporter. "He is really doing it."

Seated on a couch by the window, Phoe Wa blushed and stared at his feet. He looked like a hero to the journalists in Mawlamyine, but he was still crippled by his self-consciousness and critical of his own shortcomings. I asked the two Hinthar Media journalists what was stopping them from doing the same thing and moving to Yangon.

"It's too expensive. And we don't know anything about Yangon. How can I start from scratch and make a name for myself there?"

"It's easier when you're young, too. Like Phoe Wa," the other added. "Once you have a family it gets harder to withstand that kind of sacrifice."

When I asked if it was easy to make a living as a journalist in Mawlamyine, the two men shook their heads together. "The media situation here is getting much worse," the photo editor said.

The same statement could easily have applied to the entire country. Like every other journalist in Myanmar, the men at Hinthar Media were following the case of Ko Swe Win, the editor of *Myanmar Now*, who was reaching a critical point in his year-long legal ordeal. In March of 2017, Ko Swe Win had published an article alleging that the radical nationalist monk Ashin

Wirathu had, through his racist rhetoric, committed *parajika*—a violation of the monastic code that warrants expulsion from the monkhood. A senior monk he interviewed said that by publicly supporting the assassination of a prominent Muslim lawyer, Wirathu could be banned from the clergy.

The article instantly drew criticism from conservative Buddhists around the country. A supporter of Wirathu filed a criminal defamation suit. Police opened an investigation and arrested Ko Swe Win four months later outside the Yangon airport.

Since then, more than a dozen hearings had been held to determine whether the article had constituted defamation, but there was little public discussion over the content of Wirathu's own public statements. The clergy had banned the monk from speaking in public for a year, and Facebook eventually took down his personal page, citing content violations, but Wirathu's videos still circulated widely online, shared by the monk's many followers. There is a law criminalizing hate speech in Myanmar, but the government never brought charges against Wirathu, and never labeled his speeches as defamatory. Others said that his sermons were actually protected by another set of "Race and Religion Protection Laws," which are widely considered to be a form of institutionalized bias against Myanmar's Muslims.

In easy-to-find videos, Wirathu was candid about his views. In one video shared on Facebook, the monk could be seen preaching to a crowd of women about the dangers of marrying a Muslim man.

"Is it better to marry a drug addict or a Muslim?" he asks the crowd.

"A drug addict," they answer in unison. Wirathu smiles for a second, pauses, and then continues the list.

"A beggar, or a Muslim?"

"A beggar,"

"And is it better to marry a dog or a Muslim?"

"A dog!"

"Our religion will not disappear!" he yells to the crowd.

"Our religion will not disappear!" they shout back.

During the military regime, Ko Swe Win and Wirathu had both been jailed for speaking their minds. Ko Swe Win had spent seven years in prison early in his career, after distributing material critical of the junta. Likewise, Wirathu served nine years of a twenty-five-year sentence over his inflammatory public sermons. The military had stripped freedoms from both men for publicly expressing their thoughts, and both had been freed during Myanmar's fledgling democratic transition. One used his liberty to continue his crusade against a religious minority. The other tried to highlight the dangers inherent in such public discourse. Only one was facing another prison term. The case felt like a perfect allegory for Myanmar's debate over free speech and the rule of law—a system that had shown incredible promise, only to be quickly corrupted by the nationalist forces that were sweeping across the country.

The arbitrary application of censorship and defamation laws meant that the state could exert its authority over what was said in public. And it felt like Myanmar's civilian government was still learning how to use this power. When should the rules be enforced? Ko Swe Win was on trial for defaming Wirathu. But it was the monk who compared a group of minority people to an invasive fish species. Who was punished for speaking up, and who was permitted to speak their minds? To Myanmar's journalists, it wasn't at all clear.

While the national debate over free speech and defamation raged on, Phoe Wa told me he thought the radical religious speech was detrimental to Buddhism and for people interested in pursuing the truth. "Wirathu is not a good monk. He is full of anger, and some of what he says is opposite from Buddhism." Phoe Wa said. "I think he is popular with people who don't think so much. They don't ask themselves really if what he says is true or false, and they don't understand the truth. A real monk is not like that. A real monk wants peace."

On a local level, the national debates over free speech could exert a strange gravity. Even when the journalists at Hinthar Media were reporting on uncontroversial local stories, they were under increased scrutiny and pressure not to say anything that could cause consternation. The main story in Mon State that week was about how Myanmar's migrant workers living in Thailand had received local registration cards. Many of the migrants come from Mon State, and the money being repatriated back across the border was a large part of the local economy. But the stories sparked backlash because they were perceived as not being critical enough of the Thai authorities, who were widely thought to be xenophobic against anyone from Myanmar. Mawlimyine wasn't politically charged like Yangon or Naypyidaw, and it didn't have the frenetic economic booms of heavily Chinese-influenced Mandalay. But its reporters still had to contend with waves of online criticism and fight against both the allegations that their reporting was Fake News and the rash of *actual* false stories sweeping across social media. Even in a quiet town, where local news was slow and could be verified by talking face-to-face with people on the street corner, stories could become fodder for conspiracies. It was a telling quality and a sign of the times.

When we left Hinthar Media, Phoe Wa looked back at the building where he had started out as a reporter. "They think it's easier in Yangon," he said. "But it's not. Being a journalist is hard everywhere."

∎

Phoe Wa's home, the village of Kawkame, sits twenty minutes south of Mawlamyine, a straight shot down National Highway 8 alongside the Thanlwin River. A small and dusty place, the village's residents are quick to highlight their proximity to several important religious sites. Kawkame sits in the shadow of Taung Nyo Mountain ("The Brown Mountain"), where monks at the famous Pa-Auk Tawya forest monastery revolutionized the teaching of Buddhist meditation. The monastery is one of the world's leading centers of Vipassana meditation, and attracts devotees from across the world, who spend thousands of dollars to give up all their belongings and spend weeks sitting in the forest and practicing contemplative silence.

Phoe Wa's visit home was a chance for him to connect with his roots and remember what he felt was important. Our time in Mon State was structured by his religious devotion. Together, we spent a day visiting the pago-das and other religious sites around his village. He took me to the forest monastery and had me walk through a cavernous hall where hundreds of monks were meditating in silent unison. On the walls, excerpts from the holy text of the Dhammapada were written in Burmese and English. One said:

> *Though he has associated with a wise man throughout his life,*
> *A fool no more comprehends the truth*
> *Than a spoon tastes the flavor of the soup*

Phoe Wa snapped pictures of the monks while I tried not to make too much noise. Afterward, we walked through the forest and followed a group of nuns who were sweeping the footpaths. Everything was done in silence—the satisfaction of a simple act done with deliberateness and devotion. The sense of tranquility felt like a contrast to the rush of photojournalism, where speed can often be the defining factor of success. While we were there, I tried to square the stillness of the monastery with the dynamism and move-ment that the young photographer had such a gift for capturing.

"This is my favorite place in the world," Phoe Wa told me. "Every year when I come back here, it is a way for me to find inner peace." He wouldn't get a chance to do his two-week meditation until the New Year's holidays in April, but the quick morning tour of the monastery was a chance for him to refresh himself from the grimy feeling of Yangon and remember where he came from—a place that was quaint, quiet, and traditional.

Every time I traveled with Phoe Wa, we found a famous pagoda to visit. Every town in Myanmar has one, and five minutes down the road from the forest monastery we found Win Sein Tawya, site of the largest reclining Buddha in the world. If the Pa-Auk forest monastery was a place for careful contemplation, then the the five-hundred-and-ninety-foot-long Buddha was a noisy celebration of religious excess. Inside the Buddha's steel and concrete body, visitors could walk through four stories of museumlike rooms and stare at life-sized dioramas of Buddhist legends.

Many were grotesque and psychedelic. The depictions of Buddhist hell had particularly graphic tortures: demons stabbing sinners through the head, humans being cleaved apart by devils with axes. Other dioramas felt slightly out of place in a religious building, like one of the Buddha surrounded by a group of naked women fondling each other in the throes of sexual ecstasy. That particular story was supposed to show how the Buddha could withhold temptation, Phoe Wa told me. Several teenage boys lingered in that room for a long time.

To enter the Buddha's hollow body, we had to remove our shoes. But much of the interior was still unfinished. Workers were hammering away, their noise echoing loudly throughout the place, and several times I tripped over forgotten piles of wood and rusty nails left on the rough cement floor.

"Many visitors come to this place," Phoe Wa said after we had exited the Buddha. "I do not like it as much as the forest monastery. But I came here a lot as a child because the monk who founded this monastery is very famous in the local area. We can see his body if you want."

In a small shrine below the giant Buddha complex, the founder's embalmed corpse lay prostrate in a glass case. A few framed photos of him were posted on the window, and there was also a wax figure behind glass that depicted the monk in seated meditation.

"He was famous for his big ears," Phoe Wa said, pointing at one of the photos, where the monk's ears folded out like car doors. In the wax figure, the wrinkled ears were given extra prominence.

▪

In the center of Kawkame village, Phoe Wa's family was waiting for him. His mother, aunt, younger sister, and grandfather were all hanging out on the porch as we rolled up on the motorbike after our day of sightseeing. The house was a traditional Myanmar construction, with the main living area hoisted up on stilts and a wooden platform underneath where the family relaxed together and took their meals. The stilts allowed breeze to sweep through the house, and this afternoon it was filled with the smell of garlic and lemongrass—Phoe Wa's aunt was already hard at work preparing dinner.

Phoe Wa's grandfather had built the house by hand after World War II. Japanese forces had occupied the area around Mawlamyine during the war, and Allied bombing raids had destroyed most of the village. After the war, he and a group of young men had gone through Kawkame, repairing everyone's houses. The wood in the family home was dark and stained from years of cooking smoke. Sitting on the teak floor worn smooth from decades of use, it was easy to sense the long family history that had led to Phoe Wa.

His aunt was preparing dinner and his mother was busy helping his sister prepare for an upcoming exam, so Phoe Wa took me on a walk through the village so he could say hello to all his old neighbors. Kawkame village was populated almost entirely by women. All the able-bodied men, like Phoe Wa's father, had gone across the mountains to work in Thailand and rarely came home. The only male presence in the village were young boys playing in the dirt, and a handful of old men, like Phoe Wa's grandfather, who all seemed to be related in some way.

As we walked, Phoe Wa pointed out the village's characters. There was the big house on the corner. ("They are related to us somehow. I think their grandfather is cousins to my grandfather.") The small family next door. ("Their son has mental disorder so they keep him at home. But he is very happy.") An old uncle rode by on a bicycle on the way to a local festival, and told Phoe Wa all about the new house being built one street over. We turned a corner and were confronted by a baby cow standing in the road, which Phoe Wa said belonged to his cousin.

There was an attractive feeling of simplicity to these quiet dirt roads—an ease and comfort of movement that I had not felt anywhere else in Myanmar. A place where high school exams and feeding the cows were a family's biggest worry. Given the choice between living in Kawkame village or downtown Yangon, it seemed obvious which was more comfortable: Mom's home.

But despite being home, loneliness still clung to Phoe Wa. It struck me that he had no male role models whose example he could follow. He was part of a new generation of young people whose parents had all grown up in an isolated, violent society that preyed on anyone who dared to lift their head. They had carved out a life accordingly, only scraping by enough to fill their rice bowls each day. For a young man with a dream to stand on the frontlines of history, there was no blueprint for how to live a life. He had to do it alone.

"They go get money and they come back home. They go get more money; they come back and get married. They go get money and come back. And then eventually they die. That's their whole life. I want society to remember my name."

▪

During dinner, I kept asking Phoe Wa about his grandfather's life. He was ninety-three, one of the oldest people I had met in Myanmar. He had been born under the colonial government, lived through the Japanese occupation and the Allied invasion, and seen enough different forms of government that he'd have to count the iterations on two hands. But he stayed upstairs with Phoe Wa's sister while we ate, and Phoe Wa didn't know any of the stories off the top of his head. Instead, Phoe Wa's mom and aunt sat with us, the four of us squeezed around the small circular table, watching the occasional village neighbor cycle past on the road outside.

To welcome him home, Phoe Wa's aunt had made a point to cook specialties from Mon State. Lots of it was unlike anything I had eaten in Myanmar: pickled jackfruit with spicy pink sauce; shrimp curry; big salads of coriander leaf and tamarind. It was delicious, and I made the mistake of eating much too quickly. Once I was finished, Phoe Wa's aunt took my plate and scooped a much larger portion of everything. "Eat," she commanded.

To slow down, I asked Phoe Wa's mom what he was like as a child.

"He was very fat. That's why we call him Phoe Wa." (The name literally translates to something like "Little Fatty." His birth name is actually Than Myo Aung.) His mom started laughing. "He was so fat that he won first place in the village's fattest kid competition."

Next to me, Phoe Wa stared at his plate.

I tried to change the subject and asked what she thought of her son's journalism. "Was he always creative and curious as a kid?"

She shook her head quickly. "Nope. He wasn't curious at all. He just stayed in the house playing by himself."

"But what do you think of him going to Yangon to pursue his dream?" I asked.

"I don't think it's a good idea," she said. "I'm worried about him, of course. I'm worried that the youth there are destroying themselves with drugs. I might lose him there. Just like those boys that go to Thailand and leave their mothers alone."

Phoe Wa spoke up and said something in the Mon language, and his mom stopped talking. An awkward silence descended over the four of us. Next to me, Phoe Wa's aunt ladled another spoonful of shrimp curry onto my plate.

After dinner, Phoe Wa's grandpa came back downstairs. He sat in the room's only chair, while the rest of the family lounged on mats on the wooden platform. He wore a red longyi with holes in it, and the same loose white tank top that every old man in Southeast Asia seems to own. His teeth had mostly fallen out, and as he spoke, he scratched at the few patches of whitish stubble on top of his head, as though digging for memories.

The old man talked about Phoe Wa much more enthusiastically than his mother had. "Phoe Wa loved to come pray with me," he said. "We went to the monastery together every week. Even when he was very little, Phoe Wa knew how important that was."

The house was filled with photos. Like most Myanmar homes, a large photo of Aung San Suu Kyi hung on one wall. But there were also dozens of family photos and pictures of meditating monks. Phoe Wa's grandpa took a picture off the mantel and showed it to me. It was a photo of the monk with funny ears, whose embalmed corpse Phoe Wa and I had seen that afternoon. "We took this photo ourselves," the old man beamed, "when he visited our house."

Phoe Wa pointed to the alms bowl that the monk was holding in the photo. "We gave him some rice and little monies," he said. "It was a great honor for our family." I remembered the wax statue beneath the five-hundred-and-ninety-foot reclining Buddha: a funny-eared monk with an alms bowl, and thought of how important the world record–holding giant Buddha was to the local area. Throughout dinner, Phoe Wa's aunt had kept asking me what I thought of it, and I had struggled trying to find something to say other than, "It was very impressive looking." The giant Buddha building had been funded by small donations from families like Phoe Wa's, and its world record status gave them a fierce local pride.

The family all started laughing and joking as they remembered the funny-eared monk's visit to their house. It sparked a discussion of other important events in the village's past, with Phoe Wa's grandfather shouting out the names of the people he grew up with.

"I remember the Japanese," the old man said unprompted. "They came here and made everyone work in camps. They didn't like the people. But they liked kids, and didn't let kids work in the work camps. The kids had to carry food for them though."

The rest of the family had stopped talking to listen to the old man's story. He paused and scratched at his chin, then raised a finger. "We couldn't light candles at night back then. Because of the airplanes. And we dug holes to hide in from the bombs that fell. If you wanted to wake someone up, you had to poke them with a pin instead of making any noise."

He got up, walked over to me, and grabbed my hand.

"Are you an American?" he asked.

I told him yes, and he grew excited: "I knew some Americans a long time ago!" he shouted at me. "Back before the war. They were three Americans. They were very big people." He spread his arms to show me just how big they were.

Phoe Wa's mom butted in. "He's exaggerating. He didn't really know any Americans. He just worked as a porter on the docks carrying rice and wood in the 1930s. And an American ship came in once."

"They asked me to come to America," the grandpa countered. "One of them said that I was his special friend and that I could come with him to America."

"Did you like the Americans?" I asked him.

"Yes they were very nice. They were very rich." He nodded once, affirming that that was indeed the end of the story. Then he shook my hand and walked upstairs to sit in his sleeping chair. He seemed most of the way asleep before he even reached the top of the stairs, his feet tracing old and familiar steps in the house he had built with his own hands seventy years earlier.

Phoe Wa watched the old man disappear up the stairs, then leaned back and let his feet hang off the wooden platform. The sun had set during dinner, and the cool night air blew in from the nearby river, carrying the scent of manure and salt. "I miss it here," he said, staring up at the old ceiling beams. "Everything is easier. But I cannot stay."

•

"My goal is still just to be the most stable aspect of a failing paper!"

Kaung Htet took a swig of his Jameson whiskey and let out a big laugh. We were eating at a cheap Japanese restaurant in downtown Yangon that was popular with local journalists. Phoe Wa and I had returned from our trip to Mawlimyine, and I had asked to meet with Kaung Htet to talk about how the *Myanmar Times* was doing, and what the prospects were for Phoe Wa.

The restaurant's air conditioning didn't work, so tables and chairs were sprawled out onto the sidewalk, where we sat and watched a convict paint the fence of the police station next door. Off-duty police officers also snacked at the bar. Several of the journalists at the tables had been arrested and jailed in the past year. They sipped whiskey and talked about coverage of the civil war, while the police drank Myanmar Beer and glared. It didn't feel like a very relaxing way to escape from work.

"The *Times* is a sinking ship, I know," Kaung Htet said. "But its one that I have a large emotional connection to. That was my first journalism job."

Kaung Htet told me again that the main reason he stayed at the *Times* was to help train the next generation of photojournalists like Phoe Wa. There were certainly very few financial benefits for him to continue as a photographer there. Every time he went on assignment, he was responsible for his own insurance and expenses. If he got injured on assignment, the paper wouldn't even cover the medical expenses. He had a bleak outlook on the whole thing: "Maybe if I was shot they'd bring my body home," he said.

The veteran photographer was feeling particularly macabre, because together with Phoe Wa, he had just survived one of the most dangerous assignments of his career, and it had happened right in Yangon. One week earlier, a massive fire had broken out in the city's largest landfill, sending clouds of acrid smoke through Yangon's already polluted air. Most of the garbage at the landfill was plastic and burned quickly, and soon more than one hundred acres of trash were burning. The smoke was suffocating, and several elderly men and women in the city died from respiratory issues.

Kaung Htet and Phoe Wa had rushed to photograph the fire. Kaung Htet had done stories at the landfill before, and knew what he was getting into. "I made sure to bring a mask to cover my face," he told me afterward. "Because even when there is no fire, it smells horrible anyways."

He took his big green SUV and drove to the dump with Phoe Wa and several other colleagues. They first drove to where the firefighters were working. But later, they went out to an area of the landfill that the firefighting effort hadn't reached yet, in order to document the still-raging flames.

While Phoe Wa and the other young photographers stayed around the car, Kaung Htet trekked out into a canyon of trash, where there was nothing but smoke and ash on the horizon. He snapped photos of the hazy landscape and kept going.

"I was trying to get this specific shot," he told me at the restaurant, still coughing a bit from exposure to the smoke. "But I know that part of it is that adrenaline rush. I know it's my ego. Photojournalism is part competition. Against yourself, but also against the other photographers. You want to be the one that gets that shot."

Sipping his whiskey, Kaung Htet told me that as he went deeper into the burning mountain of garbage, he realized that he had become completely disoriented. The poisonous smoke was blinding him, and it was impossible to breathe. It wasn't until the younger photographers that had stayed by the car were able to honk the horn that Kaung Htet had a signal to follow. He moved blindly through the burning trash until he found his way back to the car.

The *Myanmar Times*'s resulting photo spread illustrated how necessary it was to put yourself at risk and be ready to sacrifice your safety in order to get the perfect shot. The photos were bleak and horrifying. They showed the strained agony of the firefighters battling an inferno without the proper equipment, as well as the aftermath of the destruction: homeless dogs covered in soot; children crying in the smoking landscape. The black, burned hills of garbage looked like something out of a science fiction movie, and were a reminder of how quickly things can be destroyed. For the thousands of Yangon residents that pulled the *Times* up into their apartments the next day, Kaung Htet's photos showed the true cost of environmental mismanagement in the seven-million-person city.

I asked Kaung Htet if he thought that Phoe Wa had that same competitive drive needed to make it as a photojournalist, and Kaung Htet told me he wasn't sure. "That's one of the things I really try to teach the young photographers," he said. But it was clear that he thought part of that motivation was instinctual. You had it or you didn't.

He thought more about Phoe Wa, considering the young intern over his whiskey. "Maybe it's a Buddhist thing," he said, "something about humility. But he's such a talented photojournalist. I just hope he learns to be a little more competitive. You need that drive. Because when you're out there really doing it in the war zone, you don't have time to think about so many things. It's just about getting the shot and then getting to safety: How do I get out of here alive?"

●

Phoe Wa told me he was proud of how he had dealt with the landfill fire assignment. It was his first experience taking photos in a dangerous place. "I was not scared," he told me. "It was exciting, you know? This was new for me. I'd never done something like that before, never seen such a big area of fire. And this was the kind of news photojournalism that I am interested in."

The assignment seemed to have hardened him, and to have put into perspective some of the things he was sacrificing in his lonely pursuit. He may have been poor and far from the people he loved, but he could put his head down and do what was required of him, and in that way he was very much like his father and grandfather and mom and aunt. More importantly, he liked his job and he was good at it—a precious feeling anywhere in the world. It felt like he had turned a corner. One evening we walked back from the *Times* office after he got off work. When we reached his hostel, he smiled and shook my hand and said something I had never heard him say before.

"Here I am . . . home."

6.

TURNING THE WHEEL

Floor of the Monastery

SRI KSETRA GOLD LEAF EXCERPT NO. 1:
Prosperity! From Ignorance spring the Productions, from the
Productions springs Consciousness, from Consciousness spring
Name-and-Form, from Name-and-Form spring the six Senses, from
the six Senses springs Contact, from Contact springs Sensation,
from Sensation springs Desire, from Desire springs Attachment,
from Attachment springs Existence, from Existence springs Birth,
from Birth springs Old Age and Death, Grief, Lamentation,
Suffering, Detection and Despair. Such is the origination of this
whole mass of suffering.

∎

When Kelasa meditated, he liked to use the Bhumisparsa Mudra. The word "Mudra" comes from Sanskrit, and means "gesture" or "seal." During meditation, a Mudra can be the way you hold your hands or body. Many of the positions refer to moments in the Buddha's life, and each one has its own symbolism and meaning.

The Bhumisparsa Mudra is made by sitting cross-legged with your left hand held across your lap, palm facing the sky, while the right hand hangs over your legs and touches the ground. In Myanmar, it is the most common way the Buddha is depicted. In pagodas and cave temples and household shrines scattered across the country, millions of gilded stone Buddhas sit cross-legged, one hand grounded to the earth, one hand turned to the heavens. The position represents the moment in the Buddha's life just before he attained enlightenment. Jealous of his position, the demon king Mara is supposed to have threatened the meditating Buddha with an army of monsters, who cried out their support of Mara. "Who will support you?" the demon king demanded of the Buddha. In response, the Buddha touched the ground, summoning the earth goddess, Prithvi, who witnessed his state of enlightenment and dispelled Mara and his demon army.

The story is an important part of the Pali Canon, a set of scriptures that form the basis of Theravada Buddhism, the doctrine practiced by 90 percent of people in Myanmar. The stories originated in northern India, where they were preserved orally. Later, they were written down on palm leaves and slices of wood in the Pali language.

The story of the Buddha and the earth goddess is often interpreted as a moment when the Buddha turned to the earth for support, rather than to a heavenly god. Some scholars believe that this allegory demonstrates a profound truth about Buddhism: the teachings of the Buddha fundamentally belong to the world, not to some higher plane. The rules of Buddhism—the *dhamma*—can be difficult, but any man or woman on earth has the power to seek enlightenment. Buddhism has a place in the real world.

Kelasa had a different interpretation. "This is the first Mudra," the thirty-three-year-old monk told me while we sat on the floor of his small monastery on a sweltering afternoon in the middle of the hot season. "It will grant me success against my enemies."

Like every monk, Kelasa's personal and spiritual journey was bound to a core religious philosophy that guided him along a path toward the same enlightenment, or Nirvana, that the Gautama Buddha reached two-and-a-half thousand years ago. When he reached that higher state of being, he would be liberated from the worldly cycle of birth, old age, death, grief, lamentation, suffering, detection, and despair. But Kelasa's spiritual journey was also deeply anchored to Myanmar's unique marriage of politics and religion. Like many monks in Myanmar, he saw a society where spiritual effects and supernatural powers were part of everyday life, where daily interactions had ramifications extending millennia into the future. Kelasa saw it as an essential part of his duty to make that connection clear to people.

"I am here to help guide the people, to show them the truth," he said to me when we first met. "This is my responsibility." Kelasa's religious belief guided him toward enlightenment, but it also gave him enemies. He saw the Myanmar state as something that was psychically and physically bound to the religion. Those that jeopardized that connection or told a different version of the "truth"—outsiders, journalists, and artists—those people stood in his way.

Only a few miles from Kelasa's rundown monastery in downtown Yangon, the over three-hundred-foot-tall Shwedagon Pagoda housed eight sacred hairs from the head of the Gautama Buddha—the historical Buddha who lived around 500 B.C.E. Shwedagon Pagoda was also supposed to hold relics from three previous incarnations of the Buddha, including fragments of a staff, robe, and an ancient water filter. The relics helped make Shwedagon the single most important building in the country, and together pointed toward the coming of the next Buddha—the Maitreya Buddha—who was prophesied to return to the earth after five thousand years to bring the pure *dhamma* to the people.

"People in Myanmar are very poor," Kelasa explained to me one day. "Compared to other countries, we have nothing. But our minds are not poor.

People can still always be happy because their minds are graced with Buddhism, and they have these properties going into their lives. That's why people always smile in Myanmar."

But Kelasa did not smile very much. In his own personal quest for enlightenment, he was facing some difficulties. The young monk was not from here; he only came to the city for a few months at a time to attend classes at the Yangon Buddhist University. He lived in a run-down monastery next to a dirty canal. The property was situated in a little garden down the steps from a busy road. Its main building overlooked the train tracks not far from Yangon's main railway station. On the raised wooden platform where Kelasa slept, studied, and meditated, passing trains shook the floor, and when he tapped his small gong, the vibrations were muffled by the rail cars thundering underneath. Every time I visited him there, we sat together on his sleeping mat, and I came away with flea bites.

Kelasa's only possessions were the alms bowl he used to beg every morning, his monk's robes, and a few razor blades for shaving his head. He had hung up a calendar on one of the monastery's wooden posts, on which he was crossing off days until the end of term. Every month was a different picture of The Lady—in her Oxford robes, speaking before parliament, reading papers at her desk. But other than that, the monk lived in simple solitude along with his pile of books from school.

"That is my sacrifice," he told me more than once. "To become a good monk, that is what is necessary."

Occasionally, a friend that he took classes with at the university came by, and the two monks practiced ancient languages together. The monastery was an ascetic place, but, squeezed into a corner by the railroad downtown, it was far from the quiet isolation of the forest monks Kelasa idealized. The neighborhood's defining landmark was the large mosque on the other side of the bridge, and the imam's call to prayer filtered in through the monastery's open windows five times a day. When Kelasa meditated, he was bombarded with external stimuli. The Bhumisparsa Mudra helped him stay grounded, he said, and it protected him from the obstacles that might impede his journey.

The curriculum at Yangon Buddhist University emphasizes language and scripture study. Graduates are expected to master ancient texts in three languages: Burmese and Pali, as well as classical Sanskrit. Kelasa also took courses in English. In his monastery, he kept a small mountain of books and periodicals, intricately stacked at the head of his sleeping mat. He called it his library. Many of the books were old photocopies of liturgical texts and other prayer books, with scripture written down in three languages. He spent five hours a day reviewing and memorizing ancient stanzas and prayers. Kelasa told me that he enjoyed the study, but that it cut down on the time he had to meditate. Like Phoe Wa, my other Buddhist friend from the countryside, Kelasa was used to meditating six to seven hours a day, but while he was in Yangon, it was much harder to devote time to the practice.

During one of our first meetings, Kelasa rifled through his books and gave me a copy of the Loka Niti. In Sanskrit, the word Niti means to "guide" or "conduct." A thirteenth century Burmese scholar compiled the Loka Niti. It contains 176 stanzas offering lessons on everything from how to gain wisdom and avoid evil to the proper behavior of a king. Kelasa told me that if I read the book, it would bless me. "Inner light lives in every person," he said. "If you don't understand, you can ask me questions."

In Kelasa's small library stacks, he also had a few copies of old airline brochures from defunct local travel agencies. Once, the monk rifled through one of them, pointing out the various holy sites scattered across the country. "If you want to really understand Myanmar and Buddhism, you must visit these places," he said. "You must go to Bagan, and Kyaiktiyo, the golden rock."

In one section of the pamphlet, the squat gray temples of Mrauk-U filled up an entire page. From the fifteenth to the eighteenth century, Mrauk-U had been the capital and most important kingdom of Arakan. It was located in the middle of Rakhine State, in western Myanmar. The temples had been a significant tourist attraction at one point, but ever since the military's campaign against the Rohingya in the northern part of the state, visits to the site had dropped off precipitously. I told Kelasa that I wanted to visit Mrauk-U but wasn't sure when I would get the chance.

"Yes. There is much violence in Rakhine State," he said, and then paused.

In Myanmar, that pause usually meant one of two things: a sigh of sadness over the state of affairs; or an observation about the dangers of Islam made with a kind of banal certitude. Both outcomes usually made it hard to continue the conversation.

"You should be careful," Kelasa continued. "Muslim people are very dangerous."

In the background, we could hear the imam on the loudspeaker, his prayers filling the swampy afternoon air. Then a train rumbled by, and we listened to the old carriages clack by underneath the building. "Do you mean Muslims in Rakhine state," I tried to ask Kelasa over the noise from below, "or all Muslims, even here in Yangon?"

"Every Muslim is dangerous," he said. Then, as his small library shook from the train passing by, the monk gave a bitter smile and touched his right hand to the ground.

■

SRI KSETRA GOLD LEAF EXCERPT NO. 2:
The rise and fall, the breaking-up, the fear, the tribulation, the repulsion, the release, the indifference.

■

At home, I flipped through the Loka Niti from time to time when I was bored. Buddhism is everywhere in Myanmar, but it was sometimes difficult to grasp how it fit into everyday lives. The lessons in the Loka Niti gave a glimpse into the world that Kelasa lived in—a place where social forces, religion, and politics swam together in a unified philosophical spectrum, with nothing separating the affairs of state from the concerns of the spirit.

Many of the Loka Niti stanzas had a gentle, lilting cadence, and I enjoyed trying to pull out meaning from the poetic metaphors. Some of them were poignant and inspiring.

28. Even the son of low parentage can be the king's counselor
Even the son of the foolish can be a sage

> Even the son of a poor man can be rich
> So don't be contemptuous of a man.

Others were harsh and judgmental:

> 121. The over-sexed has no honour
>   The over-carnivorous has no pity
>   The over-imbibed has no truthful word
>   The over-avariced has no shame
>   The over-lazy has no education.

During the late 1990s, Myanmar's military government had decided that the public would benefit from the lessons of the Loka Niti. The Ministry of Information translated some of the archaic prose into more modern language and began publishing excerpts from the stanzas in several Burmese-language newspapers, as well as the English edition of *The New Light of Myanmar*. Every few days, a new Niti excerpt would come out in paper, the equivalent of NPR reading a daily psalm for their listeners' salvation.

I had some old copies of *The New Light of Myanmar* (The "*Global*" part of the name only came in 2015), and it often seemed like the Niti excerpts at the top of the page were chosen to reflect some aspect of the day's news.

The public dissemination of the Niti excerpts lent an extra air of moral authority to the government pronouncements carried in the propaganda newspaper. The religious stanzas reinforced the notion that the state and religion were intrinsically bound. Even when the Niti excerpts had nothing to do with the day's news, they were a constant reminder that Buddhist philosophy grounded the notion of the state in Myanmar. However, the publishers had also gone to great lengths to scrub any unseemly references from the original Niti stanzas. In the little book Kelasa gave me, the introduction described that process:

> Secondly, in rewriting the contents of the Loka Niti treatise for
> the Myanmar reading public, care has been taken to see that it is

smooth and in conformity with Myanmar thought and culture and acceptable in Myanmar circles. There is no intention whatsoever to be critical of the original treatise's Pali and explanation renditions. However, some of the originals have not been published in the dailies as they reflect shades of archaic and alien thought and are thus not in conformity with Theravada Buddhist teachings as also current Myanmar thought and belief, raising some doubts.

In 2018, messages grounded in Theravada Buddhism were still one of the central government's main forms of propaganda. It was not uncommon for the modern version of *The Global New Light of Myanmar* to display full-page color photographs of government and military leaders tending to senior monks by providing meals or financial donations. Often the old, wizened monks would be sitting on elevated platforms, wrapped in their crimson robes, while the government officials knelt in piety below. Several times a week, the newspaper ran headline stories of the country's highest-ranking officials—State Counsellor Aung San Suu Kyi, Tatmadaw commander Min Aung Hlaing, President Htin Kyaw—publicly devoting themselves to these senior clergy members. The donations were a display of piety by the country's leaders and were meant to raise the public perception of their *kamma*. The army officers would often remove their military uniforms when they attended the barefooted monks, and instead dressed in traditional Bamar outfits. To this day, these ceremonies are an important part of political legitimacy for most people in Myanmar, tied to a thousand-year old tradition of political and religious forces stitching together to create the essential fabric of the country's society. The message is clear: Buddhism and Myanmar are inseparable.

■

SRI KSETRA GOLD LEAF EXCERPT NO. 3:
Prosperity! The four earnest meditations, the four-fold great struggle against evil, the four roads to saintship, the five moral powers, the five organs of spiritual sense, the seven kinds of wisdom and the aryan eight-fold path.

.

When I asked Kelasa if non-Buddhists could benefit from the Loka Niti's teachings as well, he laughed at me. "This is a land of peace," he said without irony. "Why do you come to Myanmar except to learn from the people here? Myanmar is a Buddhist land; that is why we have inner peace. That is something anyone can learn."

Many schools of Buddhism prohibit proselytization, and enforce strict rules about when a monk can talk about the *dhamma* to non-Buddhists, but it was quite common in Myanmar for monks to approach foreigners unannounced and begin talking about Buddhism, or inquire about someone's religion. Kelasa did the same. He never tried to convert me, or pressure me to learn the Buddha's teachings, but he was insistent that no one could truly understand his country without learning some aspects of Buddhist philosophy. Theravada Buddhism stresses meditation, and Kelasa thought that meditating was the single most important thing he could do as a Buddhist. "Until you have visited the monastery and meditated, you have not really seen Myanmar," he told me once.

When I spoke with Kelasa, I always had a difficult time squaring his zealotry and fear of Muslims with his genuine curiosity about how outsiders perceived his culture. Like most people in Myanmar, the young monk had had almost no contact with the outside world before 2011. His few conversations with Westerners had highlighted the fact that most only had the foggiest notions of Buddhist philosophy, but he reassured me he saw nothing wrong with my own religious background. "Christians and Jewish people have done many good things for this world," he told me. But the goodwill to outsiders always stopped there.

"With the Muslims it is different," he told me once. "They are waging war all over the world. They call it jihad. Religious war against the Buddhists and Hindus and Christians and Jews."

Like many in Myanmar, Kelasa had watched in fear as traditional centers of Buddhism had been destroyed by radical groups. He often referred to the Taliban's role in these attacks, especially the 2001 destruction of the

Bamiyan Buddhas in Afghanistan, and the group's attacks against Buddhist centers in Pakistan. For Kelasa, it was easy to believe radical preachers like Wirathu when they claimed that Muslims were targeting Myanmar next, and that no one from the outside world would help the country's Buddhists.

For that reason, Kelasa thought it was important for Myanmar to have a strong, religiously inspired leader in order to ensure the country's security. "My country needs a leader to show the truth to the world," he told me. "Someone who will stand up for the people."

The relationship between truth and faith was fragile, and everyone seemed to approach it differently. Some faithful, like Phoe Wa, had told me that truth telling and religious belief went hand-in-hand, and that real devotion would encourage people to question what they hear and steer them away from the violent messages spread by some nationalist monks. Other professionals like Kaung Htet thought that it was through rigorous reporting and adherence to strict journalistic standards that Myanmar would evolve past the point where religion dictated what the truth was. But there were many more people in Myanmar who thought like Kelasa—who started from a place of devotion and desire to follow religious authorities and grounded all truth to that fundamental core. The *dhamma* was not just a path toward spiritual paradise. The doctrine was life itself.

One day, I asked Kelasa if he agreed with Wirathu's sermons. I had recently seen an interview with the monk in which he praised the Tatmadaw's campaign against the Rohingya and called on Myanmar's Buddhists to join the military in purging the country of Muslims. Wirathu was blunt in his nationalism: if Myanmar's Buddhists cared about their country's future as a religious state, they should band together and destroy what he described as the "invading Muslim population."

"Ashin Wirathu just wants to protect his people," Kelasa said, sitting on the floor of his monastery. "His speech is sometimes too violent, but he is telling the truth to the Myanmar people. He is trying to make everyone see the truth."

"But what if his speech harms other people, like the Muslims who live here peacefully?" I asked.

Kelasa smiled and patted my knee. "Daniel, my friend, you have been deceived. That is not the truth. The Muslims do not live peacefully. They want to take away all of this and make Myanmar into a country of jihad." He waved his hand around at the religious objects in the small wooden monastery. There was not much there except for the stack of Pali prayer books and a lone statue of Buddha in the Bhumisparsa Mudra.

"That is why we need to fight. To preserve our tradition."

■

SRI KSETRA GOLD LEAF EXCEPRT NO. 5:

What are the fourteen kinds of Enlightened knowledge the Blessed
   Buddha is endowed with?
Knowledge of suffering is the enlightened knowledge of the
   Buddha –;
Knowledge of the origin of suffering –;
Knowledge of the cessation of suffering –;
Knowledge of the path leading to the secession of suffering –;
Analytical knowledge of the meaning of the Truth –;
Analytical knowledge of the nature of the Truth –;
Analytical knowledge of the etymology of the Truth –;
Analytical knowledge of the readiness of Wit –;
Knowledge of what goes on in the senses and hearts of others –;
Knowledge of the desires and inclinations of others –;
Knowledge of the "Twin Miracle" –;
Knowledge of the meditation based on extreme sympathy for
   others –;
Knowledge of the omniscience –;
Knowledge that has no limit is the enlightened knowledge of the
   Buddha.
The Blessed Buddha is endowed with these fourteen kinds of
   enlightened knowledge.

■

When Kelasa was a boy, he grew up in a remote section of the dry zone, in the middle of the country, far from any monastic center. There weren't many educated people in the town. But his uncle, a monk, stayed with the family sometimes, and had a lasting effect on Kelasa.

"I just saw his life, and he was so happy all the time. He was peaceful. Everyone else had all these problems in life, but my uncle had a simple, happy life. I wanted a life like that."

When, at age twenty, he decided to fully enter the monkhood, the boy shaved his head and shed his birth name to become Kelasa. The word is Pali, and refers to a sacred mountain in the Himalayas. It is sometimes used in Buddhist scripture to describe something as white and pure, and the name fit the monk's chaste lifestyle.

One evening we walked together to a gilded pagoda near the Yangon River. Outside, there was a large banner displaying the faces of several monks that were coming to lecture and teach. The government helped pay for these famous monks to travel and hold lectures and sermons for the laypeople across the country. Anyone could attend the public events, but because they were held in monasteries, it was rare for non-Buddhists to visit.

The advertising pictures were almost always the same: airbrushed head-shots of stern-looking monks wrapped in thick maroon robes. Beneath each picture, the monk's credentials and history were listed, along with the location and subjects of his study. A typical blurb would read:

Sayadaw Kya Myi
Sitagu International Buddhist Academy
MA Pune University India
PhD in Hindi and Sanskrit, Banaras Hindu University

Standing underneath the banners, volunteers collected donations for the temple, shaking big metal alms bowls to attract passing cars and pedestrians. There are no coins in Myanmar, so in order to make rattling noises the volunteers usually filled the bowls with small stones and bottle caps. A modern-day alms collection to compete against the noise of the traffic. The do-nation committee had a small table where passersby could collect printouts that matched the banner overhead—a handheld copy of the monk's stats, like little monk baseball cards.

The monastery was far more ostentatious than Kelasa's run-down living space. The fence surrounding the central courtyard was decorated with sev-en-headed Naga spirits, and every solid surface seemed to be covered in gold leaf. On the interior walls, someone had written excerpts from Myanmar's religious history in gold paint. I followed the story of two brothers who had made a pilgrimage to visit the Buddha, made an offering of honey cake, and were gifted with eight of the Buddha's hairs, which were enshrined as relics in a nearby pagoda.

Kelasa liked attending the lectures in Yangon; he had collected dozens of baseball cards. But he lamented the fact that young people in the city didn't seem to care so much about the visiting monks. "It is only the older people that pay attention," he told me. "The young people, when they come, they are just on Facebook the whole time. They have no respect."

In the stuffy monastery hall, we sat together with a few hundred other people and listened to the *Sayadaw* talk about the upcoming new moon and how people should be preparing themselves for the New Year's festivals, called *Thingyan*. During the holiday, which rings in the start of the rainy season, religious Buddhists around the country would begin a ritual cleansing of old impurities—a way to turn over a new leaf for a new year. In most cities, the festival had evolved into a weeklong water fight, where people used fire hoses and Super Soakers and threw buckets of water out of their apartment windows onto unsuspecting passersby. The monk talked about the importance of spiritual cleansing and of not forgetting the deeper truths beneath these traditional practices. Remi-niscence was important, he said, otherwise we will forget where we came from.

The monk giving the speech looked a bit like a rock star. He sat in front of a large LED screen, which pulsed blue, red, and green lights while his voice boomed out from five-foot-tall speakers. Advertisements for Myanmar Beer and Myanmar's national soccer team draped over the speaker units. I did not understand large parts of the sermon, so I read the beer and soccer banners which said, *We are one, We are Myanmar.*

Afterward, I asked Kelasa to help explain the sermon's gist. He told me that the monk was focused on what traditional Myanmar culture could teach us about modern problems. "This is the final month before the rains come," my companion translated. "Now is when things are most difficult. But soon we will have a chance to cleanse ourselves. The old will disappear beneath the water. But the true belief shall remain. We feel the presence of this permanence."

After the lecture, I made the mistake of inviting Kelasa to a tea shop to have dessert. Living in Myanmar, and hanging out with Kelasa, I had lost a lot of my notions about what kind of life monks lived. I had seen nicotine-addicted nuns lighting up on my block, and two bald-headed old monks comparing high scores on their mobile phone games. Kelasa ridiculed the young people on Facebook, but always took a selfie with me on his smart phone when we met. It wasn't unusual to see monks sitting in restaurants and cafés from time to time, and I thought it might be a treat to invite Kelasa to the tea shop. But his response was sharp and insistent.

"No, no!" he exclaimed. "I am a Buddhist monk. I am very disciplined! I cannot ever go to a tea shop. I have 237 disciplines to keep. I should not be exposed to evil."

When I asked what was wrong with the tea shop, he took a deep breath, and started from the beginning, as though he was explaining something very simple to a slow child: "If I am at a tea shop, I will be surrounded with bad people. There are hundreds of evils that I must protect myself from every day. People will see and they will suspect that I am not a good monk. I must stay pure. Pure mind. Peaceful heart." He paused and then added again, to ensure that I understood: "I am a Buddhist monk. That means I am very disciplined!"

Instead, he marched directly back to the old wooden monastery, where he lit a candle and pored over his textbooks. Safe in the ancient sanctuary, he could protect himself from evil.

∎

SRI KSETRA GOLD LEAF EXCERPT NO. 6:

The best way is the eightfold; the best of truth the four words; the
best virtue passionlessness; the best of men he who has eyes to see.

∎

The only benefit the loud and polluted Yangon offered a transplant like Kelasa was the chance to attend classes at the Yangon Buddhist University.
When he finished his degree, he would finally have his masters in Buddhism, and would be able to visit other temples to lecture, like the monks he
followed.

If Kelasa began teaching, he would likely start in Pyay, the city closest
to his village, where he often went for several weeks at a time to study with
the resident monks. Whenever he had time off from school, Kelasa would
take the eight-hour bus ride home and spend his vacation teaching novices
in his local monastery. Each time we met, Kelasa talked about his hometown. He told me once that his whole motivation to become a monk came
from the desire to help teach the young people in his village. "Some places,
there are no monks, no one to teach novices. If they have a monk, even
though they have no money, even though they cannot travel anywhere, they
will still enjoy their life. They will have a free and peaceful mind."

Pyay is significant for its proximity to the ancient archaeological site of
Sri Ksetra. The name means "Field of Prosperity" in Sanskrit. (It is pronounced *Tharay Khit-taya* in Burmese.) The walled city was the largest and
greatest outpost of the Pyu civilization. The Pyu were the first group of
Tibeto-Burman people to live along the Irrawaddy River valley. They likely
migrated south from central China several centuries before the Common
Era, and they established a series of city-states that together lasted a thousand years. Today, the remains of these walled cities stretch north to south

along the Irrawaddy River's banks. Most scholars believe that the Pyu cities maintained communication and trade, but were largely independent polities. They used the first common alphabet in Myanmar, which would later form the basis of the Burmese script, and used a common coinage between cities, also a first for the region. The Pyu built Myanmar's first stupas and temples, the designs of which would be repeated for millennia. Their cities were a central node along the trade routes stretching from China to India, and all the way to Rome, and through this exposure to the outside world they were able to inherit some of the political, religious, and social traditions that would go on to define life in Myanmar through the modern era.

Kelasa claimed to be a descendent of the Pyu people. He told me that the people of his village traced their bloodlines to the Pyu rulers of the Sri Ksetra kingdom. It was impossible to verify a claim like that, and almost every study of Pyu history concludes that by the twelfth or thirteenth century, the civilization had been completely swallowed by the growing Bamar empire. But when I told Kelasa that, he dismissed the history.

"My people have lived here for thousands of years," he told me one day in the dusty monastery above the train tracks. "By the grace of Buddha we survive through much hardship."

The Pyu were heavily influenced by Indian and Ceylonese missions who traveled through the region spreading the Buddha's teachings. The first wave of missionaries came from India sometime during the third century B.C.E. In the Pyu kingdoms, they found a people that had profited immensely from exposure to outside trade. Chinese histories claim that the Pyu used weapons fashioned out of gold. The king supposedly rode about in a golden litter while he was inside the city. The citizens of Sri Ksetra wore jewels and golden ornaments in their hats, and the men decorated their hair with kingfisher feathers.

By the fifth century, Theravada Buddhism—inherited from these Indian missionaries—had come to dominate Pyu religious thought. In Theravada philosophy, the figure of the king and the figure of the Buddha are supposed to share many similarities. Theoretically, anyone can become a king, just like anyone can become a Buddha, but doing so requires many lifetimes of accumulating personal merit, or *kamma*. The same miracles are supposed to occur at the birth of both the king and the Buddha, and both figures have the same spiritual markers. Together, the king and the Buddha are bound by their joint duty to protect their respective realms: the king oversees the domain of the worldly, while the Buddha supervises the religious sphere. Together, they are known as the "two wheels of the *dhamma*." A king who successfully lives up to this duty is called a "wheel-turning emperor," a *cakkavattin*. The image of the wheel-turning emperor became the archetype for the Buddhist Pyu rulers, informing everything from their architecture to their conflict resolution tactics.

The Chinese, who traded with the Pyu during the Tang dynasty, provide some of the only concurrent observations of the Buddhist kingdoms. They wrote that the Pyu were a gentle and peaceful people, and that they cared so much for the sanctity of life that they refused to wear silk, for fear of harming silkworms. Instead, even the wealthiest Pyu noblemen dressed in plain cotton robes.

This peaceful nature may have contributed to the Pyu's eventual downfall. Only a few decades after their mission to China, the Pyu's dominance of the Irrawaddy valley ended abruptly, when warrior tribes swept south from the Nanzhao kingdoms and began raiding cities along the river. These northern warriors were known as the "swift horsemen," or *Mynama*. In the year 832, these *Myanma* armies sacked the northern Pyu city of Halin, carrying off three thousand men, women, and children as slaves. The raid marked the beginning of the end for the Pyu. As the *Myanma*, known colloquially as the Bamar, raided farther and farther south, the Pyu city-states gradually lost political and economic power until their cities, religion, and social structures were subsumed into the expanding Bamar empire centered in Bagan.

Like Kelasa, generations of Bamar kings would later claim a cultural and spiritual inheritance of the Pyu culture, and incorporate Pyu traditions and myths into their own legendary history, along with the customs of other peoples in the region, such as the Mon. Pyu stupa design was replicated over and over again across the plains of Bagan. And the archetype of the wheel-turning emperor would continue to characterize the relationship between the country's political and religious leaders for centuries.

■

SRI KSETRA GOLD LEAF EXCERPT NO. 7:

Prosperity!

He who has crossed the ocean of passions, with them who have crossed, the released one with the released, the Blessed one, gold-colored like an ornament of Singī gold has entered Rājagaha.

He who is wise, entirely self-controlled, the unrivaled Buddha, the Arahat, the most happy upon Earth; his attendant am I.

■

The symbol of the wheel features prominently in Buddhist art and philosophy. The Buddha's teachings of Nirvana to his followers were considered the first turning of the wheel of *dhamma*. The rolling wheel of nature symbolizes the sanctity of the cosmic order. And the *cakkavattin*—the wheel-turning emperor—is the benevolent leader able to cut through worldly impediments as he spreads the teachings of the Buddha.

At Kelasa's monastery, there was a large image of a wheel wrought into the iron fence. The perfectly round circle, he told me, represented the perfection inherent in the *dhamma*. The wheel's rim symbolized the mental acuity that maintains an individual's practice, and the spokes stood for rigidity and discipline.

Every morning, Kelasa left his slippers on the wooden staircase and walked barefoot out onto the road, carrying his large black lacquered alms bowl. Monks in Myanmar still survive by begging in public, and for an hour Kelasa walked through the city's busy commercial heart, collecting food for the monastery. Anyone that wished could come out and meet him on the sidewalk to give a donation of cooked rice or vegetables. He also sometimes accepted donations of money, a practice that some monks in Myanmar condemn. But Kelasa told me that young monks like him did not really have a choice. It wasn't a matter of discipline, he insisted, just a fact of life. Only monks that lived in well-funded monasteries could afford not to take money, he said. "I have to travel back and forth from school. No one pays for that. I still need money, even though I am a monk."

When he received a donation, Kelasa would give a blessing. He held up a circular fan decorated with a wheel and complicated Pali inscriptions, and said a prayer for the donor. These daily interactions between monks and laypeople are a central part of the social fabric in Myanmar's Buddhist society. By donating to the monk, patrons receive *kamma*, or personal merit. (The word is often translated in English as "karma.") But contrary to the perception of poor beggaring, Kelasa and the other monks and nuns that walk through the street are in fact providing a social service. Religious Buddhists search for ways to raise their own personal merit, to better themselves in an effort to ensure good luck in a future life. Giving to the monks is one of the foundational ways of building merit. Burning incense in front of a Buddha image, chanting verses from the Pali Canon, and working at a monastery could also raise someone's *kamma*. Some rural monasteries were completely self-sufficient—they grew their own food, had small armies of monks to do chores around the property, and were well funded—but their monks and nuns still made rounds through small, remote villages in order to give parishioners a regular opportunity to raise their *kamma*.

One day, when I was following Kelasa through the busy morning rituals, I watched as an armed policeman came up to him and dropped to his knees with his hands clasped in a prayer position above his forehead. It was a startling sight—the policeman in his gray uniform and black boots bowing on the dirty sidewalk to the barefooted monk in his long crimson robes. Kelasa held up his prayer fan and slowly chanted a verse with the policeman while the traffic whizzed by. An ancient ceremony in a busy, new world. After the minute-long prayer, the cop stood up and walked back to the traffic light to direct cars.

Later, when I asked Kelasa if it was common for police officers and military men to approach him while he was begging, he looked at me like I was getting the question wrong.

"You need to understand," he told me. "The begging is not begging. The begging is about giving. They give us food. They get more *kamma*. The policeman has his job. I have mine. I am a Buddhist monk. I am not a beggar. I am just a vessel."

This idea of service—of acting as a conduit for a higher spiritual mission, and a higher, universal Truth—was what drove Kelasa. He once told me that the Truth was the highest form of the *dhamma*. But his attitude and beliefs also showed how essentially malleable the idea of truth could be in Myanmar. The Truth wasn't as simple as a set of facts people could agree on. A Rohingya Muslim's Truth was obviously different from a monk like Kelasa's. And the Truth that Kelasa and the radical Wirathu pursued felt diametrically opposed to the version that other Buddhists like Phoe Wa followed.

But truth was something more than just an unshakeable opinion. Kelasa started from a place of spiritual insight but arrived at a version of the Truth—Muslims are enemies; the nation is under attack; everything must be sacrificed to uphold our history—that many would consider flat-out wrong.

Strangely, none of the new Loka Niti stanzas addressed the idea of truth telling. But I found an old version of the book in the Yangon University Library that had escaped the Tatmadaw's early 1990s scrubbing and still contained the following one-liner:

98. Truth is weightier than sacrifice.

One of the key differences in people's versions of the Truth seemed to be what they were willing to sacrifice for it. When personal truth came from a form of universal dogma, like the extremist opinions of some of the monks, people seemed willing to sacrifice everything in pursuit of what they saw as the Truth. But more moderate truth tellers often didn't have that same zealotry, so their versions of the Truth weren't as noisy or visible.

These differences also highlighted how closely linked the idea of truth is to someone's relationship to power. Those with substantial influence over others—people like Kelasa—could largely determine how their followers believed. Every few months, the monk went home to the countryside and taught the village children how their local truths were related to the Truth. In doing so, he appealed to some larger force, and created an unshakeable narrative in the young minds.

Myanmar's monks have long used this position as arbiters of truth to interfere in national-level social and political issues. The web of monks and religious centers spread throughout the countryside has always been the most penetrating and effective network in the kingdom—it allowed local monasteries to follow and implement doctrine handed down by the council of monks known as the *sangha*, while still responding to distinctly local issues. A village's religious leaders and educators could pursue the Truth while responding to local truth.

This education system allowed the *sangha* to wield enormous influence as the essential authority between the people and their religion, and as the ultimate arbiters of truth. It allowed the clergy to interfere in the country's political affairs when necessary. Political legitimacy of a Bamar ruler was built upon public recognition of his *kamma*. Monks lent their support to the moral standing of the king and withdrew their backing when they believed the monarch was abusive or ineffective. Myanmar had a long history of leaders deposing each other in violent, scarring conflicts. But changing from one ruler to another, while disruptive, was a manageable and accepted part of political life. Impermanence is a foundational law of Buddhism. Stability instead came from the relationship between the leader and his people, and through the grounding of state power in religious thought. The *sangha* could transform a rebel into a king and make his status a universal Truth.

One of the most reliable ways for a king to prove his religious virtue was to conquer new territory and expand the empire. When Bamar kings in the river valley launched military campaigns against neighboring civilizations or upland hill tribes, they did so with the dual aim of expanding the state's economic power and buttressing the religious merit of the empire through the spread of Buddhist teachings. Kings built new stupas and temples in

conquered areas, or repaired old ones as a way of demonstrating the virtu-
ousness of their actions. They arranged marriage alliances and built tributary relationships with subjugated regions, and thus brought new subjects
into a growing Buddhist empire. In doing so, they sought to embody the
ideals of a *cakkavattin*, whose opponents eventually welcome his conquest in
anticipation of his benevolent, Buddhist rule. The *sangha*, in turn, validated
the king's religious credentials with the laypeople.

Today, Myanmar's greatest national heroes are all military leaders who
embodied the wheel-turning archetype. At different points in the country's
history, powerful men have risen up to unify the country by conquering new
territory or bringing minority populations into the fold. In schools across
the country, even in non-Bamar areas, students learn about the three military rulers who united the Bamar empire at different times in history:
Anawrahta, Bayinnaung, and Alaungpaya. Schools name sports teams after
the military leaders. Statues of the three kings stand guard over the parade
grounds in the capital, Naypyidaw, and in front of the Tatmadaw's officer
academy. In Yangon, I bought my groceries on Anawrahta Road.

Bayinnaung, who ruled in the sixteenth century, is known in Myanmar
as the "Conqueror of Ten Directions," for his habit of waging war against
practically every surrounding civilization and building the largest empire in
the history of Southeast Asia. By the end of his rule, people from modern-day Vietnam to the Manipur Hills all paid tribute to the Bamar emperor. Whenever he conquered new areas, he oversaw the construction of
new pagodas, and personally went to feed the local monks. He held mass
ordinations in the name of Buddhist purification of new regions.

The *sangha* still wields enormous influence in Myanmar, and the pat-
terns of governance and power and truth in 2018 were not so different from
those of 1518. The policeman had to appeal to Kelasa for his *kamma*; Aung
San Suu Kyi had to bow before the leaders of the *sangha* in order to stay
politically relevant; and the Tatmadaw used religious rhetoric in their campaigns against ethnic minority groups along the country's periphery. Buddhism was not just about enlightenmen—it was about personal and political
power.

When I asked Kelasa whether or not the country's leaders carried themselves as good Buddhists, he told me that they needed to show more devotion. "The *dhamma* is universal; the constitution is political," he said. "There is no higher truth than the *dhamma*."

•

SRI KSETRA GOLD LEAF EXCERPT NO. 8:

"An Arahat, fully awakened, is the exalted One, abounding in wisdom and goodness, happy, with the knowledge of the worlds, unsurpassed as a guide to mortals willing to be led, the teacher of gods and men, a Blessed Buddha." So may it be!

•

In the middle of the hot season, I took the long, bumpy bus ride to visit Kelasa's hometown of Pyay, where he still lived for part of the year. The dry zone in central Myanmar is a dusty place. A fine, dun-colored powder coats the sides of the buildings, and the air tastes charred. The Irrawaddy River, which snakes languidly through the heart of this land, provides the only hydration, and its banks blossom with soft green plant life. You can drive through miles and miles of countryside seeing little besides low scraggly bushes and the occasional old acacia tree, and then when you arrive at the river, you find an explosion of green growth. Where the watercourse moves through towns and cities of any remarkable size, the banks also fill up with heaps of plastic and other refuse—discarded coconut husks, old tires, the late-night slop from a nearby beer station.

The town of Pyay sits in a small elbow on the river, just before it begins breaking apart to fragment and drain out into the Indian Ocean. The monk's village was actually a few dozen miles out of town, in the barren countryside, but he traveled back and forth to the city to work alongside some of the senior monks in the area and to help instruct novices that came to the monastery.

Most of Myanmar's large empires and lasting cities cropped up on the banks of the Irrawaddy. The civilization's fate was bound to the course of the river. In the arid dry zone, crops almost always failed when fed by rain alone. Bagan, the first and most powerful of the Bamar kingdoms, took advantage of a wide bend in the river to sustain an area that received very little rain. Later, the royal capitals of Ava, Amarapura, and finally Mandalay used the inlets of the upper Irrawaddy to maintain regular connection to the economic centers along the southern coast.

The ancient Pyu cities, in contrast, were almost always pulled back several miles from the river and situated along smaller tributaries. The Pyu had mastered irrigation management, brickmaking, and ironwork by the second century B.C.E. At the ruins of Sri Ksetra, the largest of the Pyu cities, the full breadth of this ingenuity could be seen. I took a beat-up taxi to the archaeological site, set three miles to the east of Pyay. The driver had a collection of monk baseball cards pasted all over his windshield, commemorating the religious teachers that had made government-subsidized visits to the town.

Sri Ksetra is a large, sandy archaeological site with few visitors. Its poorly kept dirt roads twist like broken arteries through former palaces and temples. People still live within the old city walls, which describe a nine-mile-long circumference around the fortified palace and religious sites in the city's center. At Sri Kestra's height, the triple-layered wall and two exterior moats enclosed a total territory of seven square miles, far larger than the later Bamar cities of Bagan or Mandalay. Within these fortifications, a brilliant irrigation system sustained hundreds of acres of paddy field and livestock. In the event of a siege, the city could survive for years.

The fourteen-hundred-year-old city walls had mostly crumbled into small mounds of stone and rubble. Large trees were using what little was left of the fortifications to buttress their spreading root systems. Here and there workers had restored certain gates or other parts of the wall, to illustrate the beauty of the ancient Pyu brickwork.

The British scholar Janice Stargardt, who led archaeological work on the Pyu sites over several decades in the middle of the twentieth century, has demonstrated that Pyu city planning and irrigation networks at Sri Ksetra were informed by Buddhist cosmology and the credo of the *dhamma* wheel.

Through a series of locks and hydraulics, the Pyu builders were able to direct the city's irrigation canals to flow around the royal palace in an auspicious, clockwise circle, the same direction one is supposed to walk around a pagoda. The principal canals were purposely diverted to flow through the city's burial grounds before integrating into the main hydraulic system. The water's passage helped to physically realize the Pyu belief of symbolically purifying the dead and reintegrating them into the living. Stargardt and other historians have argued that both the circular flow of the water and the orientation of the city's walls were physical representations of the Buddhist Wheel of Law. Several large sculptures found around the palace in the center of Sri Ksetra illustrate the Buddha's turning of the wheel, and many other smaller plaques include the same motif. Seated in the middle of the circular city, the Pyu ruler could watch the *dhamma* wheel turn around him.

Until the twentieth century, very little was known about the Pyu people outside what could be gleaned from the ruined old cities because the few surviving written documents were very difficult to translate. For a long time, the only sources of writing were stone burial urns inscribed with the names of kings whose ashes were entombed. Most of the Pyu royal treasuries had been disturbed or raided through the centuries. The Bamar had likely carried off much of the Pyu relics and religious artwork during their early conquest of the river valley.

The mysteries persisted until 1926, when a farmer living inside the old ramparts, named Khin Ba, found a mound of rubble on his property. When archaeologists excavated the area, they found an undisturbed sixth-century stupa containing a host of ancient treasures, including forty-five old silver coins that helped confirm economic trade between different Pyu cities. But the greatest discovery was a set of twenty gold-leaf plates bound with golden wire. The plates were inscribed with sixty lines of text from the Pali Canon, separated into eight excerpts. The scriptures described the evolution and condition of someone that has attained true enlightenment. The inscriptions proved that despite an amalgam of religious traditions, by the fifth century the Pyu had adopted Theravada Buddhism as the keystone of their belief system.

The gold writing is the beginning of Buddhism in Myanmar—and the full text was displayed in the Sri Ksetra museum, translated into modern Burmese and English.

"My people, our heritage," Kelasa said when I showed him a picture of the eight excerpts. "Myanmar is a Buddhist land. This is what our enemies want to take from us."

Kelasa told me that these excerpts showed the essence of Myanmar's Buddhist history. "Daniel, you think the truth is what you read in the paper, what is changing every day. But the deeper truth is here. It is living for thousands of years. It is touching every part of life." He waved his hand at the gold-leaf texts and smiled. "This is my heritage—Myanmar traditional beliefs. We cannot afford to lose it."

7.

YOU DON'T HAVE TO BE A SOLDIER

Myitkyina, Kachin State

When I visited Bum Tsit in Myitkyina, we spent most evenings inside Red House, drinking Tuborg late into the night underneath the oil paintings of the Confluence and the topless woman.

One night, I noticed that the Red House staff had added a new sign to the wall. It said, in English:

In Wine There is Wisdom,
In Beer There is Freedom,
In Water There is Bacteria.

Bum Tsit always talked about drinking and partying at night as a natural part of being a Kachin man. But sometimes I sensed that he wanted to change. He often admonished himself for being out of shape and for drinking too much.

"I used to spend much more time in coffee shops than in beer shops," he said once. "Now it's the other way around."

Bum Tsit could have a serious and melancholy air when he was sober. But around friends, with beer flowing, he was gregarious and loud. He flirted and laughed a lot. Most nights, he invited friends to come hang out with him at Red House, where he would let them drink and eat for free. Alone except for the wait staff, we would all get roaringly drunk and play Scissors, Sword, Spear—Myanmar's version of Rock, Paper, Scissors. "You drink!" he'd shout to the loser, and everyone would laugh. It was hard not to have fun when Bum Tsit was having fun.

But late at night, awash with Tuborg, once all his friends went home, Bum Tsit grew much more introspective, and opened up about some of the stresses in his life. In the last few months, as the increasing tempo of the civil war had hurt business at Red House and the jewelry store, he had begun investing significant capital into jade. The highly controversial nature of the work made it a taboo subject with his Kachin friends, but Bum Tsit told me that as an outsider, he saw me as a neutral party who wouldn't judge him for doing what he felt was necessary to support his family.

From 2010 to 2016, while he worked in the government, Bum Tsit had been exposed to many of the region's biggest players in the jade industry and saw firsthand the massive wealth they were able to build in the secret underground economy. Now he saw his network of business, police, and political leaders as natural assets that would let him succeed as a middleman in the jade trade—buying stones cheaply from the yemase, selling to larger clearing companies, and profiting off the arbitrage. The money would go to support his large family, but it was also a way of expanding his contacts and thereby building his personal political capital and power.

He had a ready-built way to launder the money as well: the jewelry store, Red House, and the several parcels of land he still owned around My-itkyina. If he succeeded in the business, he could use them to wash the illegal cash and go from being a well-off man operating in the shadows to a truly wealthy one with insider access to the Kachin power centers. In a secret-filled industry supported by billions of dollars of illegal money, he was convinced that his connections and access to information would allow him to profit.

Throughout the spring, Bum Tsit made regular trips to Hpakan to buy jade stones from yemase like Hkun Myat. He pooled his money alongside that of his brother-in-law and a few friends for the venture, and every few weeks he would drive up to the mining town. In Hpakan, Bum Tsit would spend his nights camped out along a ridge above the slag pits, examining and buying jade from the yemase, hoping, like everyone else, to land a once-in-a-lifetime stone.

But jade has a steep learning curve, and during his monthly trips to Hpakan, Bum Tsit was quickly realizing how little he still knew about the industry. Bum Tsit and the other middleman purchasers usually did their buying at night. They would find one of the hills where thousands of yemase combed through the debris looking for discarded jade stones. The large jade companies operated twenty-four hours a day, and the massive dump trucks kept pouring the slag down onto the hillside all night. The buyers set up small stalls along the ridge. On any given night, flickering lights illuminated hundreds of the small makeshift kiosks—prospective buyers inspecting the stones with their flashlights. When a yemase found a piece of jade, he could take it up to the top of the hill and show the buyers. The stones were usually covered in mud and grime, and underneath, the exterior shells were gray and opaque from millennia of exposure to weather and erosion. The outside of a stone rarely held any reliable clues about what was inside.

During those first visits, unsure about what he was doing, Bum Tsit would spend a week at a time in Hpakan looking at stones on the hillside at night. "One day, two days—you cannot buy jade in that period of time," he told me, trying to sound confident about his new venture. "Maybe some people buy every stone that comes to them, but you see hundreds of stones each night. You have to be careful. You have to take your time with jade."

When Bum Tsit went to Hpakan, the town's various amusements were also at his disposal. He golfed and drank, and sometimes went to bars where he could watch women sing on stage. "In Hpakan, you can do anything," he said. "There are many restaurants, there is karaoke, many massage places. It is illegal massage—but no problem."

■

Jade was a path out of the challenge of everyday life in Kachin. All the powerful men that Bum Tsit knew—politicians and businessmen and military officers—were deeply involved in the jade trade. The wealth they pulled out of the Kachin mountains helped fund their influence. Bum Tsit knew that jade could help put him in a position of power as well.

But even though it was becoming a bigger part of his life, Bum Tsit rarely talked about his jade business when partying with his friends. While many Kachin viewed jade as their heritage and birthright, the business still had a seamy reputation, and no one in Kachin wanted to reveal too much about exactly how they made their money. Keeping those secrets from the people close to him was a sacrifice Bum Tsit felt like he had to make in order to succeed. "It is illegal activity," he said to me once. "If the policemen or wrong person finds out, it could be bad."

That anxiety partially explained the drinking, I thought, and maybe also his melancholy, but I didn't feel comfortable asking him. Bum Tsit was running three successful businesses and starting a fourth. And while he had long been on the periphery of the illicit dealmaking in the center of Kachin politics, this was his first time getting his hands dirty. His political and business efforts were supporting his entire extended family, and he needed an outlet.

In response, he buried himself in the new work. One night, over beers at Red House, Bum Tsit confided in me that there was much about the jade business that remained hidden to him. He told me about a recent trip he had made to Hpakan, during which he had waited in the town for days before finally buying some jade, too anxious to commit to sinking so much money into a single stone. Every night, he went to the hillside and scrutinized the exteriors of hundreds of pieces of jade. Finally, he shelled out 1 million kyats—around $750—for a stone the size of a tissue box. It was the only stone he bought during his stay. He took it to a jade cutter in town and paid another 3,000 kyats to have it sliced open with an enormous circular saw. Sliding apart the two pieces, his fortune was reveled: a white stone, richly marbled but opaque, with a thin vein of dark green twisting down the middle. It was the low-quality stone, called utility jade, that is sometimes used to make small beads for seat cushions, or sliced up into tiny squares to make floor mosaics. It was only worth about three or four dollars per kilo, not worth carrying back to Myitkyina.

"I just threw it away on the ground once I saw it," Bum Tsit said.

It seemed odd to me that Bum Tsit would go through so much work— spend a week in Hpakan, away from his businesses and family, shell out money for a hotel room, look at hundreds of jade stones, gamble a large amount of money on one—only to throw it away and come back home. The trips only seemed to make him more tired and stressed.

Even though he was a novice in the industry, Bum Tsit was a political pro, and his foray into the world of jade was an important part of his long-term plan. He was still entertaining a run for the Kachin State parliament during the 2020 elections, but jade had a powerful allure. He saw the stone as a kind of insurance—another avenue to power, similar but different to his political plans. One was "legitimate," while the other dealt in secrets. But that distinction might not matter to the young Kachin businessman if both options put him in a position of influence. The important thing wasn't a title but who he was connected to. "I want to be in a position to negotiate be-tween the two sides," he told me more than once, referring to the KIA and central government. "I already have some experience of that from negotiat-ing access into the war zone for the Red Cross. I know that the different parties trust me."

All Bum Tsit needed was to get into a position where he could use that trust to make a real difference. Jade could be the vehicle.

There was a precedent for that kind of model. Yup Zaw Hkawng, the richest man in Kachin State, had made tens of millions of dollars from the jade business. Bum Tsit told me that he looked up to the Kachin tycoon: "He has done much for Kachin people." Yup Zaw Hkawng had connections to both the Tatmadaw leadership and the generals in the KIA. He organized and funded well-publicized summits between the two parties called the "Peace-Talk Creation Group." The gatherings were nominally a neutral forum for both sides to negotiate, but they were also a place where some of the biggest players in the jade industry could meet in secret and talk business.

Bum Tsit saw this as a possible blueprint for power that rested outside of normal Kachin politics. But to succeed, Bum Tsit would need to learn more about the secretive business. Those at the top of the jade ladder had an incentive to withhold information from people at the bottom. No one knew just how many billions of dollars were at stake. Luckily, through his government connections, Bum Tsit personally knew many of Kachin State's richest businessmen. All of them had fingers in the jade trade—decades' worth of experience learning the secrets of the business—and because they recognized how they could benefit politically to have an ally in Bum Tsit, they were willing to talk to him.

I often went with Bum Tsit to meet jade merchants and mine owners. "These are important businessmen," he told me. "I get to ask about things that I couldn't learn by myself." I'd bring packs of J Donuts from Yangon and try to get them to open up during the hours-long conversations.

I always asked the jade merchants who was making out in the jade business. Their answers depended on their position in the industry, but the rule of thumb was that risk flowed downhill. Mine owners and their stakeholders were basically assured of making profit: all they had to do was pull the jade out of the ground and find the right way to sell it. These were the Tatmadaw holding companies, military-affiliated cronies, Chinese investors, and well-connected Kachin elites. Their success depended on many things, but the commercial potential of war was a common refrain among the wealthy merchants. Fighting in the mountains meant little to no oversight in the mines—so it was easy to skirt the law if you knew who to pay.

"A few palms get greased and your jade stones can be in the Chinese markets in a week," one merchant told us with a smile. "No tax that way. It's much more profitable. No reason to follow the law."

But yemase and the middlemen like Bum Tsit lived in a different, more dangerous part of the jade world, one with no guarantees. Bum Tsit had begun his jade business in one of the riskiest possible positions, and as his forays to Hpakan continued to bring losses, and as we listened to the some of the wealthiest jade businessmen in northern Myanmar tell the stories of how they made it big, one thing became very clear: if he wanted to make money in jade, he needed to break the law. "Of course there is the legal market," one merchant told us. "But everyone knows that the black market is the real business. There is a black market for jade in Myitkyina, in Mandalay, in Naypyidaw, and of course in China. You could say that it extends all across the world. That is where the money is."

Entering into the secret world of black-market jade meant dealing with criminal networks and military leaders and people whose political interests were opposed to Bum Tsit's. He considered himself a humanitarian first, and a businessman second, but the more we visited extravagant jade mansions, the better this latter path sounded. Even though it was illegal, smuggling stones to China could be a quick and dirty path to wealth and power. Bum Tsit didn't like leaving things to chance, and in the few months since he had started visiting Hpakan, he had lost thousands of dollars gambling on a product he didn't know enough about. He needed a new strategy, one that made use of his connections and his ability to keep secrets, something that was going to be more difficult as the war in Kachin grew more violent.

∎

I enjoyed escaping to the north during the winter months. While Yangon broiled under the hot-season sun, Myitkyina was still cool and gray and smoky. The breeze that blew in across the Irrawaddy carried swirls of dust through the sleepy city, and a haze hung low over the metal roofs.

During my trips north, I had gotten used to certain things, like the fruit lady that would walk by my hotel window every morning at seven. She pushed a small cart with a glass box filled with ice and pineapple and water-melon and mango. She carried a small gong that she would ring as she walked down the block. In Yangon, fruit sellers had to shout above the traffic, and the soft little *"gong"* would have been swallowed up by the trucks and loudspeakers and generators. In the Kachin city, meanwhile, there was nothing but birds chattering on the wind.

But the quiet and calm that I had grown to expect was slowly disappearing, because the war was tightening its grip on Kachin State. Throughout the hot season, life in Myitkyina felt different—more urgent and grim. UN agency trucks drove through the streets. Extra international staff for big, well-funded NGOs came and stayed in the city. For the first time, I heard people referring to the city as part of a war zone.

The fighting between the Tatmadaw and KIA usually escalated in the hot season, but this year's intensity was shocking. The Tatmadaw usually launched offensives around this time of year, when the weather and terrain conditions were most ideal for military logistics. Year after year, the pace of the war accelerated around the same time—a cycle of violence and destruction that drove forward like clockwork.

Every year when the war surged, there also came rumors that it would be the last fighting season. When I spoke to people from the KIO, they told me that they anticipated a cooling down of the tension.

"We can say that the conflict will be less and less," Dau Hka, the KIO spokesman, told me one morning in Myitkyina. "We expect change will be imposed by China."

A Tatmadaw analyst I knew in Yangon echoed this prediction, telling me that both sides were jostling for position and the fighting would draw down soon. "Just like everywhere else in the world, before they sit down to negotiate, both sides are going to try and get the upper hand on the battle-field."

But both sides also seemed prepared for a war that might never end. The KIA was confident that it had a certain advantage in the fight. The reason they had been able to fight one of the world's largest militaries to a draw for five decades, Dau Hka said, was because of a simple fact of geography. "We can keep this fight going for many years," he said. "We can just disappear back into the jungle and the mountains whenever we want. The geography is very much on our side."

Once the roads dried out at the end of 2017, the Tatmadaw launched a major offensive against KIA strongholds across the north, trying to prove that geography couldn't protect the insurgents forever. Throughout the winter and spring, the intensity of the assault steadily increased. Over the past few years, the army had squeezed KIA positions in the east, near the Chinese border. The KIA headquarters in Laiza were surrounded and under a permanent state of emergency.

"The Burmese military can easily destroy Laiza," Dau Hka told me. "They have a wide variety of artillery surrounding the city." He counted them out on his fingers, "Howitzer, 105, 120, 80, 122 millimeter. The people are under threat, but they are still there. This shows that military solutions are not the only option to the Kachin conflict, otherwise the Burmese army would have ended it a long time ago."

In response to the territory losses in the east, the KIA had secured parts of the Tanai region, a flat expanse in the northwest of the state where there were gold and amber mines that the rebels could tax. The Tatmadaw also had financial interests in the gold-mining region and focused their spring offensive on retaking the resource-rich area. The fighting was impacting life everywhere. The KIA started destroying bridges and major roads across Kachin State, limiting the mobility of not only the Tatmadaw, but also hundreds of thousands of civilians. Gas prices rose seven-fold in parts of the state where trucks could no longer reach, and staples like rice and corn were suddenly unaffordable. Civilians that had to flee their villages spent weeks at a time living in the jungle, eating nothing but tree bark and banana stems. When they had to ford rivers, the elderly, sick, and young people often had to wait until they found elephant handlers willing to carry them to safety. Eventually, the displaced people would wind up in one of the many IDP camps scattered through KIA-controlled territory, or else filter down to Myitkyina, where they would give interviews about their ordeals to the UN, the Red Cross, and other charity organizations. IDPs told stories of Tatmadaw soldiers burning Kachin villages to the ground, stealing Kachin people's property, and systematically raping women. Denial and blame flew between the government and the KIA, but not much was done to alleviate the massive human suffering. For the most part, people were on their own.

The Tatmadaw responded by stepping up operations in KIA strongholds across Kachin State. The war had even encroached on sleepy Myitkyina, home to the Tatmadaw's Northern Command. While I visited the town in early February, the KIA and Tatmadaw fought a fierce battle just across the river. The gunfire was only ten kilometers from the city center. The rebels were even contesting parts of Myitkyina itself. Early in the morning of February 3, the KIA attacked a Tatmadaw checkpoint on the western outskirts of the city. Army helicopters were taking off from the Myitkyina airport, hovering over the low hills and dropping bombs on the insurgents. When Kachin civilians were interviewed, they claimed that the bombs fell nowhere near the front lines. "They just fire anywhere, without care," one resident claimed in a televised news report. There were no real front lines in the Kachin civil war. This had allowed the KIA to hold out for so long as a guerrilla force, but it also meant that nowhere was safe for civilians.

In Tanai, thousands of villagers were holed up underground in amber and gold mines, unable to flee due to the heavy fighting. Eight months previously, the Tatmadaw had airdropped leaflets on the area warning people to leave. This was enough justification, the military said, to invade the area without warning. And now the civilians were trapped.

For Bum Tsit and the other Red Cross staff, the costs of the war were immediate and highly visible. Every week, more landmine victims streamed into the Myitkyina hospitals with nothing but their tattered clothes. Children with limbs blown apart sat stone-faced and silent on the ancient gurneys while volunteers like Bum Tsit tried to give them what little assistance was available.

As the war worsened—as he saw more and more children with amputated legs and arms—it was harder for Bum Tsit to keep up a public face of neutrality. As a Kachin man, he wanted to help his people. And as someone with political influence who was profiting off Kachin State's illegal resource trade, he felt an extra moral burden to do so. "These people are being killed just because they live near valuable natural resources," he told me. "Just stuff in the ground. I need to do something to help these people."

The Red Cross provided an outlet for his frustration. He asked to lead a team of volunteers to Tanai to bring humanitarian relief to the villagers. But the chairman of the Kachin State Red Cross forbade the trip. After a debacle in November, when the KIA apprehended a group of volunteers doing landmine awareness training in the IDP camps, the Red Cross had limited its trips into the war zone. Bum Tsit chafed a bit under the chairman's leadership style, which didn't permit many dissenting views. Bum Tsit thought that the Red Cross should do more to assist the Kachin people, but he followed his orders and directed his efforts toward raising financial aid for the victims of mine and bomb attacks.

Bum Tsit was spending twenty to thirty hours each week volunteering at the Red Cross. He would visit victims in the local hospitals, take their histories, and fill out paperwork to get their medical care paid for by the national Red Cross. One day, while he went to the military hospital to interview a double amputee, I hung around the Red Cross office and chatted with his coworkers. Bum Tsit's boss, the chairman of the state Red Cross, sat outside and smoked a big green cheroot. U Ganesh was a tall man with a prominent hooked nose and thin hair combed over to one side. He always gave me the impression of a stern grade school teacher.

When he saw that I had stayed behind, U Ganesh invited me to tea. We walked side by side in silence to a tea shop a few hundred meters down the street. One of the older Red Cross volunteers followed a few paces behind us, carrying a small box of tea. The chairman liked to bring his own tea to the tea shop. It was called "Good Friend Superfine Qingliang Tea," and he had bought it during a trip to China he had taken with Bum Tsit. When we arrived in the tea shop, the fifty-year-old volunteer went into the back kitchen and mixed the chairman's tea into a thermos.

I sipped the house tea out of a small ceramic mug while the chairman slurped on the Superfine tea. U Ganesh had a unique perspective on the war in Kachin. He was part of the large Nepali community that lived in Myitkyina. His grandparents had come to Myanmar during World War I, and his parents had settled in Myitkyina in the fifties. The chairman had spent his whole life in Myitkyina, but it was clear that he felt like an outsider, detached from the highly vocal ethnic politics of Kachin State. That morning, five thousand Kachin protesters, led by the Kachin Baptist Convention, had marched down the street that ran in front of the Red Cross office. The protesters carried signs that read, *Stop airstrikes on civilians*, and *Stop NLD government silence on civil war*, and *Stop Blocking Humanitarian Aid*.

The chairman showed me a video of the protests he had taken on his phone. When the organizers listed accusations against the Tatmadaw, the marchers called back "Urgently Stop!"

In the grainy video footage, a crowd of people waving Kachin flags and wearing traditional Jinghpaw dress marched down the road, shouting.

"Taking our jade and giving us bombs,"

"Urgently Stop!"

"Bombing Kachin State,"

"Urgently Stop!"

"Arresting and interrogating civilians,"

"Urgently Stop!"

The video ended and U Ganesh leaned back. "The Kachin marched against the Tatmadaw," he said. "And the day before, the Shan and Bamar marched together against the KIA. Everyone is mad at everyone else. And here we are in the middle. Red Cross. Neutral party." He pulled on his cheroot and a cloud of smoke shrouded his small eyes. "Even some of the Kachin are against other of the Kachin. For instance, the Lisu and Rawang militias fight alongside the Tatmadaw against the other Kachin."

Despite his skepticism about the identity politics surrounding the war, U Ganesh was highly informed about the day-to-day fighting across Kachin State. He had to be in order to coordinate the Red Cross response to the 120,000 IDPs scattered across northern Myanmar.

When I asked him why he thought the war had accelerated recently, he was dismissive.

"Why the war? Hah. That is a political consideration. Of course, the government wants to pressure the KIA into signing the ceasefire agreement. They also want to block the KIA access to funds. In Tanai there are many amber and gold mines. The KIA taxes these areas, so the Tatmadaw wants to block access."

The chairman paused for a second and relit his cheroot, puffing on it to get the ember to hold.

"One side or the other, it's all the same thing. They are just fighting for control over resources and revenues. These people marching think something will change if one side has control or the other. But for humanitarians it is the same no matter what. People are suffering. In Tanai they have blocked food from getting to the mines and the people that live there."

"It's not a good time to live in Tanai," I remarked to U Ganesh.

"Or in Myitkyina," the chairman countered. "You never know what could happen at any moment. The war could come here. When the fighting resumed in 2011, the next two years was very intense. There were explosions every day in Myitkyina." He turned and pointed to the corner across from the tea shop. "There was a mine explosion right there. Also down the street. Our staff that lived far away started sleeping in the office. If we heard only two explosions per day, we said that's OK; that's the normal level."

U Ganesh laughed at the memory and finished the rest of his tea. His cheroot had burned out while we spoke, and he put the butt back into his bulging shirt pocket. "Come," he said to me, "let us go." And we strolled back down the dusty block while the old volunteer followed silently behind with the can of Superfine tea.

•

A war that never ends builds its own narratives. The people trapped in the cycle of violence and exploitation of northern Myanmar tended to view the war as a totalizing phenomenon—the Kachin people versus the Bamar government—a conflict where the only thing that mattered was ethnic identity. But Bum Tsit had shown me that the landscape of war in northern Myanmar was far more nuanced. Individuals made up their own minds and followed their own loyalties. No one's path was completely predetermined.

Bum Tsit was adamant about that, and he was upset that more people didn't see it. So many of his friends and family members thought that being a militant was the only way to support the Kachin cause.

"Being Kachin does not mean just one thing. Too often, Kachin people think that the only way you can stand up for your people is to fight in the KIA. But I am not a fighter. I am a humanitarian. You don't have to be a soldier to be a good Kachin."

Bum Tsit's independent streak was in many ways a rebellion against the predominant narratives of the war, and against the idea of the KIA's fight as an "official" rebellion on the part of the Kachin people. That narrative had been built up over decades, as the militia had successfully convinced people in the north that Kachin youth needed to sacrifice themselves in the fight for independence. I spoke with Francis Zau Maw, an officer who told me about the rebel army's recruitment and propaganda process. He called it re-education.

"There is no conscription," he said, "But we recruit young people to join the KIA. Some are mobilized though the Pro-Team. That's what we call the propaganda team. The Pros." He laughed at this, then continued. "During the recruitment, they are indoctrinated. We teach them about our history and the Jinghpaw language and religion. They learn about economics and politics. They learn the backstory of the political military conflict."

One of the reasons so many young people flocked to the insurgency was that the KIA had done such a good job of crafting a single political narrative across the north. In the 1960s, the rebel army started deposing or killing local chieftains across Kachin State so that no traditional power structures could challenge their authority. The KIA began conscripting young men and women from all corners of Kachin society to fight against the central government, and by the mid-1970s, the army boasted thousands of disciplined troops, as well as its own parallel government systems. Having eliminated the traditional power centers, the KIA was able to construct a single dominant narrative of rebellion and a power structure that purported to stand for everyone within the Kachin nation.

But for Bum Tsit, buying into that narrative also meant giving into the same cycle of retribution and violence that had been destroying Kachin State for generations. His people had been fighting for so long, and to what end? Leaders argued about jade and gold and the billions of dollars of natural resources that supposedly belonged to the Kachin people. But becoming a militant didn't help you get richer. It didn't help your family escape Kachin State's deadly cycle of exploitative poverty. And it certainly wasn't helping the children of rural peasants avoid landmine explosions.

Bum Tsit faced a choice. He knew that joining the rebels might make him feel good for a moment, but it wouldn't really help put an end to his people's suffering. He was looking for a different path, one that would allow him to advocate for his people without sacrificing his own moral compass. Jade might be the key. But as his new foray into the business was showing him, that might mean doing a little bit of bad in the pursuit of a greater good, and it meant being alone.

■

In Red House, one of Bum Tsit's young cousins—wearing a red and green shirt with the crossed swords of the KIA—brought us plates of grilled beef and scallions, alongside bowls of sticky rice, fried eggs, and copious volumes of the mashed chili peppers that the Kachin men liked to dump on everything they ate. The young girl deposited the food, then trotted back to the bar. Despite his family's affiliation with the KIA, Bum Tsit had always been open with me about his criticisms of the group, so I asked him if he was nervous about being targeted by the militia for additional "taxes" if he got any further into the jade business.

Bum Tsit surprised me when he said that the KIA's rationale for taxing the jade trade was justified: "They need the money for the war," he replied. "To make a bullet you need money. Without any money, you won't have any bullets. Where is the money in Kachin State? Jade."

I thought about the "Pro-Team" and the KIA's public stance that they were fighting for the Kachin people's right to use their own natural resources. Many people in Kachin took that argument at face value. Bum Tsit called them the "closed-eye people." He knew the truth was more complicated: War was good for business on both sides of the front line. All it took was the right kind of marketing to make it palatable to the little people.

Bum Tsit wasn't a little person. "My eyes are open," he liked to say. However much he disagreed with the actions of the rich and powerful, he wanted to be in their position. Jade was the answer, but what was the cost? He was fully aware that investing in jade meant contributing to this cycle of exploitative violence that he wanted to end. The contradiction was in many ways the central story of his life: a man stitched thoroughly into a corrupt system, who thought that he could somehow rise above it by sheer force of will.

Bum Tsit was full of secrets and contradictions. He supported the KIA but spent years working for the military government. He wanted to get rich on blood jade and spend that money helping landmine victims. He was going to run for parliament as part of the Tatmadaw's political party, but he planned on using his position to advocate for Kachin autonomy.

Now, as he moved deeper into the world of jade, the price of keeping those secrets was becoming clear. If the public learned about his illegal business, his political career could be ruined, and with it his plan to advocate for his people. And even if those secrets never got out, Bum Tsit had to live with the knowledge of his work and the repercussions of funneling his money into an industry greased with his people's blood, and that felt like the most dangerous secret of all.

Despite the moral contradictions, Bum Tsit had made up his mind. He would put his political career on pause and cast his fate into the murky world of jade. But he needed more information if he was going to succeed like he had in government and in his other businesses. Knowledge was power in Kachin, and Bum Tsit knew whom to visit to learn those secrets.

.

"For those who want to get as much profit as possible, it is very clear. You send it to China illegally, then you pay no tax and have a big profit."

Bum Tsit and I had gone to visit Lahkri La Aung, the vice chairman of the Myitkyina Jade Traders Association, a lobbying group that supported local business interests, to learn some of the jade industry's secrets. Lahkri was an enormous player in the Kachin jade trade—a power broker with connections to both the KIA and the central government's mining authorities. He was related to the former leader of the KIO, and for years he had profited off his central position and ability to navigate Kachin politics— much as Bum Tsit hoped to do. But ever since the government had begun reforming the mining laws, he and many other Kachin jade merchants had been shut out of the industry. Now he was in the business of information— letting secrets out into the open in the hope of influencing the policymaking process and eventually getting back into the jade business.

Lahkri called this transparency. He treated secrets like a commodity, and he had agreed to sit for an interview—in the name of greater transparency—with the knowledge that our conversation would eventually be published.

Bum Tsit wanted to use the interview to learn about the jade industry, and to maybe even open the door to working together in the future. "He is a very important man," Bum Tsit told me as we drove to his house. "In fact, I am a little nervous going to speak with him, because he is so high above me."

We sat on the verandah behind Lahkri's house, late on a Sunday morning, and a young woman brought us steaming cups of green tea. The enormous property was covered in flowering trees and abutted the banks of the slow-moving Irrawaddy River. The scene radiated tranquility. Lahkri had just returned from church and wore a green cotton shirt with khaki slacks. As we talked, he occasionally glanced at his gold Rolex, and checked his notebook periodically. Behind his wire-rim glasses, the older man had sharp, probing eyes. He spoke with the assurance of someone who rarely had to explain himself.

The fact that smugglers made more money was no secret in the jade business. But how that money moved, and who was ultimately raking in the profit, was not clear to those on the outside. Bum Tsit and I both took notes as the old jade merchant explained how the smuggling networks really worked.

"The high-quality jade that comes from Hpakan is not just small stones,"

Lahkri explained. "There are big stones! Five- or ten-ton boulders. If a jade stone that size is pulled out of Hpakan today, it will be in the Chinese markets in a week. That is only possible if you use a military truck. The smugglers pay the military to carry the stones in their trucks. There is only one major road from Hpakan to China. When the public takes this road, they have to stop at all the checkpoints, which are controlled by the military. Only a military truck can cross the checkpoint without being searched."

He paused and adjusted his glasses, then continued.

"Anyone who knows how the industry works can see that there is only one way for large amounts of high-quality jade to get into China. All of this smuggling takes place on the back of the Tatmadaw."

Lahkri said that he was pessimistic about the chance for reform. "The future is not good," he said. "People talk about rule of law, but they cannot actually accomplish it, because there is so much corruption in the government."

The older businessman kept talking. By keeping the war going, he said, the Tatmadaw was ensuring long-term profitability, reaping money from areas with no governance, areas that were once Kachin territory, but were now just considered humanitarian disaster zones. "Look at some mining regions, like Tanai," he said, sweeping his arm toward the mountains in the north. "Government representatives cannot even go into the mining areas there because it is too violent. Only the Tatmadaw can go there, and it's the Tatmadaw who is making sure that there is no peace in the area, so that they can keep mining work ongoing. If the mining becomes legal because there is peace, then the Tatmadaw gets nothing. So they don't want any peace, and they keep up the illegal mining."

I asked him if the KIA was also profiting off the war and instability and lack of governance, just like the Tatmadaw. "The KIA are on the outside," he said. "They cannot have any companies operating in the mines, but they can tax the trade where they can." He explained that, as many others had alleged, when mining companies find valuable stones and the KIA intelligence officers hear about it, then they go and force the businessmen to pay. The militia threatened retribution against those that didn't cough up the money. It was a way to emphasize that they were the true owners of the land.

But, Lahkri admitted, instability in the north could also benefit the KIA. The rebels were strong enough that they could sometimes close down the road to Hpakan, freezing traffic in and out of the mines until they were paid off. This protection racket was wholly dependent on Chinese financial connections, Lahkri said. Modern technology had made the entire operation seamless and official feeling. When a KIA tax collector demanded a payment for a jade stone, or when the rebel army charged duties on the smuggling routes through the mountains, everything was done by mobile phone. Whoever was paying the bribe could send mobile money to someone in China, who would then deposit it into one of the KIO's Chinese bank accounts. Then they could show the receipt on their phone and receive an official slip from the KIA officer. The whole process took just minutes—an $800 million shakedown formalized by modern technology.

Lahkri and Bum Tsit agreed that it was important to be critical of the KIA and the Kachin elites who were profiting off the war. "Transparency is important," Lahkri said, checking his watch. "Even though it's supposed to be a democratic country now, rich people can do whatever they want." It was clear that his criticism included many of the Kachin elites who colluded with Tatmadaw leaders to profit off the instability in the north.

"We need to talk openly about Yup Zaw Hkawng and U Khun Sa," he said, naming two Kachin businessmen doing some of the largest-scale jade mining. "How they have their connections to keep their holdings? Yup Zaw Hkawng has very good relations with former president Than Shwe," Lahkri said. "And Khun Saw has good relations with Max Zaw Zaw, one of the country's biggest cronies.

"There is just as much corruption now as there was before," he said. "Tatmadaw holding companies, big crony companies, and people related to the generals, these guys are going to take everything."

Sitting on his shady verandah, Lahkri took a final sip of tea. "Anyways," he said, concluding the discussion, "everyone who is in power to check such stuff in the jade business is making money from it. There is no accountability."

∎

Whenever I visited Myitkyina, I made a point to walk down to the central market and talk to the old women who assembled there every afternoon to sell fruits and vegetables. They harvested in the morning and took rickety old motorized trishaws into the city to sell their produce at a profit—there were onions and ears of corn and big oranges filled with seeds. The old women were catty and talkative; they hooted and cracked jokes with each other. Some of them only spoke Jinghpaw or Lisu or the other local northern languages. But many were fluent in Burmese as well, a skill that was becoming more and more necessary to do business in the city. I liked to peruse the fruit stands and chat with these old women about life in the Kachin countryside. Because the government travel restrictions were so strict for foreigners, they were one of the best insights into the lives that rural Kachin families led.

The path to the market took me over the train tracks—the lifeline between this northern outpost and the Bamar heartland in the south. I would walk past the ancient YMCA guesthouse, where I had stayed during my first visit to Myitkyina more than five years earlier. At that time, the city had felt dangerous and stark. I remembered heroin addicts sprawled out on the near-empty streets, and Tatmadaw soldiers patrolling the corners. Now, however, even though the war was getting closer and closer, downtown Myitkyina was booming with commerce.

I always looked for an old orange seller named Ting Ting, who sold me bags of fruit at what she said was the "local price." Bum Tsit later told me that it was still twice as much as he would pay. But it was half what the other ladies tried to get me to pay, so I kept coming back. Plus she smiled a lot and liked to puff on enormous green cheroots. She always wore a wide-brimmed straw hat, from which her gray hair fell out to spill over her shoulders. Her cheeks were permanently puckered, with deep crevices in them—as though she had spent the last fifty years sucking on lemons. She was also permanently stooped over, a spine seemingly frozen in place from a lifetime of working in the fields. But her eyes twinkled with a kind of mischievous gleam, crinkled around the edges from laughing so much.

The first time we had met, I was still new to the Burmese language. We had just done a lesson on superlatives in my Burmese class, and I told Ting Ting, "Kachin food tastes very good. I think it is the best."

The old lady had collapsed in a fit of laughter, hid her hands behind her face, and shook her finger at me. Then she puffed on her cheroot and pointed to a papaya for me to take.

I later learned that I had used a wrong word and mispronounced a tone, so instead of saying "I think Kachin food tastes very good," I had said, "I think Kachin food fucks the best." After that, I vowed to keep practicing my Burmese tones.

But Ting Ting had a sense of humor, a rare thing in Myitkyina, where so many others were stone faced and serious. "Come back next time," she told me. "I'll be your market mama here in Myitkyina."

When I visited Myitkyina in February, Ting Ting pointed out to me that there were more and more old market women who had stopped growing their own fruit and vegetables and were instead selling produce that came from China.

"The best oranges and apples all come from China," she said to me, pointing across the road to a cart where someone had stacked piles of little, bright orange mandarins and candy-green apples. These families brought in Chinese produce on the few roads over the mountains, along with clothes and plastic goods and anything else the world's factory produced.

"It is a shame that we need everything from outside the country," Ting Ting said. "The land used to be so good, but now we cannot grow anything." I asked if she was referring to the giant, Chinese-run megafarms along the border, which specialized in monocrops of banana trees and palm oil, and which spoiled the soil. Many of these industrial farms had once been part of independent Kachinland during the 1980s and 1990s, but during the cease-fire, the KIO and Tatmadaw had secured deals with Chinese investors, selling off enormous tracts of the mountainous jungle land, which was incomparably cheap and fertile compared to what the Chinese could buy in China. Some of the Kachin elites had become rich from the land deals, but they were disastrous for local farmers, who were uprooted and forced to leave their ancestral land. The first thing the new owners often did was cut down all the valuable timber for a quick profit. But when all the old growth forest was replaced with little banana trees, there was nothing to stop the generations-old topsoil from spilling down into the rivers, leaching nutrients from the ground and turning some of the most fertile country in the world into ugly, barren hills.

"I don't know about all that," Ting Ting said, waving her hand dismissively. "I just know that thirty years ago we all fed ourselves and made all our own things. Now we need China for everything. This is all Chinese. Garbage." She gestured to the piles of plasticky clothing and children's toys spread out over a tarp on the ground next to us.

Ting Ting told me that her joints were bothering her. But since there was no functioning health center near her village, she had waited and waited and waited until she could afford to go see a doctor at Myitkyina Hospital. But even that didn't help. She hadn't been sick in twenty years, so it was her first time in a hospital in a long time. I asked why she had to save money to be seen in a government hospital, which was supposed to be free. She said that she had to pay a bribe for the receptionist to put her name down on the list, and another bribe to get her information taken by the nurse, and another bribe to get her medical records at the end of the visit. "This isn't how people are supposed to treat their elders," she said. "It is just wrong."

•

The effects of petty corruption were everywhere in the north, but nowhere was it easier to see than on the Northern Star Golf Course, with the State Director for City Development, with his baggy shirt and soft handshake. When Bum Tsit and I played with him in February, we could hear the low rumble of artillery fire from across the ridge, as the Tatmadaw fended off KIA incursions.

The rolling explosions in the background didn't seem to bother any of the other golfers or caddies in our groups. I turned and asked a doctor playing with us if the sound was what I thought. He paused and listened, marching through a kind of logical deduction out loud. "It sounds like thunder," he said. "But there are no clouds; the weather is perfect. It can't be thunder. It must be the artillery then. There is a war going on after all. I guess it is closer than we thought." He smiled at me and then swung his 7-iron.

Watching the Director, a veteran hardened by a long career as a Tatmadaw officer, it was as if there was no conflict going on at all. Every three holes, he sat down to snack at the little banquet tables that the golf course staff set up. He would sip tea, eat two or three hard-boiled eggs dipped in salt at a time, and invite me to join him.

"I eat lots of eggs to stay strong," he told me. "Every day, many eggs." The Director was in his mid-fifties, and he jiggled when he walked. But he still carried his body with the assuredness of someone who was paid to stay in fighting shape for much of his life. Off the tee, he could out-drive most of the younger players in the group.

My golf abilities were still wanting, and I rarely hit it as far as the Director. "You need to eat more eggs!" he would call to me across the fairway, flexing his biceps. When we tallied up scores at the end of each hole, I was almost always the highest. The Director called me the *gezun pelin*. The phrase translates to something like "plain vegetable," but among the Myitkyina golfers, it was slang for "loser."

Every time we played, the Director made a point to come up to me after the round and thank me for visiting. "Anything you need in Myitkyina, please come to me first," he said to me on multiple occasions.

I never appealed to the Director for help in anything. But I was sure that Bum Tsit did. Golf was a way for an up-and-coming young man to make connections and get insider information about what was happening around Kachin State. Now that he was getting into the business of illegal gemstones, Bum Tsit needed insider knowledge about what was happening in the mountains. Things like road closures and troop movements could make or break his business. Things that a military-connected Director who oversaw all the state road projects would know about.

Bum Tsit was almost always the youngest player in the group. Government officials, jade merchants, and army officers frequented the course, chatting on the fairway about events across Kachin State. It was a place where secrets could be traded like company shares, and that was the real reason Bum Tsit played golf at Northern Star, instead of the municipal course much closer to his house. After every round, we would sit at G Bar with the other golfers. The bar is part of the golf course, owned and run by the same military conglomerate that owned stakes in businesses all across the country. It looked like any other beer station in Myanmar, apart from the old golf clubs hung up on the wall. As we sipped Myanmar Beer and ate peanuts brought to us by a fourteen-year-old waiter with fuzzy, home-made tattoos running up his forearms, Bum Tsit would ply the government men and business owners for information about what was going on around Kachin State.

The parking lot outside G Bar was always filled with new Toyota Land Cruisers. In Myanmar, the cars cost upward of $200,000 after import taxes. When a government employee that made four hundred dollars a month packed his golf clubs into one of the shiny black SUVs, it was easy to infer something about his extra income.

G Bar's drab features belied the powerful gossip that was shared there. Knowledge equaled opportunity in Kachin State, and the nexus of business, conflict, and governance at the golf course made it a secret bubble of elite privilege. But Bum Tsit phrased it differently: "It's not about money; it's about power. Power to help my people." He paused for a second, thinking. "We can call it power. Or you can call it corruption."

I asked what he meant, and he pointed at himself.

"Even if we are staying within the law, there is still lots of corruption," he said. "You can use your power to do things. When I was in the government, I just had to call or write a letter, and anything could be OK."

He told me a story about bringing teak into Myitkyina. Kachin State is home to large teak forests, but like the rest of the region's natural resources, it was legally the property of the central government and the law prohibited the valuable wood from entering the city. There was a brisk trade in illegal teak, much of which went across the border to China. But the legally sourced teak had to be transported to lower Myanmar, where it was used in government buildings and fancy hotels. To most people in Kachin State, this was a blatant example of the central government stealing natural resources that rightfully belonged to the Kachin people, and as part of the state government, Bum Tsit had been in a position to do something about it.

When a local group had come to him and said that they wanted to build a new schoolhouse out of teak, Bum Tsit had agreed that the Kachin people deserved to use the wood just as much as their compatriots in the south. So when he wrote them an official letter granting permission to import the wood into Myitkyina, he took a little bit of it himself, and used it to build his house.

"This is a type of corruption," he admitted. "But Kachin is a place that I really need to help."

Bum Tsit thought if he built influence, wealth, and power by exploiting the ins and outs of daily corruption in the jade industry, he could become an insider and be a better ally for the Kachin people. But that meant being surrounded by people on both sides of the conflict. He'd need Tatmadaw allies like the Director, and well-connected KIO leaders like Lakhri La Aung. Straddling this gap between the Kachin and the rest of Myanmar, he saw opportunity.

"I'll have a strong position," he said. "My voice can stand for my people . . . So this kind of situation, like today, where everyone is fighting, I could negotiate between the KIA and the military. And if it's not possible to solve all the problems, my voice will at least be able to help in the reduction of the conflict. If there are no Kachin people in positions of power, no one will talk about us. But if I am there, then I can speak out the feelings of the Kachin people. This is what I hope and what I believe."

Bum Tsit raised his glass of Tuborg. "For the intelligence!" he cheered, and told me about his plan to start smuggling jade into China.

8.

THE FOURTEENTH STREET BLOOD TONIC

Yangon

On Tuesday nights, I'd often walk a few blocks to the gallery on Pansodan Street and drink Myanmar Beer with the artists, authors, and miscreants who collected there. In the crowded gallery rooms, stuffed with large oil paintings, Yangon's alternative crowd would congregate to commiserate about work and compare notes about ongoing projects. I liked the incongruity of drinking the Tatmadaw's beer—slogan: Brimming with Optimism—while the disjointed crowd talked about everything wrong in the country.

It was there that I met Jalin Sama. She was hard to miss—bright eyes behind big glasses and a messy bun that bounced around while she talked.

She had a voice that carried across the crowded gallery, and a laugh to match. She and her husband, Robert, had been splitting their time between New York and Myanmar since 2002. Over there, they lived in the mountains in a sprawling eighteenth-century farmhouse overlooking the Catskill Creek, where Robert sold art he purchased in Yangon and Jalin worked as an anesthesiologist at Albany Medical College Hospital. Here, they lived in a small apartment on Thirty-Ninth Street and managed Better Burmese Health Care, an NGO focused on training young doctors and delivering primary care that the government failed to provide.

They seemed to know everyone in the city, and went out of their way to help introduce me to people. Jalin invited me to tag along with her small band of physicians on remote clinic visits, and Robert kept me abreast of happenings in the local art and food scene. When we saw each other at bars or parties, I would often spend a long time talking about my research and local politics with them.

Jalin had introduced me to Bum Tsit. The former chief minister of Kachin State was a cousin of hers, and when she and Robert went to visit Myitkyina a few years previously, he had sent his then-assistant, Bum Tsit, to look after them. The young Kachin man had impressed Jalin, and like me she had a feeling that he was destined for something larger than Myitkyina-level politics. When I told her that I was studying jade and the Kachin war, she immediately thought of Bum Tsit as a good contact. Throughout the year, whenever we met in Yangon, Jalin asked me about him, and I told her about his business and family and the dangers of his new foray into jade. We talked about the difficulty of life for young Kachin people, who were faced with a stark set of choices: Become a rebel or assimilate. As Bum Tsit was learning, the middle ground had disappeared.

When I thought of a Kachin person who had chosen another path, there was no clearer example than Jalin. Her options were different than those of someone like Bum Tsit. She was from an earlier generation and was born into a family of Kachin political leaders. But unlike most other Kachin activists she had found a way to leave the revolution behind and establish herself as an independent crusader for truth and free speech.

Jalin told me that many young Kachins like Bum Tsit—having grown up surrounded by riches but unable to grasp any—were seized by an all-consuming need to build wealth, whatever the cost. She said that most influential Kachins had started off with good intentions, but that their attitudes were hardened by living in a system that was designed to disenfranchise them. "Kachin elite are part of the problem," Jalin said, explaining that people like Bum Tsit who start out trying to improve the system often become cronies themselves once they gain access to the hidden business networks that control so much of Myanmar's underground economy. But Jalin said that, instead of criticizing this behavior, poor Kachins will often think "He's a crony, but it's OK because he's a Kachin." She wanted to call out this blind patriotism, which she said stemmed from a feeling among young Kachins of being downtrodden for so long, so that they would accept any means necessary to take back what they perceived to be their birthright, especially when it came to jade.

Jalin came from the Sama clan, also sometimes spelled Thama, and I had actually read about her family long before we ever met. During the nineteenth century, when the British began military operations in the Kachin hills, the clan's leader—the Sama Duwa—had been an important player in the jade trade, and the old British gazetteer for Myitkyina district spoke about him at some length. Later, Jalin's father, known as the Sama Duwa Sinwa Nawng, had led the Kachin people after World War II, and was only a few weeks from being inaugurated president of Myanmar before the socialist revolution swept away the country's leadership.

■

Jalin's parentage automatically made her an important person in the Kachin political scene, but she was not tied to the independence movement. Unlike most Kachin leaders, she did not speak Jinghpaw, and she was Buddhist instead of Baptist. She wore this difference on her sleeve and sometimes referred to people in the north as "those Kachin nationalists."

She often took to Facebook to call out the hypocritical attitudes of certain Kachin activists and leaders. When a landslide in Hpakan killed over one hundred people, she posted about Yup Zaw Hkawng, Kachin State's richest man, whose Jadeland company had obtained massive mining consessions through its close relationship with the Tatmadaw. "The victims in Hpakan and their families deserve justice," she wrote.

Jalin told me that even this simple call for justice and what should be uncontroversial critcism of the jade magnate had rubbed some people the wrong way. Other Kachins would often say that because she was an outsider, who didn't spend all her time in Myanmar, she didn't have a right to criticize Kachin people doing what was required to build wealth for their people. That was one of the hurdles of splitting life between America and Myanmar— Jalin had an outsider's clear-eyed perspective on the problems in Kachin and the rest of the country, but it was always an uphill battle to get people to listen. But even during the three or four months a year she was in Myanmar, she spent hours each day on Facebook, criticizing the government's official positions and highlighting contradictions in her compatriots' arguments. She was incensed that people in Myanmar would cry out over abuses against rebel military groups like the Kachin and Karen armies but wouldn't lift a finger to help the defenseless Rohingya.

In Yangon, managing the clinics at Better Burmese Health Care only took a few days a week. "I feel like my real job is going online and picking fights with people," she told me once, laughing at the thought. "Not enough people here are just speaking up. I just want to show them that their views are not logical."

When a friend wrote something in support of the Tatmadaw's campaign against the Rohingya, she posted photos of Kachin women and children who were living in the forest after having been driven from their homes:

That's right. This is the same army that y'all are supporting on Rohingya issue. Do you support this too?

She told me that ethnic politics in Myanmar "didn't make any sense" once she stepped outside a local frame of reference. "Like the fact that there are these states," she said, referring to the country's ethnically based partitions. "It just makes things worse—it makes it impossible for us to ever be one people."

Jalin and Robert had been part of the resistance movement during the darkest days of the military junta, and saw their work as a continuation of that fight, trying to convince others to raise their voices. Robert often regaled me with stories about how drastically things had changed in Myanmar in the last fifteen years. He ran an art gallery focused on Myanmar art, and told me about some of the bizarre censorship rules the military had put in place. Art was supposed to have "constructive intent" and any art deemed to be "criticism" had to be publicly justified. For a while, paintings with too much black or red were considered threatening to the government, evoking as they do blood, revolution, and violence, and were covered up or censored by the military.

The biggest obstacle to reconciliation, Jalin and Robert thought, was the fifty-year hangover of secrecy, propaganda, and lies from the military rule that had ousted her father. Those five decades of terror had bred a society of mistrust, where no one could openly communicate, and the Tatmadaw used those social fissures to pursue their own interests independent of the country's social and economic development. Jalin was incensed that the military—which during the junta years was widely despised by Myanmar's population—had somehow revitalized its image through the Rohingya crackdown. Robert and Jalin fretted over this changing attitude in Myanmar, and about how people they counted as friends had transformed before their eyes over the Rohingya issue. She told me that instead of fighting over narrow local issues like resource ownership or ethnic politics, the whole country needed to rally together and show the Tatmadaw that true democratization without military interference was the path forward. Jalin believed that they could win people over one at a time, by having individual conversations, speaking to people face-to-face and laying out rational arguments that weren't based on ethnicity or national creation myths. When she read about everyday people standing up to the Tatmadaw, she went instantly to Facebook.

We need to rise up. These locals are brave. If we aren't brave enough (yet) to stand up to the guns, we should be brave enough too stand up to other forms of power abuse and mistreatments from authorities of all sectors. You know who you are. Don't make me tag you.

•

Jalin came back to Yangon every year to see her mother and push the people she knew for reform, but she also had a professional mission. Better Burmese Health Care's website described itself as a "grassroots non-profit organization working to improve health care to the poor and education of the local medical professionals in Burma."

A list of suggested donations showed how inexpensive it could be to save someone's life in Myanmar:

9 US$—one month supply of diabetic medications
6.50 US$—one month supply of blood pressure medications
7 US$—ultrasonography
20 US$—one day's (Sunday monthly clinic) salary of a senior
    BBHC doctor

BBHC was a small operation. Jalin's job as an anesthesiologist in New York was enough to fund a large chunk of the NGO and allow her to spend months at a time in Yangon. Robert raised money by collecting local art and selling it in his gallery in the Catskills.

One morning I joined Jalin and her team of young local doctors on a site visit to a remote corner of northeast Yangon. The six-person group was stuffed into the back of a pickup truck with backpacks and suitcases filled with medicine, paperwork, and laptops. The clinic was held at a monastery—the head monk had decreed that donating space for the monthly clinic was part of its duty to the local community. When we arrived mid-morning, patients were already waiting in a long, twisting line. Chickens scurried around the old wood patio, while boys in novice monks' robes did chores and watched wide eyed as the young doctors and nurses began unpacking their equipment and preparing to treat what could amount to hundreds of patients. Over the course of five hours, Jalin and her team took histories, checked blood pressures, and gave out free medication. BBHC had lots of repeat visitors with chronic conditions like diabetes, who had no other way to manage their care except through the free clinic. When Jalin treated these old men and women whose lives were unnecessarily at risk, she kept up a running narrative about the socioeconomic factors that contributed to such poor health. Like many doctors, her analysis could be blunt: "The government has totally abandoned these people. All they care about is politics. These guys will die while politicians bicker about the civil war. It's like the NGOs have to replace the government to provide services. It's totally fucked up!"

The monastery provided lunch to the team in the head monk's private meditation space upstairs. The ancient wooden building creaked and groaned as the nuns moved back and forth across the old floorboards with enormous pots of food for the visitors. People in Myanmar tend to concentrate on food and little else during mealtimes, and lunch passed mostly in silence, as though the sparse utility of their mission made other discussion irrelevant. After most of the team had filled up on rice and bitter greens and spicy fermented chili pastes, they slowly filtered down the stairs to keep the queue of patients moving. As the last person left the space, Jalin knelt alone in front of the head monk in the corner, bowed her head, and prayed.

·

My own health often felt at risk in Myanmar. Living in Yangon was a punishing experience, which was part of the reason I spent so much time traveling outside of the city: the countryside generally had less smog, cleaner water, and fewer rats. All the factors that made downtown Yangon such a fascinating and colorful place to live—the noise and crowds and piles of people crammed together—also made it feel generally unhealthy. In the afternoon, the sun fell through my third-floor windows and sent the temperature soaring into the nineties in my concrete living room. Air conditioning helped, but rolling blackouts often left me sweating alone in the darkened apartment. The restaurants and bars with backup generators were the only relief from the hot season's punishing temperatures. For all its old colonial charm, my apartment never felt like a home.

There were holes in the ceiling, and occasionally bats from the attic would find their way in. Normally they'd fly in haphazard circles until one of the ceiling fans caught them. But once, one of them flew at me in the bathroom and cut my finger. A doctor told me that I immediately needed a rabies vaccination, of which there was a national shortage. I spent the next week shuttling between Yangon's hospitals, searching for the vaccines, before eventually decamping to Bangkok for a more modern public health system. The next week I bought chicken wire from Twenty-Seventh Street and patched up all the old ceiling holes.

When it wasn't bats, the drain cut in my bedroom floor was a constant source of health anxiety. It carried water from my shower and kitchen sink to empty into the sewer sixty feet below. In the hot season, when the water level was low, the sewers backed up, and a viral twangy smell coursed up through the hole and hung heavy in the apartment.

By April, I was feeling exhausted. No matter how much sleep I got, it never felt like I was able to rest or recover. Yangon felt like it was beating me down.

"It's a problem in your blood," U Myo Tun said, as we chatted one morning at his betel stand outside the apartment on Bo Aung Kyaw Street. While he was preparing betel packets to sell to the day laborers, he suggested that I visit a special blood clinic in Chinatown.

That afternoon, I gave a pedicab driver the address from U Myo Tun and asked him if he knew about the place. Sitting in the bike's rigid steel sidecar, I tried to listen to his response, but his mouth was so full with betel spit that it was hard to make out more than a few words. Every bump in the road he'd spit, and I got a little red splash accompanied with an explanation.

"Pedicab twenty years . . ." *spit*

"Everywhere in Yangon . . ." *bump*

". . . pregnant woman to clinic . . ."

"Pedicab drivers are very healthy; we have strong legs."

He dropped me off on a busy corner at Fourteenth and Mahabandoola. I was worried I wouldn't be able to find the mysterious blood clinic, but the old townhouse was easy to spot. The Ruby Medical Hall looked like it hadn't changed in over a century, while the rest of the neighborhood had rushed headlong into the future. It was flanked by a glass high-rise on one side, and a squat, modern cement store on the other. On the second-floor verandah, a sign in Burmese read *Ruby*. On the steps leading up to the storefront, a tiny, wizened grandma sold small goods out of a plastic bowl.

"Do you need medicine," asked a stout woman in glasses sitting behind a display case.

I told her I was feeling generally unwell, and that a friend had suggested I come here to the clinic.

"You should go to the pharmacy," she said, and pointed down Mahabandoola Street. "They speak English there."

"No, no. My friend said that I needed to come here."

She shrugged her shoulders and sat back down.

A body stirred in the shadows in the back. The clinic was so empty that I was surprised to have missed another person inside. A big, round man moved from next to the staircase and came forward into the early afternoon sun.

He introduced himself as Aye Say. "Please describe your symptoms," he said to me.

I told him that I was often out of breath, and that I was having trouble sleeping, that my mind would race all night and in the morning I'd be left with debilitating headaches.

"This Blood Tonic is a cure-all," he said, and gestured to the woman to open the cabinet. Inside were three glass bottles and some old pieces of newspaper. "It will help you get up and also help your breath. It is made from all local ingredients. Mostly vegetables and legumes. Original recipe."

Aye Say told me that the Ruby Medical Hall had been on the corner of Fourteenth and Mahabandoola since 1935, selling the same Blood Tonic in the same packaging for over eighty years.

"Four generations have worked here since U Aung Khin opened the store." He started ticking off his fingers: "father; son; grandson; great-grandson."

I opened the Blood Tonic package and looked at the glass bottle. It was deep red—syrupy and ruby colored. As though it were made from real blood.

Aye Say and the woman behind the counter talked under their breath. There was some debate about exactly how much tonic I should be taking. Finally, they settled on one tablespoon with breakfast, another before bed.

"It is good for the heart and blood," Aye Say said. "It will keep you cool when you are up, up, up. This slows you down."

.

When I got home, I opened up the plastic bag and read the label on the old cardboard packaging:

Ruby Blood Medicine Liquid

Below were the instructions:

You can take it one spoon twice a day.
Can also be mixed with warm water.

A small pamphlet inside elaborated: "You can drink it with coffee, or even with alcohol. It can mix with Brandy, or gin and lime." The paper explained that the Blood Tonic could be used for:

Heart Disease
Liver Sickness
Insomnia
Bloody Stool
Those that cannot have children
Different types of menopause

I tried the blood tonic for a few weeks according to the instructions on the package, but didn't mix it with brandy or gin and lime. It had a sharp, iron-y flavor, and clung to the inside of my throat like cough syrup. I wasn't sure the traditional medicine was doing anything, but like most people in Yangon, I had few options for reliable health care. There was one international clinic in the northern part of the city, with French and Thai doctors, but it was prohibitively expensive for all but emergency situations, like the bat scratch.

When I talked to Jalin about it, she said that blood tonic and other traditional medicines were still popular for most people in Myanmar. She pointed out that for the 65 percent of Myanmar that lived in the countryside, especially war-torn areas like Kachin and Rakhine States, the setup was even worse. Local health centers there often lacked steady supplies of medicine, electricity, and water. People were undertrained and underpaid, and patients often had no choice but to rely on the cheap, readily available traditional medicines.

Myanmar has the lowest life expectancy and second highest maternal mortality rate in Southeast Asia. During the latter decades of the twentieth century, as most of its neighbors increased public health expenditures and achieved longer life for their citizens, the health system in Myanmar stagnated. By 2018, someone born in Myanmar could expect to live only sixty-six years, compared to sixty-eight in Cambodia, seventy-two in Bangladesh, seventy-five in Thailand, and seventy-six in Vietnam. Economists attribute the poor health system to a simple lack of funding. According to the World Health Organization, in 2000 Myanmar only spent three dollars per person per year on health care. (For comparison, in the same year, neighboring Thailand spent sixty-two dollars, while the United States, the largest spender, spent around $4,500 per person.) By 2015, Myanmar was spending fifty-nine dollars per person, but the country was digging itself out of a public health trench, and its people—especially those in remote areas like Kachin State—faced an uphill battle just to remain healthy.

■

It was Jalin's husband, Robert, who first invited me to Pansodan Gallery after we met at a restaurant downtown. When I visited the gallery the following Tuesday night, I met a German theologian who focused on "Kachin hermeneutics," a marine biologist who studied the dolphins in the Irrawaddy River delta, and a poet from Shan State. These were people who could stay out late drinking on a Tuesday, who didn't have to go into the office in the morning, who were one step removed from the daily grind. They were people like me.

Everyone in the gallery had a story to tell, and it was the first place in Yangon I had visited that didn't feel consumed by the local version of events. People were pursuing their own truths and sharing them freely, without fear of retribution. I could identify with the kind of good-natured cynicism among some of the expats there. But there was also a sense of ownership and support in the community of artists and academics. Most of the foreigners and locals who came to the gallery had called Myanmar home for a long time, and when they spoke of corruption and violence and racism in the country, it was with the sadness of someone talking about a sick relative.

Robert told me that Aung Soe Min, who opened Pansodan Gallery in 2006, had been one of his mentors in the art world. When Robert first started coming to Yangon with Jalin, in 2003, he went scouring the local markets, buying fabrics and paintings for rock-bottom prices. After he met Aung Soe Min and a few other gallery owners, he began developing his own curatorial style. Robert's unbridled passion for Myanmar art eventually led to him starting the Parasol Project. Each year, he bought dozens of traditionally made parasols from Pathein, a town west of Yangon known for its artisans. Then, he got local artists to paint them with anything they wanted—colorful landscapes, portraits, and abstract designs—and he and Jalin would auction them off. The auction was always a raucous affair, one of the central events of the year for the city's art community, and raised thousands of dollars for Better Burmese Health Care.

I went to the 2018 Parasol Project auction, which took place in a crowded restaurant a few blocks from my apartment. The parasols had been hung on the walls for weeks for people to look at and bid on. I bought a handful of raffle tickets, and wrote down a $250 bid for a parasol painted with a green and blue cubist-style portait of a woman's face. The art purchase would pay for twelve and a half days of a doctor's salary, or thirty-five ultrasounds. The auction was a big, boistorous party, with the restaurant filled to capacity with people holding little tropical cocktails. Jalin's mother and a young cousin took turns on the mic calling out raffle winners. Many of the physicians who worked with Jalin were there, as were many members of the funky Tuesday drinking group from Pansodan Gallery.

In the end, I was outbid on the cubist parasol. But to my disappointment, Robert said that many of the parasols ended up not getting any bids. He planned to bring them back to New York and show them in his gallery in the Catskills. Robert blamed some of it on the fact that so many local artists had chosen to paint portraits of Aung San Suu Kyi on the parasols. In the past, those pictures of The Lady had been best sellers, chic mementos for foreigners to bring back from Myanmar. But now, everything had changed.

■

Later in April, Ting Ting, my market mama in Myitkyina, called me on my phone and said she was in Yangon. She had come to the city after the doctors in Myitkyina told her she needed more specialized medical care. The family had pooled its resources, she told me, and her son had come with her to the big city. They were waiting at Yangon Central Hospital, a few miles from my apartment.

I went to visit her there. Ting Ting was sitting in the waiting room with three enormous plastic sacs stuffed to bursting. They had come straight from the bus station, she told me, and weren't even sure where they were going to stay. Once she had situated herself at the hospital, her son had gone to Sanchaung, a part of the city with lots of Kachin residents, to look for a place to stay.

Ting Ting told me she had been waiting in the hospital for eight hours, but hadn't been seen by anyone yet. She said that people in charge kept asking for money, but she didn't have enough.

She took out a folder stuffed with crinkled-up medical records and started flipping through, narrating what other doctors had told her.

"I need to take this medicine for the pain," she said, and touched her back. "And they told me I should try to exercise more. They said I need to see a . . ." she paused and showed me the English word.

"Rheumatologist," I said. But I wasn't sure how to explain what that meant in Burmese.

I left Ting Ting to try to find some help. The hospital was crowded with families like Ting Ting's, clutching their folders full of medical records and plastic bags full of personal belongings—a lottery ticket of hope in one hand, and a reminder of home in the other.

It took me most of thirty minutes to find someone who would go talk to the old woman. A middle-aged nurse smiled when I explained that my friend had been waiting for a long time and needed to see a doctor. "Everyone has to wait their turn," she replied.

■

Frontier Myanmar magazine had recently done an exposé about the widespread petty corruption in the health system in Myanmar. Su Myat Mon, the reporter who wrote the article, had visited Yangon Central Women's Hospital along with her sister-in-law, who was in labor with her first child, and found that the government-run hospital was fueled by graft. People asked for small "donations" of 1,000 kyats to do even the most rudimentary of tasks. Su Myat Mon reported that women in the maternity ward commonly paid 40,000 to 50,000 kyats in "donations" before taking their babies home.

The article was met with fury and criticism online. On Facebook, people attacked both the magazine and the reporter, and derided the report as a falsehood:

> Does it make you macho to insult others? Rather, you are the half wit who does not seem to comprehend the situation, or shall I say choose to blind sight?

> This is so not true. Doctors and nurses do not take or expect money from patients, nor they ask for it. Patients know it. Got to a hospital, pick a patient, any patient and read out this article to him or her and ask if it is true. The patients know.

So poor u r .U only know about money. We don't interest in money. We carry that bag only for our miscellaneous for medical care. 😂 😂 U r so poor & stupid. U don't know anything about our Dr life. 😂 😂 😂

Others pointed out that since it was a government-run hospital and doctors were civil servants, there was a high likelihood they weren't getting paid their normal salaries, despite grueling working conditions:

As a post-graduate doctor at YCWH, I guaranteed that my colleagues and I did not involved in such kind of corruption. We (gazetted officer level, post-graduate doctors) only survived with government pay salary and even struggled under really stressful conditions physically (including 32 hour duty) and mentally. 100% guaranteed.

Jalin had commented too:

This happens because all government staff are not paid a living wage. Surprised that this was not picked up by this reporter.

When I met with Thomas Kean, *Frontier*'s editor, he told me that he thought the government was coordinating the online attacks. *Frontier* had been the target of other online smear campaigns, especially for its coverage of controversial topics like the Rohingya and the Kachin war, and Kean said that these attacks bore the same hallmarks. We sat in a chic teahouse in downtown Yangon. He said these kinds of reactions were getting worse, but that no one else was exposing this kind of corruption, and that *Frontier* had no intention of backing down in the face of government pressure. When the country's institutions were failing its people because of graft and conflict, it was up to journalists to do their job and shine a light on those dark spots. Kean said that *Frontier* would love to publish more about corruption in the jade trade, but that people who knew the industry secrets almost never agreed to go on record.

·

After her trip to the hospital, Ting Ting told me she was diagnosed with both osteoarthritis and diabetes.

The twenty-eight-year-old doctor who treated her was still working on his fellowship. He told her that her diet was to blame for the diabetes, and said that she should eat less sugar and should find ways to get some more exercise. He didn't leave her with much hope for the arthritis—just try to manage the pain.

"I don't understand," she said to me. "All I do is work. When should I exercise?"

·

One of the young medical students training with Jalin's NGO in Yangon was the daughter of Lakhri La Aung, the Kachin merchant who had made a small fortune in jade and knew all the secrets of the smuggling networks. He wanted to send his daughter to medical school in China, but an internship with an American doctor was even more useful and prestigious, and Jalin had Kachin credentials as well.

The connections among the Kachin diaspora were powerful networking tools within the local community. Friends or relatives in America or the UK or China could unlock important doors for political lobbying and business financing. I benefitted from this network myself. Through contacts in New York, I was introduced to other Kachin dissidents and scholars who worked to reform Myanmar and Kachin institutions without resorting to picking up rifles. One was Maw Htun Aung, the country director for the Natural Resource Governance Institution, or NRGI. Maw Htun Aung also came from a wealthy Kachin family and had studied in Hong Kong, at Cornell, and at Oxford. After email introductions from abroad, we met at his office in a high-rise in the center of Yangon, not far from Inya Lake. He was intimidatingly tall, with spiky hair and thick-rimmed black glasses.

Maw Htun Aung had degrees in public administration and resource governance, and applied his considerable knowledge of extractive industry economics to studying the Kachin jade industry. He told me that the real tragedy of the jade trade was less about Kachin identity and local ownership, than the gaping hole in Myanmar's public finances—a lack of money to spend on health and education—that could be filled with all the potential revenue lost from bad governance in the north.

But unlike most others working in jade, Maw Htun Aung was optimistic about the chance for reform. For the last year, he had worked with the Myanmar Gems Enterprise, the government body responsible for oversight of the industry, to put together a multi-stakeholder policy coordination body to reform how the government recouped money from the trade.

The reform process was supposed to reduce the complexity of the jade tax system. If done correctly, it would respond to some of the complaints jade traders like Lakhri La Aung had about the regulatory framework and thereby reduce incentives to evade the official economy. The overall result would be to increase government revenues from the jade industry, which remained pitifully low. NRGI estimated that during the 2015–2016 mining season, when total jade sales equaled at least $8 billion (some estimates put it far higher), the Myanmar government only recouped $366 million. While proportionally small, it was still an enormous amount of money, and was a marked improvement from a few years previously, when only $72 million from jade sales made it out of the gemstone sector and into government coffers.

That increase in revenue, along with the push to reform the tax code that Maw Htun Aung was participating in, was all a result of increased scrutiny on the jade industry from both international and domestic stakeholders. Reports from watchdog groups like Global Witness had announced to the world that Myanmar's elites were systematically robbing the country of its resource wealth. The data that NRGI collected and made available online was only possible because in 2014 Myanmar's government—at the time increasingly sensitive to international criticism as it transitioned to democracy—signed onto the Extractive Industries Transparency Initiative. The initiative was supposed to encourage data sharing by mining companies. However, private businessmen were often wary of the reforms, and feared being held to account if sharing business records exposed their corrupt practices.

Maw Htun Aung said the new government under Aung San Suu Kyi had an even greater incentive to engage in the reform process. Over the past year, as the value of the kyat had steadily depreciated, speculators were holding onto huge volumes of jade in order to drive its dollar value up. Maw Htun Aung thought if the government could finish the reform process quickly, then maybe it could benefit from the eventual windfall. The leader of the Myanmar Gems Enterprise had promised that no one in the industry would balk at giving 5 to 10 percent of jade revenues back to the state, but it was unclear if other stakeholders could deliver. Many of the Gems Enterprise's bureaucrats were former Tatmadaw officers, and Maw Htun Aung suspected them of having dual allegiances, deliberately sabotaging the regulation process to protect their own interests. The civilian government, which was leading the negotiations, had its own problems as well—as most of the NLD representatives had little experience governing.

"There is no rule of law in Myanmar now," Maw Htun Aung said. "It is just rule by Aung San Suu Kyi."

It was a common complaint, and not just among elites from Kachin. Ethnic minorities around the country had recognized that if the NLD government couldn't deliver on its promises of reform and peacebuilding, then it was better to negotiate directly with the Tatmadaw.

"The last twenty years, the mineral sector has had the opposite of good governance," Maw Htun Aung finished. "But if we can make real progress now, the social impact will be enormous."

NRGI had created an online data visualization tool to publicize some of their findings and draw attention to the need to reform, but the information only covered money that was being reported through legal channels, and didn't take into account the vast majority of the jade economy, which was underground. Since the legal reform process only affected those who wanted to participate, the worst actors were unlikely to change. Those facts tempered optimism among many reform-minded people.

When I emailed Harvard University economist David Dapice, who has written extensively about the jade industry, his criticism had the same American frankness as Jalin's:

"Daniel: It is a bit like the drunk looking for his keys under the lamppost at night—it is not that he lost his keys there but that is where he can see things. Even so, you have to start somewhere."

■

While in Yangon, I was still transfixed by the conflict in Kachin. I spent entire afternoons searching through universities, public libraries, and private book collections, looking for old records of the jade industry and the history of the fight for Kachin resources. I almost always found mentions of the old Kachin warriors, including references to Jalin's family, and their mountain rebellion against the British in the 1880s. But most of the old history texts were written by the British themselves, and while they were long on facts and figures, they were short on analysis or empathy. There was hardly any mention of why the Kachin were fighting their colonizers. Officials in the colonial administration rarely quoted their subjects or tried to humanize them.

Instead, many of the best resources were the memories of people who had lived through Myanmar's convoluted history. It was never clear where those memories would appear, so I often struck up conversations with other people at the library.

Near to my apartment was the Sarpay Beikman translation center, where they sold essays by local scholars translated into English. Outside, there was always an old man showcasing the strangest collection of wares. One day, he had several pairs of used Qatar Airways slippers spread on the mat, each pair available for 1,300 kyats. When I asked where he got them from, he looked incredulous: "People who flew on the airplanes!"

Later, I asked why he chose the bookstore as a place to sell.

"People who spend lots of time reading like to move slow—they have more time to pause and look around. Maybe they want to buy something. Also—if you have money to spend on books, then you have something extra, maybe they want to be charitable."

A few days later, I walked the two blocks to Jalin's building to share some of the old records I had found of her family. I was heading back to Kachin early the next day to interview jade merchants, so I stopped on the ground floor to buy a package of J Donuts. Up in the high-rise apartment, Jalin's mother was preparing lunch, and the air was filled with the earthy smell of curry and rice. The walls of the two-bedroom apartment were lined with comfortable leather couches, and piles of books reaching up to the ceiling were stacked on small, rickety tables. From the balcony, their view of the city was amazing. The golden shimmer of Shwedagon Pagoda twinkled on the horizon, and in the evening they could look down at the small flower market on Anawrahta Road.

Nothing about the current setting betrayed the family's extraordinarily influential past. Jalin's father, the Sama Duwa Sinwa Nawng, had been a central figure in Myanmar's independence movement. After World War II, he represented the Kachin people during the negotiations that helped create the Union of Burma, and at the Panglong Conference he and other Kachin representatives negotiated with General Aung San to ensure that the Kachin people would have the right to self-determination. While many other Kachin leaders at the time wanted to remain within the British Empire for another five years and eventually become an independent state, the Duwa was convinced that being part of the national union would benefit the Kachin people. The failure of Myanmar's government to live up to that promise would drive the Kachin independence movement for the next seventy years.

But despite this political heritage, Jalin's life had few of the trappings of the country's other dynasties. Nothing about her lifestyle in Yangon would tell you that she could be the inheritor of Kachin chieftainship, but when she traveled north, she was treated like royalty.

The family had recently returned from Putao, in the foothills of the Himalayas in the extreme northern reaches of Kachin State. As a scion for the Sama clan, Jalin had been invited to participate in Lisu Fest, an annual celebration for the minority Kachin tribe. In the highlands, the Lisu grew little fingerling potatoes, and Jalin had brought a bag back to Yangon. Her mother had prepared them along with eggplant curry.

While we picked at the food, I showed them some of the references I had found to their family in the *Myitkyina Gazetteer*. In the 1880s, while the British were exploring the jade mines in Kachin, Jalin's grandfather had joined the rebellion against the colonizers. When Kachin chiefs around the jade mines rose up against the British, the colonial military classified the entire race of people as insurgents. The Sama clan was one of the largest in the area, and in February of 1889 a column of military policemen marched north from Mogaung to demand the Duwa's surrender. Two kilometers from the village they found a note staked in the path reading:

I, Thama Duwa, do not intend to attack the English . . . Do not believe slanders. I am helping the jade and amber mines traders in their buying and selling. Although the English are coming to attack me, I will keep out of the way. There is no blood-feud between us . . . Now people say the English will attack and destroy me. I do not know whether this is true or not; if it is true that you will destroy me, I let you know that there is no blood-feud between us.

When I read the passage to Jalin's mother, who had just finished writing a book about the family history of her late husband, she was intrigued. She said she had known about the Duwa, her husband's father, but had never heard the history of his rebellion in the Kachin hills. Like many of the local heroes in Myanmar, these rebels' stories were rarely preserved. The exploits of Bamar kings in the eleventh century were taught in primary school, but more recent heroics, like the Kachin's fight against the British, were usually only preserved through oral histories and told in small gatherings. As the civil war erased many of the old ways of life and as the oldest generation of Kachin men and women slowly died out, these stories were getting harder and harder to find.

In addition to the gazetteer, I had brought a more recent history of the Kachin people, written by the British Academy scholar Mandy Sadan, and showed Jalin's mother some of the passages about her late husband. In Sadan's book *Being and Becoming Kachin*, she discusses the difficulty of the Sama Duwa's legacy. As one of the only Kachin leaders who was Buddhist rather than Christian, and as a deputy of U Nu, the prime minister who tried to enforce Buddhism as a state religion, the Sama Duwa was deeply mistrusted by many Kachins.

Jalin and her mother thought that the Sama Duwa's negative perception among most Kachin was misguided. They worried that his important contributions to the Kachin people and the nation writ large were too often overlooked, simply because he wasn't as militant and revolutionary as other Kachin leaders.

Jalin's mother, sitting on her comfy leather couch after the meal, gestured for me to come over. She reached down into a small basket and pulled a paper off the top. It was a newspaper clipping from October 2015.

"My husband wanted to develop the country though industrialization," she started. "He wanted to build steel production facilities. He said that these resources should be made here, not imported from abroad."

As minister for industry in the young government, she said, he had pushed to build steel workshops in the northern outskirts of Yangon.

"Now this guy," she said, pointing to the picture of the young politician in the photo, "He is so proud that in these same facilities, we are now able to produce jute bags." The memory of what could have been seemed to comfort her, and the old woman laughed out loud at the thought of the fabric sacks used to pack rice and other dry goods. "Jute bags, when we could have been making steel, which now we buy from Pakistan."

Jalin later told me that when her father came south on a train from Mandalay to Yangon in 1962 for his inauguration as president of the Union, he came with his full entourage and took up an entire traincar. The group partied through the night as the train rolled south. In the morning, Jalin's mother awoke to an empty carriage, save for herself, the Duwa, and a lone bodyguard, who informed them that General Ne Win had taken over the government during the night. Press was waiting for the Sama Duwa at the train station, and his wife begged him not to make public remarks. According to Jalin, her father was undeterred, and denounced the undemocratic moves to the assembled journalists.

Over the next few days, all the ministers in U Nu's cabinet were arrested by the military government, save for the Sama Duwa. Being exempted from Ne Win's retribution gave the Kachin people even more reason to suspect him of being a traitor to the northern cause. Jalin said that her father's pardon had never been explained. She described it as both mysterious and suspicious—a gap in her family's history that has bothered her to this day.

In *Being and Becoming Kachin*, Sadan highlighted the strange relevance of the Sama Duwa's legacy today, as a new generation of Kachin navigated the treacherous political waters of simultaneously working alongside Bamar power structures and leading a civil war against them:

"For many Kachin political elites today, there is still a sensitivity about the relationship of the Sama Duwa with [Prime Minister] U Nu and a dislike of drawing parallels with their own relationships with the military regime, especially during the period of the 1994 ceasefire."

For many Kachins, the lesson of the Sama Duwa is clear: get too close to the enemy, and you risk losing your northern support. Better to keep that cooperation secret.

■

I decided it couldn't hurt to pick up a second round of Blood Tonic. After two weeks of swallowing the rubbery-feeling spoonfulls of bitter red liquid with a pinched nose, I had finally caved in and begun mixing it with gin and lime. I wasn't sure if it was the tonic or not, but I knew that I was feeling more energetic and at ease about living on Bo Aung Kyaw Street. Maybe it was the end of the hot season or a better diet or the Blood Tonic working its way through my system. But it could have also been the fact that I had finally found some friends and something like a little community in Yangon.

I shambled down the three steamy flights of dark concrete steps, careful to avoid the red pools of betel nut juice that my neighbors spit into the corners of the staircase, waved to U Myo Tun reading the newspapers at his stand, and turned left. As I walked the mile and a half from Bo Aung Kyaw Street to the corner of Fourteenth and Mahabandoola, I counted down the blocks:

Thirty-Sixth—Thirty-Fifth—Mahabandoola Park Road: The Movie Studio District
Thirty-Second—Thirty-First—Bo Soon Pat Street: Biryiani Row
Twentieth—Nineteenth—Sin O Dan Street: Chinatown

I stopped on Sixteenth and Mahabandoola to watch an ongoing construction project. Day laborers from Chin State were joking with each other as they finished their shift. Each hoisted a hundred-pound bag of cement on their shoulders and walked up a bendy, twelve-inch-wide gangway stretching from the delivery truck to the second floor of the building. They wore flip-flops and raggedy longyis, and their muscles were rippling and sweaty under the punishing afternoon sun.

I was about to turn away when I heard a bang and a shout, followed by a sudden, sickening crack. One of the workers had fallen from the walkway and shattered his leg. The white splinter of bone was sticking out of his skin and blood was streaming down across the split-open bag of cement. Yangon seemed to go silent as the man's screams echoed off the buildings, and everyone sat there looking dumbly for what felt like eternity until one of the other laborers ran into the street and screamed at a passing taxi to stop. Together, he and the driver helped hoist the injured, screaming man into the back seat of the car, and they zoomed off into the traffic toward Yangon General Hospital. They didn't slow down as they passed the Blood Tonic clinic. I thought maybe they had the right idea, and I kept walking, too.

UNTIL THE WORLD SHATTERS

In April, the fields south of the central Myanmar city of Amarapura are hard packed and brown. The dozens of tributaries snaking toward the Irrawaddy shrivel up into little muddy streams. The banks of the river are the only source of life as the watercourse churns its way south from the Kachin highlands down to the ocean. For a millennium, this area has been the heartland of the country, a flat, open rice bowl that fed the Bamar empire's aggressive growth across the region.

Not many people live in the area now. The few residents are concentrated in ramshackle villages along the Irrawaddy's banks. But the landscape is changing as new money comes into the area, and in the middle of the fields there now rises an enormous monument meant to preserve the memory and glory of Myanmar's heritage.

Its official title is the Werawsana Pagoda, but everyone knows it as the Jade Pagoda.

One government description refers to it as the "Giver of Peace, Progress, Prosperity, Good Fortune, Glory, Fame, Wealth, Immunity From all Dangers, and Wish-Fulfilling Pagoda."

It is the largest structure in the world made entirely out of jade. The project is the brainchild of U Soe Naing, a jade merchant who said that he saved up stones for twenty-five years in order to build the pagoda.

In interviews that air frequently on TV, U Soe Naing describes his personal motivations as coming from one of the foundational precepts of Buddhism: Nothing is permanent. The jade represents substantial personal wealth and a record of his hard-won rise from poor migrant worker to rich mine owner. But in Buddhism, nothing lasts forever. Reality itself evolves and perishes. The only thing that remains is Nirvana. To leave something behind, to enshrine that memory into a physical object glorifying Myanmar's Buddhist legacy, would allow U Soe Naing to build personal merit he could take with him into his next life.

In 2015, *The Global New Light of Myanmar* commissioned one of Myanmar's most renowned historians, Khin Maung Nyunt, to write an English history of the Jade Pagoda. As the structure was only a year old, the historian settled for describing its future importance:

Jade Pagoda is the land mark of Myanmar, It is expected that sooner or later this Jade Pagoda will be engraved in the List of Guinness Book of World Wonders or the UNESCO Cultural Heritage list. Due to this world's First Jade Pagoda in Myanmar, Myanmar's Hotels and Tourism Industry which is right now booming by leaps and bounds, will be further enhanced. Peoples across the world will come to learn the real condition and situation of the country and its ethnic peoples who are now unitedly on a kick off to reach the goal of a modern, peaceful, prosperous democratic state.

Khin Maung Nyunt is a respected writer. He has presented important papers about Myanmar's cross-border trade and has written a popular book about the history of Yangon's religious bells.

I frequently turn to his work as a reference point in my own research, and it feels strange to see his name attached to this kind of vapid promotional material for something that on its surface had very little historical value.

"The whole area is being urbanized," Khin Maung Nyunt wrote. "In no time Hsin Ywa, Myinhmu village that would become a cute Jade Town of international renown."

■

I visit the pagoda on a scorching, cloudless day, and the ground is incredibly hot. At most Myanmar pagodas, the floor is made of white stone to mitigate the warming effects of the sun. But the jade stones covering the grounds attract the punishing sunlight, and by the early afternoon it feels dangerous to walk on the tiles. Barefooted patrons dressed in fancy clothes shuffle from one shady area to the next, avoiding the daylight like crowds of nervous geese.

I join a small group of tourists from Yangon milling around the pagoda in a tight pack. A young woman is their guide. While she lists facts about the pagoda, kids run in and out of the small shrine rooms, and teenagers crouch together with selfie sticks to take photos in front of the different jade Buddha statues.

The tour focuses on the accomplishment of building the world's first jade pagoda. The guide is confident that the international community will soon acknowledge the historical importance of the site and will recognize Myanmar's contributions to humanity's shared heritage. She quotes almost directly from *The Global New Light of Myanmar's* official history:

"Sooner or later, the Jade Pagoda will be listed in the Guinness

Book of World Wonders, or as a UNESCO World Heritage site."

The guide also quotes other figures from the paper's history. She starts her tour by noting our place in the grand scheme of things: "The jade pagoda is located to the west of mile marker 361 on the Yangon–Mandalay Highway."

She continues: "It is 133 feet and 6 inches wide and also 133 feet and 6 inches long. The pagoda is a perfect square. This marvelous jade pagoda is made of grades A, B, C, and D jade stones. Together, these stones weigh over one thousand tons."

No one asks any questions. It feels very solemn. The tour guide brings us to each of the pagoda's small rooms, and people take pictures and move on. In each chamber, an old man stands by to sell postcards of the Jade Pagoda.

When I speak to the guide after the tour, I ask her in Burmese if there is anything else I should know about the pagoda. She replies quickly in English:

"One important thing all foreigners should know is that this is the fifth most beautiful pagoda in Myanmar," she says. "That is why many foreigners want to come visit the jade pagoda. It is an important part of our glorious Myanmar heritage."

It feels like talking to a living, breathing promotional pamphlet, but these sorts of matter-of-fact statements are common in Myanmar. Qualitative judgments are often portrayed as simple facts, especially when talking about beauty and merit.

The failure to separate opinion from fact can sometimes detract from otherwise uncontroversial details and lends a sense of arbitrariness to what should be concrete. I cannot shake the sensation that such pronouncements feel like the voice of authority commanding you how to feel. And it doesn't seem like a huge stretch to see how that type of thinking could transition from aesthetic judgments to moral ones.

■

Attitudes toward places like the Jade Pagoda can often feel like a stand-in for bigger issues affecting the country.

The official history of the Jade Pagoda notes that Buddhism itself could one day cease to exist if its adherents do not work to preserve it. In India, the birthplace of the religion, Hindu and Muslim forces long ago supplanted Buddhism. There is a real fear in some parts of Myanmar society that something similar could happen here. Religious nationalists point to the Taliban's destruction of the world's two largest standing Buddha statues in Afghanistan in 2001 as evidence of Islam's campaign against Buddhism. Public opinion polls have shown that the language of "Muslim Takeover" has permeated into nearly every corner of Myanmar's public discourse. Many people in Myanmar feel that the international community lacks empathy for what they see as an existential threat to their religion.

The Jade Pagoda's history tries to explicitly tie the temple to this effort of preserving the national religion:

"Buddhist monuments are tangible objects important for the concrete evidence of its survival," the history states. "Therefore to preserve and prevent Buddhism from total decline and extinction, it is needed to make relentless efforts."

However, in the same paragraph, the official history notes that physical structures, no matter how well built, will all crumble and shatter under the weight of time. Everything on earth suffers from impermanence. The purpose of the pagoda is not to stand as a universal monument to Buddhism. Being a physical structure, it will eventually disappear. But instead, the Jade Pagoda will bring people to Myanmar's heartland. It can act as a gathering place for the faithful. A place to remember and to attract. The only permanence comes from enlightenment. And maybe the pagoda can be part of that spiritual process for some people.

That is a view of religious heritage and the arc of history that I can understand. And it makes the arbitrary descriptions and over-the-top historicizing seem less triumphant. It is easy to criticize some of the language used to describe monuments like the Jade Pagoda, but maybe the closest highway mile marker is important if it helps you find a sense of place. If it helps you find a sense of self.

■

In Myanmar, history is often viewed as a cycle. Empires grow and contract. Enemies come and go. The cycle will continue until the world itself ends, a kind of impermanence as ultimatum.

The Bamar worldview takes the ending of history as an essential aspect of life. There is a feeling of entropy to the national myth, grounded in the same notion of impermanence that governs history's great wheel. Only by combatting that great universal decay can you break free of the cycle of destruction.

Myanmar's national anthem captures this feeling of needing to combat entropy:

> Until the world ends up shattering, long live Myanmar!
> We love our land because this is our real inheritance.
> We will sacrifice our lives to protect our country,
> This is our nation, this is our land and it belongs to us.

The song was written in 1930 by Saya Tin, a nationalist protesting against the British government. At the time, the goal of the nationalist movement was to liberate the country from the colonial oppressors and reclaim the historical heartland that belonged to Myanmar's native people. When the song was adopted as the national anthem in 1947, the country was on the verge of splitting apart under enormous internal stresses. After the chaos of the Second World War, large portions of the population were militantly opposed to being governed by the Bamar and chose to fight for their own autonomy. The anthem's lyrics reflected this dire situation: The national goal was more about avoiding something negative—destruction from enemies that threatened the state— than it was about any kind of universal affirmation. Only determination and sacrifice would hold the country together.

The anthem can still describe part of the national psyche. Myanmar's official country name is the "Union of Myanmar." The Union is supposed to refer to the diverse set of peoples and geographies that stretch from the sea to the forest, from the river to the mountains. *We are one. We are Myanmar.* But after seventy years of internal strife, there is still no consensus about what that is supposed to mean. Taken together, this history of strife and the fatalistic view toward the future evoke a feeling of foreboding. Something bad might happen. History's cycle is against us. The world will shatter. But until that day, we will make sure Myanmar remains.

The jade pagoda is just one small victory in that battle. In his history, Khin Maung Nyunt describes the ultimate reach of the project:

"To make the Jade Pagoda last as long as our planet Earth exists, the jade pagoda was constructed so that it can withstand an earthquake of 6.59 Richter scale. To enable it to meet heavy storms the bored pile technology was used. On the steel frame, iron nets and cement concretes were added."

■

After speaking with the tour guide at the Jade Pagoda, I go down to the entrance area, where there is a party-like atmosphere. It isn't yet the "Cute Jade Town of International Renown," but for every one pilgrim praying at the pagoda, there are at least three vendors down below, selling light-up LED Buddha images and handheld fans, as well as jade wind chimes and other jade house ornaments.

I buy a soda from one young woman and ask her what she thinks about the pagoda. She has a matter-of-fact perspective on the site, but it is much different from that of the tour guide. "Some rich guy wanted to become famous, so he built this pagoda out of the jade that he couldn't sell to China. It doesn't mean anything to us."

I ask her if anything exciting ever happens at the pagoda, and her friend butts in. "I heard that one time, while they were building the pagoda, a worker fell from the top and broke his leg! He had to be taken to the hospital in Mandalay to get it fixed. But that's about it. Most of the time it's just tourists coming to take pictures."

"But don't you think it's interesting that this is the world's first pagoda made entirely out of jade?" I ask, turning back to the first girl.

She cocks her head and looks at me. "Why would I care about that?"

PART III—RAIN

April 2018–September 2018

THE PINCERS OF BAGAN

In Myanmar there is an old folktale about truth and justice. When the empire was centered in Bagan, any time the king's judges needed to render a decision, they would bring all interested parties in front of an enormous pair of pincers housed in one of the city's pagodas. Both accuser and defendant had to make statements with their hands between the pincers' blades. Whenever someone lied, the pincers would chop of his or her hands. With such high stakes, no one dared to cheat their neighbors, and justice was easy to deliver.

One day, a merchant departing on a long journey asked a lay-brother at the monastery to safeguard his bag of gold. While the merchant was gone, the lay-brother thought about how he could steal the gold without losing his hand to the pincers. Finally coming up with a workable scheme, he hollowed out his staff, melted the gold, poured the molten metal in, and sealed the opening with wax. When the merchant returned from his travels and asked for his gold back, the lay-brother said that he'd already returned it.

Of course, the merchant brought a lawsuit against the lay-brother. The two were called in front of the judge and the pincers. The merchant delivered his testimony first. He put his hands between the sharpened blades and swore that he had entrusted the sack of gold to the lay-brother, and that it had not been returned to him. The crowd watched with bated breath, but the pincers remained motionless. Next came the lay-brother, walking with his staff. Before ascending the dais, he turned to the merchant and said, "Please hold my staff, friend, while I put my hands between the pincers." The unsuspecting merchant gladly held the staff while the lay-brother made his statement. With his hand outstretched, the lay-brother said that the merchant entrusted the sack of gold to him, but that he had returned the gold, which was now with the merchant. As the two stories clearly contradicted one another, the crowd expected the pincers to chop off the lay-brother's hand. When they remained motionless, the judge looked puzzled, and the crowd shouted that the pincers were useless and unjust. Someone must have told a lie, they said, but no one has been punished. They mocked the pincers.

But the judge was a clever man, and he thought the case over. Finally guessing the lay-brother's trick, he asked for the staff, unplugged the top, and retrieved the gold. The merchant received back his property, and the lay-brother was punished for his theft and lies. But due to the trickery, the pincers seemed to have become disgusted with human beings' behavior. They refused to cooperate in the rendering of judgements, and they never again sliced off anyone's hands, even though humans told terrible lies.

9.
====

MOUNTAINS

Indawgyi Lake, Kachin State

Toward the end of the hot season, people in Yangon started carrying umbrellas everywhere, and would peer up into the sky whenever they set out down the sidewalk. The monsoon skies swelled up to hang above the city like a heavy, brooding anvil, but all through the month of April and into early May they refused to break—as though they were holding back for something. The air built up heavier and heavier, and every breath felt pregnant with humid tension.

I was spending more and more time outside of Yangon, traveling to historical sites like Bagan and Pyay, and once I made a long train and bus journey to Muse, the trading town on the Chinese border. But mostly I was shuttling back and forth to Kachin.

Throughout the spring and summer, the north felt like a refuge from the marshy craziness of Yangon. The chaos and clutter were replaced by sunflower fields and a distant horizon broken only by the sharp Kachin mountains. I was trying to learn as much as possible about the effects of the war on everyday people, especially those in the countryside, where there was very little visibility or accountability. Accessing those rural areas was sometimes difficult in Myanmar, where foreigners were restricted to certain administrative areas and immigration authorities tracked people's movement.

One morning in late April, I walked down the stairs in my Myitkyina hotel and saw someone installing a new sign in the entryway. It listed twelve townships in Kachin State that required official permission to visit, and specified, in English:

You are given Punishment without any permission from the law of immigration if you go there

I spent thirty seconds trying to figure out whose permission I needed to be punished, then walked out of the hotel and boarded the 7:30 train south toward Mandalay. I was heading to a remote corner of Kachin State, an isolated lakeside community said to be a Kachin refuge long closed off from the outside world. The historical accounts I had dug out of the old libraries in Yangon had described the Kachin mountains as a nearly impenetrable barrier keeping the outside world at bay. I wanted to see the wilderness firsthand, and to learn if the mountains could still offer protection today. KIO officers had told me that geography would protect the Kachin people forever. But geography was also the reason for a lot of the current economic and political mess. The rugged and remote northern mountains had given the Kachin people refuge and riches, but they had also painted a target on their backs. It had given outsiders a reson to try to conquer the area. I hoped that by visiting an area that was said to still be a glimpse into an old, isolated way of life in the mountains, I could hear a new perspective about the meaning of Kachin land, history, and identity.

As the train blasted its whistle, the sky sizzled with lighting and black clouds pulsed overhead. But the ground stayed dry. Then with a jolt the train moved south, rocking slowly back and forth, as the passengers quickly dozed off.

■

Four hours later, I disembarked in Hopin and hired a motorbike driver to take me two hours west. Workers were slowly constructing a new road over the mountains to Indawgyi Lake, Myanmar's largest body of freshwater. On the road, my driver seemed determined to test how fast he could drive over the new asphalt speed bumps. We passed by several construction crews and police outposts. In northern Myanmar, the farther away you travel from the railroad the less government there seems to be. These lonely police and military outposts—with one or two dozing young men, rifle muzzles hanging low in the dirt—felt more like stubborn reminders of a faraway power than any kind of local authority. The outposts were almost all accompanied by small, hastily erected pagodas slathered in gold paint. As we zoomed past them, my driver would bow his head toward the religious structure and murmur a short prayer under his breath and the motorbike would swerve a bit toward the shoulder.

There was a sense of harsh remoteness to Indawgyi Lake. At first glance, it appeared untouched by Myanmar's wider violent upheavals. The largely untamed wilderness around the lake felt like a protective barrier against outside forces. But it was easy to see where that was changing. Along the lakeshores, large swaths of elephant grass had been cleared for future construction, and the water was swollen with the detritus of new infrastructure. Enormous piles of discarded plastic marked the movements of construction crews on the new road.

Just before our arrival in the village of Lonton, the driver pulled his motorcycle off the road and straight into a small river, where he sloshed water over the engine to cool it down. I gestured to the rainbow slick of oil drifting downstream toward the lake and asked if that was a problem. "It doesn't matter," he said, and pointed at the other men washing their motorbikes in the stream.

■

In the late 1880s, fresh off their military victory against the Bamar kingdom in Mandalay, when the British sent men into northern Myanmar to "pacify" the Kachin tribes, they considered Indawgyi Lake a strategic lynchpin for the district. The lake had long been an economic hub and a natural converging point between the region's three major ethnic groups, the Shan, Kachin, and Bamar. Colonial administrators in Mandalay thought the lake would naturally prosper with the right kind of investment, so on a stormy February morning in 1888, Major Charles Adamson arrived by boat with a team of soldiers. Surrounded by the sharp peaks of the Kachin highlands, Adamson wrote in his journal that he "could see the clear water glistening in the sunshine and just stirred by the slight breeze which was blowing." The major noted that he found the scenery "very diversified and pleasing."

Adamson and his men were finishing a two-month tour of the northern hills, where their purpose was to secure the allegiance of as many Kachin chiefs as possible. The British military had annexed upper Myanmar three years previously, but much of the far north was still ungoverned and unknown to the colonizers. Government administrators in Mandalay referred to these mountainous peripheries as the colony's "Frontier Areas," and planned to rule them as distinct political entities. They believed that the key to exerting the crown's authority in these remote jungles would be a form of indirect rule. While the heavily populated, mostly Bamar areas in the south were subject to direct rule by British officials, people in the mountains would remain under traditional local governance structures, with only a modicum of colonial oversight.

This system—a version of divide-and-conquer tactics based on geography and ethnicity that were common practice throughout the British Empire—would exacerbate many of the already simmering disputes and differences between the mountain-dwelling Kachin and the neighboring groups from the valley and lowlands. Geography had always been tied to political differences between population groups in Myanmar. The colonial policies would institutionalize that separation for decades and hamper efforts toward national reconciliation for generations to come.

Adamson was a thoughtful, if occasionally condescending, observer of his surroundings. The major captured the events of his journey in a memoir titled *A Short Account of an Expedition to the Jade Mines in Upper Burmah, in 1887–1888, With a Map.* Of the difficulty of foot-travel in the northern hills he wrote:

> A journey which in March, when the country is dry, may be done in two days, might be absolutely impracticable in December, when the water had not yet sufficiently dried up; and a road which was good three years before, would, if not frequently used and kept open, be absolutely useless, even if it could be found, at the present time.

The mission was subjugation, and the colonial soldiers were not shy about demanding it. Adamson traveled through the jungles with 150 foot-soldiers, 25 cavalry, and more than 300 pack mules, as well as two trundling mountain artillery pieces and a pair of elephants. (Adamson abandoned the elephants after only a few days in the jungle, recognizing the sheer impracticality of such huge beasts moving through the difficult terrain. But several times during the expedition, he ordered the mountain guns to launch artillery shells at faraway mountaintops, leveling small clearings in the forest as an easy way to frighten villages into submission.) The quick securing of allegiance was paramount, because Adamson's commanders in Mandalay were convinced that controlling the northern mountains—filled with rubies, teak, rubber, gold, and jade—would pave the way to great financial returns.

The administrators were blunt and transactional in their demands: An end to nationalist resistance and an agreement to pay taxes were the only requirements needed to declare a village effectively pacified. By this metric,

Adamson's expedition was largely a success. The major secured the allegiance of nearly every Kachin chief he met, and brokered a deal with the
chiefs of the Kansi clan, who controlled access to the jade mines in the
mountains to the northwest. With the flow of the precious stone secured,
the British believed that they would soon be able to tap into the lucrative
cross-border gemstone trade between Kachin and China.

By other metrics, the mission was less successful. Despite Adamson's
victory in "forcibly reaching the Jade Mines," the British military would
spend the better part of the next decade trying to secure the region—visiting each area of the Kachin hills in turn, surveying the land, and trying to
convince the local chiefs of the benefits of agreeing to subjugation. Every
autumn, the British sent a group of more than one hundred military policemen, called the Jade Mines Escort, to "control the disorderly rabble that
assembles there during the cold season." Nevertheless, profits from the jade
trade eluded the colonial overlords, and they lashed out at Kachin chiefs,
whom they suspected of hindering their progress or harboring insurgents.

The colonial administrators sometimes considered these people and
their livelihoods in terms of assets and liabilities, an expendable feature of
the land that they could use or abuse at will. When the British launched
punitive raids on Kachin leaders, like Jalin's grandfather, they described the
results in detached, clinical prose:

> Forty-six villages containing some 639 houses were burnt and
> 509,000 lbs. (about 227 1/4 tons) of paddy destroyed. It is
> impossible to estimate the enemy's loss. Seventeen dead bodies were
> found: their loss was probably heavier, but the jungle was too thick
> to allow of a correct estimate being made. Sixty-three buffaloes
> and four cows were killed. The losses amongst the troops were four
> killed, one a British Officer who died from the effects of a wound
> in the foot from a *panji*, and thirty-five wounded; total killed and
> wounded thirty-nine.

Adamson had already spent more than two decades in Myanmar and knew most of the country well, but he was still impressed by the wilds of the north. Around Indawgyi Lake, he found a rugged, untamed landscape that challenged his soldiers. The men could rarely see beyond the five-foot-high elephant grass growing on the banks. Twice, the strong winds on the surface of the lake forced the boats aground, where the soldiers found little but trees filled with vultures and the tracks of wild elephants and tigers. Despite the natural bounty of the lake, few people were living there; almost every village Adamson found was abandoned.

The lake, which at one point had been the site of economic cooperation, had erupted in chaotic violence in 1883. A small-time trader from the lake, claiming to be the reincarnation of a legendary Shan warrior prince called Hawsaing, managed to rally four hundred Kachin warriors to his cause. He spent most of the next year raiding Shan and Bamar towns and caravans throughout the district. In a pattern that would repeat for more than a century, the king in Mandalay responded to this northern rebellion by sending in an enormous military force from the south. The soldiers marched through the rebel's home, burning everything.

Nearly five years after this short conflict, Adamson's party could only find a smattering of inhabitants anywhere around the lake. The company camped near a village called Lonton on the western bank, where Adamson interviewed several residents. Writing in his journal, he concluded that, "It was from this district that the Kachins started when they rebelled and attacked the Burmese. They forced all the inhabitants of Endaw to join them, burning and plundering all those villages where the inhabitants dared to oppose them."

The next day, Adamson circumnavigated the lake and quickly departed. But the Major left with a sense of optimism, recognizing the economic potential of the region:

"There are not more than 100 houses in the whole place. I expect that in ten years there will be ten times the number, and that the place, instead of being a desert, will be a highly cultivated and flourishing province."

∎

Foreigners that visit Lake Indawgyi are only allowed to stay in Lonton village, the same spot on the western bank that Adamson's men explored in 1888. It is still not much more than a small collection of wooden shacks sandwiched between the asphalt road and the water's edge. While most of the lake feels cut off from the rest of Myanmar, protected by a ring of mountains and thick jungle, Lonton village has the feel of a lonely military outpost. The single guesthouse is right next to a Tatmadaw fort. Every evening at sundown, the soldiers dragged two large barbed-wire barriers across the road and harassed anyone coming back and forth. The guesthouse manager told me that this was for the village's protection. "There is KIA in the mountains."

The economic paradise that the British had hoped for more than a century earlier was still a struggling backwoods area caught between sides in a war with no end. While some of the wilderness had been tamed, and the jade money was flowing down from the nearby mountains, none of the natural wealth appeared to have improved the lives of the lakeside residents. Rebel forces stood guard in the mountains west of the lake, mining gold and felling trees to sell for their war effort. Southern businessmen slashed the forest. And all through the week, enormous empty dump trucks trundled north on the bumpy road toward the jade mines of Hpakan.

On my first afternoon in the village, two teenagers approached me on the shore of the lake. "Hey, bro, what are you doing here?" one of them asked in English. It wasn't a combative question, just genuine curiosity about why I was visiting the lake. The young man introduced himself as Naw Seng. He was wearing tight black jeans and a flannel button-down shirt, which seemed unnecessarily warm for the hundred-degree weather. Almost all the men in town wore longyis and loose-fitting tank tops, but Naw Seng cut an urbane look. He had long coiffed hair and black plastic glasses frames without any lenses.

Naw Seng told me he was seventeen years old and was born and raised in Lonton village. He was from the southern section of town, which he called the Kachin ward. There was a clear line running through the village: Buddhists lived in the north, around the pagoda and the Tatmadaw outpost, while Kachin Christians were gathered in the south, surrounding two stone church buildings—one for the Baptists, another for the Catholics. Naw Seng asked me if I wanted to tour the Kachin area with him.

This was something that would often happen when I visited desperately remote areas like Lonton village. Smart local kids—always boys—would latch onto me for the day. Naw Seng had spent a few years going to school on the outskirts of Yangon, and now all he could think about was leaving the village. "I want to get out of here, bro," he told me. "There is nothing to do here." When I asked what he did at night he said, "Nothing, just look at my Facebook."

Naw Seng told me his father worked in the jade mines, and rarely came home to visit the family in Lonton. The teenager lived with his mother, who sold rice that she grew on a small plot of land. He told me that he didn't see a future for himself in the town, despite the fact that his family had lived there for generations. "This place is dying," he said, while we stared at a small pile of plastic that had washed up into the reeds. "I care about the lake, but there is nothing for me here. I cannot stay here."

I asked him about the resource-rich geography around the lake, which many Kachin consider to be their birthright. "I'm not interested in that. My father and uncles, they care. But look at it. The Bamar have taken everything from the Kachin. That's why we all just want to get out of here."

Later, Naw Seng showed me his house, a small one-story wooden structure with a fence of crooked branches and a few goats and chickens milling about in the dirt. On the road outside, the government had erected a public awareness billboard instructing the Lonton villagers how to preserve the lake. The faded sign showed cartoon pictures of fishermen, each with a big red X over it:

Do not electrocute fish.
Do not poison fish.
Do not use explosives to catch fish.
Do not harvest fish while they are spawning.

I asked Naw Seng if other warnings should be posted to the sign. "The government should help fight the pollution," he said. I asked if the KIA, which operated illegal gold mines nearby that released mercury into the water table, should be held responsible for damaging the lake.

Naw Seng thought for a moment. "That is just a story that the Tatmadaw says," he replied. "The KIA only hide in the mountains so they can fight for the Kachin people. The Tatmadaw wants to take our land."

•

Naw Seng was a music fan, and as we walked south toward the fields nearby Lonton, he quizzed me on my favorite musicians. He knew far more about the American pop scene than I did. He asked me what my favorite Justin Bieber song was, and when I told him that I didn't have one, he was disappointed. "Justin Bieber is my favorite singer," he said. We walked for a while in silence, then he asked me, "Is Justin Bieber Satan?"

I was tempted to say yes, but instead asked, "Why would you think that?"

"Someone at the church told me that." Then he was silent for a bit more. "I want to be a singer," Naw Seng blurted out, "But I cannot." He flipped his hair and gave a teenager's dramatic pause. "You can guess why."

I spent a couple hours walking around the Kachin part of town with Naw Seng, trying to figure out why he thought he couldn't be a singer and listening to him talk about his plans for the future. None of them involved staying in Kachin State. His dreams all lay "out there"—in Yangon or in Mandalay or further afield in Bangkok and Los Angeles. If he couldn't be a singer, he told me, he would like to be a fashion model, a burgeoning profession in a country that had only been exposed to social media for a few years. And if that didn't work, he could always be a tour guide with his good English, he assured me.

Naw Seng promised to show me a pretty section of the lake, but we couldn't find the path, and then got lost trying to work our way through a neighbor's farm. It seemed strange that after living in such a small village his whole life, he could still get lost going for a short walk. After a while he told me that I was walking too fast, and suggested we go back and walk back up the main road where the ground was flatter. "I don't ever walk around here," he explained, breathing heavily. "I only take the motorbike or stay at home. My family and my ancestors all lived in Lonton, but for me the roots are gone. I don't know the village as well as the rest of my family."

Naw Seng liked to point out all the trash on the side of the roads and kept saying how shortsighted and foolish the other village residents were. "People that throw it on the side of the road are selfish," he told me. "It is bad for the lake." When we passed the canal where my motorbike driver had washed his engine, Naw Seng said that the little stream had been backed up for the past two years, because people keep using it as a place to throw their rubbish.

The only places in Myanmar with government-run garbage collection services were Yangon and Mandalay. Out here in the countryside, there was no way to dispose of trash other than littering or burning it. A local NGO had constructed rubbish bins out of old fishing net, but it was clear that the bins hadn't caught on yet. When I asked Naw Seng what he did with his trash, he admitted that he threw it on the side of the road, because he didn't know what else to do with it.

Our walk led us back through the Buddhist section of town. The area around the village school ground was bustling with activity. The next day was the full moon, and the entire village would celebrate with an elaborate ceremony. Hundreds of young boys from the area would use the auspicious holiday as an opportunity to become novice monks. They would march up and down the main street in colorful regalia, accompanied by musicians and lavishly ornamented elephants. I asked Naw Seng if he would go to see the parade, and he reminded me that as a Christian Kachin, he didn't hold any special fondness for the full moon. "But anyone in the town can go," he said. "They make it so that it's the whole town that celebrates, not just the Buddhists. All of the soldiers will come out too, to cheer on the parade."

We followed the perimeter of the school, watching as the older men in town organized the chariots and parade floats for the next day, then continued on back to my guesthouse.

That night, dark clouds rolled in over the giant lake, and the wind came in hard from the east. The power went out in the little village, and all I could see from the guesthouse was the Tatmadaw outpost, silhouetted by lightning.

•

When you speak to Kachin people about their home, the first thing that most people talk about is the importance of the mountaintops, the hundreds of little valleys, and the furrows that guide the streams that feed together at the Confluence to form the Irrawaddy River. Land is livelihood. Land is history. Land is identity. Awng Li, a Kachin philosopher and theologian who studies traditional Kachin spirituality, told me once that the northern mountains were the center of Kachin identity, and that the spirit of every Kachin person is tied to that land. "Even if a Kachin person meets another in San Francisco or London, they will ask where their family is from. What clan, what area? That is how we know who we are."

The Kachin are not the only ethnic group that links their cultural heritage to this rugged geography. Myanmar's northern mountains are part of a chain running from northwest Afghanistan to the highlands of central Vietnam, containing some of the most varied sets of wildlife, peoples, and histories of any region on Earth. State control over these highland areas has proven historically difficult. The traditional political powers of Asia all arose from low-lying, flat river valleys conducive to wet rice cultivation. In the seventeenth century, a state like Myanmar's power was directly correlated to its ability to sustain a large amount of manpower and project that force outward. Feeding and controlling these large populations required ease of commerce, quick communication, and sustainable infrastructure, as well as a liberal use of forced labor. The steep mountain highlands, with their hostile locals and difficult terrain, made moving supplies and people extraordinarily difficult. An army that could march one hundred miles a week on flat land may have only been able to cover half that distance in the mountains. That distance might be even less if other geographic features were taken into account: deadly strains of local malaria; temperatures that could range from broiling in the day to freezing at night; and above all, an enemy familiar with the local terrain.

These geographic hurdles add up to something the political scientist James Scott has called "friction of distance" in the Southeast Asian highlands. In his book, *The Art of Not Being Governed: An Anarchist History of Upland Southeast Asia*, Scott describes how these hostile mountain environs provided refuge for groups whose way of life was threatened by the growth of the monolithic state structures of the lowlands. Instead of being coerced into labor or conscripted into military service in the Bamar kingdom, the Kachin and hundreds of other small communities like them survived in these safe spaces, which Scott refers to as "shatter zones." He describes these areas as places "where the human shards of state formation and rivalry accumulated willy nilly, creating regions of bewildering ethnic and linguistic complexity." Whereas the lowland empires encouraged sameness and homogeneity in its subjects, these asylum areas welcomed a diversity of political, social, and religious structures. The mountains provided shelter for those who rebelled—groups like the Kachin—who refused to assimilate to what they saw as the tyrannical rule of the southern Bamar. The geography offered physical, social, and spiritual protection.

Today, close to one hundred million people live in these highlands, which for centuries have provided secret refuge from the power of the lowland empires. Living in these mountain communities has always required a high degree of mobility and a way of life tied directly to the features of the land that is so hostile to outsiders. Life was different in the mountains. Instead of stationary rice cultivation, most highland clans practiced roving slash-and-burn agriculture. They were mobile and hard to find. While the Bamar developed a top-down system of imperial rule, many Kachin groups thrived under an arrangement of participatory politics that encouraged dissent. And while Buddhism spread across all of the lands touched by the Bamar kingdoms, the Kachin followed an animist tradition based on worshipping traditional spirits known as *nats*. The same held true for many of the Naga, Chin, and Karen minority groups around Myanmar's mountainous periphery. These populations were able to maintain their traditional religious identities until the arrival of missionary groups toward the end of the nineteenth century, and today many are Christian rather than Buddhist.

Across Asia, mountain communities were often characterized by their dissent from and objection to the political projects of the lowlands. As empires expanded, it was the newly swallowed minority populations which were forced to work as slaves and soldiers in rigorously ordered class systems. Escaping those laws meant moving into the mountains where the lowland armies could not function. In that sense, the mountains acted as a form of justice for minority groups, a way of balancing the scales.

This tradition of mountaintop autonomy continues today in places beyond Southeast Asia. Despite decades of war in Afghanistan and Pakistan, state authority has yet to fully arrive in many mountain communities. And in India's far northeast, the hill tribes of Arunachal Pradesh stand apart in their autonomous Himalayan enclave. In the mountains, old secrets still live on.

That isolation could also become a commercial asset. Beginning in the late 1980s in eastern Myanmar, the Wa people carved out a completely autonomous state in the steepest parts of the Shan hills. Despite being nominally part of Myanmar territory, the Wa state functioned with complete economic and political impunity, maintaining a standing army thirty thousand strong, financed mainly through the narcotics trade. But its enclave status made it enormously valuable for the Chinese to launder money and tamper with Myanmar politics. Today, the Wa are almost entirely controlled by China, which has placed "advisors" in every part of the Wa government. Isolation as a kind of branding, and mountaintop autonomy for sale.

Some analysts allege that Laiza, the KIA mountaintop stronghold on the border with China, functions in a similar way. On the Myanmar side of the border, steep mountain paths and enemy batallions and landmines prevented any kind of regular economic life. But the roads into China were freshly paved and safe. KIA officials used Chinese banks and Chinese cell phones and Chinese weapons. And Laiza was only a three-hour drive to the

Chinese jade trading town of Ruili. The KIA's war let gems and drugs and people traffic back and forth over the border, but often it was Chinese businsses and criminal networks that profited the most.

These kinds of exploitative economic arrangements had changed the meaning of life in the mountains. For the Kachin, the northern geography had long been seen as a defense against the power of the Bamar kingdom. But unlike most other highland areas in Asia, the Kachin hills are also home to unparalleled natural wealth. Once the outside world got a glimpse of what lay underground, the mountains transformed from an asset to a liability. Like other groups around the world that suddenly found themselves in possession of commodities that other groups need or value, the Kachin were both blessed and cursed by their access to resources. Objects like jade, which held no intrinsic value but was coveted by outsiders, became a reason for war. For centuries, the Kachin were able to fend off these incursions. But the modern world and its war machines and earth movers had finally broken into the mountain refuge. Indawgyi Lake was supposed to be a glimpse of old Kachin, and while it was still cut off from the rest of the world, that isolation could no longer be considered a source of strength. The mountains now seemed primarily like an enormous hurdle keeping rural people away from all the benefits of Myanmar's economic development—a marker for inequality that you could read on a map.

With the loss of this highland autonomy also came the gradual loss of much of the unique cultural and political identity tied to that geography. The secrecy of the mountain communities was being forgotten by the younger generation. Awng Li, the theologian, described to me how the loss of unconquered safe spaces in northern Myanmar had made it extremely difficult to find Kachin people who still practiced the traditional spirituality that he studied.

Awng Li told me that much of the Kachin history related to land was carried down through the oral tradition, and that these stories were at risk of disappearing. Devoid of a connection to their homeland, younger people no longer remembered the creation stories beyond what they heard in church. When I asked Bum Tsit, in Myitkyina, if he remembered the old stories, he said no. "My grandmother and aunt know more about that. When I go to the Kachin traditional festivals the old people will tell the stories. But for me it is not as important."

"Oral tradition passes the myths and stories down through the generations," Awng Li said. "The wisest must recite stories about god and creation. That man is a diviner. He speaks in a language humans cannot understand. He is able to communicate in the language of the spirits, through the good spirits, about the plan of the Supreme Being . . . That is an inborn heritage. We are part of creation. But not owners of it."

•

Formerly the heavens high were not,

The stable earth had no existence.

Where since were fixed the heavens high,

The fleeting cloud alone appeared.

Where now the solid earth is seen,

The fairy-fowl alone was found.

—Excerpt from "Kachin creation myth," from *The Kachins, Their Customs and Traditions* by Ola Hanson

•

In the morning, I watched from the small balcony of the guesthouse as the handmade pirogues motored out into the center of the lake, which shone with a pale stillness under the still-heavy sky. On the shore, old women gossiped while they beat wet clothes against the rocks. The absence of young people was conspicuous. In any other small town in northern Myanmar, it was common to see the younger generation engaged in household work and the daily commerce of village life. Or, if their parents could afford it, they would stream up and down the road in morning packs on the way to school. But Lonton had a strange emptiness. Small children played together in the village's green spaces, and the older generation managed the handful of beer stations and sundry shops along the main stretch. But the middle generation seemed to have all disappeared; the group that would make up the future of Lonton was missing. Naw Seng was one of the few young men that I met the entire time I spent on the lake. And the stillness of the morning seemed to reinforce what he had told me the day before: "For me, the roots are gone."

That morning, I rented a bike and went up the west bank of Indawgyi Lake, hoping to find a famous floating pagoda where Major Adamson's boat had smashed against the shore during a storm in 1888. The woman that rented me the old bicycle warned me to stay on the road. "There was fighting yesterday between the Tatmadaw and KIA, just on the other side of the hill."

The road passed through miles of desiccated brown farmland. Much of it was staked with barbed wire covered in signs that said "Jadeland Companies." Jadeland is a conglomerate owned by the richest man in Kachin State, Yup Zaw Hkawng, and some local groups were worried that his investments around the lake would lead to further environmental mismanagement. Shadowy businessmen, the "cronies" close to the Tatmadaw, had purchased most of the virgin land around the lake, and were planning on building luxury resorts that would supposedly cater to both domestic and international tourists once the road to the lake was finished. Locals complained that no one would come and the hotels would just be used to launder money. But they held out some hope that the construction projects would offer short-term jobs for unemployed young men—something a little closer to home than the jade mines in Hpakan.

Steven Tsa Ji, the director of a local development policy organization, scoffed at the investments around Indawgyi. "They are just getting ready to build hotels," he told me. "It is just like the Hukawng Valley," he said, referring to a famed forest in a remote area of Kachin State that had been set aside as a tiger preserve, only to be secretly logged by developers like Yup Zaw Hkawng once attention had shifted elsewhere. Well-connected businessmen would do the same around Indawgyi Lake, Steven told me—using hidden government connections to purchase vast swaths of land and using construction projects to launder dark money while the locals waited for a promised economic windfall that may never arrive.

More than a century after the British colonial expedition to the lake, outside businessmen saw the region around Indawgyi the same way as Major Adamson: as an untapped economic resource that would thrive with external investment and management. And the locals were still mostly an afterthought—an expendable feature of the mountains.

In 2014, the area around the lake was designated a UNESCO World Heritage site. It became subject to certain environmental regulations to protect the lake's unique biosphere. Endangered species like the Burmese peacock turtle and the white-rumped vulture live in Indawgyi, and the lake functions as an important site for migratory water birds from across Central Asia and Siberia.

The UNESCO designation came with recommendations to protect the lake: less fishing; less pesticides; fewer mercury-dumping gold mines. Human waste from Buddhist pilgrims that flock to the area in February needed to be better managed. The UNESCO designation called for the promotion of sustainable, traditional agricultural and fishing practices to preserve the lake.

Community-managed ecotourism could replace lost income for locals, but business was slow to pick up. Get-rich-quick schemes like artisanal gold mining had continued. The local authorities were forced to acknowledge that the environmental protections were not as strong as they hoped. On the map that I picked up at the tourism center, the western mountains were labeled with a skull and crossbones and a written warning not to venture near the gold mines that the KIA operated.

I rode past miles of barbed-wire-fenced farmland abutting fine lakeside real estate. The vista was forlorn and beautiful. The cloudy reflection coming off the lake indicated the coming storm, and the wind carried the sharp iron twang of a sky preparing to dump rain, but the road stayed dry. Every so often, it would curve through a small village, where someone would sell pressed sugarcane juice or little bags of yellow mango. The sky was steely and dark, and lightning began flashing over the western mountains. Occasionally the sound of sporadic rifle fire would echo down to the lake, but whether it was hunters or soldiers, I could not tell.

I had given teenage Naw Seng my mobile phone number, and that day, he sent me more than a dozen text messages during my bike ride. One read: "Where r u? Let's go to look the view and I want speak in English and also I just want to be free with you bro."

Another said: "Are you boring with Lonton? Are you boring with me?"

The rental bicycle broke down just as I reached the floating pagoda. Instead of looking for someone to help me re-attach the pedal, I got a boatman to carry me and the bike back to Lonton village for 10,000 kyats. On the water, I asked him how things had changed since the lake had become a special preserve and construction began on the road. "It feels like all the Kachin left," he told me. "The fishermen come from outside and they take all the fish from the lake." He dipped a hand in the water and looked at me.

"They say there is more money. They say that they will make it a place for tourism and that we will all benefit, but that will never happen while the fighting continues. You are one of the only Westerners I have had as a customer. Only Myanmar people visit. Buddhists come to see the pagoda."

The boatman continued: "The rains will come soon. Then I will go to the pagoda and meditate for one week."

For most people in Myanmar, especially for devout Buddhists, the rainy season was a time for cleansing and rebirth—marking the beginning of a new year and a chance to plant new seeds. But it could also be a time of violence. When the rains come through, floods and landslides clear away villages, changing the landscape. It is a force that comes and goes and is mostly invisible, but which changes things in a permanent kind of way.

■

The tourist office was empty when I returned. I was ready to go back to the guesthouse when a young woman trotted across the road from a small restaurant stall to open up the building and take back the busted bicycle. She apologized and said that since there were hardly any tourists these days, they didn't do regular maintenance on the bikes.

Later, I met up with Naw Seng and we walked through the Kachin ward and talked about the KIA. Naw Seng's parents named him after one

of the greatest heroes of the Kachin independence movement, who led battalions of Kachin fighters against the Japanese during World War II, and
then against the central government during the 1950s and 1960s.

I asked the teenage Naw Seng what he thought about his namesake and
he said that he had been told stories of the famous warrior when he was a
kid, but that the name did not inspire him to join the fight.

"Do you want to know why there is fighting?" he asked me. "It's because
the Bamar want to take this," and he swept his arm at the lake and surrounding mountains. "They want Kachin State to be theirs. But I will not
fight them."

Like most Kachin people, Naw Seng had cousins and uncles who fought
for the KIA. But no one from his immediate family had joined the revolution. Naw Seng said he supported the rebellion, but had learned from his
father to distrust the KIA's leaders for profiting alongside the Tatmadaw at
the expense of the poorest Kachins.

"If the KIA did not make peace, then the Bamar people would not have
taken so much from us," Naw Seng said, referring to seventeen-year ceasefire
between 1994 and 2011. "The KIA leaders don't represent all the Kachin
people. They are rich and we are all poor. My father says that is why we had to
go to war. Because these are our mountains. Not Bamar. This is Kachin land."

Lonton was an economically depressed place with few opportunities. It
seemed like the kind of environment that would encourage idle young men
to take up arms. But when I asked Naw Seng if he ever thought of joining
the insurgency, he was quick to shake his head. "I am too afraid to fight," he
said.

Naw Seng had even fewer choices than someone like Bum Tsit in Myitkyina. In the city, an enterprising and smart young person could at least
make some outside connections and start a business, even if it meant com-
promising on some of their values. But for Naw Seng and the rest of Lonton,
there was really no option other than to take up arms or leave Kachin State.
That was one of the hidden costs of the northern war that was often absent
from newspaper articles—how perpetual violence and mismanagement
closed in around families until it forced people into decisions they wouldn't

otherwise make. That's why Lonton had so few young people; they had all made the inevitable choice to leave.

Indawgyi Lake laid bare many of the contradictions of the Kachin civil war. Making peace in the 1990s had cost the Kachin people the security of their mountain refuges and the natural wealth that they considered a birthright. But the long, painful civil war of the 2010s was only making the situation worse. Peace was costly, and war seemed pointless—and this limbo sapped hope from the next generation of Kachin. For a young man like Naw Seng, there were few good choices. Even the idea of being a singer was too fraught for him. "A Kachin cannot be a pop singer," he finally told me after I pressed him on why he thought his dream was impossible. "You can only become popular if you sing about the war and the politics and old Kachin traditions. I don't want that."

Instead, he dreamed simply of leaving home. And the brief glimpse of a life outside Indawgyi—a new road, a foreign tourist, a Justin Bieber song—only added to his determination to leave his ancestral home behind and start something new that had nothing to do with Kachin State or its mountains or its war or its jade money.

It was my last evening in Lonton, and Naw Seng said that he wanted to walk me back to my guesthouse to say goodbye. When we passed by the military checkpoint, he put his head down and swept his bangs over his face. "I don't like this place," he said to me in English as we walked. "They see every Kachin as an enemy."

■

I had come to the lake to try to understand how the ancient sources of Kachin strength—geography, a sense of community, and beautiful, rugged wilderness—functioned today. But the mountain strongholds that Adamson's men had encountered were long gone. In many ways, the Major's parting thoughts about Indawgyi Lake still rang true today:

It was hoped that with unlimited rice plains, a magnificent lake swarming with fish, a Government that would enforce peace, with open water communications and in the near future a railroad, this beautiful country would recover prosperity. All that can be said after a generation has passed is that "it is only beginning to recover from the devastation caused by the Kachin rising of 1883" . . . So much easier is it to destroy than to restore.

The morning I left the lake, the skies finally opened up and dumped silver sheets of water. On the way back to the train, my motorbike driver didn't stop on the side of the road to pray at the new pagodas, and he didn't talk to me at all. Instead, he clenched his teeth and steeled himself as he drove headlong into the downpour.

The hot season was over. The rains had come.

10.

VOICE OF THE YOUTH

Yangon

On a steamy Yangon evening, several hundred young people gathered at a public park near Kandawgyi Lake to watch and listen to some of Myanmar's most popular music groups. The security guards out front had confiscated glass bottles and aluminum cans for safety reasons, but provided plastic grocery bags for people to pour their beers into and sip through straws. When audience members put their hands in the air and moved to the music, limp bags of beer sloshed everywhere, showering nearby dancers.

The concert, titled Voice of the Youth, was a showcase for punk, heavy metal, and rap—genres that were traditionally underground, but were quickly gaining momentum in Myanmar. Part of the reason for the surge in popularity was the explosion of mobile Internet and Facebook during the last few years that had made it possible for bands to communicate directly to their fans and arrange and advertise concerts in a matter of hours. But much of the new music was also popular because of its subject matter. The young musicians spoke to the country's youth about all the topics that had been taboo until very recently: alienation against a militarized system, questioning of authority, doing drugs and having sex.

The crowd was the most eclectic I had ever seen in Myanmar. Transgender women walked about in groups without concern. Young men in flat-brim caps and Jordan sneakers huddled together and bounced to the hip-hop beats. Heavy metal fans with enormous dyed mohawks were head-banging near the front of the stage. There were even a few men sporting Nazi regalia on top of their denim jackets and studded metal belts.

Toward the end of the night the punk rock band Side Effect took the stage. Like all good rock bands, the four musicians wore all black and had carefully sculpted facial hair. Side Effect's music was overtly political. Unlike a lot of modern bands in Myanmar, they didn't sing about chasing girls or going to clubs. Their songs were about making yourself heard and about the hollowness of modern commercial culture. The band had been together since 2004, and had helped grow the punk rock scene from small do-it-yourself shows held in secret into a commercially viable art form with a significant following. In the process, they had become one of the most well-known and influential music groups in Myanmar, which brought their anti-establishment message to young people across the country. The band had toured in Europe and America, and had recorded their recent album at studios in Germany and France. At the concert, they were the most polished band on stage. Live music in Myanmar could often be more about emotion than musicianship. Bad tunings and poor harmonies were balanced by unbridled dancing and a palpable feeling of tension being released. The sound reflected the fact that it was difficult to find the time, space, or money to be a professional musician in Myanmar—most bands just lacked practice. But Side Effect exuded the confidence and stage presence of a seasoned group.

Halfway through the set, the band's lead singer and songwriter, a thirty-six-year-old who called himself Darko C, turned to the crowd and asked the young concertgoers to split in two. Then he instructed them to yell at each other: I hate you! I love you!

"What feels better?" he asked the crowd. Then he brought up the taboo subject: "This song is about Meikhtila."

It had been four and a half years since Buddhist mobs had massacred local Muslims in the central Myanmar town of Meikhtila, and it was an event that was almost never spoken about. For many people in the crowd, it was the first time that they had heard the word "Meikhtila," being publicly used to refer to the killings. "It's the secret everyone knows about but is afraid to say," said one concertgoer next to me.

In Side Effect's tribute, the memory of the massacre came alive in a heavy, driving bass line and cascading electric guitar riffs. In his lyrics, Darko railed against what he saw as the hypocrisy of the Buddhist rioters, and the feeling that there was no way to reverse the terror that had taken place.

Are you a believer or a murderer
or the devil crushing voiceless people?
The smell of your hatred
stinks when you spread your
message in the air
Look what you've done

The young people in the crowd thrashed and screamed to the angry music. The remnants of the plastic beer bags were ground into a soggy pulp against the asphalt. When Darko crooned—*We wont forget this!*—one concertgoer near the stage screamed into the sky and tore at his shirt until the buttons went flying. During a night of largely happy and upbeat dancing, the mood had suddenly become a lot darker. There was a sense of anger and loss in Side Effect's music. Even the people that didn't understand all of the song's English lyrics said later that they felt the importance of the song. "It's more than words. All of Myanmar feels this loss and sorrow," one young man told me. "This is the truth that our government doesn't want us to know. But we remember."

•

Sectarian and ethnic fault lines can be highly visible in Myanmar. Geographic regions are named after dominant ethnic groups. Certain urban areas are commonly referred to as "Muslim neighborhoods." On Myanmar TV shows, it wasn't uncommon to hear characters refer to a South Asian person as "*kalar*," a word that is considered a racial epithet in many communities. But intercommunal violence was for the most part restricted to the peripheries of Myanmar's society. The battles between ethnic militias and the Tatmadaw took place in remote mountains. And in the case of Rakhine, the Muslim targets of Buddhist mob violence had already been erased from most facets of Myanmar's society through decades of propaganda. These sorts of battles happened in the shadows, which made it easy to not think or talk about them. In cities like Yangon, they were rarely discussed in public except when the Tatmadaw proclaimed its victories in the media. Government officials made it clear that other public discussion of these unsightly events was both unpatriotic and harmful to national security.

Even foreigners living in Myanmar, many of whom worked in the humanitarian space, were mostly careful about where and when they discussed things like the violence against the Rohingya. In private, most people referred to it as a genocide, but there was a prevailing sense within the expatriate community that there were very few places in Myanmar where you could say the same thing publicly. Many of my close friends worked for international humanitarian or development agencies, within the UN system, or at Western embassies in Yangon. At one time or another, most of them said they were nervous to bring up these subjects with their local colleagues, who nearly all supported the Tatmadaw's campaign in Rakhine. "I can't believe how much we all capitulate to this national craziness," a friend who worked on refugee issues told me. "I feel like we're going to look back at this twenty years from now and really regret not speaking up louder. Are we like the people who didn't say anything in Rwanda in 1994?"

One of the few places where it was easier to publicly air dissenting views was in the arts and music community, where alternative crowds were more accommodating of unpatriotic ideas. That was one reason why the Side Effect shows attracted such a diverse group of fans—everyone from drag queens to drug dealers could identify with Darko's lyrics and the sense of not really belonging in modern Myanmar.

A few weeks after the concert, I sat down with Darko and he explained to me why he had written a song about Meikhtila when no one else in Myanmar would talk about the killings. Sitting in a coffee shop, he was still visibly distraught over the memory of the 2013 massacre:

"The Meikhtila incident hit me really hard. It showed us all that this violence was not just about the Rohingya people, like the government was saying. The real problem is inside. It's towards Muslim people."

The massacre had capped off a season of sectarian violence from 2012 to 2013 that had shaken the musician's belief in himself and in his country. Like most Bamar people, Darko grew up in a religious household. Almost all of his friends were practicing Buddhists. His only information about the violence against the Rohingya came from people he knew living in Rakhine State, who told him that the fighting in the region was only due to Muslim terrorists conspiring against the local Buddhist population. But after the Meikhtila riots, the singer began to believe in a different truth: that it was Myanmar's government and religious authorities who were perpetrating a conspiracy against not just the Rohingya, but all the country's Muslims. In protest, he renounced his Buddhist faith and declared to his friends and family that he was becoming an atheist.

"Buddhism was like a threshold for my thoughts," he explained. "It was something stopping me from going further. Because Buddha supposedly said one thing or another, and he can't be wrong, it meant that I couldn't think beyond that."

It was not such a dramatic leap for Darko to accept that the government would conspire against a minority group to disenfranchise them. As a rebellious youth growing up under the yoke of military rule, he had learned to fear and evade the reach of the government's propaganda and intelligence arms. Later, as a young songwriter, he had been required to submit all his lyrics to the censorship board before he could record his songs, a process that he despised. In an interview Darko gave to the *Los Angeles Times*, he lampooned the censorship process: "They are not musically literate at all," he said. "They are from the military. They got promoted . . . They are stupid, man. You can't negotiate with them."

Through the censorship board and other restrictions on free expression, the military government had systematically outlawed a lifestyle that the teenage Darko aspired to. He and his friends were all rock music aficionados who looked up to American musicians and a lifestyle that was completely foreign in Myanmar. For years, he had followed bands in other countries as they lashed out against everything they saw wrong in the world, or else just poked their finger in the eye of the authority for the fun of it. Darko had grown up rebelling against his teachers and hating his government, but when he became an artist he found himself in the absurd position of being censored by the very regime he was protesting against.

Like the country's journalists, Myanmar's musicians saw 2012's relaxing of censorship laws as a once-in-a-lifetime opportunity. Musicians were no longer required to get censorship approval before recording. For Darko, it was a chance to finally write down all the forbidden thoughts that he had bottled up, and he quickly found a growing audience that responded to his message. He told me he saw the new freedoms as a new responsibility. He started writing about taboo subjects like Meikhtila, screaming outward to larger and larger crowds the secrets that Myanmar's government wanted to keep in the dark.

■

One challenge for musicians in Myanmar was finding venues to play. Even in Yangon, there were hardly any public spaces where young people could get together and listen to music. The lack of free space wasn't so much a policy as it was a social hangover from decades of artistic suppression, when impromptu youth gatherings of any decent size were illegal. If there was nowhere easy for young people to meet, then there was nowhere for them to foment rebellion against the government.

To Darko's displeasure, the camaraderie of shared struggle and artistic experience that had defined his youth in Yangon had mostly disappeared in Myanmar's modern culture.

"Nowadays it's more about separation," he complained. "Everyone just puts on their headphones and they don't give a shit about what other people are listening to, or what other people like."

In 2014, Darko and the rest of the musicians in Side Effect started partnering with a Danish NGO called Turning Tables to change that culture through music education workshops. The programs aimed to promote and empower local music scenes as a vehicle for free expression. Side Effect had fans all over the country, so when they showed up in a new city, it was usually easy to attract participants to the workshops.

Turning Tables referred to the programs as "Social Cohesion Workshops." One of the organization's volunteers explained to me how it was supposed to work: "We go to these cities where there is very little support for young musicians, and we get people from all different backgrounds together who share a common love of music. Then we spend a week teaching them songwriting skills, and through that process they learn to communicate with each other as peers." Turning Tables had a mobile recording studio, and at the end of the weeklong workshops the participants got to record songs that they had written together and take something tangible home.

Darko had led workshops in some of the most socially divided places in Myanmar, like Kachin and Rakhine States. In these areas, the musicians sometimes had a difficult time connecting with the local youth, who tended to be suspicious of outsiders. In Rakhine, Darko said that there was too much open hostility and overt Buddhist nationalism to make the programming effective. And in Kachin State, they were treated like outsiders and it took days of meetings before they found someone who was willing to vouch for them within the community.

In the end, it was a sense of common grievance, in addition to a common love of music, that brought the Kachin participants together with the Yangon punks. "There was a real solidarity," Darko said. "I think maybe it's because not many other people have come and just said, 'We don't like what the government did to you.' But we went there and said that."

His message was blunt: "You hate the Burmese military. Of course you do. Fuck them. But we hate the Burmese military too. Fuck them!"

That kind of plain-spoken aggression worked because Side Effect's workshops and music targeted young people that naturally felt alienated from the mainstream views within their own communities. In some ways, the messages were similar to the arguments that opposition groups had been putting forth in Myanmar for most of the past seventy years: It's OK to be different from the majority; there is strength in diversity of views.

Darko acknowledged the similarities, but cautioned against comparisons between his antiestablishment message and those put out by ethnonationalist forces.

"That is a political debate—Will they be part of the Union? Will they have a federal governance system?—but what are we doing on the ground level. If the Kachin and the government sign a cease-fire, there will be peace on one level. But real peace between individual people will take centuries to work out. We need to fill that gap. We want to talk about who you are, regardless of ethnicity and religion. It's about something deep within you: Who are you?"

It was a common message that could appeal to a certain set of youth across the country. Anger at authority, often undirected, could be channeled into the creative outlet of music. Do something constructive with your feelings.

There was another aspect of dissent Darko was trying to build in these new social spaces. By bringing people of different backgrounds together to share a common passion, identity did not have to be tied to religion or ethnicity, as it almost always was in Myanmar. If you ask someone who he or she is, they wouldn't have to automatically respond by saying "I am Bamar," or "I am Muslim." They could say, "I'm a guy who likes painting," or "I'm a guitarist."

Darko had a broader understanding of identity than many people in Myanmar. "You don't choose where you come from," he told me once. "But a Rohingya and Rakhine poet can have a deeper connection than two Bamar people."

Side Effect's success in piloting these programs around Myanmar gave Darko some small hope for the future, even if he didn't like to admit it. Whenever I asked him if he was optimistic about the direction of the country, he always pointed out all the horrible things happening: the civil war, the genocide against the Rohingya, the failings of the local media. But like most people in Myanmar, he believed that his young son would grow up to have a much better life than he did. That was a shared belief across the country that made life in Myanmar feel very different from life in the West. Polls from YouGov, Cambridge University, and the Pew Research Center show that most people in America and Europe do not believe that the next generation will have an easier go of it. But in Myanmar it is accepted as a sure thing. Despite the difficult history and the horrors of some of Myanmar's ethnic violence, there was an optimism about life that could be felt in cities like Yangon—places that were developing commercial ties to the outside world. It was also sobering to realize the consequences of that thought: People in Myanmar believed things were getting better, even when life for some of those on the margins of society was getting steadily worse.

.

Most political dissidents, when they spoke publicly, talked about constitutional reform, the need for an open electoral system, and the importance of a free press. Darko, on the other hand, had an unvarnished contempt for anything written by the local media, and an almost equal hatred of the foreign press. "They all just pick the headlines that make it most interesting, in order to sell their publication," he told me. "Of course there is truth underneath part of it. But there is a lot of bullshit there."

A lot of Darko's rejection of the news media stemmed from a trip he made to Rakhine State, where he visited a local NGO run by a fan of Side Effect. The man was a Buddhist, and Darko expected that he would have been a virulent hater of the Rohingya. But instead he felt sorry for the poor farmers living in decrepit villages and went out of his way to show Darko how difficult life was for the Muslim residents in Rakhine.

"Just seeing these people—they are just human beings. They are like everybody else. Just like these kids in Yangon, listening to the same music," Darko told me, remembering the trip. "And I was like, 'Oh God, I've been lied to.' Nobody wrote about these things. Nobody wrote about how they are just normal people."

Darko let out a short bark of laughter.

"And no one gives a fuck about them. It really changed my mind. That's when I started hating the local media."

For Darko, a skeptical attitude was the most natural thing in the world. Growing up in a city cut off from the rest of the world, it had felt like the government had weaponized secrecy to use against its own citizens. Outside information was actively condemned. In the newspaper every day, and on billboards and in publications across the country, government propaganda posters listed the official goals and desires of the people of Myanmar:

OUR THREE MAIN NATIONAL CAUSES
Non-disintegration of the Union—Our Cause
Non-disintegration of the National Solidarity—Our Cause
Consolidation of National Sovereignty—Our Cause

PEOPLE'S DESIRE
Oppose those relying on external elements, acting as stooges, holding
   negative views
Oppose those trying to jeopardize stability of the State and progress of
   the nation
Oppose foreign nations interfering in internal affairs of the State
Crush all internal and external destructive elements as the common
   enemy

Not all residents of Myanmar wanted to "crush all internal and external destructive elements," but there was little anyone could do except keep their heads down and try to survive. People lived in constant fear of the military intelligence apparatus—anyone could be labeled an "internal destructive element," and government spies and surveillance were a ubiquitous part of life. Secret informants lurked in tea shops and taxi stands, listening for subversive comments. By one estimate, the military eventually recruited up to one fifth of the population to spy on their friends, family, and neighbors. If you opposed the National Causes, or the People's Desires, you could end up being dragged to Insein Prison, where, after the secret police tortured you, you would likely confess to your crime whether or not you committed it.

There were lots of stories about people being turned in to the secret police by their friends or family members after accidentally saying the wrong thing. One of the most popular tales involved a Yangon taxi driver in the early 1990s, when there were few cars in the city. Everyone in Yangon seemed to know this driver, who had supposedly picked up a customer who started ranting about how stupid the government was. Normally, no one would engage like that with a stranger, but because the customer was so adamant and vocal, the driver nodded and grunted in agreement as he drove through city. Then at the end of the trip, before the customer got out, he leaned forward and showed the tape recorder he was holding. "Just remember, I can send you away whenever I want," he said. Then he just got out. The story was supposed to show how crazy everyday people could act when they had power over someone else.

In the junta years, one of the only reliable outlets for people looking for alternative views was the radio. All local stations were housed on military bases, because information was seen as such a critical part of the government's fight against rebel groups. The strict social controls did not stop people from secretly listening to nighttime broadcasts from the BBC or the Voice of America, which came in from abroad. But because of the fear of informants, it was difficult for people to share the information they gleaned from their twilight listening sessions with anyone else.

It was not an easy place to grow up if your favorite band was Metallica, as Darko's was. He attributed his skepticism toward the system as mostly coming from his father, who had gone to sea as a ship's engineer and traveled around the world. When he would come back to Yangon, he would bring his son new music that he had picked up on his trips, and Darko was sometimes one of the first young people in Myanmar to hear about new music from abroad.

Aside from the occasional CDs that his father brought back, Darko and the other rock music aficionados living in military-run Yangon had to wait for cassette tapes to make their way over the border from Thailand. As a teenager, Darko would search through the recordings in secondhand shops, looking for new punk and heavy metal releases. Most of the rock music he could get his hands on was more than a decade old. In the mid to late 1990s, the Yangon rockers were finally getting their hands on the American hair metal that was popular in the 1980s. If someone heard of other music they wanted to listen to, they could go to a store and request a mix tape to be made. The owner would source originals from Thailand and make a cassette, which the customer could come and pick up a few weeks later. But for the most part, everyone listened to the same stuff. "You could write down all the names of the bands that every rocker in town listened to," Darko remembered. "Metallica, Judas Priest, Slayer, it wasn't very diverse, because it only came from three or four music stores."

These record stores would churn out duplicates of cassette tapes, copying them over and over for the young men that came in. The albums were illegal, but no one really enforced the copyright laws for something as obscure as heavy metal. The English lyrics attracted less attention, so a lot of the international music was able to escape the censorship board's unilateral bans. Sailors like Darko's father could bring back music from abroad, and through the record stores the music would circulate through Yangon's rock scene.

The difficulty of finding music created a natural camaraderie among the young men, which solidified the small scene. When Darko picked up his new tapes, he would bring them to tea shops, the only public areas with tape decks and good hi-fi sound systems from Japan. He and his friends would sit and sip their drinks and wait their turn to use the stereo. Only one tape could be played at a time, so if something sounded good, Darko would go to the next table, ask who the musician was, and make friends.

In 2002 the country's first Internet cafés opened, and for a select group of people, the new utility changed their lives. There were almost no Burmese language websites at that point, so the Internet still held little real benefit for most people in Myanmar. But Darko was a student at the University of Foreign Languages, and he and his peers now had an outlet that was denied to almost everyone else in the country. He would make the long trip down to Bo Aung Kyaw Street, climb up a dark staircase covered in betel spit, log into a computer terminal, and search for what was happening outside of Myanmar. The café's patrons had to submit their entire download and search history, and an attendant sitting at the front would make a printout of every website visited to submit to the authorities. At the café, the young students could download foreign music and carry it away on USB sticks. It would take thirty minutes to download a song on the slow connection, and power cuts were frequent, but it opened a window to the modern world.

Seeing what else was out there, however, only made the situation in Myanmar seem worse by comparison, and spurred Darko to find a new path. "We felt left behind," he said. "So many things were blossoming outside of Myanmar. Why can't we have it here? That's why I wanted to start the band. Not to be like someone else, but because we felt like we had to do it. If we didn't do it, then no one else was going to."

The plans piled up, but in the meantime Darko had to make money. He and his girlfriend opened up a fabric store, and he wrote music that other bands performed. It was a far cry from the punk lifestyle that he had dreamed of as a student. Then, at the end of the rainy season in 2007, the country erupted into protests. In response to fuel shortages, thousands of monks took to the street to protest the military government. In a highly symbolic gesture, the monks turned their alms bowls upside down, refusing to accept donations from the military and denying them the chance to raise their personal religious merit. In effect, the monks had declared that the military was unfit to rule.

Like most people, Darko didn't think that the protests would be able to accomplish much. "How would prayers to the Buddha stop the military?" he remembered thinking. But as more and more people flooded Yangon's rainy streets and closed down the city, Darko joined in the protests, which had been given a name: the Saffron Revolution.

He and his girlfriend went home to the garment shop and started making red armbands for people to wear in solidarity with the monks. Despite his initial skepticism about the monks' protests, he found himself swept up in the action. It was the revolutionary movement he had been waiting for.

"We thought that we were finally going to win," he said. "When things start to happen—anywhere in the world—it's about movement! Capturing what is happening all around right now, and capturing your feeling about it."

As part of the resistance effort, he linked up with friends from university who were filming a covert documentary about the protests. Darko was assigned a code name, and given times and locations to meet other conspirators, whom he only knew by their code names. They would pass videotapes from one to another, smuggling the illegal footage out of the country. Darko only did a few hand-offs before one of the other agents was disappeared, which in Myanmar meant arrested and tortured and possibly killed. The tapes he helped transport were eventually compiled into a documentary called *Burma VJ*, which was nominated for an Oscar in 2009. The movie captures the electric moments of those wet September days, as the people came out to the streets charged with the sensation that something new was happening.

But in the end, the Saffron Revolution became the revolution that wasn't. The monks fell to a hail of bullets, and the videotapes showed the destruction of the protesters. Soldiers fired indiscriminately into the crowds of dissidents, who huddled inside darkened stairwells and told each other to be brave. In one part of *Burma VJ*, a hiding protester says, "Don't run! If we must die, we will die," while another yells "Hide! They are shooting into the stairwell."

After the protests ended in carnage, Darko was so mad at the government's response that he considered joining one of the ethnic militias, just so he could kill Tatmadaw soldiers. His friend, the Side Effect drummer Tser Htoo, was an ethnic Karen, and together they thought of signing up with the Karen National Union's army. But when he found out that the army only accepted ethnic Karen soldiers, he had to look for other avenues for rebellion. Music was the only option left.

∙

Like punk scenes anywhere in the world, the Yangon concerts seemed just as much about style and fashion statements as they were about music. People wore lots of tight black jeans and T-shirts; there were hardly ever any longyi wearers. Long hair and mustaches were common, as were big metal jewelry pieces. Many of the older guys that hung out at the shows were heavily tattooed with skulls and other occult symbols.

Occasionally, people at the shows also sported swastikas and other Nazi symbols on their clothing. The phenomenon wasn't restricted to the punk rock scene. It was not uncommon in Myanmar to see young men wearing Nazi regalia (I never saw a woman wearing a swastika). But there seemed to be a higher concentration among the rebellious young men that were naturally drawn to the underground music scene. Another of the country's most famous music groups, Iron Cross, was named after the German war medal, which is often associated with the Third Reich.

The swastikas were worn with a flagrant and banal pride that made it disconcerting for anyone who had grown up fearing Nazi symbols. There didn't seem to be any shame about sporting Nazi armbands or even having swastika tattoos. Never once did I see anyone publicly reprimanded for wearing Nazi clothing.

The broken cross was a symbol of peace and good luck long before it was a symbol of hate. In Southeast Asia and India, the swastika appears in Hindu, Buddhist, and Jainist artwork dating back to at least 3000 B.C.E. Its use predates the Nazis by millennia. But there was no confusing the black, red, and white swastika, turned on its diagonal; there was only one group that used that symbol.

Nazi and fascist ideology was clearly at odds with Darko's vision of music being a universal bond that could bring people together and break down cultural barriers. The presence of Nazi supporters in the music scene irked him, and when I asked him about it, he got visibly upset. He knew plenty of young musicians that had gone down that path. "They don't realize that if Hitler ever saw them, he would kill them like that," he said to me, snapping his fingers. "We are everything he didn't like: short, brown, non-Aryan people. I try to tell these kids that, but they don't listen."

I sometimes went out of my way to try to interview these swastika-clad youth, when it felt safe. Once, at a hotel in Pyin Oo Lwin, the city that hosts the Tatmadaw military academy, the young bag boy that took my luggage was wearing an oversized denim jacket covered in Nazi patches. The Death's Head emblem of the SS was etched onto the back, and swastikas covered both sleeves. The SS flag was sewn on the lapels.

The boy was thirteen years old, and he said that he was a big fan of the band Iron Cross. When I asked him why he wore the jacket, he said quickly, "Hitler was a strong leader. He was a hero for his people."

The owner of the hotel was watching us from the reception desk, and the boy kept glancing over my shoulder, as though fearful that his explanation of the jacket might somehow hurt the hotel's reputation. The next night, he wasn't wearing it anymore, but I approached him again and asked about the Nazi regalia. "It makes people afraid," he said. "There is nothing in this town. This is a military town. I am very poor; no one cares about me. But when I wear this jacket people give me more respect."

I asked the hotel owner if he had told the boy to remove his jacket and he said yes. "Was it because of the symbols on it?" I asked.

"Yes. I don't know what all of them mean, but I could tell it was upsetting you, so I told him to take it off while you were here."

There were young kids like that at some of the punk shows, who seemed to be trying to intimidate people they met without having to speak with them. But Darko told me that the connection between Nazi fascism and mainstream Bamar culture was deeper and darker than most people liked to admit. It wasn't only about wanting to shock people. "Some of these kids wearing the Nazi stuff really buy fascism," he told me. "This idea that you do all necessary things to make the country great. Military leaders are all great heroes in Bamar history. Anawrahta, Alaungpaya, these guys killed a lot of people, but they are portrayed as heroes. I think that a lot of people look at Hitler in that same way. They think that Germany was for Germans, and Jews aren't supposed to be there, that Germany was poor because of the Jews."

These Nazi-era arguments were eerily similar to the rationalizations often given in Myanmar to explain why the Rohingya didn't deserve the same protections as the rest of the country. They were outsiders that weren't part of Myanmar's natural races, immigrant parasites that siphoned resources from the rest of the country and plotted to undermine the Buddhist state as part of a global Islamic conspiracy.

Darko thought education was to blame: "They hear the story in school, in textbooks—that Hitler killed millions of Jews. But I don't know why that doesn't stick. Maybe they don't make the point of how horrible these things really were."

Myanmar has a history of Judaism—the mayor of Yangon in the early 1930s was an Iraqi Jew—but it was also true that most young people in Myanmar have never met a Jewish person, which made stories about the Holocaust seem like ancient, irrelevant history. Just like how for most people in America, the idea of the Khmer Rouge killings, or the scale of death and destruction during Mao's reforms in China, could sometimes feel abstract.

Myanmar's own history is filled with Buddhist kings that killed and enslaved hundreds of thousands of ethnic enemies in the effort to mold the Bamar state. History is written by the conquerors, and the Bamar were very good at that.

■

When Darko and Side Effect led a workshop for young musicians in Mawlamyine, close to Phoe Wa's home village, I traveled with them. For one week, the professional musicians worked with the local youth to build communication skills and record songs. Then, on the last night, they hosted a free concert with some of the biggest names in Myanmar's rap, punk, and heavy metal scenes.

There had been trouble getting permission from the town's authorities, who were linked to the military. But eventually they had allowed Darko to set up the show in the middle of downtown Mawlamyine.

The musician was upbeat about the progress they had made. "Six or seven years ago, these guys wouldn't have given a shit about me. They wouldn't have listened to what I have to say. But now we can sit down and have a discussion. We can tell them why it's important for us to do this process. We can begin to spread the seeds. Today, I'm talking to you about this openly, without fear. I never thought the country would be like this."

The night of the concert, close to one thousand young people filtered into downtown Mawlamyine. Phoe Wa was in town, and I tried to convince him to come by telling him that Darko was an interesting example of how people could tell the truth in Myanmar. But Phoe Wa said he'd rather spend time with his girlfriend and left the show after only a few minutes.

The energy at the concert was electric. Young people from all over Mon State came into the city to hear musicians that they would ordinarily have had to travel days to see. It looked like most of them wore whatever clothes showed the most loyalty to their particular scene. The hip-hop kids were mostly outfitted in NBA jerseys and flat brimmed caps. The metal and punk guys wore aggressive T-shirts that said things like *We hate this fucking system*, and *I hate everyone*. One young woman wore a shirt that said *Problem Child* in lettering made to resemble blood.

There were also a few Nazis, as at practically every concert in Myanmar. And other decorations indicated that not all the concertgoers had such an open attitude toward outsiders. One young man who was dancing wildly and throwing back cans of beer had a jacket that read: *No Human Rights For ~~Terrorists~~*.

But mostly the concert felt like a small-town festival that happened to have really angry music blaring out of fifteen-foot-high walls of speakers. Occasionally, toothless skinny old men in longyis would shamble through the back part of the crowd, looking somewhat lost. One bald guy standing next to me was tapping his feet to the rap song being performed. He said that he was seventy years old and had never seen anything like this before. I asked if he liked the music and he shook his head.

"It sounds like garbage. No one cares about the classics anymore. And these clothes are too strange." But he kept smiling and moving his legs to the beat.

Mawlamyine is one of Myanmar's largest cities, but large public events like this only happened a few times a year, and it was rare for alternative music groups to tour through the provinces. The streets around the public park were completely blocked by parked motorbikes and street vendors. Anyone in the neighborhood with something to sell came down to the concert. A few old women with coolers sold beer and soda on the corner. One man was selling grilled squid tentacles skewered on long bamboo sticks. Another man had come to the punk concert to sell his collection of Hello Kitty and Angry Birds balloons.

There was a group of scantily dressed transgender women that showed up halfway through the show. They mostly huddled together in a knot of colorful sequins, laughing loudly and shooting glances at the few Western men in attendance. It was still very rare to see groups of openly transgender people in public. In a provincial area like Mawlamyine, it was even more unusual. The women said that they came from small towns scattered all over the area and stayed in touch on Facebook. When they heard about the concert, they planned to come to the show together. It was one of the few times a year where they could be themselves openly. One of the women had even brought along her boyfriend. He mostly stood off to the side, looking like any other young man who had been forced to accompany his girlfriend on a night out with her friends. But whenever the group moved through the crowd, he offered his elbow to his girlfriend and pushed through the dancers to find her a good spot.

I had never seen such an open display of tolerance in the country. At the concert, Myanmar's social rules seemed to break down, which was exactly Darko's goal. If Side Effect could host programs like this all over the country—reach out to all those kids in Myanmar who felt like they needed a different way to express themselves, and then find a way to keep these kids connected afterward—then he might really be able to build the kind of social space he wanted, where identity meant something beyond ethnicity and religion, where two singers could have more in common than two people from the same ethnic group.

Like any good concert, the atmosphere was infectious. Despite being filled with some of the most aggressive-looking people in the country, the punk scene was the most welcoming and friendly environment I encountered in Myanmar. It was completely unlike the punk and hardcore scenes I was familiar with from America and Europe. The young kids in the crowd didn't go around breaking things or starting drunk fights after the concert. They didn't graffiti anything. Instead of a bar, people who wanted a break from dancing congregated under a banyan tree shrine.

Darko always referred to the progress made in other countries' music scenes when he talked about his hope for Myanmar. But there was something unique to the local scene that could never be replicated outside of the country. Punk and heavy metal were born in the West. To this day, they provide an outlet for young people to rebel against authority. But in New York or Berlin or Tokyo, those angry youths are rebelling against a system that is generally open and free, even if it has its problems. In Myanmar, something else was happening. The young rebels were questioning a society that was decidedly not open and free. In many ways, mainstream Myanmar celebrated its lack of openness. Outside views were ridiculed and condemned. The specter of authoritarian history, and the campaign against free information that came with it, clouded every aspect of social dialogue.

At their concerts, the Myanmar punks were creating a mini ecosystem of progressive freedoms inside a repressive nationalist state.

▪

At the end of every show, Side Effect played "The Change," their most well-known song. It was a bouncy anthem with lots of long wailing "oh-oh-ohs" and audience clapping. Anywhere else, the lyrics might have sounded a bit cheesy and melodramatic, but in Myanmar, the song took on a darker significance. Darko had written it in 2013, a few months before the Meikhtila massacre, during the height of Myanmar's transition, when it seemed like everything was changing for the better.

"It makes me happy to play it," Darko said. "To remember that moment, full of hope, thinking that we could make a difference. It's a good feeling."

Hey, can you hear me saying
That I've been always waiting
To be the one to make a real change
That's my dream
I'm not hiding, man
But we've been living in a
place where even dreams
have been traded
for fucking gold

11.

THE LONGEST ROAD

The North

"Secrets are important in Kachin," Bum Tsit told me once. I didn't fully appreciate how true that was until he became a jade smuggler.

In July, he called me from Ruili, the trading town on the Chinese border where jade merchants from Myanmar went to cash in on their stones. He had just struck a deal with a Chinese trader for two thousand dollars and was on a high. "It was so easy," Bum Tsit said over the phone. "He just came and bought it like that. I didn't have to do very much at all."

At the end of the hot season, after consulting with dozens of old businessmen who had become rich in the jade industry by breaking the law, Bum Tsit had decided to change his business model. He found a new partner—an old classmate that he called Guy, who had grown up in the mountains near Hpakan, and whose entire family worked in the jade business. Guy had a knack for choosing the right stones from yemase sellers, so while he purchased all the jade in Hpakan, Bum Tsit kept his mouth shut and his wallet open, using his political and business connections to set up meetings and manage the smuggling operation.

There was a clear power dynamic between the two men. We visited Guy at his house, which felt like the polar opposite of Bum Tsit's custom-built teak palace. The small compound had three little wood structures covered in tarp and rusty tin. The floors were caked with dirt. The two men talked business while a baby boy walked around shirtless, cheeks bulging out like a chipmunk while he sucked on a rambutan pit. Every time he finished one of the fruits, his older sister would peel another and pop it into his mouth.

With Guy's skill, Bum Tsit saw himself moving beyond small-time jade purchasing. He didn't want to be like the gamblers in Hpakan, who could spend all their money on a single stone, only to cut it open and lose everything. "The only people who should cut open jade are really rich people," Bum Tsit said. "We don't have enough money to afford the loss, so we don't cut anymore."

Instead, for the past few months, Bum Tsit had been shuttling between Myitkyina, Hpakan, and Ruili—managing the family businesses, purchasing jade, smuggling stones across the border, and turning a small profit in China. He had fully thrown his lot into the jade smuggling business. But the reality of that life had turned out to be an exhausting cycle that required him to spend most of his time on the road and kept him away from friends and family. The jade business had consumed his life. He told me he felt like he was on a road that he couldn't get off, because at every turn he caught a glimpse of larger and larger future riches.

About once a month, he visited Hpakan, purchased around a hundred kilograms of jade, and paid a smuggling company to carry them to China. He made unique marks on all of his stones, so that he'd be able to identify them among the others when they arrived in Ruili. When the jade arrived safely in China, the smugglers would alert the merchants they worked for, who would then descend on a clandestine warehouse. The smugglers had a good reputation for never losing a stone, and their service was cheap—only seven dollars per kilogram.

Smuggling networks have operated between China and Myanmar for centuries. Ever since the Ming dynasty mandarins began sending merchants into the jungle to hunt for gems, businessmen have tried to find ways around the paperwork and taxes and people with outstretched palms along the border. Little has changed in the past three hundred years. Armed groups who control territory along the frontier often have their own arrangements with the smugglers. Both the Tatmadaw and KIA worked with and profited from the smuggling networks, something that Bum Tsit was well aware of.

But as a way to protect his conscience, Bum Tsit was deliberately keeping himself in the dark about how the smugglers he hired crossed the border with so many jade stones. When I asked him how the smuggling operation would work, the man who prided himself on access to information waffled. "They never tell you how they carry the stone," he said. "It's for their protection as well."

Regardless of whom the smugglers were paying—the Tatmadaw or the KIA—it was a secret that Bum Tsit didn't want to know. It was dangerous knowledge, so he protected himself with a kind of calculated ignorance. If Bum Tsit didn't know which group his money was going to pay off, then he didn't know which side of the war he would be funding. He wouldn't have to guard another secret.

Bum Tsit's stones were mixed in with those of larger jade businesses, and when he collected them in Ruili, he often met businessmen with military connections or hidden Chinese investors. Many of these more established jade companies maintained their own trading houses in Ruili and permanent stalls in the large, open-air jade market, where old men would sit and sell stones every day. For those companies, Ruili was the most important node in the green vein—and the markets produced a steady stream of jade money.

For smaller operations, like Bum Tsit and Guy's nameless two-man enterprise, that time and effort was often contracted out. Like every other twist and turn of the lucrative jade stream, enterprising people had come up with ways to profit in this niche. Bum Tsit worked with a man who had set up shop in Hotel Ruili. The entire hotel was rented out by these jade vendors. Each guest room had been converted into a jade showroom—stones were stacked on the dressers and end tables, stuffed into drawers, spread out across the bed. There was a small chair in the corner where the vendor sat all day and watched over the stones. His job was to both guard and to sell the jade. He worked like an auctioneer, trying to inflate the price, and took a 5 percent commission off the final sale. Often, the sale was made while Bum Tsit was out of the hotel, and he never met the Chinese men who bought his jade stones. Other times, the buyer was thousands of miles away, viewed the stones only through video chat on a mobile phone, and then transferred money through a banking app.

Despite the quick and easy money that came with his new life, Bum Tsit told me he did not like Ruili. The jade boomtown had a dirty, abusive feeling to it. Like border towns everywhere, it attracted particular types: outlaws, misfits, people who cut deals on the margins and were comfortable with ambiguity. On paper it seemed like the kind of crowd Bum Tsit might fit in with, but he said it made him uncomfortable. Ruili was a melting pot for greedy, hard men from across the region, and Bum Tsit's Myitkyina-oriented political connections were less useful on this side of the border. He said that he sometimes felt lost in the city, and if things went wrong he had far fewer friends he could call than in the Kachin State capital.

The one silver lining to Ruili was how Myanmar's politics disappeared when people crossed the border. People coming back and forth across the border didn't bring any news with them that wasn't business related. The only thing that mattered was jade, an industry still governed mostly by unspoken rules. No one negotiated jade prices in the hidden folds of merchants' robes anymore, but new customs were alive and well, and every ethnic group had a well-defined niche: Kachin men were mainly responsible for supplying stones to the market, either by smuggling them across the mountains or serving as middlemen between Chinese companies and small-time businesses in Kachin State. Shan people living in the town mainly ran jade trading stores, while Bamar busissmen worked as shopkeepers or gemstone cutters. In Ruili, Kachin and Bamar jade men drank side by side in the bars without mentioning the war. Even Rohingya Muslims were welcome—they had long made up a substantial part of the Ruili jade scene, successfully carving out a section of the market cutting gems and operating small stalls in the open-air jade market and repatriating money to their displaced families through informal moneylenders scattered across Southeast Asia. Here in the jade stream, none of the Myanmar Buddhists cared about the Rohingya. Everyone shared the single-minded pursuit of cold, hard cash.

Ever the pragmatist, Bum Tsit described the lack of ethnic tension much the same as he talked about the petty corruption he had witnessed in the government, when Tatmadaw cronies and the KIA worked hand-in-hand to enrich themselves: "Everyone is cooperating. It's just business."

But the more time Bum Tsit spent in Ruili, the clearer it was becoming that he and the other Ruili traders were only swimming in a small tributary of the jade stream. Many of the men he met there had been doing the same thing for decades. With patience and a little bit of luck they turned small profits week after week and slowly built wealth. But no one was becoming an overnight millionaire. Even with all the connections Bum Tsit had made, the elite network of investors and military men who controlled most of the industry were happy to keep their arrangements secret, and did not welcome new blood.

For Bum Tsit, the untempered greed in the jade business was both revealing and repellent. He told me that it wasn't how he was brought up to behave. Despite his deepening participation in the jade trade, he was still a staunch advocate for the poor people—mostly Kachin—who were most affected by the industry's reckless avarice.

Earlier that month, he had sent me videos on Facebook of a recent disaster in Hpakan. A mining company detonated explosives and the resulting landslides had killed dozens of yemase. Bum Tsit had been in the mining town at the time but wasn't able to do anything to help the miners. The Red Cross could have responded, but Bum Tsit said he was no longer volunteering with the organization. "Jade has changed my life," he admitted over the phone. "But not the way I wanted. There's no time to volunteer anymore."

It was becoming clear that to succeed as a jade trader, Bum Tsit would have to abandon practically every other aspect of his life. He had already given up on his political ambitions for 2020, because the underground jade stream looked like a much quicker path to power. But that decision hadn't turned out exactly as he had anticipated. It didn't free up any extra time for the things that he always told me were most important—Bum Tsit almost never saw his family or friends, and had no extra bandwidth to manage Red House or the jewelry store. Worst of all, chasing the stone had put an end to his humanitarian work. He defended his actions by saying that once he had the power and influence that would come from being wealthy with jade, he could afford to help Kachin's most vulnerable. But life on the road was hard, and it was wearing Bum Tsit thin.

After spending a week in Ruili, Bum Tsit had sold the large stone for two thousand dollars, and a few others for around six hundred dollars each. He left the remainder with the vendor in Hotel Ruili and hoped that they would be sold by the time he returned in a month. All together he and his partner made a profit of 4 million kyats on the trip—almost three thousand dollars.

"The profit is small, but it is steady," Bum Tsit said. He already had plans to expand. "I can hire one person to stay in Hpakan just buying jade for me and sending it to Ruili all the time. Then I can get another person living in Ruili selling all the jade. Then I'll be making profit all the time. Every week."

In the north, being self-sufficient was an important part of the path to wealth and power. In Kachin, if you didn't have to rely on anyone else, it meant your allegiance wasn't for purchase, that you could be trusted, that secrets were safe with you.

Over the phone, Bum Tsit told me he still had a long way to go. "The jade business is a long road. But now we are standing on our own."

∎

The next month, I met Bum Tsit in Myitkyina, which was sticky and green toward the end of the rainy season. He had just gotten a call from the smugglers that his newest batch of jade stones had arrived in Ruili, and we spent a few days together while he prepped for the road.

I brought a box of J Donuts up with me from Yangon and came to Bum Tsit's palatial house one Saturday, where he was lazily scrawling through Facebook on his phone. A big mango tree outside had spilled pulpy fruit over the ground, and fat black flies were droning around in a baritone sugary haze. Bum Tsit's three dogs—David ("it's a girl but we gave it a boy's name"), Windy ("it was windy when I bought her"), and Rooney ("for Manchester United")—were napping on the marble floor of his living room, where framed stone mosaics of Jesus and the apostles were scattered with photos of him in his graduation robes and stoic, staged family portraits—the mandatory wall decorations in any Kachin household. Unlike the Bamar homes in the south, there were no pictures of The Lady.

We were going to a birthday party for his nephew that afternoon, and he told me that these brief respites at home, when he could disengage from the jade world and concentrate on his family, were now some of his favorite moments. After years of longing to be out in the countryside helping IDPs or finding jade or influencing the peace process, now that he was forced to spend so much time in the road, it was the comfort and calm of his family that he was missing most.

His road trips to Ruili were also dangerous. Beyond the fact that he was regularly breaking the law, the trip to the Chinese border brought him through treacherous mountain paths and skirted around the frontlines of the KIA and Tatmadaw's forever war. The areas were littered with minefields and unexploded ordnance, a danger he knew well from his time in the Red Cross.

Bum Tsit and Guy normally met up at Guy's house to make the trip to Ruili together. Every time before leaving, Guy's young daughter would tell Bum Tsit, "Please take care of my daddy and bring him home safe."

Even though the rainy season was supposed to bring a lull to the fighting, the war was still raging, especially around the Tanai region, with its rich amber and gold mines. Yup Zaw Hkawng's Peace-Talk Creation Group kept calling for the Tatmadaw to return to the negotiating table, but the military's campaign of maximum pressure was delivering results. The KIA was being forced out of long-held positions and the Tatmadaw was securing important mining sites. Every time Bum Tsit set out through the mountains to China, he risked getting further entangled in the war.

The birthday party was at a cousin's house. This was the part of Bum Tsit's family that was closest to the KIA, and included generals and rebel intelligence officers. The men in the family were well traveled from their advocacy work for the KIO, but the family was still poor. They all slept in a single room, and the living area was stacked with what felt like everything they had accumulated in their lives. The floor and walls were covered in cheap plastic adhesive wallpaper, each surface with a different pattern. Fifteen members of the family were crammed into the living room to sing birthday songs and gossip. They passed around plates of fried meat and bitter greens that I recognized had come from Red House, along with the ubiquitous Tuborg beers the Kachin men loved to drink in the evening. For dessert there were rambutans and watermelon. Conversation grew tense after an hour, and Bum Tsit told me that since he had stopped doing business with his brother-in-law and begun working with Guy, the family dynamic had changed. The air was also heavy because, for the first time, a very important person was missing from the birthday celebrations. Bum Tsit's grandmother had died less than six months earlier, and the hole she left was obvious.

With the family matriarch gone, Bum Tsit had become the leader of his extended clan. He had long supported his family financially, but now he had to take on the twin emotional burdens of leading the living and satisfying his ancestors. During the birthday party, he was unusually quiet, and we didn't stay long before leaving to meet some jade businessmen.

Bum Tsit was still regularly meeting with wealthy jade merchants he knew through his old government connections, hoping to learn some secret that would lead to a big break. So many of the successful Kachin businessmen had started off like Bum Tsit in the 1970s or '80s, only to be in the right place at the right time to unearth a "life-changing stone." But many of the self-made merchants said the same thing: these days, with military control over nearly the entire trade, it was harder than ever for a young man like Bum Tsit to climb the jade ladder. Elites on both sides of the war had rigged the industry with financial help from China.

The more he became involved in jade, the angrier Bum Tsit became over its injustice. Before his grandmother had died, she had spoken to him of the once impenetrable Kachin mountains where she and her siblings had grown up, hidden from the outside world, free to pray and live and speak the way they wanted. But that version of Kachinland was nothing but a story for Bum Tsit's generation. They had watched as industrial explosives and earth-moving equipment had systematically destroyed the mountains; as every year the rivers grew more polluted; as landslides leveled villages and crushed innocent lives; as heroin use decimated a generation of young people; as billions of dollars' worth of gemstones slipped out of the country, untouched by locals; as wealth beyond their wildest dream was flaunted in their faces, forever out of reach; as the national army dropped bombs on its own people to secure mining areas; as IDPs trekked through the forest looking for safety; as the rich got richer and the poor got poorer; as the safe spaces in the north disappeared; as villages burned; as women were raped; as the choices for a young person thinned; as everything was reduced to us versus them; as children were birthed, raised, and buried knowing nothing but war. All along, the green vein coursed steadily out from Kachin to China, a river of wealth that poisoned almost anyone who dipped their toes.

In the end, all that was left was bitterness and anger toward the rigged system, and I had a hard time seeing how Bum Tsit rationalized his new jade smuggling business. He wanted to build political power so that he could find a solution that could stop the fighting and suffering in Kachinland. But to do so he was investing in an industry that fueled both sides of the war machine. It was one of the contradictions that seemed to be at the heart of his very personhood. "We fight, but we work together," he had told me when we first met. But now he told me that he was less interested in acting as a bridge between his people and the central government, and was spending more time secretly using his connections to support the KIA.

"The Kachin people really need my help," he told me. "Kachin people have no opportunities and so they need Kachin people like me with the power to solve their problems . . . I have a strong position."

It wasn't just Myanmar's minority groups that had reason to be upset. All that jade wealth was money that the government should have been recouping. Jade money should have been able to rebuild bridges and hire more teachers and give doctors a living wage, so that old ladies didn't have to trek all the way to the capital to receive care, and didn't have to bribe nurses to get seen. But instead, jade was paying for the enormous teak mansions behind the shady banyan trees in northern Yangon and arms shipments for the KIA. One of the bizarre injustices of the Kachin war was how few people outside of the north understood the massive scale of this underground economy. The jade theft was largely a secret contained in the deep furrows of the Kachin mountains. Journalists for *Frontier* or *The Irrawaddy* occasionally ventured up north to report on the war, and Kaung Htet sometimes printed photo essays showing conditions in the jade mines. But these outlets were mainly oriented toward foreigners or local elites who were the least affected by the theft of these resources. Most people in the country understood next to nothing about the jade industry.

For those in power, that was a good thing. The hidden wealth in the far north was a dangerous secret they hoped to keep. When Myanmar's truth tellers—journalists and activists and artists—tried to expose it, they were intimidated, charged with defamation, and sometimes shot. But it was impossible to deny that the people of Myanmar were the victims of one of the biggest natural resource heists in human history.

It was difficult to see how Myanmar could find justice for such a situation. Most Kachin people thought that armed resistance was the only way to seek revenge on a system that seemed to only respond to strength. "Enough negotiating," said one of Bum Tsit's cousins who worked for the KIO. "This isn't just a game. This is our people."

But how much of the fight for independence was about preserving Kachin autonomy, and how much was about well-connected individuals like Bum Tsit abusing a broken system to enrich themselves at the expense of some the country's most vulnerable people?

That question affected everything. The war destroyed lives and land-scapes and long-held identities, and for what? Like the mighty Irrawaddy River, it started in Kachin, but its force rolled across the entire country.

.

My last trip to Myitkyina was the first time I felt scared in Myanmar. Earlier that summer, I had published the first articles from my jade research. I had written about the jade war and possible collusion between the KIA and Tatmadaw in *The Diplomat*, and described some of the horrible labor conditions faced by the yemase in *Frontier*.

I wasn't doing anything illegal, but many parts of my life in Myanmar would look suspicious to the government if someone gave me more than a passing thought. My apartment was leased in another person's name. I had never even met the owner. My landlord was a Swiss NGO and once every three months I paid one of their employees in cash. I had never registered an address with the police or immigration officials, and I was doing all my work on a series of tourist visas that I'd get on periodic trips back to Bangkok. Any digging would have also shown that my fellowship at Columbia was funded in part by the US government as a program meant to groom future national security professionals. In a country with a penchant for conspiracy theories, it was a perfect reason to deny someone access. Whenever I applied for a new visa, I worried that someone in the Foreign Ministry would check my record, label me undesirable, and deny me reentry.

For most of a year, I was able to stay below radar. But then I left the country for two months and began publishing my jade stories. When I came back to visit Bum Tsit and Phoe Wa and others, things suddenly felt different.

In Myitkyina, two muscular young men followed me every time I left the hotel. They'd walk behind me until I got into a cab or entered a building, then lurk around for a few minutes before heading back to the hotel. When I walked to the market to visit Ting Ting, my market mama, they lingered in the background, pretending to look at sneakers. They were ham-fisted and obvious, and didn't seem interested in being subtle. They stayed on the same floor of the hotel as me, and whenever I came back in the evening, I saw them standing on the balcony, smoking and staring down at me. By the time I'd climbed to the third floor, they'd be hanging in the hallway, watching the staircase, and would glare at me until I shut the door to my room.

One morning at breakfast, one of them approached me and asked in excellent English what I was doing in Myitkyina?

"I'm just visiting some friends," I told him.

"This is a dangerous place to visit. There is a war going on. You could get hurt."

"It seems very safe to me."

"What is your job?" he asked.

I told him the truth. "I'm a student. Doing research about Myanmar's history."

"I'm an officer in the army. Intelligence division."

"Very impressive," I said. "Are you stationed here in Myitkyina?"

"No, no. From Mandalay. I'm just here for vacation."

I told him to enjoy his trip, finished my eggs and toast, and left the hotel quickly. Later that day, when someone from the KIO office picked me up in a truck to bring me to a meeting, I told him about the two army men. He turned the radio off and made a U-turn. He drove twice around one of the traffic circles, checking his mirrors again and again. "It's OK. We are not being followed," he said.

I'd come to the KIO office to learn about the prospects for renewed peace talks. Francis Zau Maw, the KIO officer I met with, told me it was unlikely the two sides would find a peace deal any time soon. He said the fighting had been especially fierce in 2018 because the Tatmadaw was feeling emboldened after its successes against the Rohingya, and had redoubled its efforts to secure profitable mining areas in the north. Francis told me that as the war in Kachin entered its eighth year, thousands of new IDPs had been driven out of their homes over the fight for resources.

I liked talking to Francis. He was open with me about the fact that for people in power the war was just as much about business as it was about ethnic identity. He said the KIO's grievances were mostly about the Tatmadaw's economic tactics. For instance, the Tatmadaw had bombarded a KIA battalion near Myitkyina, forcing it to move, then signed an agreement with Chinese companies to establish a special economic zone in the area, blocking Kachin businessmen from working there. In the Tanai region, they had displaced thousands of Kachin families to secure amber and gold mines they could operate in secret away from civilian regulators. Across Kachin State, everywhere the Tatmadaw had attacked KIA strongholds and pushed the rebels out, they had sponsored road-building projects that would partition the region and sever connections between KIA-held territories.

Francis identified jade businessman Yup Zaw Hkawng and his Jadeland company as a major culprit. "He is building lots of the roads," he said. "I can send you data about his cooperation with the Chinese and the Tatmadaw."

Francis was a big, round man who smiled a lot. He was defiantly friendly and cheerful, despite the topic of conversation. After listing all the KIO's grievances with the central government, he waved his hand dismissively. "We can find lots of reasons to fight," he said, laughing. "But the important thing is that the KIO help the Kachin people stay Kachin. We are at risk of losing our identity. We are up in the mountains, trying to preserve our way of life," he said. "But it is slowly disappearing."

The fighting had been especially terrible for the tens of thousands of Kachin IDPs living outside of government control. Foreign aid groups operating in Myanmar, like the International Rescue Committee or Mercy Corps, were forbidden from working on the KIA side of the line, so the IDPs only received assistance from the rebels, the Kachin Baptist Church, and occasionally from the local branch of the Red Cross. Many Kachin thought the government's denial of services to these IDPs was a way to pressure the most vulnerable Kachin to abandon the KIA and return to areas under central government control.

When I got up to leave, Francis asked about the two army men at the hotel, and I told him that I thought I was being followed. He patted me on the back as we walked out of the office and looked sad even though he was still smiling. "You can't come here anymore. We're having enough trouble as it is."

A cache of weapons had been found in a house next to their property a few months back, and the military had been putting even more pressure on the KIO, threatening to close down the Myitkyina office. The Kachin Independence Organization didn't want any more attention. It would be my last interview with the group.

.

Later that day, I met a family of IDPs who had fled the fighting earlier in the year. There were several IDP camps in Myitkyina, but there was no way for me to go visit with my military tail. Instead, with the help of a friend, I arranged to meet a father and son in a small restaurant alongside the Irrawaddy River, where I ordered noodles and plates of fruit for the three of us. They were two of the thousands of villagers who had fled fierce bombardment and land skirmishes in the Tanai region. With the help of the Red Cross, including Bum Tsit's Youth Brigade, they had settled in Myitkyina, where they hoped to spend only a few months before moving home.

The father, who asked me to call him Nan, said that his family's farm grew pineapples and rice, and they had a few chickens, but that he and his brothers had long worked in the gold mines for extra cash, operating dredging machines and panning by hand in the streams. The work was dangerous and dirty, but it helped Nan raise extra money to send his kids to school, and it let him purchase his wife a small silver bracelet after the birth of their second son. In the spring, the Tatmadaw had bombarded and eventually occupied his village. "They dropped papers a year ago saying that we should leave, but nothing happened," Nan said. "Then they started dropping bombs."

At one point, one of the villagers had tried to flee for help on a motorbike, but a soldier, likely nervous on the front line for the first time in his young life, shot the man as he drove out of the village. After that, Nan and the others had decided to abandon their previous lives, and the family escaped into the jungle.

Nan said that while they were in the forest, he had survived in part by eating tree bark so that his children could eat the only rice the family had. "You have to chew tree bark for a long time before you can swallow," he said.

His seven-year-old son had never been to Myitkyina or any other moderate-sized city before the fighting, and was overwhelmed. The IDP camps where they were staying were sparse and depressing, but they were considered the lucky ones. Myitkyina was under government control, so it was easier for humanitarians to come work in the camps. The Kachin IDPs who were in KIA-controlled territory had even less.

The boy was Nan's youngest son, born right after the KIA went back to war against the Tatmadaw in 2011. Nan said that once the fighting started, his wife had become too stressed, and was unable to give birth again. His son had grown up knowing nothing but civil war, and Nan was worried that he wouldn't be able to adjust to a normal life.

The boy had never seen the Irrawaddy River before. The whole time his father and I talked, he leaned out over the railing and looked down to the water rushing past—muddy and thick—south across the heartland of Myanmar toward the Andaman Sea.

"It's beautiful," he said.

.

While Bum Tsit was preparing for his road trip to Ruili, he got a call from Zung Ki, a famous Kachin singer he was friends with. We drove to meet him in a rugged SUV called a Toyota Kluger that Bum Tsit had bought after selling his luxury Nissan sedan. The Kluger was made for the mountains, and was a good car for Bum Tsit's regular trips to the jade mines, but it wasn't the most practical vehicle for Myitkyina's smooth asphalt. While we bounced down the darkened road on the Kluger's stiff suspension, Bum Tsit told me that Zung Ki was from his parents' generation. That age gap was important: it meant Zung Ki was from the group of Kachin men that grew up in an independent Kachinland before the 1994 ceasefire. Most of that generation had a single-minded loyalty to the KIA, and Bum Tsit liked to use that fact to distinguish himself as a younger, more pragmatic Kachin patriot. While Bum Tsit didn't see anything wrong with doing occasional business with the enemy if it advanced some larger strategic purpose, someone like Zung Ki would think of that as a kind of betrayal of the Kachin people.

Zung Ki was a singer for the revolution. He often made trips to Kachin IDP camps, where he sang his popular songs and played guitar. He also sometimes went to the KIA headquarters in Laiza to party with the troops, among whom he was a celebrity.

Zung Ki's most popular songs didn't glorify war or jade or the life of the soldier. They were about the everyday aspects of Kachin village life that were increasingly disappearing as the war permanently transformed the north from an independent polity to an extension of the Bamar state.

In "Harvest Season" he wrote about old agrarian traditions—*happily welcome the harvest season . . . loud sounds of jungle birds and black spider monkeys*—that had mostly been replaced as industrial farming had proliferated across Kachin State.

Many Kachin men are gripped by a kind of machismo attitude, but Zung Ki was the most flamboyant person I had met in Myanmar. When Bum Tsit and I arrived to meet him at a little roadside bar, on the outskirts of the city, he hopped up to hug Bum Tsit from behind, beer in hand. "He is my boyfriend," Zung Ki said to me. "No sex," he said in a reassuring voice. "Just love."

"He says that to everyone when he gets drunk," Bum Tsit said.

"No Bum Tsit," Zung Ki said. "You're my special man."

We sat down to a plate of Kachin snacks. Highlighted in the center was a platter of cold noodles mixed with shaved pork liver and fresh basil and mint. You were supposed to take a pile of noodles, liver, and herbs into a small bowl, and cover it in a spicy, sour green sauce. It went great with cold beer, and Zung Ki and his two young, heavily tattooed friends had already finished more than twenty bottles. The empty glasses were scattered across the table and ground.

The restaurant had lots of posters up advertising the national soccer team. The posters had seemingly appeared overnight across the country in the spring, as Myanmar played in qualifying matches for the FIFA Asian Cup. The team ended up losing most matches in spectacular fashion, but the posters stayed up, along with their ubiquitous slogan: *We are one, We are Myanmar.* The motto seemed especially strange in a place like Kachin—a willed sense of unity that was so obviously at odds with the spirit of the people. To the Kachin, it seemed obvious that this was just another propaganda scheme on the part of the central government, further proof that the politicians and generals from the south couldn't be trusted.

Zung Ki pointed at the poster and shouted, "They are all liars, talking about unity. We care nothing about the national team. Actually it should be 'One take all, all get none.'" He hiccupped and swigged from his beer, and one of the younger men spoke up. "It doesn't matter if you are Kachin or Bamar or Shan or Lisu. If you are weak, you suffer. If you are powerful, you take."

"It's true," Zung Ki said, still hiccupping. "This is the story that the world needs to hear about the Kachin people. Many Kachin are poor and weak, and our leaders only pretend to stand up for us. But really, they only help rich people like Yup Zaw Hkawng and others—they just use the war to keep getting rich, and the poor keep getting poorer."

Zung Ki finished his beer, then pointed at me and switched to English. "You also have this problem in America."

I told him that I agreed. That richer people in America tended to get richer, while poor people stayed poor. "But we aren't having a civil war," I pointed out.

"You don't know what you're talking about," the singer accused. He swept back his thick mop of graying hair and pointed a finger at me. "I know. I've read about it. There are nine groups of people in the United States. Nine levels. It is related to the order people receive their benefits." He put down his beer and started counting on his fingers, while I struggled to keep up in my notebook.

"The first is the Red Indian. They are the first American people. So all the opportunities go first to them.

"Then is the politicians—the senators and presidents. The third group is the Jew Rich People. The fourth is billionaires. Then you have normal American people." He pointed toward me.

"The sixth is people from Korea and Vietnam. They are war refugees, and they have already been in America for forty years.

"Next is people from Mexico and Europe. Number eight is Chinese people. Then lastly you have all the rest of Asian and Southeast Asian people. Like Myanmar's people."

He paused and looked at me, nodding. "Kachin refugees who accept US citizenship, they are at level nine. How can they reach level two or three?"

I wasn't sure how to respond, so I said that while there was social stratification in America, it wasn't nearly as simple as he had described it. "Plus," I said, "your list doesn't include Black people, who often have a very hard time in America."

Zung Ki nodded and said, "They are like us, the Southeast Asians. Last place in America."

"Also," I said. "The Native Americans, the ones you call 'Red Indian,' are some of the poorest people in the country. They have very little access to health care and most people have totally forgotten about them. In many ways they are like the Kachin—their land was taken and their traditional ways have been lost throughout the country's history."

Zung Ki waved his arm at me, clearly upset. "You don't know anything about America!" he yelled. "For example. That's why Jimmy Carter wasn't reelected in the 1970s. Because he didn't support the Jewish people."

Bum Tsit stood up and tried to calm his friend down.

"I know what I'm talking about Bum Tsit!" Zung Ki yelled at him, still speaking in English so that I could understand. "I don't have to bow down for some foreigner."

Bum Tsit made a couple of self-deprecating jokes that made everyone laugh. The singer sat down and kept swigging his beer, but it was clear that the night was almost over.

Later, back in the car, Bum Tsit apologized to me for his friend's behavior "He gets like this when he is drunk. It is not good. It is shameful."

I told him not to worry about it, but it was a strange way to end the night. Zung Ki's conspiracy theories and accusations were off-putting, but in a way, I could understand them. He and the other Kachin men lived in a world laced with secrecy, where outlandish stories were often completely true. During my time in the north, I would hear stories about how the central government was systematically poisoning the Kachin youth, or how there were spy satellites watching the university, or other implausible justifications for Tatmadaw victories in the war. In Myanmar, it often felt impossible to know exactly what was happening, so explanations that offered some kind of order and told a good story were easy to latch on to. In the beginning, I often dismissed these theories, but the more I learned about elites plundering the region at the expense of the poor, the more credence I gave them. Whether or not the stories were grounded in fact, they rang true to the people telling them, and that collective belief shaped reality on the ground.

Zung Ki spent his career singing about a disappearing way of life and trying to raise the spirits of a people who, for generations, had been fighting for their right to live their own way. Powerful outside groups had been trying to rob them of their wealth and identity for centuries. Who in that situation wouldn't agree that people in power distribute wealth and benefits along discriminatory, ethnic lines? And who could prove that that wasn't true?

The KIA also had a role in promoting that idea. The collective belief that the system was rigged gave young men and women very good reasons to volunteer to fight. Those that wanted to help their people, but who didn't have access to economic power like Bum Tsit, had few options other than to become a rebel. The war continued. Government stayed far away. And the green vein kept flowing.

On the way back into town in the Kluger, Bum Tsit tried to cover for his friends. "They don't know any better," he said. "But some of what he says is true. Jade helps the rich people get richer, and the poor people stay poor. . . . It shouldn't be that way."

I thought of where Bum Tsit fit into this picture. He certainly wasn't poor. But he was a far cry from the old merchants and generals in their mansions whose jade businesses gave them control over billions of dollars of the underground economy. When I met him, Bum Tsit seemed like one of the few people who occupied something like a middle ground, who would use his position of power to improve governance in the north and help the little people of Kachinland. But as the inequities of the industry became clear, and as his jade business took precedence over every other activity in his life, his goal of helping poor Kachins seemed more and more a distant idea, a theoretical ends to justify the illegal activity.

Bum Tsit was a good, kind-hearted man, and one of my best friends in Myanmar. But I couldn't help but notice that he had changed once he became a smuggler. Jade was a business; helping was a hobby. As Jalin had warned me: Many powerful Kachins start with pure intentions but get corrupted in their pursuit of influence and money. The current of the green vein and the civil war that swirled around it were too strong for someone like Bum Tsit to swim against. You either stayed afloat or you drowned.

My friend seemed to recognize the same thing. "Even if you sacrifice everything," he said, "the result will be the same. Because the system is broken."

The Kluger bounced over a pothole and Bum Tsit gripped the wheel and we continued in silence down the darkened road.

■

One important aspect of traveling to Ruili was that the trips gave Bum Tsit a secret back door to visit the KIA headquarters in Laiza, the mountaintop town on the border with China. When he had gone there in the past to visit his brother, a cadet in the rebel army, he had been able to take the road from Myitkyina and drive unimpeded across the front line. But government controls had gotten stricter in the last year, and the only way into the garrison town now was by crossing in from the Chinese side of the border. During his last trip to Ruili, Bum Tsit had stopped for two days to see his brother and some of the other recruits.

Laiza feels more like China than Myanmar—a product of the roads connecting the city directly to Yunnan Province. Everyone in the city uses Chinese yuan and Chinese SIM cards, and the hotel signs are in Mandarin. It's the people themselves that make the mountaintop refuge part of Kachinland. Units of KIA soldiers in battle dress march through the city's streets in the morning and spread across the grassy fields to do calisthenics in the pre-dawn mist.

Bum Tsit thought it was important for him to maintain a connection with the rebel army. He had liaised with them in secret since 2012, when he had first exchanged emails with the KIO leadership to help set up peace talks between the rebels and the central government. Bum Tsit trafficked in information, and both sides had secrets that could help him build influence. Even though he had given up on running for political office in 2020, he still needed the KIA's support for his jade business and his smuggling operation. That support put him at risk. If the Tatmadaw or the police learned what he was doing, they could arrest him for fraternizing with enemy forces. Because of the KIO's business presence across much of the north, most Kachin people could be accused of the same crime. It was just a question of who was high profile enough to target. So Bum Tsit had to keep his contact secret.

But after his grandmother's death, Bum Tsit also felt more pressure to show his loyalty to the Kachin cause. He always described himself as a humanitarian first and a businessman second, even if jade had taken over his day-to-day life and completely eclipsed any of his charity work. But for Bum Tsit, the humanitarian title was a kind of armor that he wore to help justify his actions. He told me that his trips to the KIA headquarters were about helping young Kachins neglected by the government. IDPs there had no support, and Tatmadaw bombs and artillery perpetually threatened Kachin civilians who lived in Laiza. Most of the world had forgotten about this last corner of Kachinland, but jade gave Bum Tsit the means to help—even if it was something small like buying a goat and roasting it for the young recruits. It was an easy way to rationalize his smuggling operation. Even though he was directly contributing to the industry at the heart of the civil war, he used his profits to personally help poor Kachin people, which gave him a great deal of satisfaction. When he visited Laiza, Bum Tsit could still feel like a humanitarian first, a businessman second.

■

When I invited him out for a drink at Ledo Bar in downtown Myitkyina, Bum Tsit said he didn't like the place, and passed. "Watch out for drug addicts there," he told me.

Ledo Bar was one of the only modern restaurants in the city—it re-minded me of some of Yangon's hipster bars—and it attracted a crowd of young and wealthy people. Most were related to Tatmadaw commanders and Chinese businessmen involved in extractive industries who used Myit-kyina as a base for their operations. The few Kachin who spent time there tended to be from a handful of well-connected families. I went there to meet Yup Sin Wa Lee, the son of Yup Zaw Hkawng, the richest man in Kachin State. He had made a fortune in jade and used it to build roads and create jobs for Kachin locals. I had seen his projects at the Confluence and around Indawgyi Lake. Most people saw Yup Zaw Hkawng as a conscientious Kachin businessman who gave back to his people, but behind the scenes, the jade kingpin was intertwined with both the Tatmadaw war machine and the KIA, and used his connections to enrich his family.

"Yup Zaw Hkwang is no different from the other leaders in this county who want to keep the war going," another Kachin jade merchant with de-cades of industry experience had told me. "He is close to Than Shwe and Ohn Myint," he said, referring to Myanmar's former military leaders whose families own large parts of the jade industry. "But because he talks about Kachin people and sometimes gives some of his money to charity, people here think he is a good man."

One of the ways Yup Zaw Hkawng raised his public profile was by holding regular meetings of his own peacebuilding initiative, called the Peace-Talk Creation Group. It was one of the only independent organiza-tions that had succeeded in getting Kachin and Bamar stakeholders to sit at a table and talk, but it was also a forum for people with business interests in Kachin State to gather. Important deals about resource sharing came to-gether on the margins of these meetings, establishing who could control which areas of the Hpakan jade mines. It was a place for men with guns and money to carve up land and share information. Yup Zaw Hkawng organized it all and made a killing. This was Bum Tsit's hero—someone that worked in the shadows, whose access to information and important people made him powerful, but who presented a public face of neutrality and pro-Kachin humanitarianism.

During my dinner with Yup Sin Wa Li ("Just call me 'Sin,' bro") I asked him about his family's commercial empire. Jadeland Companies had become an enormous conglomerate in the north, and Sin oversaw all the road-building projects. Before starting work for his father, he had gone to school in Massachusetts, where he got a degree in construction management. Afterward, Sin had returned to northern Myanmar to help the family grow its empire. In Yangon, where he kept an apartment, he was known for riding in an enormous black Jaguar sedan around the city's poshest neighborhoods.

Sin was accompanied by his friend, who introduced himself to me as "Da Rock," and was so swollen with muscles that he had a hard time scratching his back. He wore a tight black shirt with the KIA's crossed-swords emblem and lettering that said "let's help IDPs."

Da Rock said he had studied geology but couldn't find a job, even in the jade industry. "Kachin young people graduate but can't find jobs, so they just all end up working in the mines and doing drugs," he said. Instead of joining them, Da Rock had opened a mixed martial arts gym in Myitkyina and taught self-defense, mostly to wealthy local Kachin and Chinese women.

Da Rock ordered passionfruit juice while Sin and I drank beer. Sin told me that like his friend, he was trying to show the Kachin people the path to self-improvement: "I keep telling my friends they should get in business with China. The money comes a lot faster that way."

He told me his goal for the next few years involved "working on all the roads between Kachin State and China." He was extremely confident that the project would be profitable. "I'm trying to privatize all of them. All the border crossings, too."

I asked if he had to deal with security concerns or got any pushback from angry locals, and how the relationship between the Tatmadaw and the KIA affected his business.

"Well, there's war at the moment, of course," he said. "The war doesn't really hurt the business though. In some ways it makes it easier. There isn't much traffic, so that just makes construction easier."

He talked about the beautiful forests in the remote mountains where his construction crews were working. One of the war's effects was that the abandoned areas of the north had proliferated with plant and animal life. "You just have to throw a net in the river and you catch fish like that," he said, snapping his fingers.

The logs from the ancient jungle trees, he said, were wider than some of their trucks and difficult to chop down. He sold them to Chinese trading companies to finance the road building. Despite the war, Sin said, money was easy to come by. "It's actually quite easy to get financing. The Chinese in particular are really eager when it comes to construction."

Those connections—the cross-border financing between local magnates and outside Chinese investors—all of it was contingent on agreements with the Tatmadaw. The reason Francis at the KIO office was so upset about Jadeland's construction projects was that they were taking place in territory that had once been KIA controlled but had been taken by the Tatmadaw. Once the roads were built, it would make those gains permanent and extend the government's commercial access across Kachin State.

The bar we were eating at—Ledo Bar—owed its name to the first major road-building project in Kachin State. The Ledo Road was cut during World War II to connect India to China. It was the brainchild of General "Vinegar Joe" Stilwell, the American who led the Burma Campaign. The Ledo Road was the culmination of a dream that had its origins with the British explorers who trekked across Kachin in the 1830s and imagined a highway to the markets in China's interior. It wasn't until the horrors of World War II and the need for the allies to resupply China that enough manpower was dedicated to cut through the mountainous jungles and lay the road. It was made possible by Kachin and Chinese soldiers, working together against the Japanese.

Sin told me that Kachin–Chinese cooperation was similar today. "That's where the future is," he said "Most people here are stuck looking backward. Ethnic politics and all that mess. But in this part of the world, all roads will lead to China. They are building the next generation, and we are going to get rich off of it. At least, some of us are."

He said his dream was to build a Jadeland corporate headquarters in Myitkyina. "I want to show local people it's possible. That they don't have to go to Mandalay or Yangon to make money. Kachin people have no confidence now. A Burmese businessperson has so much more capital and power than someone from Kachin. Comparing the two is like comparing an American business with someone just in Yangon. It's a completely different league."

I left Sin and went back to Red House to finish the night with Bum Tsit, drinking Tuborg in front of the oil paintings of the Confluence and the naked Western lady.

When I told him about the Jadeland road building projects, and the logging and the privatization of the border and the general arrogance of how Sin described his position of power in Kachin, Bum Tsit smiled bitterly and raised his glass: "For the intelligence . . ."

No one lives through war unscathed, no matter how strong they are. The war destroyed families like Nan's, and was erasing the traditional Kachin identity that Zung Ki sang about, and would help make Yup Zaw Hkawng and his son richer. Bum Tsit had tried to find a middle ground, but in the end would likely fail, a victim of both the war and its narrative, which sucked in anyone and anything that got too close. The only ones who could stay adrift were the ones floating on a pile of cash.

Bum Tsit wanted to navigate this confluence of forces in the north and find his own path. But the river only flows in one direction, and like almost everyone else in Kachin, Bum Tsit had been swept up by its inevitable pull: He had sacrificed his own independence—and a large part of his identity—in the hope that by getting his hands dirty he'd be able to better help his people.

Bum Tsit's great tragedy was that the choice of whether or not to get embroiled in the war was never more than an illusion. It was never his to make. The system of collusion and corruption among Myanmar's privileged few forced the decision on almost anyone born in the northern mountains. People like Sin and other elites—both Kachin and Bamar—made these choices behind the safety of locked doors. And no matter how much he learned, no matter how many secrets he kept, for now Bum Tsit was still on the outside looking in.

■

On my last day in Myitkyina—a steaming morning in late August—Bum Tsit picked me up in his Toyota Kluger. I waved bye to the two army guys lurking outside the hotel and drove north. The car was already packed for his next trip into the mountains, but Bum Tsit said that he wanted to show me something before he left.

We drove out of town on the Jadeland-built road toward the Confluence. I thought we were heading back to the river, but after a few miles we turned left on a dirt road and pulled into an enormous open pasture. "This land is all owned by the church," Bum Tsit said. We drove through fields of electric green grass, still wet from the last monsoon downpour, and did not speak much. The fields were filled with row upon row of little white rocks, and it took me a few minutes to realize they were tombstones.

Bum Tsit parked in the middle of the field and stepped out. "Watch out for the pigs," he said, pointing to a section of the ground that was torn up, where three fat gray pigs were waddling about between the graves, sniffing the dirt. "They roam here wild."

We stepped gingerly through the graveyard, and Bum Tsit pointed out old stones marking his family members, many of whom had been in the KIA. He pointed to a headstone that was too old and faded to read: "He died in the war. My cousin or something." Bum Tsit's father was buried somewhere in the field, but he didn't want to visit the grave. He had personally buried at least six of his family members here. They had originally been in the Dugaht-awn ward cemetery, in his neighborhood, but when the government had destroyed the old graveyard to make way for a new development, Bum Tsit had to dig up the bones himself and bring them to the new cemetery.

"This place is a VIP cemetery, for people who have served the country," Bum Tsit said. His grandfather had been a state education director for many years, securing a place for all of his family members.

We walked through the rows as Bum Tsit talked. The ground was lumpy and overturned. The hog trenches made it look like the dead were coming up out of the ground, and their spirits were not so far away at all.

We found his grandmother's grave. She had died in the spring, at the age of ninety-three, from complications from a blood clot in her right leg. She had raised Bum Tsit when his parents left, in the early years of his life that he still called "a bitter history." For seventy years, she had farmed and prayed and led the family safely through generations of war, everything a Kachin matriarch was supposed to do. The extended family—the cousins and the in-laws and the grandchildren, even the uncles and brothers in the KIA—had come to see her on her deathbed. I had visited her and Bum Tsit when they came south to visit a doctor six months earlier. After consulting with Jalin—one of the only doctors he could trust in Myanmar's broken medical system—Bum Tsit had spent around $10,000 for a flight to Yangon and two operations in a private hospital that doctors hoped would give her a few more years. He spent a week sleeping on couches in the hospital corridors, where relatives who worked in the big city and who didn't often visit Myitkyina came with envelopes of cash. Bum Tsit had propped his grandmother up on the hospital gurney as she held hands with the visitors and chanted guttural, haunting prayers. Bum Tsit told me it was a mix of Christian hymns and traditional Kachin chants, giving thanks to her creator. After a week in the hospital, she and Bum Tsit flew back to Myitkyina. She immediately had complications, and died within a couple weeks.

At the grave, Bum Tsit bowed his head and touched the headstone and muttered something under his breath. In English, the white stone said:

IN LOVING MEMORY OF
OUR BELOVED MOTHER AND GRAND MOTHER
HPAJI DU JAN, LASI ROI JI
AGE—93
ASLEEP IN JESUS ON 19TH MARCH, 2018
"EVERYONE WHO LIVES AND BELIVES IN ME
WILL NEVER DIE—EVER."
—JOHN 11:26

Bum Tsit was now the head of the family; he listed all the people he was responsible for supporting. His aunt and his brother. His mother and his younger sister and his nieces and nephews and cousins. Bum Tsit had also recently proposed to his girlfriend, whose father was a KIA general. As the groom, he would have to organize and throw a party for upward of two thousand guests. The expenses and responsibilities kept piling up, and the jade road he was navigating kept getting longer.

After the graveyard, we visited a holy mountain nearby, where the church had built a large public altar for people to pray. Bum Tsit had never talked much about religion, but since his grandmother had died, he told me he had been spending more and more time at church.

On top of the mountain, above a long a set of concrete steps, stood a large circular chapel with individual prayer rooms built around the edge. Bum Tsit and I each chose a room for private thought. "Watch out for snakes," he told me before going into his room. "They sometimes hide in here because of the warmth."

Inside the tiny room there were no snakes or hogs or hidden drug addicts. But there was a small mat to kneel on, a candle that had burned most of the way down, a handful of translated prayer books, and a little notebook where people could leave messages. On the cover it said in English, *Happy Day. Every time you smile, I smile.* Most of the messages were in Jinghpaw, with a few Burmese notes mixed in, and an occasional Bible quote in English. I flipped open to a page where someone had written:

Thanks GOD For everything. You lead me always I can't stay, I can't breathe without you. Blessing me, bow to you.

On another page someone had written the date—July 18, 2018, and asked for an end to the war.

Please beloved GOD on high. Let us find peace and live once more in harmony with fellow men. Let the fighting stop and let us return in peace to our land. Your Kachin children pray to you almighty GOD.

It was a bright, sunny day, and the concrete steps were dappled with shade when I walked out of the prayer room. I sat on a bench and waited for Bum Tsit, who spent a long time praying. I heard his voice carrying out along with the chapel's other devotees—a droning hum of faith on top of the windy mountain. Afterward he came and sat with me on the bench and we watched as groups of young Kachin men and women came up the steps to pray. It felt like the most relaxing spot in the north. People were laughing and joking with each other and commenting on how beautiful the day was.

"This is a Kachin mountain," Bum Tsit whispered. "It's sacred for these people. But we can lose all of this."

He paused for a second and closed his eyes. "She lived for so long; she saw so much history. That whole time, she would come and pray for peace. I am very sad that when she died, the Kachin were still not free."

12.

THE PEOPLE UNDER THE STAIRS

Yangon

In the late afternoon, when the sun dipped below the old brick apartment buildings and the city let out a collective exhale, Bo Aung Kyaw Street was quiet. The deadening, radiant heat receded into the shadows, and the humid air sizzled like it was shedding something. The trucks would halt their deliveries for the day, and the street vendors packed up their wares and started walking back home—the broom sellers and the mango slicers and the betel hawkers all finished. Even the rats and the pariah dogs seemed to take an hour off, sulking back into the shadows and napping through till sunset.

It was my favorite time to walk through the narrow downtown streets. Even after nearly a year in the city, many parts of Yangon were still mysterious, and the landscape was changing all the time. Sometime early in the rainy season, a series of stores had opened on my street, all of which seemed to focus on refrigerators and air conditioning. Like most Yangon businesses, the stores all spilled out onto the streets, where dozens of porters—mostly teenage boys—lounged about on giant thrones of cardboard refrigerator boxes. The store names revealed their owners' global ambitions—Glacier World, Master Electronics, Multi World—and each left their doors open so that frigid blasts of air coursed out onto the steaming sidewalk, an in-the-flesh advertisement for what you could expect from their products. One of the boys outside Glacier World saluted me as I walked by. "Welcome to the coolest block in Yangon," he said.

Downtown Yangon was a warren of surprises that never got old. Services and stores that might be invisible in any other city were right in the open. A couple of blocks over from Bo Aung Kyaw was a street filled with printer repair shops. I sometimes took my noodles there, and watched the old men fix the broken machines. One afternoon, I saw a young writer, notebooks and pens hanging out of his pockets, bring in his ancient personal printer on the back of a pickup truck. I recognized his type. He stood nervously aside and bounced on the balls of his feet while the repairman opened the machine and poked around. Taking a rectangular black piece out, he walked out onto the sidewalk, where a stream of late afternoon sunlight shone on the old contraption. With a small horsehair brush, he briskly cleaned the mechanism. Dust and old printer debris flew out into the street, swept up in the wake of a passing van. The ghosts of Yangon stories filtering out into the air, never to be told again.

My fellowship was coming to an end, and I knew what I was going to miss most—the hidden personal stories and memories of old Yangon stacked so tight and high on top of each other that they threatened to collapse the whole city.

For Phoe Wa, these stories were the beginning of his love affair with Yangon. After more than a year scrimping and scrounging and saving, he had finally found something in the city he cared about. He found people facing hardships worse than his, whose stories he could share to the world.

After the two photographers had reported on the Yangon dump fire at the end of the hot season, Kaung Htet decided that Phoe Wa had spent far too long as an unpaid intern. If the photography department didn't have the money to hire him, at least another section of the *Times* could put his considerable skills to work. Kaung Htet reached out to the Lifestyle section and convinced them to hire his young protégé.

The new job was much more demanding than the internship. Phoe Wa was responsible for finding and pitching his own stories, reporting and writing them in English and Burmese, and providing photographs.

On Bo Aung Kyaw's middle block, the young photographer crouched in an archway and pointed his camera into the dark recesses beneath the staircase of a moldering colonial building. A sharp metallic clanging echoed out of the shadows. In the dark pit beneath the staircase a single bare bulb illuminated the scene: a beefy middle-aged man in a black T-shirt and longyi, bending over an ancient water pump, searching for the leak. Tools and extension cords and old lifeless pumps were all stacked in the dark corner. The workshop was tiny—only a few feet in either direction—but for Bo Bo it was his professional water pump repair storefront. In a cramped city, every square inch counts, and any space that can be given an address is available for rent. The repairman explained his personal setup to the young photographer, who was busy taking notes.

Phoe Wa sat with the man for a long time, asking about his family history and how he had come to work under a staircase in downtown Yangon.

Bo Bo's den was small, but it was filled with the personal touches that only come when someone spends many hours in a space. A small plastic mirror hung on the wall, and extra clothes and umbrellas were stacked along the tables in the back. Despite his dirty work, Bo Bo went to great lengths to take care of himself: His fingernails were trim and clean; his hair was slicked back with gel; he carried a fashionable leather bag. He told Phoe Wa the building was one hundred years old, and his father had lived and worked under the stairs for forty-eight of those years. After he died, Bo Bo inherited the space and used it as his workshop. When his family started living under the stairs, less than two million people lived in Yangon. Now there were more than seven million. Even though he operated out of a pit in an ancient building, he was arguably more a part of the city than any new gemstone magnate in a flashy new mansion on Inya Lake.

Bo Bo's only problem with the space was that potential clients were sometimes unimpressed by his office, and opted for professional-looking repairmen with larger stores.

Phoe Wa's interview with Bo Bo ran in the Lifestyle section of the *Myanmar Times*'s weekend edition. It was titled "The People Under the Stairs," and included interviews with four of downtown Yangon's most forgotten inhabitants.

"You point out to any building in Yangon and you can be sure someone is living or working under the stairs," Phoe Wa wrote.

Another staircase dweller he interviewed was a seamster named Ko Myo Myint, who worked and lived in a thirty-two-square-foot space. After living in a cramped dorm for more than a year, Phoe Wa understood how Ko Myo Myint felt:

"He says he has a taste of what death feels like: his house is not much bigger than a grave."

Ko Myo Myint told Phoe Wa that living under the stairs was "disgusting." His chief complaint was always having to cover his food with a second plate—to protect his dinner from the dust that rained from the ceiling whenever someone walked up or down the stairs.

"Stairwells usually host electric meters and leaking water pumps, not human beings," Phoe Wa wrote in the *Times* article. "But many who cannot afford a more decent accommodation in Yangon have made them their homes."

When he described the underlying conditions, Phoe Wa made sure to highlight that the staircase dwellers live among us like regular people, that they aren't so different from the rest of Yangon's residents:

> They used to be the homes of the poorest workers, but some who
> now [consider] themselves to be part of the middle class are also
> dwelling there. They are technicians, sales assistant in mobile shops

or shopping malls; they sell groceries on the street, books or DVDs. Some, like Ko Myo Myint, have decided it could be a place to do business in.

But other examples showed how little respect most staircase dwellers got from the general public:

U Lin Lin Soe also lives under a fly of stairs. He works in a computer shop on Seikkan Thar Street. He seldom loses his cool, but he cannot tolerate people urinating in the staircase anymore. "I'm really fed up. You can't imagine how bad the smell is," he says.

The project had helped Phoe Wa find his voice. He told me he didn't think he was doing anything special, just talking to these people like humans, without ignoring their concerns. "They are good people who just want to be treated like everyone else," he said. While Phoe Wa could still be cripplingly shy in public, when he was reporting his humility and soft-spokenness was more of an asset than a liability. He could win people's trust. He was an easy person to open up to.

Phoe Wa and I both loved the hidden stories of Yangon, and we sometimes compared notes about the odd places we found. He told me about the women in northern Yangon who walk around collecting ladies' hair in giant plastic bags to sell for wigs at roughly twenty dollars per kilo. And I told him about the street full of one-room movie production studios I had stumbled onto. Each storefront specialized in a different genre of film. One made romance movies, another horror, and another action. If you didn't nail your pitch with the first producers, you could add a love story and try again next door.

One day the two of us walked by a narrow shop front on Anawrahta Road, between Twenty-Seventh and Twenty-Eighth Streets. Living under the stairs, in a building held together by grime as much as by masonry, was a man repairing fans and blenders. Technicolor plastic fan blades stacked six feet high were piled all around the tiny room, as were the metal blades and unspooled motors of dozens of electric blenders. He replaced fan blades for one dollar, and repaired blenders for three. The man had found a niche in the rotating blade market, and had all the trappings for success. Only in Yangon could such low-grade commerce operate street side on one of the busiest thoroughfares in the entire country. His secret: he lived under the stairs.

•

Unlike hard news reporting, the Lifestyle pieces rarely had any follow-up stories, so Phoe Wa started each assignment from scratch. During any downtime he had, he listened to the radio and browsed Facebook, or took the train to random parts of Yangon and just listened to what people were talking about, searching for scoops. He knew the city well from his first few jobless months, when he had gone on a self-guided tour of all of Yangon's important pagodas and monasteries, and he found himself returning to some of his old haunts looking for new stories.

The Lifestyle section was printed in both English and Burmese, so its stories reached a much wider audience than some of the *Times*'s hard news reporting, which was curated for each version of the paper. When I spoke with Fabien Daudier, Phoe Wa's new editor, he admitted that the Lifestyle section had a reputation for fluffy stories, but he was trying to push his team to address more meaty issues. Under Daudier's leadership, the section had reported on LGBTQI rights and feminism in the Burmese version of the paper, topics that were especially touchy in Myanmar. "Every topic that's interesting is controversial," Daudier said, and as an editor he encouraged the young reporters to take risks and write about subjects they found interesting.

Daudier said Phoe Wa was a good young reporter to work with because he took that guidance to heart. "He likes to write about these forgotten people," Daudier said. "Every week he gets better at it. . . . When he interviews subjects, his questions are more on point. Every time he manages to dig a bit deeper."

At the weekly staff meeting for the Lifestyle section, editors would review the upcoming stories and assign work to Phoe Wa and the other reporters. He was often tasked with covering fashion shows and doing food reviews, but told me he found the daily grind and pseudo-advertorial side of the business boring.

When he pitched his own stories at the meetings, he always came back to the same theme: Yangon's hidden population—the city's least visible and most vulnerable people. Phoe Wa had a penchant for giving these stories dramatic titles. In addition to the "People Under the Stairs," he had written stories about boat captains in the Yangon River ("Ride the Tide or Die Trying: The unsung tale of ordinary heroes risking their lives so you can get to work"), vendors on Yangon's commuter train ("Victims on the Trains"), and amputee trishaw drivers ("Single Leg Bike Race").

Phoe Wa called the subjects of his articles the "grassroots people," and told me that their stories showed the injustices of life in modern Myanmar. "These are the hidden truths that we all forget about," he said. "People don't know about how hard life is for most people in Yangon because no one shows them. For some people these stories aren't important. But people need to know about this."

Phoe Wa estimated it took him at least a week to properly research, write, and photograph each of the stories. He normally took around one thousand photos for a feature, which he would whittle down to around twenty-five before his editors chose a handful to go into print. Even though he still struggled writing in English, his characteristic ability to capture movement shone through in his photographs. In "Ride the Tide or Die Trying," the cover shot was of a shivering little boy with a skewed baseball cap, his mother shielding him with one arm while their shared umbrella sloughs off sheets of water on a rainy season morning. In the background, a boatman looks pensive as he regards the river's rough waves. A single family's hardship—but an easy stand-in for the dangers faced by every traveler in Myanmar.

The movement and action in the pictures helped make the stories seem less like charity pieces or poverty journalism and more like sympathetic snapshots of real people doing the hard work of simply living in Yangon.

Phoe Wa told me that when his friends in Mon State read his articles online, they were shocked that life in the city could be so difficult. To most people in the countryside, like Phoe Wa's old colleagues at Hinthar Media, Yangon existed only in the imagination—a cosmopolitan paradise of teak palaces and beautiful people and wide boulevards with lots of cars—all the glitzy imagery that the Myanmar press normally published.

At Kaung Htet's urging, Phoe Wa had also begun branding himself on social media. He set up an Instagram profile and started regularly posting his photos on Facebook. When the monsoon rains created enormous landslides in Mon State, Phoe Wa took pictures for the *Times* and showed his pictures of the relief efforts online.

"Phoe Wa and a few others at the *Myanmar Times*, they have a lot of potential," Daudier told me. "I do believe they will become well-known or influential journalists."

.

Reporting on meatier stories gave Phoe Wa a lot more confidence, but he said the bigger change was having money in his pocket. Of the $350 salary he now made every month, he sent $130 back to his mother in Kawkame village. That alleviated his feeling of *A Na*, and still left him plenty to feed himself well and save up for journalism trainings and English classes he wanted to take. He could afford to make regular trips back to Mon State to visit his family and do freelance photography work on the way. He started getting known in the Lifestyle section for his stories about rural parts of Mon State that few people had heard of.

The new job also meant he had money to take his girlfriend on dates. With Phoe Wa's encouragement, she had moved to Yangon from Mawlamyine and enrolled in a nursing course. Phoe Wa said she was confident she'd be able to find a good-paying job in a private hospital.

Phoe Wa still lived in the hostel two blocks from my apartment, but the situation had drastically improved. Instead of thirteen men, there were only six living there now. Phoe Wa was now the longest-tenured resident, so he got to sleep next to the wall. He even began feeling a kind of camaraderie with the other migrants. "We all understand each other," he said. For the first time, he was less nervous about being robbed and finding food to eat, and more concerned with the normal sorts of things that twenty-three-year-old guys in Yangon worried about: what his hair and clothes looked like, how much to save for his own apartment, where to take his girlfriend for dinner.

Phoe Wa's yearlong ordeal had come to an end. He no longer felt like he had to "walk five steps" for every one that his friends made. He had become acquainted with his limits and learned about how resourceful the city could make someone. It put him in touch with a lifestyle that no one in his family had previously experienced. He said it made him a better Buddhist as well, because he had trained himself to meditate and pray in a place that was anything but calm.

During the summer, Phoe Wa's grandfather had died at age ninety-three. When it was obvious that the elder wasn't going to make it, Phoe Wa rushed back to Mawlamyine to be with his family. He sent me anguished Facebook messages, including a photo of his grandfather on his deathbed.

"I am happy to take care of him before he dies," he wrote. The old man hadn't lived long enough to see his country finally become truly free, but he had seen his grandson succeed in carving out a new life for himself and his family that the older generation would have never thought possible.

Strangely, Bum Tsit's grandmother and Phoe Wa's grandfather died within a few months of each other. Each was ninety-three years old when they passed. For both young men, the year ended with a family leader gone, and the youngest now in a position to carry the family into the future.

•

Phoe Wa's star was shining brighter and brighter. He was developing his own recognizable brand and had begun attracting a small following on Facebook. But the *Myanmar Times* was still floundering, and journalism as a whole in Myanmar was suffering regular setbacks.

Both the civilian government and the Tatmadaw were becoming more and more hostile toward journalists. When the NLD had first come to power, people had given the politicians the benefit of the doubt, believing that they wanted to change the law but were confounded by the Tatmadaw's veto power in parliament. But every month that passed without the civilian government coming forward and proposing any legal change, and the more Aung San Suu Kyi remained silent over abuses carried out against reporters, the less The Lady seemed like a human rights icon. A local free speech organization called Athan (which means "Voice") would later report that in their first three years of being in power, NLD officials brought suits against thirty-six journalists; almost all were for "online defamation."

On Facebook, Phoe Wa wrote to me explaining why the country's print media was suffering:

> Myanmar people are busy with their livelihood, so they have no time and not interest in reading political articles but, few people do read. And also the amount of readers are decreasing. Games take position as a huge part of their life.

Anyone who spent time online in Myanmar knew that Facebook was also one of the primary drivers of anti-Rohingya racist sentiment. The social media site had fueled xenophobic attitudes and failed to police hate speech and fake news. In March of 2018, the United Nations published a scathing report of the tech company's activity in Myanmar, declaring Facebook to have had a "determining role" in the anti-Rohingya violence. It later came out that Facebook didn't have any employees based in Myanmar and only a handful of censors who could read Burmese, so much of the content that would have been scrubbed in other countries was shared freely in Myanmar. In April 2018, Mark Zuckerberg promised to hire more Burmese-fluent censors, and that summer the personal accounts of key military figures like Commander-in-Chief Min Aung Hlaing were suspended, but little was done to delete the hate-fueled propaganda that was already floating around the web. Even months after Facebook officially acknowledged the problem, the social media site was riddled with racist commentary.

On August 25, 2018, one year after the ARSA attacks, I went on Facebook and easily found posts describing Rohingya as "dogs," "maggots," "kalar," "terrorists," "whores," and "rapists." People suggested they should be lit on fire and fed to pigs and raped and stabbed. "Send them to Allah quicker," read a commonly shared meme: a slick of bold white Burmese letters over the characteristic pink and purple pastels that make Facebook messages so easy to digest.

Despite the poisonous speech and demonstrable falsehoods, Facebook remained a major news source for Myanmar's younger generation. Phoe Wa posted on the platform nearly every day, as did most of his peers. After growing up in a society cut off from the outside world where even communication between family members had to be monitored, Facebook's open market feel and near limitless capacity for free speech was a high that wouldn't soon wear off. Nothing indicated that Phoe Wa's generation was likely to ditch the Internet in favor of newspaper subscriptions any time soon.

One of the ways the *Times* responded was by increasing its online presence. If it couldn't get young people to buy the paper, maybe it could attract them through targeted online marketing. The paper hired a local director and announced that it would air a documentary on itself. In the trailer, a narrator with a deep voice talked about the newspaper like it was a mysterious character in a Hollywood drama:

> What does it mean to be the heartbeat of a nation? For *Myanmar Times*, it's more than just the source of news, knowledge, and entertainment. It's the meanings we give it that make it more than just a good creation story. To discover what *Myanmar Times* means to the hearts and souls of the men and women whose very spark starts the nation's pulse, we just asked.

In the short video, some of the paper's editors and reporters looked directly into the camera and said what they thought about the paper.

Nanda, a senior reporter, said, "*Myanmar Times* means understanding both sides."

Kang Wan Chern, the paper's chief editor, said, "For me, *Myanmar Times* means truth."

Kaung Htet said, "For me, *Myanmar Times* means honesty."

For some in Yangon, the video felt cringey and desperate. If the *Myanmar Times* wanted to rehabilitate its image, it could have invested in more investigative reporting into important issues like corruption or the violence in the north. A year after the start of the Rohingya crisis, the *Myanmar Times* was still following the editorial directives that the government had intimidated them and many other local papers into following. The *Times* still didn't print the word "Rohingya" without any modifiers like "self-described" or "so-called." The editors sometimes tied themselves in knots trying to avoid the word: "The persecuted majority-Muslim ethnic group in northern Rakhine who are not Kamans . . ." The publishers refused to invest in deeper reporting or stand up for hard-hitting journalism, but they happily coughed up money for a slick online video.

■

The government's intimidation techniques were working. On September 7, the trial for Wa Lone and Kyaw Soe Oo, the Reuters reporters who were arrested while they reported on government massacres of Rohingya civilians, came to end after nine months of dramatic and at times bizarre testimony.

The case made headline news in Myanmar every week. As policemen dragged Wa Lone and Kyaw Soe Oo back and forth from Insein Prison for regular court hearings, photographers snapped photos of the handcuffed reporters. In every picture, Wa Lone, wife by his side, gave two thumbs up as a reminder to the world that he had done nothing wrong and was still fighting for free speech in Myanmar. Zarni Phyo, a *Myanmar Times* photographer, would later win an award from the Society of Publishers in Asia for his pictures of the two journalists.

The news coming from the hearings was bleak. Early on, the court indicated that the government was within its rights to try the two reporters under the Official Secrets Act. Conviction under that statute could mean up to fourteen years in prison.

The case was deeply troubling for Myanmar's journalists, especially considering how farcical some aspects of the hearings seemed. One policeman gave testimony as a state witness and described the night of the arrest. Under cross-examination from the reporters' defense team, the policeman admitted that he was reading from notes that he had written on his palm. The notes read, "No. 3 road and Nilar road junction," the checkpoint where the police had arrested the two reporters. The prosecution claimed that the vehicle stop was random, and that the police hadn't known that the two men were journalists. That story conflicted with the reporters' own account: that they were victims of a setup operation. They had been arrested almost immediately after leaving a restaurant where they had been handed incriminating documents by police officers they didn't know. Under pressure from the judge, the officer on the witness stand told the court that the notes on his palm were there to aid his memory, because he had forgotten details.

During the hearings, another policeman, Captain Moe Yan Naing, came forward to say that the police had been ordered to entrap the two reporters. The police captain was then promptly arrested and sentenced to a year in prison under the Police Disciplinary Act. From Insein Prison, Moe Yan Naing told assembled reporters, "Putting me in prison stops other police officers from saying the truth."

Throughout the hearings, the Reuters journalists were adamant. "The role of an independent media is crucial to solve the Rakhine crisis," Wa Lone told reporters at the courthouse in February. "If we are not reporting about the right information, the government will not know the real situation on the ground."

The *Myanmar Times* was covering the court proceedings, but unlike some outlets, like *Frontier* and *Irrawaddy*, it rarely voiced any support for the reporters.

Phoe Wa and I often talked about the case, and I was struck by how unsentimental he could be about his colleagues' imprisonment. Sometimes he thought it was a terrible affront to human rights in Myanmar; but other times it only registered as a kind of life lesson that he needed to absorb.

When we first discussed it, not long after Wa Lone and Kyaw Soe Oo were arrested, Phoe Wa was still struggling to feed himself and scrounging for sleeping space and scraps of stories. At that moment, the only lesson he took from the case was about self-preservation: "It's not just these two. Many reporters and photographers were arrested by the police," he said. "We need to learn from their mistakes. We learn what they did, how they worked, why they were arrested. We have to be careful."

Later, after the reporters had been held in Insein Prison for several months and once Phoe Wa had a more steady job, he allowed himself to get angry. "They were just doing their jobs," he said. "They shouldn't be arrested for trying to learn secrets. That's the job of a reporter."

Most journalists found it troubling that the *Times* wouldn't take a public stand against the government's prosecution of the Reuters reporters. It issued no editorials in defense of a free press, and didn't criticize the seemingly arbitrary application of the rule of law. After all, it was the job of many reporters to learn government secrets, and the state hadn't prosecuted anyone under the Secrets Act since the NLD had come to power. Unable or unwilling to come to the reporters' defense, the publishers had effectively ceded the narrative to the state-run media. But over the previous year, the public had seen just how quickly someone's life could come undone if they took a stand against the country's nationalist forces. No one inside the country was going to come to their aid. When reporters asked NLD politicians to weigh in on the Reuters case, they said that it was a matter for the judiciary, and no one else should get involved. Much like Phoe Wa, the *Myanmar Times* was also taking a lesson in self-preservation, to the detriment of journalism across the country.

A few days before the sentencing, I called Phoe Wa to ask how it might impact his reporting. "We feel like we are not safe when we write stories, when we do investigations," he said. "We are not protected."

One of the prosecution's arguments against Wa Lone and Kyaw Soe Oo was that they had saved contact information of rebel soldiers on their phones. "But all reporters, we have these phone numbers," Phoe Wa told me. "They can arrest us any time if they want."

During Wa Lone's and Kyaw Soe Oo's sentencing on September 7, presiding judge Ye Lwin said the two reporters "tried many times to get their hands on secret documents and . . . did not behave like normal journalists." He sentenced both reporters to seven years in prison.

As soon as he read out the verdict, power failed and the court was plunged into darkness.

■

The next day, the *Myanmar Times* led with a picture of a spear going through a newspaper and a caption that read "Who's Next?"

But the righteous anger against the decision was instantly caveated by the paper's editorial. Titled "The Week: A difficult time with a glimmer of hope," it opened:

> This week proved to be another difficult one for the government and the country because of intense international criticism following the sentencing of two Myanmar reporters to seven years in prison for violating the Official Secrets Act.

There was nothing in the three-hundred-sixty-one-word editorial actually condemning the verdict, and no mention of any domestic criticism. Instead, after ninety-three words about the trial, mostly focused on the difficulties brought on by international denunciation of the case, the paper devoted one hundred forty words to recent economic hardships faced by Air Mandalay, a commercial carrier that had ceased operations due to rising fuel costs.

The one so-called glimmer of hope was that the Tatmadaw had met with three armed groups that made up the Northern Alliance. The KIA, by far the largest of the alliance's rebel groups, did not attend. But the editorial was nonetheless upbeat:

> The two sides agreed to meet again next month at a still unspecified place, leading to hopes for a positive outcome in the near future.

■

Myanmar's internal upheavals show what happens to the idea of truth when public trust disappears. In Myanmar's case, that public trust never really existed, and without a concerted effort on the part of the central government to build trust, people seek comfort in tribal communities and put confidence in local leaders' abilities to say what is real and what is not. That voice of authority could be a radical Buddhist monk like Kelasa or Wirathu. It could be a flawed politician like Aung San Suu Kyi or a steadfast military commander like Tatmadaw Chief Min Aung Hlaing. It could be an insurgent militia, or it could be "rebellion-lite" in the form of an outsider like Darko. It could just be the mass echo chamber of a platform like Facebook. Unfortunately, trust was rarely placed in the hands of journalists. Hard news reporting that challenged the status quo was not a part of most people's lives, and those who reported it were rarely given the opportunity to weigh and determine the difficult matters of truth and secrets in modern Myanmar. Too often, the only way they shaped public dialogue was through the abuses they suffered at the hands of the government.

Phoe Wa and other photographers were able to shine by focusing on issues that were noncontroversial. But investigative journalism basically stopped there. Every truth teller in Myanmar came to a threshold—a line their thoughts and actions and words should not cross.

But truth is linked inherently to justice, and the outside world was not content to let Myanmar's warped version of the truth interfere with the need to seek justice for one of humanity's most horrifying acts in recent decades.

In September 2018, a United Nations fact-finding mission presented a report to the Human Rights Council in Geneva. The group found that impunity for crimes—especially war crimes committed by the Tatmadaw—had robbed Myanmar's victims of justice for decades. The report concluded that Myanmar's leaders, and specific Tatmadaw commanders, were responsible for mass killings and sexual violence, and suggested that the International Criminal Court open an investigation into crimes of genocide.

Despite mountains of evidence, the legal case for genocide was still a difficult one to make. After years of well-intentioned hand-wringing over the issue of genocide, international law had established that the deciding factor for the crime is "genocidal intent." Other atrocities, like Ethiopia's Red Terror, the killings during India's partition, or the ethnic cleansing of Kosovar Albanians, were never legally ruled as genocide because intent is such a subjective and difficult thing to prove.

Considering the Tatmadaw's rigid chain of command, its history of deliberately trying to erase the Rohingya as a legally recognized ethnic group, the level of organization behind the killings, and quotes attributed to commanders during the operations, the report concluded that there was sufficient evidence of genocidal intent to bring the investigation to court, and named six Tatmadaw generals directly responsible for crimes committed during the 2017 operations. These included Commander-in-Chief Min Aung Hlaing, as well as the commanders of the Thirty-Third and Ninety-Ninth Light Infantry Divisions, Generals Aung Aung and Than Oo, who were alleged to be directly responsible for perpetrating rape, murder, and arson across dozens of Rohingya villages.

In addition to the charge of genocide, the fact-finding group concluded with significantly more certainty that the Tatmadaw had committed crimes against humanity and war crimes, not only in Rakhine State, but also in Kachin and Shan States during its eight-year fight against the KIA.

According to the UN experts, the Tatmadaw regularly targeted civilians, used rape and sexual violence wantonly, and deliberately fueled exclusionary rhetoric on the basis of ethnicity. It wasn't exactly hard for UN experts to find evidence of xenophobia in the Tatmadaw's official stance. The Tatmadaw's own directorate of public relations was clear about how the military considered ethnic groups like the Rohingya undesirable: "Despite living among peacocks, crows cannot become peacocks."

Unlike most other authorities that purported to tell the truth in Myanmar, the UN mission established a level of transparency by explicitly defining its version of the truth:

Factual findings are based on the "reasonable grounds" standard of proof. This standard was met when a sufficient and reliable body of primary information, consistent with other information, would allow an ordinarily prudent person to reasonably conclude that an incident or pattern of conduct occurred.

Through interviews with 875 victims and eyewitnesses, satellite imagery, written documentation, and photos and videos, the UN experts painted a truly harrowing picture of events. In a section of the report labeled "Human Rights Catastrophe," the authors described the Tatmadaw's organized sexual violence against Rohingya women:

> Rape and other forms of sexual violence were perpetrated on a massive scale. Large-scale gang rape by Tatmadaw soldiers occurred in at least ten village tracts of northern Rakhine State. Sometimes up to 40 women and girls were raped or gang raped together. One survivor stated, "I was lucky, I was only raped by three men." Rapes were often in public spaces and in front of families and the community, maximizing humiliation and trauma. Mothers were gang raped in front of young children, who were severely injured and in some instances killed. Women and girls 13 to 25 years of age were targeted, including pregnant women. Rapes were accompanied by derogatory language and threats to life like, "We are going to kill you this way, by raping you." Women and girls were systematically abducted, detained and raped in military and police compounds, often amounting to sexual slavery.

The report also made clear that the anti-Rohingya campaign served a distinct political purpose for the Tatmadaw, noting in the introduction that, "Since independence, the numerous ethnically-based armed conflicts have been used by the Tatmadaw to justify its power, presenting itself as the guarantor of national unity."

A year after the genocide began, it was clear that the campaign against the Rohingya would haunt the country for generations. The sheer scale of human misery, the Tatmadaw's terrible attempts to cover up the crime, and Aung San Suu Kyi's refusal to stand up for her country's most vulnerable people had returned Myanmar to the status of an international pariah state, just as it was beginning to climb out of its own self-imposed exile.

For the moment, whether justice would actually be rendered was an unanswerable question, as both military and civilian leaders signaled that they would not cooperate with any international investigation.

Two months after the UN report came out, Min Aung Hlaing ordered the release of seven soldiers from the Thirty-Third Light Infantry Division who had been convicted of massacring ten Rohingya civilians at Inn Din— the same massacre Wa Lone and Kyaw Soe Oo were reporting on when they were arrested. The seven soldiers had been sentenced to ten years in prison, but were released after less than a year. In jail, they were known to receive preferential treatment; guards allowed them cigarettes and alcohol that were off limits to other prisoners.

The amnesty for the soldiers was widely viewed as a way of bolstering support for Min Aung Hlaing's eventual presidential campaign. One sure way to garner popularity in Myanmar was by liberating the soldiers who sacrificed themselves to save the Bamar heartland from dangerous ethnic minorities living in the periphery. Some people thought Aung San Suu Kyi's defense of the Tatamadaw was an attempt to hold onto that same nationalist support. But many expected the general to unseat The Lady in the next national election; the genocide had made him one of the most popular figures in the country.

■

At Hyper Pub, Phoe Wa could finally afford to buy me a drink. The one good thing about Myanmar Beer is that it is almost always ice cold. The Tatmadaw may have largely ignored the health and education systems during its time running the country, but it had always found a way to ensure its most popular product arrived to the consumer convenient and cold. The napkin holder in the center of the table was also a Myanmar Beer–branded piece of plastic. One side had the soccer team's logo, *We Are One; We Are Myanmar*, which felt as bad a motto as it ever had.

The willed sense of unity that the government and military were trying to impart on the country had never felt cheaper. In the face of charges of genocide, it sounded more like a nationalist credo meant to deflect any kind of self-reflection or criticism than a sincere vision for Myanmar.

The other side of the napkin holder said *Brimming With Optimism*, which maybe helped explain the first. Even though the country's leaders were entrenched in a backward-looking worldview, Myanmar's youth was still gripped by a sense of optimism for the future. No matter how bad the situation for journalists seemed to get, every time we met, Phoe Wa told me how much better his life was now than when he was growing up. Despite the stark economic inequality, the ethnic wars, and the disappearance of truth and transparency from public discourse, his current setup still felt like a dream, he said, one that would have been unimaginable ten years previously. With that historical perspective, *Brimming With Optimism* wasn't so off base.

But certain groups were still left behind in the new Myanmar, including Phoe Wa's grassroots people. He told me that now that he was in a position to influence the public—no matter how small the paper's audience was—it was his responsibility to illustrate how difficult life in Myanmar still could be. Someone didn't have to be from a maligned ethnic minority to be suffering. The system wasn't fair, and it was worth taking a risk to tell that truth. "Journalism can open our eyes and ears," he told me. "It's very important, and I love this job."

After working in the Lifestyle section for several months, Phoe Wa pitched an idea: the next time he was in Mon State, he would drive fifty kilometers south of his village and take a boat to the Kyaikkami lighthouse, situated on an island about a mile out to sea. The story would be a profile of a lighthouse keeper, a job that most people take for granted, Phoe Wa said.

His editor agreed, and during his next trip home, Phoe Wa spent several days on the island with a lighthouse keeper named Aung Ngwe. Later, after the trip, Phoe Wa told me the island's solitude was unnerving and reminded him of a horror movie.

In the twelve-hundred-word feature, which he titled "The Lighthouse Keeper," Phoe Wa set the stage for drama:

> Occupying the edge of the coastline, lighthouses can be
> metaphorical gateways to the chaos and intrigue of vast oceans.
> They can also be places of loneliness and personal reflection.

During his time with Aung Ngwe, Phoe Wa had gotten the lighthouse keeper to open up. He told the story of how, several years previously, Aung Ngwe had been stranded on the island with a colleague during a storm. The other man, named Win Zaw, was bitten by a snake and slowly died from blood poisoning over the course of three days. Aung Ngwe told Phoe Wa he almost went mad as he waited for the rescue boat to come, sharing an island with a dead man whose phone kept ringing every thirty minutes. The veteran lighthouse keeper said he had to convince himself that the other man was just sleeping until the boat arrived.

"Whenever I approach the doorway, I see him sitting outside, lifeless. That image of him will never leave me," Aung Ngwe told Phoe Wa.

"The Lighthouse Keeper" was the first story I read by Phoe Wa in which he delved into the history and social context of his subject, letting his words take center stage instead of his photography. His readers learned that there are twenty-six general and local lighthouses along Myanmar's coast, that you have to be under thirty-five and a good swimmer to qualify as a lighthouse keeper, and that the typical salary is around 160,000 kyats per month—about $118—a third of a junior reporter's salary. He also wrote about how in some cases lighthouse work had been a form of sentencing for political prisoners under the military government. Phoe Wa called it a "punishment of loneliness."

Aung Ngwe had not committed any crime, Phoe Wa reported. But after his son died, the grief caused him to walk out on his family and start living on the street. Only when his estranged wife asked a friend to help him get a job did Aung Ngwe learn about the opportunity at the lighthouse.

Now he split his time between the island and the shore. One shift on the island lasted between four and six months, during which the lighthouse keepers had to fend for themselves—fishing, gathering firewood, and repairing the light when needed. A lighthouse keeper made paltry money. But according to Phoe Wa, the stark solitude of the job held a mysterious allure.

Preparing themselves mentally for the isolation and the ocean breeze, the waves and serenity, they start to miss the lighthouse. Then they head off to the island again for another stint.

•

The next time I spoke to Phoe Wa, he was getting ready to exhibit his work in a gallery for the first time. A San Francisco–based organization put together an event called "Building Bridges Yangon," and invited Phoe Wa to display his photo essay of the Sky Dragon Lion Club, the pictures he had published many months before that had first caught my attention. The event was a mixed media exhibition featuring photography, augmented reality experiences, noise art, and video installations. It was hosted at the Old Tourist Burma Building, a recently renovated colonial landmark from 1905 in the heart of downtown Yangon.

The exhibition was opening on the eve of Martyrs' Day, the national day of mourning commemorating the 1947 assassination of General Aung San. The whole city was preparing for a day of patriotic contemplation, and *The Global New Light of Myanmar* urged its readers to focus national efforts on repairing the linkages between Myanmar and other countries.

"We must listen to the speech of all sides carefully," one article read. "Through this productive dialogue we can be [more able] to identify the common ground and can build trusts and expectations."

The promo material for Building Bridges hit many of the same notes. The exhibit would be an artistic union between cultures. From Myanmar to the world.

Phoe Wa's selection validated his considerable talent and exposed him to Yangon's exploding art scene—along with the strange characters and wealthy patrons that came with it—but he was characteristically humble about being chosen. "It's a good chance for me to meet foreign artists," was all he said, "a good chance to get involved and get good exposure." One of the things he had learned over the past year was that the key to success as a journalist in Myanmar is to have foreign contacts. Kaung Htet and Min Zayar Oo—whose photos regularly appeared in Reuters, *The New York Times,* and *National Geographic*—were the defining photographers of their generation not because they were so well known domestically, but because they were the ones telling Myanmar's story to the rest of the world. Foreign contacts were everything, because the local market for good reporting was still so small.

Building Bridges hosted a mix of twenty-seven emerging local and international artists, all under thirty. Many of the local artists' work focused on economic inequality, diversity, and social cohesion—the forces that had plagued Myanmar since independence. The same forces that had driven an assassin to gun down General Aung San in the Secretariat Building more than seventy years ago.

One of the most popular works in the exhibit was a photo essay called "Below 3 Feet," by local photographer Kaung Swan Thar. The title referred to the tiny spaces beneath the train tracks that Yangon's railway employees leased out as homes to the city's poorest families. The little wooden hovels— far more suitable for lumber storage than for raising children—went for twenty dollars a month or one dollar a day. Families unfolded sleeping mats and brought in electric stoves and crammed their clothes and belongings into the space and made it a kind of home.

In the gallery, the artist had constructed a tiny, claustrophobic crawl- space meant to resemble the amount of space these families had, and mounted photos on the walls. The tiny space made it feel impossible to ever stretch out, and it was difficult to look at more than one photo at a time, because your face was never that far from the wall. Inside the dark space, it became impossible to look away from the images of poverty: a child crawling out of the tiny hole in the morning with *thanaka* paste smeared on his face; a mother and son curled up squatting, peeking out into the rain; a woman surrounded by a pile of plastic refuse, staring at the smartphone in her hand. The faux voyeurism of the whole thing—Yangon's bourgeoisie in an air-conditioned gallery crawling into a facsimile of poverty to experience what was actually happening a few blocks away—was a feeling that didn't go away easily.

Wealthy foreigners and Yangon hipsters crowded the opening and moved from work to work listening to the artists explain their craft. In a white polo and tight blue pants, Phoe Wa introduced his photo essay to a small group that nodded politely and murmured in museum voices.

His pictures were printed on three shimmering pieces of long black fabric hung from the wall on elegant, hand-carved wooden bars. An enormous fluffy white and black Chinese dragon mask was mounted above. The bright colors of the Sky Dragon Lion Club's costumed dancers stood out on the Tourist Building's freshly painted white walls. The brash physicality and over-the-top motion in the pictures set Phoe Wa's work apart from the inward-looking and contemplative feel of many of the other pieces on display.

I had looked at these pictures dozens of times while following Phoe Wa, and had spent hours going over his photography. But one thing I hadn't noticed when I first saw this photo essay many months before was how young the acrobats were. They danced with the violence and energy of boys with nothing to lose, but would carry their missteps with them forever in the form of shattered knees and concussed brains and broken teeth. They looked like young artists on the verge of success willing to sacrifice everything for their work, as though the dance they shared was more important than family or friends or food.

That night, for Martyrs' Day, *The Global New Light of Myanmar* posted an editorial on the meaning of sacrifice:

The spirit of martyrdom is simple. A martyr is someone who prioritises the people's interests and subordinates personal interests. Martyrs devote themselves entirely to the welfare of the people and the country, even at the cost of their own lives . . .

Martyrs' Day was born of the people. We wish all the people remember this. Essentially, the people decide a country's destiny.

Taken together, the photo exhibit and the day's news offered a refractory lens into the meaning of sacrifice, youth, and destiny in Myanmar: A little bit of the truth. And something else kind of like it.

THE JETTY

Two young men and two young women sit on the jetty, drinking Yoma Beer. The day is coming to a close and the ferries are taking the commuters back across the Yangon River to Dala. Most are tiny little twelve-seater pirogues powered by pounding diesel outboard motors that shatter the evening's quiet. A storm is brewing and the cloudy sunset sky is throwing sharp contrasting colors across the jetty as the little boats struggle through the choppy waves in the river. Most are filled with bright orange life jackets, but no one is wearing them.

The young men and women on the jetty sip their beer and watch the boats while the sun dips down. They have bags of sunflower seeds and between mouthfuls one guy keeps throwing a handful of kernels out into the air. The seagulls circling the pier dive for them, but inevitably miss as the seeds fall into the water to be churned apart by the boats' wakes.

An old green boat, turned mostly brown with rust and grime, is docked at the jetty, loaded with sacks of rice from the country's interior. A Muslim boatman with an orange, henna-stained beard kneels on the roof, praying west toward Mecca and the sunset. The noise of the ferries and the seagulls and the beer drinkers drowns out his prayer, and no one seems to notice him. When he finishes, he wraps up his prayer mat and starts washing his clothes in the river, hanging them up to dry on the boat's handrail.

"My name is Abdul Razak and I come from Mandalay," he says in perfect English when I ask. "But I am leaving this place. This boat is going to Thailand and I will not come back."

"Why not?"

"It's simple. My family needs money. I cannot make enough here in Myanmar. I am the father. That means I need to work. To sacrifice."

I nod and leave him in peace and walk back to sit with my feet hanging off the jetty and watch as the little boats swim by underneath. Passengers aching and tired from a day of work sit in silence. Everyone seems to be contemplating the river, carrying its swell of muddy water from the country's interior, rushing out toward the Andaman Sea and beyond.

Eventually, the young men and women finish their beers and run out of sunflower seeds and leave the jetty. The ferries run out of commuters and dock for the night and cede the riverway to the enormous container ships that will plod up and down until morning. The jetty grows quiet as the gulls swoop away to wherever they sleep. A strong wind is blowing and it carries the stinging metallic scent of oncoming rain.

The only sound is Abdul Razak, quietly singing to himself on the roof of the rice boat, waiting for the storm.

Acknowledgements

This project evolved out of my own lived experience. There was no real beginning, middle, or end to the research and writing, and there were plenty of dead ends and detours that did not make the final cut. In hindsight, I wish I had enlisted a more diverse range of voices in my research. For instance, while I spoke to people in the Tatmadaw, I never convinced any of them to go on the record with me. And while I spent plenty of time speaking with women in cities like Yangon and Myitkyina, it was very difficult to interview women and girls in the interior. When you come into a remote village in northern Myanmar and start asking questions, it's mostly only the men who come out and talk to the strange, sweaty foreigner speaking bad Burmese.

Additionally, I am acutely conscious that this story could be better written by someone from Myanmar, someone who understands the nuances of Burmese better than me, who has lived this history, and who has tasted its warped effects on truth. In the end, this was a story I wanted to learn more about, and not having found any book on it, I decided to write one myself.

This project would not have been possible without the friendship, love, and support of many people. I might never have returned to Myanmar if Charlie Sennott hadn't helped convince me to take a pen and notebook and not look back. Likewise, my aunt Meredith Moss gave me some much-needed advice about following your heart and doing what makes you happy. The Boren Fellowship and Columbia University gave me the freedom to explore Myanmar as I wished, and I am deeply grateful to my professors at Columbia, especially Roy Kamphausen, Yumi Shimabukuro, Austin Long, and Alexis Wichowski, for helping me think through old problems in new ways. David Dapice and Tommy Vallely at the Ash Center at Harvard University were the first ones to highlight for me the importance of jade in

Myanmar's political economy. For me, the green vein will always run in part through Cambridge. Richard Hughes was a wellspring of knowledge and an incomparable guide into the world of jade, gems, and Myanmar history.

In Myanmar, I was dependent on the support of far too many people to name here. Ben and Chantal helped make Yangon feel like home. Scott and Aryiani and Kate and Talia were a refuge of peace and calm in the chaos of the city. Jalin and Robert took me into their lives both in Yangon and in New York. I'd also like to thank Moe Chit of Moe Myanmar Language Center for teaching me how to speak Burmese and giving me the vocabulary necessary to conduct most of my research. Of course, I depended most of all on the incomparable hospitality of the people of Myanmar. Phoe Wa, Bum Tsit, Kaung Htet, Darko C, Kelasa, Hkun Myat, Naw Seng, and Zahura Bekam opened their lives to me with generosity, patience, and poise. To all those named in this book, as well as those whose identities have been obscured, I thank you from the bottom of my heart.

My trip to the Rohingya refugee camps would have been a failure without the unparalleled assistance of Riton Quiah. Shannon Tiezzi at *The Diplomat* helped me become the first person in Abuja, Nigeria, to get a journalist visa to Bangladesh. I am deeply thankful to both the members of the Rohingya refugee community and their neighbors in Cox's Bazaar with whom I spoke.

Andrew Scheineson, Anne Berman, Mandy Sadan, Amara Thiha, and Jalin Sama, in addition to several people already named, read versions of this story, in part or in whole, and gave me invaluable comments. Thanks to my agent, Sharon Pelletier at DG&B, for taking a shot on a first-time author. And to my editor, Ryan Harrington at Melville House, for believing so fully in this story and for the longest, easiest, most productive conversations about writing I've ever had.

Finally, and most importantly, thank you to Afra, for being, throughout this project, the best mountain-hiking, whale-watching, crab-munching, "cheesecake"-ordering, art-loving companion I could hope for. No matter where we find ourselves on the globe, with you I am more myself.

Notes on Sources

This is primarily a work of reportage, and most of the information in this book comes from face-to-face conversations and my own observations. However, I also found the following sources useful for providing context and history to Myanmar's complicated issues.

CHAPTER 1

For information about the state of journalism in Myanmar, I relied on reporting from *The New York Times*, Reuters, *The Wall Street Journal*, *Financial Times*, *Myanmar Times*, *Frontier Myanmar*, and the *Bangkok Post*, as well as Human Rights Watch, Amnesty International, and the Committee to Protect Journalists.

CHAPTER 2

Francis Wade's book *Myanmar's Enemy Within: Buddhist Violence and the Making of a Muslim "Other"* was an excellent introduction to the history of the systematic persecution of the Rohingya. Reporting and analysis from the International Crisis Group, Human Rights Watch, and Amnesty International were essential for understanding the 2017 Rohingya exodus.

CHAPTER 3

For an introduction to the Kachin people, I recommend Ola Hanson's *The Kachins*; Edumnd Leach's *Political Systems of Highland Burma*; Bertil Lintner's *The Kachin: Lords of Burma's Northern Frontier*; and *The Kachin: Religion and Customs*, by A. Gilhodes. For information about Myanmar's civil wars, I found the following works helpful: Bertil Lintner's *Burma in Revolt*; Ashley South's *Ethnic Politics in Burma: States of Conflict*; and *Burma: Insurgency and the Politics of Ethnicity*, by Martin Smith, as well as reporting and analysis from *The Irrawaddy*, the BBC, and the Myanmar Institute for Peace and Security.

CHAPTER 4

Information on the history of Myanmar's jade mines can be found in *The Myitkyina District Gazetteer*, edited by W. A. Hertz, as well as *Stone of Heaven: Unearthing the Secret History of Imperial Green Jade*, by Cathy Scott-Clark and Adrian Levy. For information on jade, gems, and gemology, I found Richard Hughes's essays enormously insightful. And for information on China's historical and religious relationship with jade, I turned to Berthold Laufer's *Jade: A Study in Chinese Archaeology and Religion*.

A 2015 report from the British NGO Global Witness called *Jade: Myanmar's "Big State Secret"* claims that in 2014, Myanmar jade was worth $31 billion, a figure that would equal roughly half the country's GDP. The report contends that a small group of crony businessmen and former military leaders control the vast majority of the industry, and that Tatmadaw officers in Kachin State often build enormous wealth by personally extorting jade businesses.

Global Witness spent a year mapping the business holdings of friends and family members of Than Shwe, the former leader of the Tatmadaw and de facto dictator of Myanmar from 1992 to 2011. According to the paper, Than Shwe's family owns stakes in at least nine separate mining areas in Hpakan. In 2013 and 2014, the companies owned by Than Shwe's sons reported $220 million in jade sales through legal channels. The black-market revenues may be far larger. The report ties Than Shwe's family to Chinese investors and to leaders of the United Wa State Army—an opposition group of narco-traffickers that have been heavily sanctioned by the United States.

The biggest losers in the fight over jade, according to Global Witness, are the people of Kachin State, who "are seeing their livelihoods disappear and their landscape shattered by the intensifying scramble for their most prized asset." The report highlights that current mining practices are "weighted heavily in favour of a powerful elite connected or allied to . . . the military, who use networks of anonymous companies and proxies to disguise their identities."

The grim conclusion to the Global Witness analysis is that jade is fueling a conflict without end: "The notion of Kachin State being ungovernable allows this elite to perpetuate the idea that applying transparency reforms . . . to the jade business is not possible. This sustains the secretive, abusive and highly lucrative status quo."

The report is controversial among some in Myanmar, because it details the theft of military officials but largely ignores the corrupt activity of the KIA. One Tatmadaw analyst I spoke to told me that the Global Witness team got much of their jade information from Kachin leaders, many of whom felt locked outside the industry, and wouldn't spill the beans on the Kachin mining practices.

One local industry leader, meanwhile, told me that he had seen Chinese trade data showing that the jade business was worth at least $40 billion per year, but that the Myanmar government had urged the Chinese not to publish the information. "The difference would be too embarrassing for the government," the jade trader told me. "People would ask: where did all the money go?"

Meanwhile, the Natural Resource Governance Institute put KIA's stake in the jade trade in the low single digits. "I wouldn't say their stake is more than 3 percent," Maw Htun Aung, NRGI's country director, told me. He also said that measurements from 2014 and 2015 might not be accurate anymore, because those years saw a production glut. Mine owners were fearful of future NLD reforms and flooded the market with jade. However, the statistic that stabilizes the industry—the information that drives everyone from the million-dollar investor to the yemase on his hands and knees—is the fact that the price of imperial jade, the ultra-rare stone that makes up only 0.01 percent of all jade, never wavers. At $25 million per kilogram, the stone of heaven can change anyone's life.

CHAPTER 5

For invaluable insight and commentary on Myanmar's history, I recommend the following books: *A History of Burma*, by Maung Htin Aung; *The River of Lost Footsteps*, by Thant Myint-U; and *A History of Myanmar Since Ancient Times*, by Michael Aung-Thwin.

CHAPTER 6

I benefited from the Inwa Institute's excellent library of books on the history of Buddhist nationalism, as well as Donald Smith's *Religion and Politics in Burma*, "School, State, and Sangha in Burma," by Nick Chesman, and reporting from the International Crisis Group. For information on Buddhist theology and doctrine, I turned to *The Buddhist World of Southeast Asia*, by Donald Swearer. More on the Pyu can be found in the many works of Janice Stargardt, especially *The Ancient Pyu of Burma*.

CHAPTER 7

For a richly detailed account of Kachin identity and the politics of Kachin State, I recommend two works by Mandy Sadan: *Being and Becoming Kachin: Histories Beyond the State in the Borderworlds of Burma*, and the anthology she edited, *War and Peace in the Borderlands of Myanmar: The Kachin Ceasefire, 1994–2011*.

CHAPTER 8

Information about Myanmar's public health system primarily came from the World Health Organization and the Organization for Economic Cooperation and Development.

CHAPTER 9

For an immersive account of the influence of geography on diversity and independence in Southeast Asia, I turned to James C. Scott's book *The Art of Not Being Governed: An Anarchist History of Upland Southeast Asia*. While there are many excellent commentaries on the British colonial history in Myanmar, I found the following secondary and primary sources most useful: *The River of Lost Footsteps*, by Thant Myint-U; *The Pacification of Burma*, by Charles Crosthwaite; *The Gazetteer of Upper Burma and the Shan States*, edited by James G. Scott; and *Mandalay to Momein*, by John Anderson.

CHAPTER 10

For information on music and social cohesion, I recommend visiting Turning Tables's website: www.turningtables.org.

CHAPTER 11

I learned about jade smuggling from a variety of in-person and academic sources. Reporting from Global Witness tackles this hidden subject, as does Henrick Møller's essay "Attack of the Burmese Dogs: Ethnicity, Jade Trade, and Conflict in the Sino-Myanmar Borderlands," and many papers by Wen-Chin Chang, notably "*Guanxi* and Regulation in Networks: The Yunnanese Jade Trade between Burma and Thailand, 1962–88."

CHAPTER 12

Further information on press freedom and protections for journalists can be found from the Committee to Protect Journalists, Reporters Sans Frontières, the International Press Institute, Human Rights Watch, and Amnesty International, among others.

Selected Bibliography

In addition to the below works, I used contemporary reporting from the *Nikkei Asian Review*, *The New York Times*, *The Wall Street Journal*, *The Washington Post*, Reuters, Associated Press, CNN, *Financial Times*, *Asia Times*, *The Diplomat*, *Frontier Myanmar*, *The Irrawaddy*, *Myanmar Times*, and *Bangkok Post*.

BOOKS

"Report on the Administration of Burma During 1892–93." Government Printing. Rangoon. 1893

"Selection of Papers regarding the Hill Tracts between Assam and Burmah and on the Upper Brahmaputra." Bengal Secretariat Press. 1873

"The British Burma Gazetteer: In Two Volumes." Government Printing. Rangoon. 1879

"The Imperial Gazetteer of India." Vol. XVIII. Clarendon Press. Oxford. 1908

Adamson, C. H. E. "A Short Account of the Expedition to the Jade Mines in Upper Burmah, in 1887–1888, With a Map." J. Bell and Co. Newcastle-upon-Tyne. 1889

Anderson, John. "Mandalay to Momien: A Narrative of the Two Expeditions to Western China of 1868 and 1875 under Colonel Edward B. Sladen and Colonel Horace Browne." Macmillan and Co. London. 1876

Appadurai, Arjun, ed. "The Social Life of Things: Commodities in Cultural Perspective." Cambridge University Press. Cambridge. 1986

Bayfield, G. T. "Narrative of a Journey from Ava to the frontiers of Assam and back, performed between December 1836 and May 1837, under the orders Lieutenant-Colonel Burney, Resident at Ava." Rangoon. 1837

Brown, G. E. R. Grant. "Burma Gazetteer: Northern Arakan District (or Arakan Hill Tracts)." Vol. A. Government Printing. Rangoon. 1960

Chang, Wen-Chin & Tagliacozzo, Eric, eds. "Burmese Lives: Ordinary Life Stories Under the Burmese Regime." Oxford University Press. Oxford. 2014

Chang, Wen-Chin, and Tagliacozzo, Eric, eds. "Chinese Circulations: Capital, Commodities, and Networks in Southeast Asia." Duke University Press. Durham. 2011

Cheesman, Nick, Monique Skidmore, and Trevor Wilson, eds. "Myanmar's Transition: Opening, Obstacles and Opportunities." ISEAS–Yusof Ishak Institute. Singapore. 2013

Chhibber, Harbans L. "The Mineral Resources of Burma." Macmillan and Co. London. 1934

Crosthwaite, Charles. "The Pacification of Burma." Edward Arnold. London. 1912

Davies, H. R. "Yun-nan: The Link Between India and the Yangtze." University Press. Cambridge. 1909

Daw Kyan. "Selected Writings of Daw Kyan." Yangon University Press. Yangon. 2005

Farrelly, Nicholas and Cheesman, Nick, eds. "Conflict in Myanmar: War, Politics, Religion." ISEAS Yusho–Ishak Institute. Singapore. 2016

Fellowes-Gordon, Ian. "The Battle for Naw Seng's Kingdom." Leo Cooper. London. 1971

Gilhodes, A. "The Kachins: Religion and Customs." White Lotus Press. Bangkok. 1996

Goette, John. "Jade Lore." Ars Ceramica. Ann Arbor. 1976

Grantham, S. G. "Burma: Part 1. Report." Census of India, 1921. Vol. X. Government Printing. Rangoon. 1923

Gray, James. "The Niti Literature of Burma." Trubner and Co.. London. 1886

Griffith, William. "Journals of Travels in Assam, Burma, Bhootan, Afghanistan, and The Neighbouring Countries." 1847.

Guy, John, ed. "Lost Kingdoms: Hindu-Buddhist Sculpture of Early Southeast Asia" Yale University Press. New Haven. 2014

Hall, D. G. E. "Burma." Hutchinson University Library. London. 1960

Hanson, Ola. "The Kachins: Their Customs and Traditions." American Baptist Mission Press. Rangoon. 1913

Harvey, G. E. "History of Burma: From the Earliest Times to 10 March 1824 The Beginning of the English Conquest." Longmans, Green and Co. London. 1925

Hertz, W. A. "Burma Gazetteer: Myitkyina District." Vol. A. Government Printing. Rangoon. 1960

Htin Aung. "Burmese Folk Tales." Oxford University Press. London. 1948

Htin Aung. "History of Burma." Columbia Universtity Press. New York. 1967

Htin Aung. "The Stricken Peacock: Anglo-Burmese Relations 1752–1948." Martinus Nijhoff. The Hague. 1965

Khin Maung Nyunt. "Myanmar Traditional Monthly Festivals." Inwa Publishing House. Yangon.

Khin Maung Nyunt. "The Selected Writings of Dr. Khin Maung Nyunt." Myanmar Historical Commission. Yangon. 2004

Lammerts, D. Christian, ed. "Buddhist Dynamics in Premodern and Early Modern Southeast Asia." ISEAS–Yusof Ishak institute. Singapore. 2015

Laufer, Berthold. "Jade: A Study in Chinese Archaeology and Religion." The Mrs. T. B. Blackstone Expedition. Chicago. 1912

Leach, Edmund R. "Political Systems of Highland Burma: A Study of Kachin Social Structure." The Athlone Press. London. 1959

Lintner, Bertil. "Burma in Revolt: Opium and Insurgency Since 1948." Westview Press. Boulder, CO. 1994

Lintner, Bertil. "Land of Jade: A Journey Through Insurgent Burma." Kiscadale Publications. Kiscadale, Scotland. 1990

Lintner, Bertil. "The Kachin: Lords of Burma's Northern Frontier." Asia Pacific Media Services. Hong Kong. 2014

Luce, Gordon H. "Phases of Pre-Pagan: Language and History." Oxford University Press. Oxford. 1986

Michael Aung-Thwin & Maitrii Aung-Thwin. "A History of Myanmar Since Ancient Times: Traditions and Transformations." Reaktion Books. London. 2012

Myanmar Ministry of Information. "Loka Niti."

Ni Ni Myint. "Burma's Struggle Against British Imperialism 1885–1895." The Universities Press. Rangoon. 1983

Pope-Hennessy, Una. "A Jade Miscellany." Nicholson & Watson. London. 1946

Pradhan, M. V. "Burma, Dhamma, and Democracy." Mayflower Publishing House. Bombay. 1991

Sadan, Mandy, ed. "War and Peace in the Borderlands of Myanmar: The Kachin Ceasefire, 1994–2011." Nordic Institute of Asian Studies, Studies in Asian

Topics, no. 56. Copenhagen. 2016

Sadan, Mandy. "Being and Becoming Kachin: Histories Beyond the State in the Borderworlds of Burma." Oxford University Press. Oxford. 2013

Scott, J. George. "Burma: A Handbook of Practical Information." Daniel O'Connor. London. 1921

Scott, J. George. "Gazetteer of Upper Burma and the Shan States, in Five Volumes." Government Printing, Burma. Rangoon. 1901

Scott, James C. "The Art of Not Being Governed: An Anarchist History of Upland Southeast Asia." Yale University Press. New Haven. 2009

Scott-Clark, Cathy & Levy, Adrian. "The Stone of Heaven: Unearthing the Secrets of Imperial Green Jade." Little, Brown. New York. 2001

Seekins, Donald M. "Historical Dictionary of Burma (Myanmar)." The Scarecrow Press. Lanham, MD. 2006

Smard, R. B. "Burma Gazetteer: Akyab District" Vol. A. Government Printing. Rangoon. 1957

Smith, Donald. "Religion and Politics in Burma." Princeton University Press. Princeton. 1965

Smith, Martin. "Burma: Insurgency and the Politics of Ethnicity." Zed Books. London. 1991

South, Ashley. "Ethnic Politics in Burma: States of Conflict." Routledge. Abingdon, UK. 2009

Stargardt, Janice. "The Ancient Pyu of Burma, Vol 1: Early Pyu cities in a man-made landscape." Publications on Ancient Civilizations in South East Asia. Cambridge. Institue of Southest Asian Studies. Singapore. 1990

Steinberg, David I. "Burma/Myanmar: What Everyone Needs to Know." Oxford University Press. Oxford. 2010

Swearer, Donald K. "The Buddhist World of Southeast Asia." SUNY Press. Albany, NY. 2010

Thant Myint-U. "The Making of Modern Burma." Cambridge University Press. Cambridge. 2008

Thant Myint-U. "The River of Lost Footsteps: A Personal History of Burma." Farrar, Straus and Giroux. New York. 2006

Thant Myint-U. "Where China Meets India: Burma and the New Crossroads of Asia." Farrar, Straus and Giroux. New York. 2011

Wade, Francis. "Myanmar's Enemy Within: Buddhist Violence and the Making of a Muslim 'Other.'" Zed Books. London. 2017

Yule, Henry. "A Narrative of the Mission Sent By the Governor-General of India to The Court of Ava in 1855, With Notices of the Country, Government, and People." Smith, Elder, and Co. London. 1858

ESSAYS, ARTICLES, AND TALKS

"Direct Communication between Upper Assam and Northern Burma." *Proceedings of the Royal Geographical Society and Monthly Record of Geography, New Monthly Series.* Vol. 14, No. 6, pp. 404–407. June 1892

"Imperial Green Jade: Britain's Fruitless Quest for Burma's Jade Mines." www. Inwa-Advisors.com. Accessed September 24, 2017.

Myanmar EITI. "Myanmar Extractive Industry Transparency Initiative Annual Activity Report: July 2015–June 2016," Nov. 2016

"Treaty Between Alaung-hpaya and the British East India Company in 1757." *SOAS Bulletin of Burma Research.* Vol. 3, No. 1, pp. 123–125. Spring 2005

Ardeth Maung Thwanghmung. "Beyond Armed Resistance: Ethnonational Politics in Burma (Myanmar)." *Policy Studies.* Vol. 62. 2011

Baker, George. "Observations at Persaim and in the Journey to Ava and Back in 1755." *SOAS Bulletin of Burma Research.* Vol. 3, No. 1, pp. 99–122. Spring 2005

Ball, Sydney H. "Historical Notes on Gemstones." *Economic Geology.* Vol. XXVI, No. 7, pp. 681–738. 1931

Ball, Sydney H. "The Geologic and Geographic Occurrence of Precious Stones." *Economic Geology.* Vol. XVII, pp. 575–601. 1922

Bauer, Andrew, Paul Shortell, and Lorenzo Delesgues. "Sharing the Wealth: A Roadmap for Distributing Myanmar's Natural Resource Revenues." Natural Resource Governance Institute. February 2016

Booth, Anne. "The Burma Development Disaster in Comparative Historical Perspective." *SOAS Bulletin of Burma Reearch.* Vol. 1, No. 1, pp. 1–23. Spring 2003

Buchanan, John. "Militias in Myanmar." The Asia Foundation. July 2016

Burney, H. "Some account of the Wars between Burmah and China, together with the journals and routes of three different Embassies sent to Pekin by the King of Ava; taken from Burmese documents." *Journal of the Asiatic Society.* No. 66. June 1837

Chang, Wen-Chin. "Guanxi and Regulation in Networks: The Yunnanese Jade Trade between Burma and Thailand, 1962–88." *Journal of Southeast Asian Studies*. Vol. 35, No. 3, pp. 479–501. October 2004

Chang, Wen-Chin. "The everyday politics of the underground trade in Burma by the Yunnanese Chinese since the Burmese socialist Era." *Journal of Southeast Asian Studies*. Vol. 44, No. 2, pp. 292–314. June 2013

Chang, Wen-Chin. "The Trading Culture of Jade Stones Among the Yunnanese in Burma and Thailand, 1962–88." *Journal of Chinese Overseas*. Vol. 2, No. 2, pp. 269-293. November 2006

Cheesman, Nick. "School, State and Sangha." *Comparative Education*. Vol 39, No. 1, pp. 45–63. 2003

Christian, John L. "Anglo-French Rivalry in Southeast Asia: Its Historical Geography and Diplomatic Climate." *Geographical Review*. Vol. 31, No. 2, pp. 272–282. April 1941

Christian, John L. "Trans-Burma Trade Routes to China." *Pacific Affairs*. Vol. 13, No. 2, pp. 173–191. June 1940

Dapice, David. "A Grand Bargain: What It Is and Why It Is Needed." Ash Center at Harvard Kennedy School. August 2016

Dapice, Daivd. "Rakhine State Policies: Considerations for the New Government." Ash Center at Harvard Kennedy School. October 2016

Dapice, David & Vallely, Thomas. "Choosing Survival: Finding a Way to Overcome Current Economic and Political Quagmires in Myanmar." Ash Center at Harvard Kennedy School. October 2016

De' Conti, Nicolò. "Early Fifteenth Century Travels in the East." *SOAS Bulletin of Burma Research*. Vol. 2, No. 2, pp. 110–117. Autumn 2004

E. G. "The Burma-China Frontier Dispute." *The World Today*. Vol. 13, No. 2, pp. 86–92. February 1957

Ehrmann, Martin L. "Burma: The Mineral Utopia." *The Lapidary Journal*. August, October, and December 1957

Ferguson, Jane M. "Who's Counting? Ethnicity, Belonging, and the National Census in Burma/Myanmar." Bijdragen tot de Taal-, Land- en Volkenkunde, Vol. 171, No. 1, pp. 1–28. 2015

Franco, Jenny, Hannah Twomey, Khu Khu Ju, Pietje Vervest, and Tom Kramer. "The Meaning of Land in Myanmar." The Transnational Institute. Amsterdam. January 28, 2016

Global Witness. "Jade: Myanmar's 'Big State Secret.'" London. October 2015

Horsey, Richard. "Buddhism and State Power in Myanmar." International Crisis Group. Asia Report No. 290. September 5, 2017

Hla Hla Kyi. "Natural Resources and Local Community: The Case of Jade Production and Local Community in Lonekhinn-Hpakant Jade Mine Area, Kachin State, Myanmar." *International College of Mekong Region Journal.* Vol. 3, No. 2, pp. 62–75. July–December 2015

Hughes, Richard. "Jade Buying Guide; Jade Auction Record." Lotus Gemology. www.Lotusgemology.com Accessed August 21, 2017

Hughes, Richard. "Burma's Jade Mines – an Annotated Occidental History." www.ruby-sapphire.com. Accessed August 14, 2017

Irwin, Emma & Shortell, Paul. "Governing the Gemstone Sector: Lessons from Global Experience." Natural Resource Governance Institute. May 2017

Jones, Maria. "An Exploration of Jade." Thesis. Eastern Michigan University. 2004

Kachin Development Networking Group. "Kachin State Natural Resources Development Policy Discussion Paper." June 2015

Kachin Development Networking Group. "Saving the Ngo Chang Hka Valley." August 2017

Kachin Development Networking Group. "Valley of Darkness: Gold Mining and Militarization in Burma's Hugawng Valley." 2007

Kambani, Stephens M. "The illegal trading of high unit value minerals in developing countries." Natural Resources Forum. Vol. 19, No. 2, pp. 107–112. May 1995

KIO Technical Advisory Team. "The Kachin Peace Process." 2017

Laichen, Sun. "Ming-Southeast Asian Overland Interactions, 1368–1644." Dissertation for University of Michigan. 2000

Leach. E. R. "The Frontiers of 'Burma.'" Comparative Studies in Society and History. Vol 3, No. 1, pp. 49–68. October 1960

Lieberman, Victor B. "Ethnic Politics in Eighteenth-Century Burma." *Modern Asian Studies.* Vol. 12, No. 3, pp. 455–482. 1978

Lieberman, Victor. "The Qing Dynasty and its Neighbors: Early Modern China in World History." *Social Science History.* Vol. 32, No. 2, pp. 281–304. Summer 2008

Luce, Gordon H. "Chinese Invasions of Burma in the 18th Century." *The Journal of the Burma Research Society.* Vol. XV, pp. 115–128. 1925

Luce, Gordon H. "Geography of Burma under the Pagan Dynasty." *The Journal of the Burma Research Society*. Vol. XLII, pp. 32–52. 1959

Luce, Gordon H. "Note on the Peoples of Burma in the 12th–13th Century A.D." *The Journal of the Burma Research Society*. Vol. XLII, pp. 52–75. 1959

Maran Hkawn Tawng. "The Socio-Economic Conditions of Kachin Under Colonial Rule (1886–1948)." PhD Dissertation, University of Mandalay. 2014

Meehan, Patrick. "Drugs, insurgency and state-building in Burma: Why the drugs trade is central to Burma's changing political order." *Journal of Southeast Asian Studies*. Vol. 42, No. 3, pp. 376–404. October 2011

Michael Aung-Thwin. "The British 'Pacification' of Burma; Order without Meaning." *Journal of Southeast Asian Studies*. Vol. 16, No. 2, pp. 245–261. September 1985

Møller, Henrik Kloppenborg. "Attack of the Burmese Dogs: Ethnicity, Jade Trade, and Conflict in the Sino-Myanmar Borderlands." Paper presented at the symposium "Regionalization of Development," Chiang Mai University. 2–3 July, 2017

Mowry, Robert D. "Chinese Jades from Han to Qing." *Archaeology*. Vol. 34, No. 1, pp. 52–55. January/February 1981

Mya Maung. "On the Road to Mandalay: A Case Study of the Sinonization of Upper Burma." *Asian Survey*. Vol. 34, No. 5, pp. 447–459. May 1994

Myanmar Ministry of Information. "Constitution of the Republic of the Union of Myanmar." 2008

Natural Resource Governance Institute. "The Resource Curse: The Political and Economic Challenges of Natural Resources Wealth." NRGI Reader. March 2015

Norins, Martin R. "Tribal Boundaries of the Burma-Yunnan Frontier." *Pacific Affairs*. Vol. 12, No. 1, pp. 67–79. Mar 1939

Nwattiwong, Naritsara. "A Journey Through Burma [in 1888]." *SOAS Bulletin of Burma Research*, Vol. 2, No. 2, Autumn 2004. Translated by Kennon Breazeale.

Pemberton, R. Boileau. "Abstract of the Journal of a Route Travelled by Captain S. F. Hannay, of the 40th Regiment, Native Infantry, in 1835–36, from the capital of Ava to the Amber Mines of the Hukong Valley on the South-east Frontier of Assam." *SOAS Bulletin of Burma Research*. Vol. 3, No. 1, pp. 197–227. Spring 2005

Pollak, Oliver B. "A Mid-Victorian Coverup: The Case of the 'Combustible Commodore' and the Second Anglo-Burmese War, 1851–1852." *Albion: A Quarterly Journal Concerned with British Studies*. Vol. 10, No. 2, pp. 171–183. Summer 1978

Sakhong, Lian H. "The Dynamics of Sixty Years of Ethnic Armed Conflict in Burma." Burma Centre for Ethnic Studies. Analysis Paper No. 1. January 2012

Steinberg, David I. "Burma Under the Military: Towards a Chronology." *Contemporary Southeast Asia*. Vol. 3, No. 3, pp. 244–285. December 1981

Steinberg, David I. "Myanmar 1991: Military Intransigence." *Southeast Asian Affairs*. pp. 221–237. 1992

Steinberg, David I. "The Problem of Democracy in the Republic of the Union of Myanmar: Neither Nation-State Nor State-Nation?" *Southeast Asian Affairs*. pp. 220--37. 2012

Steinberg, David I. "The Socialist Republic of the Union of Burma State Economic Organizations Concerned with Trade." *Contemporary Southeast Asia*. Vol. 4, No. 1, pp. 107 113. June 1982

Steinberg, David I. & Youngsmith, Barron. "China's Burma Connection." *The Brown Journal of World Affairs*. Vol. 12, No. 2, pp. 69–74. Winter/Spring 2006

Su, Elizabeth. "Jadeite Markets in China." Thirty-fourth International Gemmological Conference. Vilnius. 2015

Symes, Michael. "An Account of an Embassy to the Kingdom of Ava, Sent by the Governor-General of India, in the Year 1795." *SOAS Bulletin of Burma Research*. Vol. 4, No. 1, pp. 59–208. Spring 2006

Thant Myint-U. "The Hidden History of Burma: Race, Capitalism, and the Crisis of Democracy in the 21st Century." Talk given at the Center for Strategic and International Studies. Washington. November 20, 2019

Thaw Kaung. "Palm-leaf Manuscript Record of a Mission Sent by the Myanmar King to the Chinese Emperor in the Mid-Eighteenth Century." *SOAS Bulletin of Burma Research*. Vol. 6, Parts 1–2. 2008

United Nations Human Rights Council. "Report of the Independent International Fact-Finding Mission on Myanmar." August 2018

United Nations Human Rights Council. "The economic interests of the Myanmar military: Independent International Fact-Finding Mission on Myanmar." September 2019

United Nations Office on Drugs and Crime. "Evidence for enhancing resilience to opium poppy cultivation in Shan State, Myanmar; Implications for alternative development, peace, and stability." March 2017

United States Treasury Department, Office of Public Affairs. "Treasury Implements Termination of Burma Sanctions." October 7, 2016

Visser, Laurens J. "Bulding Relationships Across Divides: Peace and Conflict Analsysis of Kachin State." Centre for Peace and Conflict Studies. 2016

Woods, Kevin. "A political anatomy of land grabs." Transnational Institute. March 10, 2014

Woods, Kevin & Kramer, Tom. "Financing Dispossession: China's Opium Substitution Programme in Northern Burma." Transnational Institute. Amsterdam. February 2012

Yang Chiu Mei, Ou. "A Mineralogical Study of Burmese Jadeite Jade." Thesis. University of Hong Kong. 1985

Zöllner, Hans-Bernd. "Hermeneutics Revised: In Search of the Religious-Political Hermeneutics in Myanmar." Text was an extended version of a talk given in Berlin on June 12, 2017

Index